# INFORMATION

*The Key to Life*

## Dr. Werner Gitt

First printing: September 2023

ISBN: 978-1-68344-341-4
ISBN: 978-1-61458-835-1 (digital)
Library of Congress Control Number: 2023934588

Please consider requesting that a copy of this volume be purchased by your local library system.

**Printed in the United States of America**

Please visit our website for other great titles:
www.masterbooks.com

For information regarding promotional opportunities, please contact the publicity department at pr@nlpg.com.

Master Books®
A Division of New Leaf Publishing Group
www.masterbooks.com

# Table of Contents

## Terms Used for Large Numbers

The names of many large numbers differ between American and British/ German usage. This book uses the naming conventions of American English.

| Large number terms | American English | British English |
|---|---|---|
| Thousand | $10^3$ | $10^3$ |
| Million | $10^6$ | $10^6$ |
| Billion | $10^9$ | $10^{12}$ |
| Trillion | $10^{12}$ | $10^{18}$ |
| Quadrillion | $10^{15}$ | $10^{24}$ |
| Quintillion | $10^{18}$ | $10^{30}$ |
| Sextillion | $10^{21}$ | $10^{36}$ |
| Septillion | $10^{24}$ | $10^{42}$ |
| Octillion | $10^{27}$ | $10^{48}$ |

# FOREWORD
by William A. Dembski

In the first chapter of Romans, the Apostle Paul makes clear that the attributes of the physical world give sufficient evidence of God to render atheism not just intellectually untenable but also morally repugnant. Ignorance of God's power and glory is never innocent but always willful. Thus, Bertrand Russell's famous quip that if asked at the pearly gates why he disbelieved in God, he would respond "not enough evidence," has never seemed, at least within Christian theology, as particularly exculpative. The physical creation has always been enough to convince humanity of God's power and glory, and to assert the opposite has always been a mark of foolishness (cf. Ps. 14:1).

Professor Werner Gitt was one of the first Christian thinkers to see the profound connection between the mathematical theory of information and evidence of God's activity in the world via a spoken word (cf. Gen. 1 and John 1). Thus, this book is the sequel to an earlier book titled *In the Beginning Was Information* [G15]. But what exactly about the physical world gives evidence of God? If the universe were a giant homogeneous pudding, it might be difficult to discern God's power and wisdom in creation. But the world is not a pudding. It is a space-time continuum, the mass-energy of which is hierarchically distributed with precise structures at each level of organization. In particular, cosmology and biology both give evidence of God. The focus of this book is on biological design. It argues that the vast complexity and precise organization of DNA — its information! — provides conclusive evidence for the activity within the world of a non-material entity. Information, as this book demonstrates, is inherently non-material — it lies beyond the reach of any reductive materialism.

Werner Gitt, by contrast, argues that information of the sort that we see in living systems could not have come about by material processes devoid of intelligent guidance. In this regard, Werner Gitt's thinking parallels that of many design theorists this side of the Atlantic. The intelligent design movement, from the start, has seen the crucial role of information as a marker of intelligence and the inability of purely material factors to capture the notion of information. Our emphasis has been a bit different from Werner Gitt's, focusing on statistical and complexity-theoretic properties of patterns associated with the activity of intelligent agents. Werner Gitt is aware of this work and draws connections with it at the end of this book. Yet his approach to information is broader than that of most American design theorists, focusing also on the semantics, pragmatics, and end-directedness (what he calls "apobetics") of information.

My strong endorsement of this work should not be interpreted as a blanket acceptance of every one of its claims. Thus, I would encourage readers to keep in mind that the intelligent design movement, broadly conceived, contains some diversity of views. There is agreement on core issues: intelligent design proponents agree that information is a primary and irreducible feature of the created order, that purely material forces are unable to account for information, and that natural selection cannot create the sort of information that we encounter in biology (in particular, materialistic theories of evolution are bankrupt). Nonetheless, individuals within the intelligent design community hold a diversity of views on the precise details and timing of key events in the formation of the cosmos and of life.

As a mathematician with experience in reading technical literature, I found the organization and notation of this book quite accessible. Readers without this background or experience, however, may experience something of a "culture shock." I would encourage such readers to exercise patience and plow through what for many will be new terminology and notation. Some of this terminology may seem idiosyncratic. In part this is an unavoidable consequence of this book being a translation from the German language. But it is also the result of hammering out a new vocabulary to define novel concepts. Sitting on my shelf is a massive encyclopedia of physics dated 1992. In it the word "information" appears neither as an entry nor in the extensive index. Information, as applied to the natural sciences, remains in its theoretical infancy. This book helps to advance the discussion and move it to maturity.

Although I speak and read the German language fluently, having lived in Germany for five years, I was delighted when in 1998 I was able to purchase the then recently completed English translation of *In the Beginning Was Information....* I'm delighted that this expanded and refined sequel to that work is likewise available in English. I appreciate its scientific insights. But even more I appreciate its commitment to our God and Savior, Jesus Christ, who is the Word — the INFORMATION — made flesh.

William A. Dembski, Research Professor in Philosophy at Southwestern Seminary in Ft. Worth, Texas, and Senior Fellow with Discovery Institute's Center for Science and Culture. With doctorates in both mathematics and the philosophy of science, he is a prolific author who published the first academic monograph on intelligent design (*The Design Inference*, Cambridge University Press) and founded the first intelligent design research center at a major university (Baylor University's Michael Polanyi Center).

# PREFACE

We live in the Information Age. Computers (processors of information) play a central role in our society. Indeed, no branch of science, technology, government, or private industry could do without this revolutionary and timesaving tool. Indeed, the term "information" has become a key word for our understanding, not only of technological processes, but also of biological systems.

But what is information? Claude Shannon was among the first to tackle this question and to develop a mathematical theory for studying it. Unfortunately, Shannon's definition of information falls short of being all-encompassing. It does not consider certain essential attributes of information such as meaning and purpose. In fact, it is suitable for handling just one relatively superficial aspect, the statistical attribute.

As an information scientist I took up the challenge and have spent more than 30 years researching the concept of information. The realization that information was by no means an attribute of matter but rather a distinct non-material entity was a breakthrough for me. This position stands in stark contrast to all those publications that are influenced by the widely accepted materialistic worldview.

After working out a definition of information, I succeeded in formulating scientific laws for this non-material entity, information, from which it is possible to draw sound arguments. Some of these scientific results were published in the German book *Am Anfang war die Information* [G25] (translated into English as *In the Beginning was Information*) and in two English-language articles [G26].

Thereafter, the book was substantially altered and extended, appearing in 2016 in German under the new title *Information: Der Schlüssel zum Leben* (*Information — the Key to Life*). Since then, the German version has gone through multiple editions and refinements, all of which to date are incorporated in this English version under the same title.

This version of the book also reflects the cumulative efforts of a number of others over the years, in translating, editing, and correcting. To all of them I would like to express my very heartfelt thanks for all the effort, time, and patience invested.

This book has been structured into two parts. Chapters 1 through 8 address exclusively scientific matters and the resulting conclusions. We begin by first establishing a precise definition of Universal Information (UI), and then formulating empirical statements derived from observations of human (natural and machine) languages.

Next, we take an extensive look at the fundamental aspects of scientific laws of nature. From the empirical statements derived, we then propose six scientific laws and nine corollaries of Universal Information. Finally, through careful study, we have determined that all living organisms contain UI in their DNA and belong within the UI definition domain. Thus, the scientific laws of UI apply to all of life, and by using them as premises we are able to draw sound arguments. This is discussed extensively in chapter 8.

In chapter 9 we go beyond the boundary of science and demonstrate that the Bible is a divine source of UI, extending beyond human intellect. By means of mathematical-probability reasoning, we determine that the Bible is an absolutely trustworthy source of truth. Additionally, we demonstrate by comparison that our previously drawn scientific conclusions agree with biblical revelation.

In this age of materialism-based science, people believe what they regard as science and reject the Bible. Why is this? Modern science rests on two unjustifiable pillars. One is materialism, claiming that all phenomena in this world are caused exclusively by mass and energy. The other pillar of modern science (a corollary of the first) is that mass and energy possess the ability to self-organize over time. These are principles whereby God is completely excluded from all scientific thought processes. Both of these pillars are toppled by the scientific laws of Universal Information.

This book refutes materialism, atheism, and the theory of evolution, and confirms the existence of an almighty and all-knowing God. What was stated almost two thousand years ago in the New Testament (Rom. 1:19–21) is here supported with scientific arguments,

> since what may be known about God is plain to them, because God has made it plain to them. For since the creation of the world God's invisible qualities — his eternal power and divine nature — have been clearly seen, being understood from what has been made, so that people are without excuse. For although they knew God, they neither glorified him as God nor gave thanks to him, but their thinking became futile and their foolish hearts were darkened.

My hope and prayer is that this book will "light a fire" and also encourage many to dig ever deeper for the truth. If this is done with unhindered sincerity, then in the end a person will turn toward the living God of the Bible — the scientific evidence demands it!

# INTRODUCTION

There is an ancient war between creationists and secular evolutionists. This war has intensified over the past few centuries, most notably after the publication of Darwin's *On the Origin of Species* (1859). Science is one of the primary fronts in this war; however, philosophy, theology, law, economics, the arts, education, and essentially every area of human activity are also involved.

Many people are convinced that this war is based upon the concept of "religion vs. science," "blind faith vs. confirmed facts," or "emotion vs. rationality." This is a misconception which results only in arguments that are tangential to the central issue. If the main issue is not framed properly and addressed directly, it will never be dealt with in a rational manner. However, there is a two-pronged approach that may lead to a solution.

First, it is vital to understand that this is not a "science vs. religion" matter. Both sides are unquestionably ideological and, as such, can be defined as religious. If this is not understood, people will continue talking past each other and addressing matters that never deal with the primary issue.

Evidence of this problem lies in the common evolutionary argument that their position is not religious and not metaphysically based. They seem convinced that the creation position relies entirely on religious beliefs while the evolution position is based entirely on solid scientific facts. The physicist-philosopher David Bohm in "Sketches, Further Remarks on Order," from the 1969 book *Towards a Theoretical Biology*, has a cogent remark here:

> It seems clear that everybody has got some kind of metaphysics, even if he thinks he hasn't got any. Indeed, the practical "hard-headed" individual who "only goes by what he sees" has a very dangerous kind of metaphysics, i.e., the kind of which he is unaware. … Such metaphysics is dangerous because, in it, assumptions and inferences are being mistaken for directly observed facts, with the result that they are effectively riveted in an almost unchangeable way into the structure of thought. What is called for is therefore that each one of us be aware of his metaphysical assumptions, to the extent that this is possible.[1]

In their attempt to silence creation opposition, evolutionists have tried to use modern science to undermine points being made by the opposition, in particular any statements which appear to have a biblical basis. Evolutionary arguments are disseminated through every possible medium: education, entertainment, government, and daily news programs. Essentially, this has amounted to a form of propaganda which is often devoid of scientific facts. The sad truth is that this propaganda to which the public has been constantly exposed has caused many Christians to doubt their own faith. Our goal then, from a Christian perspective, is to help build up the faith of our brothers and sisters in the Lord while presenting the facts and logic regarding a number of evolutionary arguments.

There are some major weaknesses in modern science which need to be exposed. One, for instance, is an argument over what "reality" means. Both Kant (18th century) and Kuhn (20th century) argued that our perception of reality is distorted as it passes through our sensory receptors and is then subjected to complex electrochemical processing in our brain. Kuhn explained that concepts and assumptions already programmed within our brains can also alter our perceptions of reality. Within the last twenty years, the term "worldview" has been adopted to represent those neural programs that alter our perceptions.

---

1. David Bohm, "Further Remarks on Order" in C.H. Waddington (ed.), *Towards a Theoretical Biology: 2 Sketches* (Edinburgh University Press, 1969), p.41f.

Very simply put, a worldview is what you believe to be true and thus is the basis for the way you interpret what your senses tell you, as well as determining your actions and reactions in everyday life. What you believe to be true will be based on what you have learned, what you have been taught, your assumptions, and your own experience. The two worldviews that will be addressed in this book are those of the *biblicists* (those who believe the Bible is true) and the *materialists* (those who believe only what their senses can determine is true).

Biblicists and materialists are in continuous conflict. A person who believes that the Bible is true also believes that it was inspired by God Himself and thus takes precedence over what our senses might tell us, or how we interpret what our senses might tell us. A materialist believes that he is free of any metaphysical or religious trappings and is depending entirely upon what his senses inform him is true, as well as on his own ability to interpret and understand those sensory inputs. As such, neither position is neutral, for as much as the former depends on the accuracy of God's Word, the latter depends on faith in the ability of his own brain and senses and is in axiomatic denial of any other ultimate source of knowledge. Thus, both are, in essence, religious views.

So, while Christians have a bias *for* God and the Bible, materialists have a bias *against* God and the Bible. Evolutionists, as materialists, also have a strong bias that restricts science to material processes only. These biases are parts of their respective worldviews, based upon their respective frameworks of ideas, assumptions, axioms, etc. No one is exempt from having their worldview affect or bias how they perceive things and how they think about things. Thus, the argument that Christians should be disqualified from science because of their bias is fallacious. In fact, it is historically verified that most of the individuals who initiated formal studies in various fields were Bible-believing Christians: Kepler, Newton, Faraday, Maxwell, Boyle, Mendel, Pasteur, and many others.

The foundation for all of this is naturalism, which claims that all phenomena are the results of natural causes and can be explained entirely by natural laws. "Nature" is thus defined as "the entire material universe and its phenomena." Materialism is defined as "the doctrine that everything in the universe was and is caused and explainable solely by mass and energy and the laws that govern these." This either leads to the conclusion that a circular argument is involved or that materialism and naturalism are synonymous. Unlike naturalism, however, materialism is unambiguously defined:

> The cause of all phenomena is matter, and determinism is the foundation of all scientific progress and criticism.[2]

> What are living things made of? Are there special substances that are found in living things but not in nonliving material? Is there a special "spirit" or "essence" that living things possess? Does life have a physical and chemical basis that we can hope to understand and describe in the same way we do something that is not alive, like an automobile engine or a calculator? To answer these questions, we must first examine the world around us ... a world made up of matter and energy.[3]

The fundamental assumption of the modern scientific establishment is that reality consists solely and entirely of time, space, mass, and energy — mass and energy defining "matter." As a result of this assumption, it requires that scientists explain all observed phenomena in terms of space, time, and matter alone, and also that matter must be able to self-organize over time. This is the worldview of secular science today.

This worldview, which excludes from the outset even the possibility of a creator or god, is by definition a metaphysical stance. It is not a matter of science, but a presupposition based upon ... what? Perhaps only on a desire for God not to exist?

Such a position logically leads to the conclusion that evolution must be true, as nothing other than natural forces and laws is permitted in the range of explanations. Complexity, intelligence, organization — all must be the result of physical processes. This, however, is also what they are trying to prove, and therein lies the logical fallacy of *petitio principii* (assuming the conclusion in the premises). Interestingly, they generally appear to be unaware of their involvement in this fallacy and fail to see how their own worldview is affecting the objectivity of which they boast. Once again, we see Bohm's quote ringing loud and true.

The inescapable fact is that, one way or another, we are all biased. Classical science, however, had instituted a system of checks and balances

---

2. Claude Bernard (1800s), cited in Arthur Custance, *The Mysterious Matter of Mind* (Grand Rapids, MI: Zondervan, 1980).
3. Kenneth R. Miller and Joseph S. Levine, *Biology* (Upper Saddle River, NJ: Prentice Hall, 2000)), p. 45.

as a way to eliminate as much bias as possible. This was done by welcoming the participation of scientists who had varied, and sometimes opposing, worldviews/religions. Controversy was tempered by mutual respect. This system is no longer in operation; only one worldview is permitted in standard science journals. Sadly, this is usually true for both the creation and evolution journals. This strict adherence to the orthodoxy (of either side) is the subject of a quote by Sir Karl Popper in his 1984 book *The Myth of the Framework: In Defense of Science and Rationality*:

> I hold that orthodoxy is the death of knowledge, since the growth of knowledge depends entirely on the existence of disagreement ... discussion between people who share many views is unlikely to be fruitful, even though it may be pleasant; while a discussion between vastly different frameworks can be extremely fruitful even though it may sometimes be extremely difficult, and perhaps not quite so pleasant (though we may learn to enjoy it).[4]

The first point is the necessity of showing that both sides of the creation/evolution debate are not only subject to bias but are dependent upon a metaphysical foundation. The second point is that it is necessary to debate the issue in terms of a decisive topic or subject, and not some ambiguous issue. Is there such a decisive subject? In this book we have treated the subject of "information" as that decisive subject. We believe this subject can get to the heart of the matter and help us decide which position is correct.

The word "information," as it is used in everyday language, is somewhat vague and subject to confusion. It is generally used to denote some meaningful knowledge that is to be learned or communicated. However, when information is being considered in terms of engineering — e.g., for storage and transmission purposes — no meaning is required nor is it relevant. Because the word "information" carries different meanings, we have unambiguously defined it by identifying its four distinguishing attributes. In order to avoid ambiguity or misunderstanding or conflation with other uses of the word "information," we have labeled this definition "Universal Information," often abbreviated as UI.

---

4. Karl Popper, *The Myth of the Framework: In Defense of Science and Rationality* (Oxfordshire, UK: Routledge, 1995).

Proceeding carefully, certain laws about Universal Information can be formulated. The very existence of Universal Information challenges the worldview of materialism. The possibility of an intelligent source is examined, as well as whether or not this intelligent source is non-material.

We then examine the particular coding system found in DNA, and discover that the information conveyed within genes is indeed UI. Using this DNA evidence and scientific laws governing UI as premises, we are able to develop sound, logical deductions. This leads us to the following conclusion: the God of the Bible exists, and He is responsible for originating and embedding Universal Information into biological life.

The truth is a powerful thing: it does not allow a person to remain undisturbed. Some embrace and follow the truth. Some reject it outright. Others prefer to ignore it, employing what might be termed "intentional ignorance." How a person reacts to the truth is a willful decision that produces unavoidable consequences in that person's life.

If materialism is embraced, then we invent our own standards of right and wrong and are accountable to no one for our decisions. If, however, the Bible is right, then there is an absolute standard of right and wrong and we are to be held accountable for not only our decisions, but our attitudes and actions as well. In Paul's letter to the Romans, he states:

> For since the creation of the world God's invisible qualities — his eternal power and divine nature — have been clearly seen, being understood from what has been made, so that people are without excuse (Rom. 1:20).

Let us take a look.

# PART ONE

# Information

*Chapter 1*

# VARIOUS MANIFESTATIONS OF INFORMATION

Following are some examples of complex systems, about which the question must be asked: What is the reason this system can function in such a remarkable way?

## 1.1 The spider's web

Figure 1 shows a section of the web of a *Cyrtophora* spider. The mesh size is approximately 0.8 mm x 1.2 mm. The circle in the lower picture indicates the part that has been highly magnified by an electron microscope to provide the upper picture. The design and structure of this web is exquisite, and the spider uses the available material quite economically. The required rigidity and strength — stronger, weight-for-weight, than steel or indeed any other man-made fiber including Kevlar — are obtained with a minimal amount of material. Spiral threads do not merely cross the radials and the two sets are not attached at the points of intersection only. Instead, they run parallel over a short distance and then they are tied or "soldered" together with very fine threads.

This spider's web gives the appearance of skilled architectural planning and proficient weaving. The spider's body chemically synthesizes the silk it uses for spinning the web using a computer-like controlled

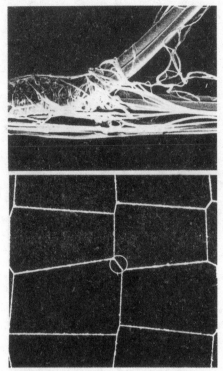

Figure 1: The web of a *Cyrtophora* spider.

manufacturing process. Where did this apparent architectural, engineering, and chemical ability come from? How were these instincts instilled into the spider? Where did the information come from? Most spiders are also active in recycling: they eat their own web in the morning and chemically process the material for re-use in manufacturing a new web.

If we want to answer these questions, we have to be willing to look at the way in which *information* plays an essential role.

## 1.2 The spinnerets of *Uroctea*

The spinning spigots of *Uroctea* spiders are shown in Figure 2 under high magnification. The female has 1,500 spinnerets, only a few of which appear in Figure 2, where threads can be seen emerging from two of them. Silk having the required tensile strength is produced in the "factories" located directly below the spinnerets. These complex processes have a computer-like control and, in addition, all the required equipment is highly miniaturized. How is it possible that such a complex and minutely detailed manufacturing process can be carried out without mishap? It is because the system contains a controlling program that has all the required processing **information** (see chapter 5.9.2, Operational Universal Information).

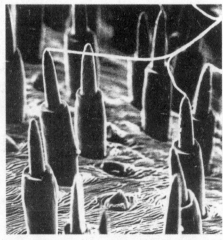

Figure 2: The spinnerets of *Uroctea*

## 1.3 The *Morpho rhetenor* butterfly

The South American butterfly *Morpho rhetenor* is depicted in Figure 3 under various magnifications so that the detailed structure of its wing scales can be seen (*Scientific American*, Vol. 245, Nov. 1981, p. 106). The wings exhibit marvelous colorful patterns, metallic blue above and brown underneath. The wings were analyzed for pigmentation, but none was found. How then can this colorful beauty be explained?

The detailed structure of the wings becomes apparent at 40×, 280×, and 16,000× levels of magnification. At

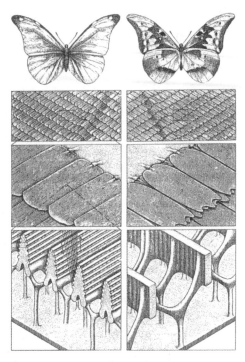

Figure 3: The South American butterfly *Morpho rhetenor* with wing surface sections under different magnifications.

the lower magnifications the structure resembles roof tiles, but at magnification 16,000× the secret is revealed. The structure is quite extraordinary: on the left side of Figure 3 is a regular grid of precisely constructed wedge-shaped ridges spaced at intervals of about 0.00022 mm. This pattern is repeated so accurately that the maximum deviation is only 0.00002 mm. What is the purpose of this marvelous structure, which would be impossible for us to manufacture with this precision?

A certain physical effect is utilized here in a fascinating way. It can be explained in terms of a simple example: when one drops two stones into a pool, concentric waves spread out from each point of impact. At some points of contact these waves cancel out and at other points they enhance one another. This effect is known as wave interference, and it is this effect on light waves that results in the observed colors. When the sun's light rays strike the stepped grid, called a *diffraction grating*, some colors are canceled out and other colors are enhanced. The grid spacing and the wavelengths of the incident light are precisely tuned to one another.

Furthermore, the deep black edges are caused by another fine structure: the scales are covered with pits about 0.001 mm across, with a high refractive index. Almost all light entering this pit is not reflected to an observer, but back into the material, so it appears almost completely black — blacker than any paint.

Another butterfly, *Lamprolenis nitida,* has two "blazed" diffraction gratings interspersed on single scales, which give two main color signals.

Did this simply happen accidentally, where everything is precisely formed to produce a special physical effect? That stretches credibility. It appears that, once again, the answer is most likely linked to **information!** (see chapter 5.9, Production Universal Information).

## 1.4 The development of human embryos

What happens during the nine months of human gestation is incredible. During the first four weeks of the new life, billions of cells are formed, and they arrange themselves according to an apparent plan to shape the new human being. Around the fifteenth day the first blood vessels appear. A few days later, within the tiny breast of the 1.7-mm-long embryo, two blood vessels join to form the heart, which begins to pump blood through the minuscule body before the end of the third week. The tiny new heart provides the developing brain with blood and oxygen. In the fourth month the heart of the fetus[1] is already pumping 30 liters of blood per day; at birth this volume will be 350 liters.

After two months the embryo is only three to four centimeters long. It is so small that it could literally fit inside a walnut shell. At this stage all organs are already developing — including lungs, eyes, and ears, even though they are not used yet. During the following months the organs increase in size and assume their eventual shape.

Various stages of human embryonic and fetal development are shown in Figure 4 [B3]:

A: A four-week-old embryo that is 4.2 mm long:
    1) Boundary between back and abdomen
    2) Incipient shoulder groove

---

1. **Fetus:** After 12 weeks no new organs begin to form. When organogenesis (embryogenesis = the growth and differentiation of cells at the sites of new organs during the first 12 weeks) is concluded, the embryo is referred to as a *fetus* (Latin for "offspring") and its further growth is known as fetal development.

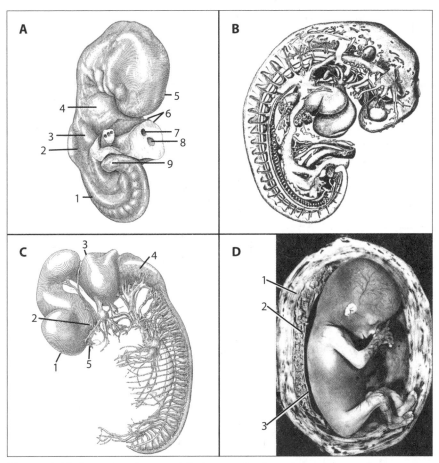

Figure 4: Various developmental stages of a human embryo.

3) Liver bulge
4) Heart bulge
5) Eye
6) Thin and thick part of the navel funnel
7) Anulus umbilicalis
8) Anulus umbilicalis impar
9) Coccyx

B: The embryo at four weeks when it is 4.2 mm long with internal structures exposed.

C: The exposed nervous system of a two-month-old embryo that is 17.7 mm long:

1) Telencephalon (= the front part of the first brain vesicle)

2) Optic nerve
3) Cerebellum
4) Medulla oblongata
5) Olfactory lobe (sense of smell)

D: Three-inch (75-mm) fetus shown inside the uterus:
1) Placenta
2) Myometrium (= muscular wall of the womb)
3) Amniotic membrane (the amniotic fluid has been removed)

How is it possible that embryonic development does not entail a disorderly growth of cells, but is systematic and purposeful according to an apparent timetable? A precise plan, in which all stages are programmed in the finest detail, underlies all these processes. In this case, also, **information** is the overall guiding factor.

## 1.5 The organ-playing robot

Would it be possible for a robot to play an organ? In Figure 5, Vasubot, a Japanese robot, enthralls music lovers. It has two hands and two feet that are able to manipulate the keys and the pedals as it reads sheet music by means of a video camera. The notes are converted to the required

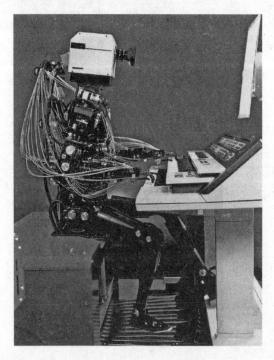

Figure 5: The organ-playing robot, Vasubot. This robot was exhibited at EXPO '85 in Japan. It was developed by Prof Ichiro Kato of Wasedo University, and was built by Sumitomo Electronic Industries. The robot is now on display in the official Japanese Government building EXPO '85 (tsukuba). This illustrates the capabilities of this level of technology and its limitations, i.e., this robot can only perform that which has been pre-programmed.

robotic hand and foot motions. This robot can read and play any piece of music without first having to practice it. The reason for this ability is that information is provided in a program together with all the required mechanisms. If the program is removed the robot cannot do anything. Information is the essential ingredient.

Consequences: Looking at the above examples, all of which are non-random in behavior or organization, we must consider that built-in information is their common factor. None of these systems could operate if their intrinsic information were removed. To better understand the processes occurring in living as well as in inanimate systems, it is necessary to study the concept of information in much greater depth. Werner Strombach, Professor of Informatics at Dortmund (Germany), briefly expressed an idea with which I could agree:[2]

Whoever can identify the original source of information holds the key to explaining the world. [S13]

---

2. I would add that it is not clear from the statement whether God is being referred to or whether He is excluded. The question of the source of the information is acknowledged to be of fundamental importance, but without the Spirit of God no one can really understand this world, even if they could logically and correctly answer the question about the source of the information. If the Bible really is the Book of Truth, as it so often indicates (e.g., John 17:17), then it is actually the Bible that is the key to understanding the world.

*Chapter 2*

# THE FIVE LEVELS OF
# UNIVERSAL INFORMATION

## 2.1 The search for the right scientific term for "information"

Good science and logical deductions require that critical terms in any field be unambiguously defined. Although everyone has an idea of the meaning of the term "information," it has not been unambiguously defined. We attempt to correct this here, and to select a suitable term for the "information" we will be working with intensively in the following chapters.

Why do we need a special term for this "information"? Firstly, we are defining information in a new way, and to avoid confusion with the other uses of the term "information," we need to give it a new name. Secondly, the term "information" appears in all kinds of scientific publications. Biologists refer to "biological information" when they investigate communication processes in living systems. Engineers use the term "statistical information," physicists use the term "algorithmic information," Intelligent Design proponents use the term "complex specified information." However, they all have one thing in common — they have not developed a *precise* definition of the information to which they refer. The meaning of the term "information" has remained superficial and vague. We cannot begin to develop an exact scientific theory if confronted with such a poorly defined term. In order that the term "information" used in this book should not be confused with existing definitions, we need to use a new meaningful name. This new term will fulfil the following requirements:

- The word "information" must appear in it, as the theory we are describing is surely an "information theory."

- The new term should not suggest affinity with specific scientific disciplines, but rather be applicable in a general sense.

- It should be an appropriate term for an entity governed by scientific laws. As scientific laws are themselves universally applicable, the term should suggest this universality.

- The term must be sufficiently broad and inclusive to cover systems completely unknown today, should they fall unambiguously within the domain of the definition.

- A precise definition will draw sharp boundaries between systems that are either included or excluded, and the more precise the definition, the sharper the boundaries. Precision and generality are, though, not necessarily contradictory terms. Although our definition is of necessity restrictive due to its precision, it loses none of its universality thereby.

- The communication systems we used as objects of our study were human natural languages (written) and human machine languages. Study of these revealed two separate classes of human communication systems. The one we studied intensely was based upon an abstract symbol set that leads to abstract sequences of symbols (words) that are designated with meanings derived from the entities they represent. This abstract attribute allows for the development of a great number of words (vocabulary) while using a minimum number of symbols (alphabet). The other communication system we encountered uses symbols that were not abstract; i.e., they resembled or had an inherent physical relationship with the entities they represented. Except for a brief discussion of this system that we designated as Mental Image Information (MII), we have left it for further study. The first system with abstract symbols is not only more versatile in forming a large number of abstract words but can be highly specified as to the meaning of each word. This broad capacity for numbers of words and potential to be defined unambiguously speaks of its universality.

Following discussions with several scientific colleagues, I have settled on the term **Universal Information (UI)**. This expression is neutral with respect to any specific discipline; nevertheless, it expresses its intended general applicability. However, it will be necessary to use the ambiguous term "information" as we work toward the specific definition we are seeking. Let us turn our attention to the definition of this new entity — Universal Information.

The subject of our study will include natural human languages and human machine languages. First, we will identify five attributes of Universal Information starting at the lowest level (*statistics*) and then work progressively through the higher levels of *syntax* (including thereby the code), *semantics* (meaning), *pragmatics* (action), and *apobetics* (purpose).

## 2.2 Necessary conditions for Universal Information

Let us start by describing a 1,500-year-long mystery regarding information. Figure 6 is a picture of icons cut in stone as they appear in the graves of pharaohs and on obelisks of ancient Egypt. Do they convey a message? Do they have information? To find out, we need to make three checks involving symbols, sequence, and order, which are the necessary conditions (NC) identifying information.

**NC1:** To present information, a set of symbols is required. This first condition is satisfied, because the stone carvings display various different symbols such as an owl, water waves, a mouth, reeds, etc.

Figure 6: Egyptian hieroglyphics

**NC2:** These symbols must occur in a generally irregular sequence. These irregularities differentiate it from an artistically composed array of similar ornaments. This condition is also satisfied, as there are no regularities or periodic patterns.

**NC3:** The symbols must be presented (drawn, printed, chiseled, engraved, etc.) in some recognizable order, such as in rows, columns, circles, spirals, or some other perhaps very complex (yet recognizable) distribution. In this example, the symbols appear in columns. With these three conditions met, it now seems possible that the given sequence of symbols might comprise information. However, it could also be that the Egyptians simply loved to decorate their monuments in this way. Similar to some of our patterned wallpapers, they could have chosen to decorate their walls with those shapes that we call hieroglyphics.[1] The true nature of these symbols remained a secret for 15 centuries because no one could assign meaning to them. This situation changed when one of Napoleon's men discovered a piece of black basalt the size of a normal table-top near the town of Rosetta on the Nile in July 1799 (see Figure 7). This stone, known as the Rosetta Stone, was exceptional because it contained inscriptions in three different languages: 54 lines of Greek, 32 lines of Demotic, and 14 lines of hieroglyphics. The 54 lines of Greek contained 468 Greek words an`d there were 166 different hieroglyphs in a total of 1419 hieroglyphic symbols. The Rosetta Stone played a key role in the deciphering of hieroglyphics, and its first success was the translation of an Egyptian pictorial text in 1822.

Once the meaning of the entire text was found, it became clear that the hieroglyphics contained information. Although enigmas remain, today hieroglyphic symbols are understood.

Figure 7: The Rosetta Stone (kept in the British Museum in London). Top: 14 lines of hieroglyphics; center: 32 lines of Demotic; bottom: 54 lines of Greek.

---

1. From Greek *hierós* = sacred; *glýphō* = carve, engrave. Since the Ptolemaic period, they were called *tà hieroglyphikà grámmata* (= 'the sacred engraved letters') in Greek.

𓏏𓉐𓏺𓄿𓂝𓂋𓂻𓆑𓏏𓄿𓆓𓏏𓇋𓇋𓇋𓇋𓇋𓆑𓂋𓀀𓂝𓂧

Rather one bushel from God, than five thousand ill-gotten.

𓇋𓄿𓏤𓏺𓂋𓏺𓏏𓆑𓏏𓄿𓄿𓆑𓂋𓄿𓂝𓄿

Keep your tongue from evil speech and you will be well-respected.

𓅓𓄿𓀀𓂝𓂋𓏺𓀁𓂋𓄿𓄿𓅓𓀁𓄿𓀀𓅓𓄿𓂋𓂻𓄿

Do not rob from the poor or do violence to the weak.

Figure 8: A computer printout of some proverbs translated into hieroglyphics.

**Decoding hieroglyphics:** The Greek text was easy to read and to translate, and in Cairo already it was found to be homage to King Ptolemy, inscribed by priests of Memphis in the year 196 B.C. With the obvious assumption that the contents of all three texts were identical, it appeared to be possible to decipher the pictorial writing, symbol by symbol. This assumption proved to be correct, but the decoding process became somewhat of an adventure, since a 1,400-year-old prejudice stood in the way. Horapollon, an Egyptian from the fourth century, had described hieroglyphics as being a purely pictorial script — as indeed it seemed to be. But this assumption resulted in some bizarre findings. A decisive step forward came when a Swedish linguist, Åkerblad, studying the Demotic text, recognized all the proper names appearing in the Greek version as well as the words for "temple" and "Greeks." Subsequently, Thomas Young, a physicist and physician, recognized the names "Berenice" and "Cleopatra" in the cartouches (the symbol groups appearing in the ovals in the sixth line from the top in Figure 7). Instead of looking for pictorial symbols, Young boldly suggested that the pictures were phonetic symbols representing sounds or letters. But he then shied away from the idea just as everyone else had before him. Here we see again the inhibiting effect that prejudices can have on finding the truth. The eventual breakthrough was made by the French founder of Egyptology, Jean François Champollion (1790–1832). He correlated single hieroglyphic symbols with the corresponding Greek letters appearing in the names "Ptolemy" and "Cleopatra" and could then begin the deciphering.

P T O L M Y S

K L E O P A T R A

This example of hieroglyphics has given us some idea about the nature of information. But that is, necessarily, just the beginning.

A complete characterization of the information concept requires five attributes: statistics, syntax, semantics, pragmatics, and apobetics. Information is presented as language (i.e., formulated, sent, and stored). An abstract alphabet comprising individual symbols is used to compose words (code). Then the (meaningful) words are arranged in sentences according to the rules of the relevant grammar (syntax) to convey the intended meaning (semantics). Universal Information must obviously also contain the action/s expected by the sender (pragmatics) and their intended purpose/s (apobetics).

## 2.3 The lowest level of information: Statistics

When examining a book or computer program we may consider the following questions:

- How many letters, numbers, and words make up the entire text of the system?

- How many single letters does the system's alphabet contain; e.g., "a, b, c ..., z" or "0, 1"?

- How frequently do certain letters and words occur?

To answer these questions, it is irrelevant whether we are dealing with actual meaningful text, with pure nonsense, or with random sequences of symbols. Such engineering investigations are not concerned with content, only with statistical aspects of the material medium used to convey the information. These matters all belong to the first — the lowest — level of information, namely, the *statistical level*. The statistical level can be seen as the bridge-overlap between the material and non-material realm. This is the level for which Claude E. Shannon developed his mathematical concept of information when he was working out a system to enable information to be transmitted more quickly via the then new transatlantic telephone cable. What was important to him was how the symbols themselves could be put into a condensed form, not whether they had any meaning. The meaning was presumed but not necessary. For instance, a shorter way of saying "n times n times n times n" is $n^4$. But it does not matter what n is, or what it represents. This is the sort of thing Shannon was interested in doing — this is called stochastic, or statistical information.

As explained in Appendix 1, Shannon's Theory of Information is suitable for describing the statistical aspects of information, i.e., those quantitative properties of languages that are manifested when information is encoded into a material medium. From an engineering perspective, meaning and grammar are not important for a given sequence of symbols. We arrive at the following definition:

> **Definition D1:** Information, according to Shannon's theory, is any sequence of symbols without regard to its origin or whether or not it is meaningful.

*Comment:* The statistical evaluation of a sequence of material symbols is a quantitative concept that may be measured in bits (binary digits).

According to Shannon's definition, the information content of a single message (which could be one symbol, one sign, one syllable, or a single word) is a measure related to the probability of its being received correctly. Probabilities range from 0 to 1 and so this measure is always positive. The information content of a number of messages (signs, for example) is found by adding the measures related to the individual probabilities according to the summation rule.

When somebody uses many words to say next to nothing, then, according to Shannon, this message is nevertheless assigned high information content because of the large number of letters used. But if somebody else concisely expresses the essentials of that same statement in very few words, his message is assigned a much lower information content. In another example, which expression, (a) or (b), contains more information?

- "Two plus two equals four"
- "2 + 2 = 4"

In one sense, both (a) and (b) contain the same amount of information. However, within Shannon's work, where the number and statistical frequency of characters are the measure, (a) contains more information than (b).

A representative in the American Congress once made the point:

The Lord's Prayer consists of 56 words, and the Ten Commandments comprise 297 words. The Declaration of Independence contains 300 words, but the recently published ordinance about the price of coal comprises no fewer than 26,911 words.

Which of these contains the most information? According to Shannon's theory, the ordinance about the price of coal does. The usefulness of Shannon's theory is limited to the level of statistical analysis, especially useful in the physical realm of engineering.

Because Shannon's definition of information is concerned exclusively with statistical interrelationships and measures that exist between sequences of symbols, meaning is not considered or evaluated. Statistical information is unsuitable for deciphering or evaluating meaning. A good comparison would be a sound level detector at an opera. The detector is able to indicate the sound level in decibels but it tells us nothing about the meaning either of the words or of the musical score in this opera. The scope of Shannon information is analogous to the output of this sound level detector. Thus, if we want to include the concept of meaning within the definition of information, we need to move to a higher level of Universal Information. The five levels being referred to here are illustrated in Figure 9.

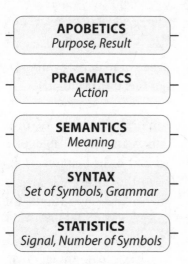

Figure 9: The five levels (attributes) of Universal Information (UI)

## 2.4 The second level of information: Syntax

When we look at something written in English it is obvious that the letters do not appear in random sequences. Combinations like "the," "car," "father," etc. occur frequently but we do not find certain other possible combinations like "xcy," "bkaln," or "dwust." In other words:

- Only certain combinations of letters are allowed, e.g., agreed-upon words of the English language. Other combinations do not belong to the language.

- The arrangement of words in sentences is not arbitrary; they follow rules of grammar.

In order to form information-bearing sequences of abstract symbols, both the construction of words using individual letters and the arrangement of words into sentences are subject to very specific rules, all based on conventions that exist for each language. This is referred to as syntax (Greek syntaxis = structure; the arrangement and interrelationship of words in grammatical construction).

> **Definition D2: Syntax here includes all the structural characteristics of the presentation of information.** The second level is independent of meaning (semantics) and pertains to the set of abstract symbols itself (the code) and the rules governing how they are assembled into sequences, including words, vocabulary, and grammar.

In considering this level, it will be helpful to subdivide its aspects into two distinct categories.

A) The code: the set of abstract symbols (the basic units) used for presenting information

B) The actual syntax: the interrelationships of the symbols (grammar)

### A) The code: A system of symbols for presenting information

A set of abstract symbols is required at the syntactic level for the presentation of information. Most written languages use letters and numerals, but a very wide range of conventions exists: Morse code, hieroglyphics, various data processing codes, international flag codes, musical notes, and the various hand signs used in the many different sign languages across the world used by and for the deaf.

> **Definition D3: A code is a uniquely defined set of abstract symbols.** "Abstract" here means that the symbols have no inherent relationship or resemblance to the reality that they are being used to represent.

Several questions are relevant:
 – How many abstract symbols are available in the set?
 – What criteria are used for constructing the code?
 – Which code should be used?
 – What mode of transmission is suitable for a given code?

– How can we determine for an unknown system whether a code is present or not?

**Number of abstract symbols:** The number of different abstract symbols (represented by n) employed by a coding system can vary greatly and depends mainly on the purpose and the application. In computer technology usually only two switch positions (on and off) are possible, and so binary codes were created comprised of only two different abstract symbols (such as 0 and 1). The various alphabet systems used by different languages generally range from 20 to 35 letters (these are the abstract symbols). This number of letters is sufficient for representing all the sounds of the language concerned. Certain script is not based on elementary sounds — pictograms are employed with each one representing a single word so that the number of different symbols is incalculable. Some examples of coding systems with the required number of abstract symbols are:

- Binary code ($n = 2$ abstract symbols, all electronic data processing codes)

- Ternary code ($n = 3$; Morse Code may be thought of as a ternary code with the three abstract symbols: "." (dot), "–" (dash) and " " (space))

- Quaternary code ($n = 4$, e.g., the genetic code consisting of four letters: A, T, C, G)

- Quinary code ($n = 5$)

- Octal code ($n = 8$ octal digits: 0, 1, 2, ... , 7)

- Decimal code ($n = 10$ decimal digits: 0, 1, 2, ... , 9)

- Sedecimal (hexadecimal) code[2] ($n = 16$ hex digits: 0, 1, 2, ... 9, A, B, C, D, E, F)

- Hebrew alphabet ($n = 22$ letters)

- Greek alphabet ($n = 24$ letters)

- Latin alphabet ($n = 26$ letters: A, B, C, ..., X, Y, Z)

- Braille ($n = 26$ letters)

---

2. Sedecimal system: This is used for representing numbers with base 16 (Latin *sedecim* = 16). A commonly used name for it is the "hexadecimal" system, which is a hybrid derived from both Greek and Latin: Greek *hexa* = 6, Latin: *decem* = 10. An acceptable alternative to sedecimal would be "hexadecadic" from the Greek word for 16.

- International flag code ($n = 26$ different flags)
- Russian alphabet ($n = 32$ Cyrillic letters)
- Japanese Katakana writing ($n = 50$ abstract symbols representing different syllables)
- Chinese writing ($n > 50,000$ pictograms)
- Hieroglyphics (in the time of Ptolemy: $n = 5,000$ to $7,000$; Middle Kingdom, 12th dynasty: $n$ = approx. 800)

**Criteria for selecting a code:** Coding systems are not created arbitrarily — they are optimized according to criteria related to their use, as is shown in the following examples:

- Pictorial appeal (e.g., hieroglyphics and pictograms)
- Small number of abstract symbols (e.g., Braille, cuneiform script, and binary code)
- Speed of writing (e.g., shorthand)
- Ease of writing (e.g., cuneiform)
- Ease of sensing (e.g., Braille)
- Ease of transmission (e.g., Morse code)
- Technical legibility (e.g., universal product bar codes and postal bar codes)
- Ease of detecting errors (e.g., special error-detecting codes, like a test for divisibility by three)
- Ease of correcting errors (e.g., Hamming code)
- Ease of visualizing tone sequences (musical notes)
- Representation of the sounds of natural languages (alphabets)
- Redundancy for counteracting interference errors (various computer codes and natural languages; written German has, for example, a redundancy of 66%)
- Maximization of storage density (e.g., compressibility of data)

**Choice of code** is aligned to the **mode of communication**: If a certain mode of transmission has been adopted for technological reasons (based upon some physical or chemical phenomenon), then the code must be suited to that technology. In addition, the concepts of the sender and the receiver must be in tune with one another to ensure certainty of information transfer (see Figure 10, chapter 2.7). The following is an overview of various types of existing messaging systems:

- Acoustic transmission (conveyed by means of sounds):
  - Natural spoken languages used by humans
  - Mechanical transducers (e.g., loudspeakers, sirens, and fog horns)

- Optical transmission (carried by light waves):
  - Written languages
  - Technical drawings (e.g., for constructing machines and buildings, and electrical circuit diagrams)
  - Technological flashing signals (e.g., identifying flashes of lighthouses)
  - Flag signals (e.g., semaphore)
  - Punch cards (an early mode of computer data entry); mark sensing
  - Bar codes (product ID, postal)
  - Sign language

- Tactile transmission (Latin *tactus* n. = touch; adj. *tactilis* = tangible) (Signals: physical contact):
  - Braille writing
  - Music rolls; barrel of a barrel-organ

- Magnetic transmission (carrier: magnetic field):
  - magnetic tape
  - magnetic disk
  - magnetic card

- Electrical transmission (carrier: electrical current or electro-magnetic waves):
  - telephone
  - radio and TV

**How to recognize a code.** In the case of an unknown system it is not always easy to decide whether one is dealing with a real code or not. The following five necessary conditions (**NC**) must be fulfilled simultaneously for a given set of abstract symbols to qualify as a code:

**NC1:** An unambiguously defined set of abstract symbols must be present, which may be arbitrary in nature. [Again, "abstract" here means that the symbols have *no inherent physical relationship or resemblance* to the reality that they are being used to represent.]

**NC2:** The sequence of the individual symbols must, generally speaking, be irregular/aperiodic:
Examples of aperiodic symbol sequences:

1. •─ ─••• •─• ─ ─ ─ •─ ─ ─• ─•• ─ ─ ─ ─ ─•
2. A brown dog
3. qxst wzyr gffqtr

Counter-examples (periodic sequences):

4. ─ • ─ • ─ • ─ • ─ •
5. ⊓⊓⊓⊓⊓⊓⊓⊓⊓⊓⊓    ──────────────────
6. abc abc abc abc

Note that nos. 1–3 may each represent the use of a code to convey a coded message, though as no. 3 suggests, not necessarily; aperiodicity is a necessary, but not sufficient condition to indicate the existence of a code. But none of the counter-examples 4–6 indicates that a code might be present.

**NC3:** The symbols appear in clearly distinguishable structures such as in rows, columns, blocks, spirals, or perhaps in some other very complex (yet recognizable) distribution.

**NC4:** At least some symbols will generally recur.
Examples:
1. (English) People live in houses.
2. German) Der grüne Apfel fällt vom Baum.

---

**Pangrams:** A perfect pangram is a sentence comprising all the letters of the alphabet where each letter is used once only. No such 26-letter sentence in English is known without using abbreviations and/or obscure/doubtful words, and is highly artificial. The well-known sentence that retains meaning while showcasing all 26 letters as compactly as possible still requires 35 letters to do so: *The quick brown fox jumps over the lazy dog.*

It is difficult to construct meaningful sentences without using some letters more than once. Sentences where no letters are repeated are often rather chaotic, for example:
- Big fjords vex waltz nymph (22 letters)
- Vixens jump; fowl quack (19 letters)
- Quick nymphs beg fjord waltz (24 letters)

**NC5:** It can be decoded successfully and meaningfully (e.g., hieroglyphics). In short, the receiver is able to understand the meaning conveyed by the code. This requires semantics, the next level in the hierarchy of attributes.

## Sufficient conditions (SC) for a code

**SC1:** A code system is established with certainty if it can be decoded successfully and meaningfully (e.g., hieroglyphics). In short, the receiver is able to understand the meaning conveyed by the code. This requires semantics, the next level in the hierarchy of attributes.

## Sufficient conditions for a non-code (SCn)

It is important to be able to identify something which might appear to be a code system, as being a non-code system. There are two sufficient conditions (SCn) for this. A sequence of symbols *cannot* be an abstract code if:

**SCn1:** It can be explained fully on the level of physics and chemistry, i.e., its origin is exclusively of a material nature.

Example: The periodic signals received in 1967 by the British astronomers J. Bell and A. Hewish were at first thought to be coded messages from space sent by so-called "little green men." It was, however, eventually established that this "message" had a purely material origin and a new type of star was discovered — pulsars.

**SCn2:** It is *known* to be a random sequence (i.e., when its random origin is known or communicated). This conclusion also holds when the sequence randomly contains valid words from a known code.

Example: we run a random character generation program and obtain the following output:

AZTIG KFD MAUER DFK KLIXA WIFE TSAA

Although the German word "MAUER" and the English word "WIFE" may be recognized in this sequence, this does not contain Universal Information according to SCn2 because our knowledge of the program informs us that it is a *random* sequence.

These fundamentals of the "code" theme were first published by the author [G6] in 1982 and they have withstood scientific scrutiny for nigh on half a century. According to our experience, the presence of a code signifies a preceding intellectual process, and its meaning, among people, depends upon an agreed-upon syntax. We thus have the necessity of intelligence at the second level of information. We are now in a position to formulate some fundamental empirical statements (ES):

---

**ES 1:** A code is an essential requirement for presenting Universal Information. A code is a necessary, but not a sufficient, condition for identifying or for generating Universal Information.

**ES 2:** The allocation of meanings to, and the determination of meanings from, sequences of abstract symbols are intellectual processes, based on convention.

**ES 3:** Once the code has been defined by a freely agreed convention, this definition must be adhered to thereafter.

**ES 4:** If the information is to be understood, the particular code must be known to both the sender and the receiver.

**ES 5:** A code system is always the result of an intellectual process, and thus requires an intelligent originator.

---

In ES 5, "intellectual process" and "intelligent originator" seek to express the fact that matter by itself cannot generate a code. All experience shows that only a reasoning being with free will, intelligence, and a creative ability to plan can achieve this. The ability to think is a necessary prerequisite, and thinking must involve information processing.

The language researcher Helmut Gipper defined "thinking" as follows [G4, p. 261]:

> The intellectual activity of a living being can be regarded as "thinking" if it succeeds on the basis of its biological construction plan and its brain structure not only to remember and use practically

the experiential data received through its senses, but also to freely link them in the sense of if – then relationships and, thereby … to draw simple conclusions and find solutions to problems.

Thinking is not to be confused with the instinctive ability of animals without room for decision. Thinking presupposes freedom of choice. The building of a spider's web, a bee's honeycomb, or even the language of the bees have nothing to do with thinking — however complex, useful, or amazing these abilities may be. These are inborn, rigid programmed behavior patterns that allow minimal variations within specified boundaries.

Although instinctive behaviors do not involve thinking, most, if not all, are directed by informational control systems. For example, the code systems of communication within the animal kingdom were not invented by them but are, according to Figure 22 in chapter 5.2, completely created.

---

**The German system of Postal Codes:** Empirical Statements 1 through 5 can be easily demonstrated by means of a well-known example of a code system, the system of postal codes introduced in Germany on July 1, 1993, using a five-digit code. The entire federal state was divided into 26,400 new postal delivery districts. 1,700 major customers with more than 2,000 postal deliveries daily were given their own codes. In addition, 16,500 codes were used for post-box addresses. The first digit designates the region around a particular city (e.g., 1 for the region in and around Berlin; 2 for Hamburg and environs; 8 for Munich and environs), and the second digit generally designates a large town. The third to fifth digits represent the postal districts within a town or region. The allocation of five-digit codes to postal districts was executed by an expert team of 8 persons (ES 1, sender of information as a team). In accordance with ES 4, the code must be known to both sender and receiver. In order to achieve that, the greatest print contract in history was placed: 40 million Postal Code Directories, each weighing more than 2 kilograms, with 1,000 pages, were printed and given to all households. The code system was permanently established after exhaustive consultation (as per ES 5, a code system has to be thought out *via* an intellectual process).

---

In Figure 10 the expression "rejoice" appears in different languages and coding systems. This observation leads to another important empirical statement:

---

**ES 6:** Any given sequence of Universal Information (UI) may be represented by any other code system of UI.

---

გიხაროდეთ
أفرحوا
Радуйтесь
džiaukitės
örüljetek
verbly julle
rejoice


Figure 10: Different codes expressing the same meaning. The word "rejoice" is represented by means of a selection of different coding systems. From top down: Georgian, Arabic, Russian, Lithuanian, Hungarian, Czech, German (Braille, Morse code, shorthand), and English.

**NOTE:** ES 6 does not imply that a complete translation is always possible. It is often very difficult, when translating from one language to another, to convey metaphors, turns of phrase, ambiguities, and figures of speech. Also, words for certain objects or concepts in one language may not yet be present in another.

ES 1 through ES 6 demonstrate that fundamental statements about Universal Information can be formulated even at the relatively low level of codes. If, for example, one finds a code underlying any given system, then one can conclude that the system had an intellectual origin. In affirmation of ES 5 no one would have suggested that the hieroglyphics were caused by a purely physical process such as the random effects of wind or water, even before it was decoded successfully and meaningfully (NC5).

The following are some properties common to all coding systems:

- A code is a necessary prerequisite for presenting, transmitting, and storing information.
- Every choice of code must be thought out beforehand.
- Devising a code is a creative intellectual process.
- Matter is the carrier of codes but cannot *originate* codes (for instance, electrical impulses can carry speech from phone to phone, but the electrical impulses do not originate the speech).

**Definition D4: Syntax is the set of all rules in a language, regardless whether it is a natural or machine language, or one of logic or mathematics.** Syntax defines allowable combinations of basic symbols in a given language to form more complex elements (e.g., letters into words, words into sentences, and sentences into paragraphs) and establishes the rules for making those definitions. It encompasses a language's morphology, phonetics, and vocabulary. In short, syntax determines what structures are and are not allowed in a language.

## B) Syntax per se

Consider the following questions:

a) Sender-related:
- Which of the possible combinations of abstract symbols are actual defined words (lexicon and spelling)?
- How should the words be arranged (i.e., sentence construction, word order, and style), linked with one another, and inflected to form a sentence (grammar)?
- What language should be used for this communication?
- Which special modes of expression are used (style, aesthetics, precision of expression, and protocols)?
- Are the sentences syntactically correct?

b) Receiver-related:
- Does the receiver understand the language? (The content is not yet relevant.)

The following sample sentences illustrate various aspects of the syntax level:

- The hungry wolf pursues the nimble deer. (proper sentence)

- The bird singed the song. (semantically possible but syntactically wrong)

- The green freedom persecutes the thinking house. (semantically nonsense but syntactically correct)

- Twas brillig, and the slithy toves did gyre and gimble in the wabe.[3] (syntactically correct, but with mostly meaningless words)

- The baker dumb tomcat automatic even honor. (no syntactic structure but meaningful words)

- Molf ortan kinker deffel glauch legeslamp. (totally impossible to understand: no syntactic structure; no meaningful words)

The syntax of a language includes all the rules that describe how individual language elements are to be combined. The syntax of natural languages (basic communication from person to person) is much more

---

3. From *The Jabberwocky* by Lewis Carroll. Note that in spite of the meaninglessness of the words, the poet's skillful choice of syllables does indeed arouse the feeling of meaning in the reader's mind.

complex than that of formal artificial languages (such as computer codes or musical notes). The syntactic rules of an artificial language must be complete and unambiguous because, for example, a compiler program that translates programs written in a programming language (source code) into another machine language cannot call the programmer to clarify syntactic issues.

Since any encoding and the assignment of meaning thereto rests solely on an agreed convention, knowledge of this convention is essential for both the sender and the receiver. This knowledge is either transferred directly (e.g., by being introduced into a computer system), by inheritance (as in the case of instinctive biological systems), or it must be learned from scratch (e.g., mother tongue or any other natural language).

No person enters this world with an inherited knowledge of some language or its concepts. The acquisition of ability and knowledge in a language involves learning the relevant vocabulary and grammar. This is so even where the learning is largely effortless, as in a young child exposed to the language(s) in its surroundings. The vocabulary and grammar themselves arose from "agreement."

## 2.5 The third level of information: Semantics (meaning)

> **Definition D5: Semantics refers to the meaning that has been assigned to words, phrases, sentences, etc.** Meaning is established through an unambiguous definition of the object or concept that is represented by the words, phrases, sentences, etc.

Whether we read a novel, directions, or a communication of another kind, we are not nearly as interested in the individual letters, or even the grammar, as we are in the meaning of what has been written.

Symbol sequences and syntactic rules are prerequisites for representing information. However, the essential characteristic of the conveyed information is not the selected code, neither is it the size, number, or form of the letters or the method of transmission such as the written word on paper or through optical, acoustic, electrical, or tactile signals.

**The essential characteristic of Universal Information is the actual message being conveyed; i.e., the sense, the meaning. This essential attribute is called the "semantics."**

Although semantics is a central attribute of Universal Information, it plays no role in issues concerning storage and transmission. The cost of a telegram, for example, does not depend on the importance of the message but only on the number of letters or words or syllables. Both the sender and the receiver are mainly interested in the meaning, and it is meaning that changes a sequence of symbols into Universal Information. So now we have arrived at the third level of Universal Information, the *semantic* level (Greek *semantikós* = having meaning).

Questions concerning semantics include:

a)  Sender-related:
    • What is the sender's purpose or goal?
    • What meaning is contained?
    • What information is implied in addition to the explicit information?
    • What stylistic means are employed for conveying the information, e.g., metaphors, idioms, and parables?

b)  Receiver-related:
    • Does the receiver understand the information?
    • Is the message meaningful?
    • What background information is required for understanding the transmitted information?
    • Is the message true or false?

---

**ES 7:** An important aspect of Universal Information is that it has been transmitted by someone and is meant for someone. A sender and an intended receiver are always involved whenever and wherever there is Universal Information.

---

*Note:* Some information, such as a personal letter, is directed to a single receiver; some information, such as a book or newspaper, is directed to a wide range of receivers; and some information is not directed to any receiver other than the sender, but is simply self-expression, such as diarizing, talking to oneself, or writing a shopping list for oneself. Finally, there is information which is intended for a receiver, but which never gets there, such as a letter lost in the mail.

Here, at the semantic level, is the first time we have *meaningful* information.

We may now formulate additional empirical statements.

> **ES 8:** Semantics is a necessary attribute of Universal Information.

The statistical and syntactic properties can be altered appreciably when information is represented in another language (e.g., translated from English into Chinese) **but the meaning is not intended to change.** In fact, if the meaning *does* change — as when a message is poorly translated — then we hear people say that the message (i.e., the information) has been "lost in translation."

Universal Information is always an abstract representation of something else. Universal Information is encoded in abstract symbols that represent what is being discussed. For example, the symbols in today's newspaper may give information about an event that happened yesterday, or perhaps the event happened in another country. Sequences of abstract symbols play a substitutive role — they are used to convey a reality or a system of thought. Thus, the information itself is not the actual object, act, event, or idea being discussed. It is the means of communicating concerning those things.

Because meanings represent intellectual concepts, the point of origin must also be intellectual. Consider, as an example, the following chain: author of a radio program (**sender**) → transmission equipment → radio tower → radio antenna → car radio → and finally the car driver as the **receiver** of the information. Random electrical noise will not yield a message to the driver, other than suggesting that his radio is not working properly — which is simply an inference he would draw, rather than the result of receiving a meaningful message.

> **ES 9:** Universal Information leads back to an intellectual source (sender) by tracing its progress backwards along the chain of transmission.

We may formulate an additional empirical statement that allows us to distinguish and identify Universal Information:

> **ES 10:** Universal Information cannot originate from random, unguided physical-chemical processes.

The notion of guided and unguided processes is critically important. Unguided physical-chemical processes yield outcomes that are wholly determined by physical laws. There is no end goal in these processes — they merely happen in accordance with the natural laws that govern them. Thus, purposeful outcomes are not possible for unguided physical-chemical processes. This holds true even if we consider probabilistic laws, such as are involved in quantum mechanics, since these do not manifest goal or purpose any more than deterministic natural laws. As a consequence of this unguided aspect of purely natural physical-chemical processes, they are incapable of generating meaningful Universal Information. What the data they provide can do, however, is to demonstrate the interconnectedness of cause and effect.

A necessary requirement for generating meaningful information is the ability to select from alternatives, and this requires an intelligent, volitional source. Recall the earlier discussion of syntax. Both code and syntax originate only from intelligent agents (e.g., humans). Unguided, random processes cannot do this — not in *any* amount of time — because this selection process demands continuous guidance by intelligent beings *that have a purpose*. If this purpose involves communicating information, then it entails the use of a language. Language and communication of information are not the result of unguided processes. An unguided process does not require intelligence, but a guided process does. A guided process involves intelligence doing the choosing, guiding, and specifying a direction and intent (see "Guided processes and natural law," on following page).

A language is any suitable way of expressing meaning. Universal Information can be transmitted or stored on material media only when a language is available. The information itself is invariant, regardless of any change in either the transmission system (e.g., acoustic, optical, or electrical) or the storage system (e.g., brain, book, computer hard drive, magnetic tape).

ES 5 and ES 9 categorically link information to a sender (an intelligent source of meaningful information). Whether or not information is understood by some receiver does not change the fact that this information exists. In modern times, the carvings in the Egyptian obelisks were seen as human workmanship (and as likely representing information) long before they were deciphered; it was obvious that they could not have resulted from random processes. The meaning of the hieroglyphics could not be understood until after the Rosetta Stone was found in 1799. Nevertheless, these hieroglyphics represented Universal Information since the time that they were carved into stone.

**Guided processes and natural law:** Consider water flowing in a river. It does so according to natural (scientific) laws and without guidance. In this state it will flow, erode the riverbed, deposit silt in a lake or in the ocean, etc. — all natural phenomena. Let us now introduce purposeful guidance. We build a dam and direct that same water to flow through a specific route (pipes) so that it propels generator blades to produce electricity that allows lights to be turned on, and for refrigerators, televisions, and computers to run. Could that water have produced equivalent results with nothing other than unguided natural laws? What if we allowed countless billions of years — would that make it any more possible? In this we see that guidance is what allows for processes to run in a direction *contrary* to the direction of natural laws. It's not that guidance allows us to violate any natural laws (as may appear to be the case in a refrigerator, where electrical energy is directed through a machine to extract heat to make the inside of the refrigerator colder). It's that things are purposefully selected and directed (i.e., guided) so as to attain a goal that unguided processes would never have attained, because of the *sheer impossibility* of that goal happening *without* this direction/guidance. This is because unguided physical laws naturally and invariably take us away from the desired goal. The Second Law of Thermodynamics, for example, does not allow heat to flow from a colder body to a warmer one. Yet, with a refrigerator (a purposefully created machine) we accomplish precisely that objective while always complying with natural laws (see chapter 2.4).

Meaning is expressed through various forms of human languages:

1. Natural languages and dialects: at present there are approximately 5,100 active natural languages and dialects on earth. In addition, there are the various sign languages used by the deaf. It is interesting to note that deaf children born to hearing parents will invent their own "home sign language" in order to communicate. Language ability thus appears to be inherent in humans.

2. Artificial languages: Esperanto, semaphore, traffic signals.

3. Formal artificial languages: logical and mathematical calculi, chemical symbols, musical notation, algorithmic languages, programming languages like Ada, Algol, APL, BASIC, C, C++, Fortran, Pascal, PL/1.

4. Special technical languages: building and construction plans, block diagrams, diagrams depicting the structure of chemical

compounds and electrical, hydraulic, and pneumatic circuit diagrams.

A common property of all languages is that defined sets of abstract symbols are used and that definite rules and meanings are allocated to the individual symbols or language elements. Every natural language contains units like morphemes, lexemes, idioms, and, in natural languages, entire sentences that serve as carriers of meaning (formatives). Meanings are assigned to the formatives of a language, and the sender and receiver must mutually agree on these assignments to make sense of any communication. Natural languages employ many devices for encoding meaning. Several of these devices are: morphology, syntax (grammar and style), phonetics, intonation, and gesticulation, as well as numerous other aids like homonyms, homophones, metaphors, synonyms, polysemes, antonyms, paraphrases, anomalies, metonymy, irony, etc.

Every communication process between sender and receiver consists of formulating and understanding the meaning of the words in some language. In the *formulation process,* the thoughts of the sender generate meaningful words that are to be transmitted by means of a suitable language. In the *comprehension process,* the symbol combinations (words, etc.) are analyzed by the receiver and converted into their corresponding meanings. It is universally valid that, in the case of the communication of information, the sender and the receiver are both intelligent beings. It can also be said that if there is no intelligent receiver, but there is information being encoded, the particular system used for transmission, acquisition, processing, and storage of the information must have been created by intelligence (Figures 21 and 22, chapter 5.6).

## 2.6 The fourth level of information: Pragmatics (action)

**Definition D6: Pragmatics in this context refers to the action that the sender desires or expects of the receiver.** The expected action may be either explicit and/or implicit within the message.

There is a Russian saying that "the effect of spoken words can last one hour but a book serves as a perpetual reminder." Books can have lasting effects. After one has read a manual on software, for example, one can use the system that is described in it.

Many people have read the Bible and this book has motivated them to act in entirely new ways. This consequential aspect of reading of the

> **Minister for Semantics:** Former U.S. president Harry S. Truman (1884–1972) composed the following light-hearted memorandum during his period of office: "I have recently appointed a *Minister for Semantics* — a very important portfolio. His task is to provide me with expressions that appear to be heavy with meaning, to teach me how one can say yes and no in one sentence without becoming entangled in contradictions, to work out a word combination which will make me appear to be against inflation in San Francisco, and supporting inflation in New York, and, finally, to show me how one can wrap oneself in silence but still tell all. You will agree that such a man would save me a lot of trouble." (Source: *Reader's Digest*, February 1993, p. 168) Truman was actually more concerned about the *effects* of his words than their meaning, and this is on a level above semantics. He seemed unaware that he was actually looking for a Minister for *Pragmatics* (or even *Apobetics* — discussed later).

Bible caused Blaise Pascal to say:"There are enough passages in Scripture to comfort people in all spheres of life and enough passages to alarm them."

**Information demands action by a receiver.** For our purposes it is immaterial whether the receiver acts or thinks according to the sender's wishes, responds negatively, or ignores it. Even the shortest promotional slogan for a laundry detergent can promote a market preference for it, i.e., customers start buying that brand.

Up to the semantic level the question of the sender's intended purpose(s) with the transmitted message is not apparent. However, every transmission of information takes place because the sender wants to achieve a certain outcome involving the receiver. In order to achieve the intended outcome, the sender considers what is needed from him to attain that goal. We have now reached an entirely new level of Universal Information that we call pragmatics (Greek pragmatikós = "practical" from pragma = "act").

Questions arising in the area of pragmatics include:

a) Sender-related:
- What response or action(s) does the sender want from the receiver?
- Should the action be formulated explicitly, or should it be implicit?
- Is the response or action required or desired by the sender to be performed in only one predetermined way or are there degrees of freedom?

b) Receiver-related:
- To what extent does the received and understood meaning influence the thinking and behavior of the receiver?
- What is the receiver's actual response?
- Does the receiver respond in a way that achieves the sender's purpose?

> **ES 11:** Universal Information always includes a pragmatic aspect.

The pragmatic aspect might:
- be non-negotiable and unambiguous so as not to allow any degree of interpretive freedom; e.g., a computer program or a military command
- allow a limited freedom of choice (like some parental requests of children)
- allow considerable interpretive freedom of action (as in the case of a person choosing what to wear to a function described as "very casual")

Note that even if the receiver deviates considerably from the desired action expressed by way of the semantics, this does not detract from the validity of ES 11.

The use of language does not involve the mere linking of sentences together, but that requests, complaints, questions, instructions, teachings, warnings, threats, or commands are formulated in order to obtain some kind of response by or in the receiver. Computer scientist Werner Strombach [S12] defined information as a structure that achieves some outcome in a receiving system. He has thereby drawn attention to this important attribute of Universal Information — pragmatics.

We can distinguish between two classes of action:

a) Fixed:
- Programmed actions (e.g., mechanical manufacturing processes and the operation of data processing programs)
- Trained actions (e.g., police dogs, dolphins, horses, and elephants)
- Instinctive animal behavior

b) Flexible and creative:
  - Learned activities such as social manners and manual skills
  - Reasoned/intelligent actions (as when choosing a route from a roadmap)
  - Intuitive (human) actions
  - Volitional (human) actions, involving intelligence and free will

Here, too, we can construct a statement from experience:

---

**ES 12:** Universal Information is sent to cause the receiver to perform some action or respond in some desired way.

---

This response-initiating effect of Universal Information is valid for both inanimate systems (e.g., computers or an automatic car wash) and living organisms (e.g., trained actions of animals and humans).

The pragmatic, i.e., the "expected response" attribute of Universal Information is much more profound than it may appear at first. The desired response that the sender has in mind is not one that would be likely or expected to occur by unguided physical-chemical processes. If it were something that would be expected to happen in the natural and normal course of events, the transmission of the information would not be needed.

Unguided physical-chemical processes always occur in the direction mandated by the natural laws of physics and chemistry, i.e., toward a state of equilibrium (the lowest energy and most stable state). On the other hand, physical-chemical processes guided by Universal Information are almost always directed into states of *disequilibrium*, i.e., unstable high-energy states. Examples are nearly unlimited:

1. The cultivating, planting, irrigating, and harvesting of an agricultural field. The field left untouched by man, i.e., without any intelligent intervention, would produce a mixture of weeds, grasses, shrubs, trees, etc., with much less yield, if any, for human needs.

2. Transporting employees from Los Angeles, USA, to Berlin, Germany. This would be impossible without machines and implements.

3. Preparing and serving a meal.
4. Protecting against a dangerous hazard by developing and installing an automatic safety device.

All these examples (and countless others that may be given) require machines that utilize energy to power implements specifically designed to either perform or facilitate the desired actions. Manpower utilizes the most exquisite of machines (namely, the human body) that can perform a multitude of actions by itself. However, the performance of the human body is greatly expanded by the use of mechanical implements designed, constructed, and operated by man. Manpower has also been augmented by using animal power, e.g., horses, oxen, and elephants, as well as machines powered by steam, internal combustion engines, electric motors, and so on.

Man's development of these machines and implements required the use of Universal Information during the creative thinking process, in the development of designs and plans, and in organizing all the steps and parts required for assembling the final product. The purpose of all of man's development of skills and technology has been to improve or make possible the performance of some action. Man's ability to successfully accomplish this depends primarily upon his capacity to create and utilize Universal Information.

Repeated observations of Universal Information's pragmatic attribute in a large variety of messages demonstrate the following empirical statements:

> **ES 13:** When the pragmatic attribute of Universal Information is expressed in the material domain it always requires a **machine.**

> **Definition D7:** A machine is a material device that requires energy to perform a specific function(s).

Universal Information, creative power, and matter are all necessary for the construction of a machine. It is Universal Information that determines and directs the assembling of the material system into the necessary configuration, thereby creating a machine. This means that tracing backwards through the manufacture and design of any machine capable of performing useful work will lead to the discovery that Universal Information was there at the outset, and that this originated from an

> **ES 14:** Universal Information and creative power are required for the design and construction of all machines.
>
> **ES 15:** The existence of a functioning machine invariably means that Universal Information is affecting, or has affected, the material domain.
>
> **ES 16:** Machines operate within the physical-chemical laws of matter (mass and energy).
>
> **ES 17:** Machines cause matter to consistently function in specific ways and consistently produce results never achieved solely by unguided physical-chemical processes.

intelligent source. Without intelligent input, raw energy cannot perform useful work. Information is necessary to design and produce a machine capable of harnessing raw energy and storing or utilizing it in goal-oriented fashion.

While the finished machine will mostly not exhibit any "fingerprint" of information, the existence of a machine, as defined above, will always imply an informational process in its design and construction. Information qualifying as Universal Information always conveys an expected action for an intended purpose. This means that the receiver must be a living organism capable of responding to Universal Information or a machine capable of functions (actions) directed by Universal Information. Within the material domain, both of these systems must have energy available as well as machinery capable of harnessing the energy and performing the work (action).

Although Universal Information cannot be quantitatively measured, the amount of work performed and the amount of energy utilized to perform the work can be measured quantitatively. The amount of energy used to perform a given unit of work could be utilized to assess the value of the Universal Information controlling the design, construction, and operation of the system. The smaller the amount of energy required for a machine to perform a unit of work, the higher its efficiency. The higher the efficiency of a machine, the higher the value of Universal Information and the higher the intelligence required to create the Universal Information essential for the development and assembly of the machine. In chapter 8.4 the reader will find a general discussion of machines, with examples from simple to extremely complex. Additionally, in chapter 10.2.1, the reader will find a discussion assessing the value of a given sequence of Universal Information.

## 2.7 The fifth level of information: Apobetics (purpose)

> **Definition D8: Apobetics** refers to the intended goal, the purpose, that the sender wishes to achieve. This was preceded by thought processes and actions to bring about that goal.

A goal can only be achieved by a preceding action (pragmatics). The action can be accomplished by the sender, the receiver, or by a man-made machine. In each case, the sender must first develop Universal Information to plan the sequence of events required to accomplish his goal.

The poet Goethe once wrote:

Some books seem to have been written, not to teach us anything, but to let us know that the author has known something.[4]

Such a less than worthy motive for writing a book nonetheless highlights something of fundamental importance: the sender is in pursuit of a goal which he seeks to achieve through the receiver. For example, a marketing firm (the sender) puts out a promotional slogan aimed at the customer (the receiver) to help a production division achieve good sales (the purpose). In the New Testament, John mentions a completely different purpose for his information:

I [the sender] write these things to you [the receiver] who believe in the name of the Son of God so that you may know that you have eternal life (1 John 5:13).

From these examples we begin to see that with any piece of Universal Information some purpose is being pursued.

We have now reached the highest level of information, namely, **apobetics** (this is the teleological aspect, the question of purpose; derived from the Greek *apobeinon* = result, success, conclusion). The term "apobetics" was introduced originally by the author [see G5] in linguistic consistency with the titles of the other four levels. For every performed action and achieved result on the side of the receiver, there was a preceding purpose, plan, goal, or concept involved. The teleological attribute

---

4. J.W. von Goethe, No. 417 in *Maxims and Reflections*, translated by Bailey Saunders, 1892.

of Universal Information is the most important because it concerns pre-meditation. Any piece of information involves the question: "What is the purpose of this information?" The following examples should elucidate this aspect:

- Computer programs are always written with a purpose (e.g., to solve a set of equations or to manipulate some data).

- A chocolate manufacturer uses a promotional slogan to entice customers (receivers) to buy his brand.

- Man is endowed with the ability for natural language that can be used for communicating with other people and formulating goals.

- God gives us a purpose for our lives through the Bible; this is discussed more fully in chapter 9 of this book.

Examples of questions in the realm of apobetics are:

a) Sender-related:
   - Has the sender described or implied an unambiguous purpose?
   - What does the sender want to achieve?
   - Can this purpose be recognized directly, or can it only be indirectly deduced (implicit apobetics)?
   - Has the sender encouraged or motivated the receiver to perform the sender's expected action(s) and thus achieve the sender's intended purpose(s)?

b) Receiver-related:
   - What purpose is achieved through the actions of the receiver?
   - Does the result obtained from the receiver correspond to the purpose the sender had in mind?
   - Did the receiver achieve a purpose that the sender had not intended? For example, the evaluation of historical documents could lead to actions or conclusions never intended by the author of the historical documents (the sender).

The receiver may respond to the sender's intention to varying degrees:

1. Completely (i.e., doing *exactly* what the sender wanted/requested). Example: A command in the form of a computer program (it responds *exactly* as it was programmed).

2. Partly. Example: Directives given to average children (they might respond to what is asked but not necessarily deliver fully what was expected; e.g., they respond to the instruction "clean your room" but may do so in "their own" way).

3. Not at all. Example: Directives given to disobedient children (e.g., they receive the instruction "clean your room" and do nothing at all).

4. By doing something other than, even the exact opposite of, what was requested. Example: Directives given to rebellious children (e.g., they receive the instruction, "Be home by 10 p.m." and respond by staying out past midnight).

An achieved result, however, may not have been mentioned or may not even have been imagined by the sender (e.g., documents from previous centuries with trivial contents that provide historians with important clues not necessarily intended by the sender).

In this case, also, we can formulate significant empirical statements with respect to apobetics:

**ES 18:** Every piece of Universal Information has purpose (is teleological).

**ES 19:** The teleological aspect of Universal Information is the most important, since it comprises the sender's purpose.

*Comment:* The total effort involved in the four lower levels is actually only necessary as a means for attaining the sender's purpose. The teleological (apobetic) aspect may often seem to overlap or even coincide entirely with the pragmatic aspect. However, unbundling the two is generally possible. **Apobetics** begins the process by an intentional purpose and subsequent plan in the mind of the sender, whereas **pragmatics** achieves this purpose (goal) by the receiver's performance of an action/actions.

Whenever the teleological attribute is minimized or deliberately ignored, we should be aware of the associated violation of ES 18. For

> **Information on epitaphs:** It is immaterial whether the originally intended goal, or even an entirely different goal, is achieved. The following anecdote demonstrates that even epitaphs may have far-reaching apobetic consequences. I was very moved by the testimony of a Ghanaian professor of architecture who had submitted his doctorate several years prior in Brunswick. He told me about a cemetery near Accra in which, even today, crosses on graves tell of the first missionaries to Ghana. The epitaphs show that they died of tropical diseases a few days after they arrived.
>
> On the face of it we would say that these people had failed in their purpose. God set an end to their lives without them passing on a single word of the gospel and without them seeing any fruit. Now this Ghanaian friend was telling me that the silent witness of these crosses had given him the decisive impulse to come to faith. It had become clear to him that the love of God had moved these people to the extent that they had risked their lives in order to tell other people about it.
>
> Here we see that God's ways are often not what we expect. What seems futile to us in our time (Greek: *chronos*) may be booked as everlasting fruit in God's time (Greek: *kairos*). The missionaries had gone out with the aim of winning Africans to faith. Now, after a long time, someone was testifying that the goal had been reached. Today, in his mother tongue, he shares the gospel with many of his students. Could those missionaries, in their hour of death, have suspected that their goal would be achieved, even after such a long time and in such an indirect way?

instance, evolutionary doctrine deliberately attempts to suppress any hint of purpose. In the words of G.G. Simpson, an American zoologist: "Man is the result of a materialistic process having no purpose or intent; he represents the highest fortuitous organizational form of matter and energy."

To complete this section, several more empirical statements follow.

> **ES 20:** The five attributes of Universal Information (statistics, syntax, semantics, pragmatics, and apobetics) are valid for both the sender and the receiver.
>
> **ES 21:** Within Universal Information the syntactic, semantic, and pragmatic levels are interlinked in such a way that each lower level is a necessary prerequisite for the realization of the level above it.
>
> **ES 22:** Although the apobetic aspect is achieved last, it is conceived in the sender's mind *first* and is the impetus for the message (Universal Information) and its subsequent effects.
>
> **ES 23:** There are no known natural laws, processes, or phenomena by which unaided matter can give rise to Universal Information.

## 2.8 Summary

It should be clear from the above that Universal Information comprises many interrelated levels. Despite Shannon's great contributions for resolving engineering problems associated with storage, processing, and transmitting information, Shannon's theory concerns itself with only a small and relatively insignificant aspect of the full nature of Universal Information. This may be clearly seen from the discussion of the five levels of Universal Information. Many authors who consider only one or two levels of Universal Information do not recognize the limitations that this imposes and thereby make contradictory statements and draw erroneous conclusions.

An important example is that it is not possible to find answers about the origin of biological systems by considering only the statistical level. Even more importantly, considering only the statistical level implicitly imposes a limitation on biological systems *a priori*. This *a priori* limitation is the claim that *only* chance and natural events were involved in the origin of these biological systems. But this is an *ideological* position based on the assumption of materialism, and not based upon science. This is one avenue by which materialistic ideology has been and continues to be smuggled into science, namely by *assuming* materialism to be the only reality.

Even treatises with impressive mathematical complexity bring no further clarity if their mathematics is restricted to the level of Shannon's theory. Well-founded conclusions are only possible when the sender/receiver issue is treated systematically at *all* levels of Universal Information.

The empirical statements formulated thus far (1 through 23) are derived from experience. These statements have all been tested in real situations. In chapter 5 we will use some of these empirical statements as we formulate scientific laws.

Figure 9 exhibits, in hierarchal form, the five levels that make up Universal Information: statistics, syntax, semantics, pragmatics, and apobetics. Using ES 7 and ES 20 we can make the following general observation: these five aspects, as shown in Figure 11, are relevant for both the sender and the receiver.

**Origin of information:** ES 2 describes how Universal Information is developed. First the sender has at his disposal a set of symbols (characters) that have been selected and accepted. The sender then uses one symbol after another from the set to create units of information, namely, words, sentences, and other informational structures. This is not a random process but instead requires the application of intelligence. The sender has knowledge of the

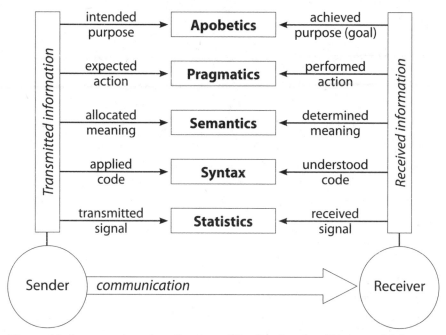

Figure 11: A comprehensive diagram of the five levels of Universal Information. Whereas Figure 9 simply listed the five levels of Universal Information, we can now incorporate our further observations that each of the five levels is always relevant for both sender and receiver.

language he is using, and knows which sequence of symbols he needs in order to specify his meaning, expected action(s), and intended purpose(s). These steps demonstrate that the generation of Universal Information is a mental/intelligent process. Intelligence is an attribute that has never been observed in inanimate matter and, as a result, we can claim that inanimate matter is incapable of generating Universal Information. In the below addendum 2.9 "The worldview of materialism" we will examine this important point in more detail.

**Understanding information:** On the receiver's side, the process involves deciphering (ES 2 and ES 4) instead of developing a message. The receiver must know the set of symbols that has been used in the message. Using his own intelligence and his knowledge of the language, the receiver can decode the symbols, words, and sentences to understand the meaning of the message, hopefully performing the expected action(s) and thus achieving the sender's purpose(s). Generating and understanding Universal Information forms the basic scheme of all communication processes.

## 2.9 Addendum: The worldview of materialism

Generally speaking, within the materialistic worldview, phenomena occur via only two types of processes: (1) "chance" events (also called "random" events) or, (2) events that are directed according to natural laws, and thus must necessarily occur. The Nobel laureate biologist Jacques Monod exemplifies this view in his book *Chance and Necessity,* in which he argues that these two processes (chance and necessity), alone or working together, serve to explain every single aspect in the universe. Let's examine each of these processes.

**1)** The key feature of chance/random events is that they are non-directional, i.e., without any objective or purpose, by definition.

For random events every possible outcome has an associated probability of occurring, without any preferred direction or outcome.

The antithesis of "random" is "directed, guided, designed, or purposeful." When an event is random, this implies that there is no way to predetermine what the outcome is going to be other than in a statistical sense. Nonetheless, while statistical predictability may appear to violate the unpredictable ("chance") aspect of randomness, it does not. Predictions based on statistical methods are always statistically confined, meaning that they may or may not occur and are invariably constrained by the margins of uncertainty.

Mathematics then exposes chance as a non-viable candidate for producing results equal to those obtained by Universal Information. This is because even in what may be considered a relatively "simple" situation — such as the unguided assembly of a protein comprised of 500 amino acids — the natural resources (time, space, and matter) of the entire universe would be exhausted long before the event would occur by chance.[5]

In short, chance alone could never reasonably explain such events.

---

5. Proteins are formed by combinations of any of the 20 different amino acids. Thus, the total number of possible sequences having 500 amino acids is 20 raised to the exponent 500 — approximately $10^{650}$ possible sequences. The chance assembly of *one specific* sequence (protein) is therefore 1 out of $10^{650}$. By any reasonable standard, the probability of this happening is essentially zero; i.e., it is "impossible." Hence, chance alone cannot explain the emergence of this sequence. While functional variance of proteins exists, their number is insignificant when compared to the total number of possible sequences. To illustrate, even if in our example there were $10^{100}$ functional variants, that number may as well be zero when compared to $10^{650}$. Furthermore, this calculation is extremely conservative in that only one variable (namely, the sequence of amino acids) is considered. Other relevant variables, such as chirality, are not being considered here. It should be noted that these other variables would all make the chance formation of the specific protein even *less* likely.

2) Events determined according to natural laws are also incapable of producing an intelligent outcome, primarily because the outcomes are wholly determined, i.e., there is no "choice" involved or even possible. For instance, a stone that is dropped from a height cannot choose to fall, it *must* fall, as determined by the force of gravity. By definition, intelligence demands that choice, *free* choice, be both available and exercised.[6]

Outside of any direction/guidance (such as that provided by the DNA/RNA system), amino acids assemble to form many different kinds of molecules — sometimes even polypeptides (but never functional ones). This is due to the fact that, unguided, amino acids under varying environmental conditions merely follow deterministic physical-chemical laws. This means that a given sequence of amino acids is as equally likely to occur as any other sequence of the same length under the specified conditions. However, the formation of functional proteins requires peptide bonding of left-handed amino acids in a very narrow range of sequences — a result that processes determined solely by natural laws have not been shown to be capable of producing. Chance, as we saw earlier, cannot account for the emergence of this specific sequence either.

Materialists assume that chance and deterministic processes somehow combine to produce "intelligent results" that exhibit great organized complexity, function, and purpose. This has never been seen to happen — it is an ideological assumption lacking any empirical foundation. Yet they believe it because their ideology (worldview) demands it. In other words, to admit the alternative — that chance and deterministic processes are *not* capable of generating highly organized complexity with functional, purposeful outcomes — would immediately demolish the materialists' worldview/religion.

The discussion in this chapter is preparation for the Theory of Universal Information presented in the next chapter, in which a succinct and unambiguous definition of Universal Information will be given and its definition domain will be closely examined.

---

6. **The etymology of *intelligence* expresses this concept.** The word *intelligence* stems from two Latin words: the preposition *inter*, meaning "between" and the verb *lego*, referring to "an act of choosing or selecting." Thus, the etymology of intelligence indicates an act of "choosing between alternatives." The layman's notion of intelligence reinforces this. We regard a person as "intelligent" when that person makes (i.e., selects) the right choice (among all possible choices), selects the proper route (among all possible routes), selects the right answer (among all possible answers), and so on.

*Chapter 3*

# THE THEORY OF
# UNIVERSAL INFORMATION

## 3.1 Materialistic views of information

Judging from modern discussions surrounding the term "information," as dealt with, for example, by Janich [J1], Ropohl [R4], Völz [V2], [V3] and Wills [W6], we see that they are consistently characterized by two factors:

- they have a materialistic foundation

- they are liberalist, inasmuch as they try to integrate diverse philosophical trends

Many authors (e.g., Konrad Lorenz, Manfred Eigen, and Bernd-Olaf Küppers) follow a program of "Naturalization of the Information Concept," as Janich [J1, p. 172] calls it. As such, information is seen as an object within the scientific theories of natural structures and, without further consideration, is integrated into physical theories as a phenomenon within the domain of matter (mass and energy). Thus, Küppers answers the question, "What is life?" with the following equation [K5, p. 17]: "Life = Matter + Information."

Küppers thereby specifically notes that he considers both information and life to be *material* entities. However, as shown in chapter 6, Küppers' equation contains a fundamental error. This is demonstrated simplistically yet graphically in Figure 12. Figure 24 (chapter 5.10) emphasizes hierarchically the disparity between the three phenomena: matter, information, and life.

Figure 12: Adding information to matter does not give life.

Ropohl proposes to define the term "information" very widely [R4, p. 3]: "I should like to defuse the philosophical squabbles by declaring various information terms as allowable and by working out their common denominator." I concur with the critics of his thesis in the following quotation [G15, p. 22]:

> This approach strikes me as if in physics one would want to accept different energy and momentum ideas on the basis of consensus. One cannot expect anything scientifically useful to emerge from such an approach. The law of conservation of energy has gained its outstanding significance just because it was formulated precisely. Only its strict scientific formulation makes it possible to successfully use it universally in all kinds of technical, physical, biological, or astronomical applications. I should also like to see a similarly clear formulation of the term "information." The most powerful scientific statement is always achieved with the successful formulation of a natural law. The definition of the term "information" was covered very comprehensively in [G6] and consequently several scientific laws about information were discovered and formulated. The concept was designated for the first time in a scientific periodical [G10] as a theory of Universal Information.

There are only two possible scientific approaches in response to a natural law (after one has made the effort to understand and test its statements). One either:

- accepts it, and applies it to cases not yet investigated, or
- tries to disprove it.

We note that scientific papers dealing with the topic of biological evolution consistently assume that information can emerge spontaneously from matter alone (e.g., [B6], [D2], [E2], [K1], [K6], [O1], [R3]). However, no one has been able to demonstrate such a process. As a result, two methods have been used in an attempt to make plausible a phenomenon that has never been observed:

1) By computer simulations (as seen in [G27]) or theoretical calculations (as seen in [B6]).

**Objection:** Even the most impressive simulation is only a simulation and is never the same as a real-life process. Computer simulations are always theoretical constructs and, out of necessity, must incorporate considerable simplifications. These simplifications are sometimes accepted in the study of physical systems because only certain parameters are to be studied. It is impossible to include or consider all influencing variables or their interactions. What is then simulated is always a reduced representation of reality. How much more does this apply when life itself (the complexity of which has thus far proven to be beyond man's comprehension) is the subject under investigation?

2) By experiments with bacteria.

**Objection:** Here we have to bear in mind that information is already present in the life-forms used. The fact that these living organisms are capable of performing unforeseen and astonishing adjustments and adaptations under special experimental conditions says nothing about the origin of new information but rather speaks about the ingenious "programming" that directs such flexibility (see also chapter 7.7).

**Changes within a species:** Consider the following analogy: to test a complex but unknown computer program, the computer is fed a particular set of parameter values. If the parameters lie within certain limits the program can run a thousand times without revealing some of its properties. Not until a wider range of variations in the parameters is used will certain branches in the program be executed and thus reveal new properties of the program. The human programmer has structured his program correspondingly, knowing the range within each parameter. If, indeed, there is a Creator, and we are part of the creation, then it is self-evident that we are less capable in every area than the Creator. Thus, what we can do with a computer is almost infinitely less than a Creator could do in the creation. The Creator could easily introduce infinitely more possibilities within biological programs to allow living organisms to adapt to changing environmental conditions (e.g., programmed genetic variability). No new information is created with all these adaptations — contrary to the view so often propounded by evolutionists — but rather information *already present* is activated and selected on the basis of changed environmental parameters. It might also be noted that, in sexual reproduction, the combining of the parents' genetics is known to produce differences in not just appearance, but the timing and execution of various traits. Siblings look different from not only their parents, but from each other, due to the large number of different ways their parent's genes are able to combine in each of them.

## 3.2 The Theory of Universal Information

This book introduces a Theory of Universal Information[1] (TUI) that is not prone to the above materialist or liberalist biases and weaknesses. The characteristics of the TUI, which will be further expounded upon, are as follows:

- The term *Universal Information* will be defined succinctly, unambiguously, and universally.

- The nature of Universal Information is treated in accordance with reality, not as a physical entity as happens in the materialistic theories, but rather as a phenomenon that originates from a mental (intelligent) process. This is corroborated by our experience and observations. The fact that in all observable phenomena information needs a material medium to store and transmit it does not make it a material entity. For instance, if one deletes a program from a computer, the mass of the computer remains completely unchanged. The actual essence of a computer program is the idea, the *Universal Information* that originates only from intelligence. The UI itself is a non-material entity, as described in chapter 5.5.

---

1. The "Theory of Universal Information" (TUI) was first used in a scientific publication [G13] in order to document that we are not dealing with another philosophical concept about the term "information," but rather about an unambiguous definition and a set of scientific laws that can be observed and tested worldwide. The word "theory" is used here in the sense of Section 4.1 (see index keyword "theory").

- Universal Information laws, just like the laws regarding mass and energy, are discovered through observation and experimentation. For this reason, these laws are appropriately designated *scientific laws* of Universal Information. Just as natural (scientific) laws of physics and chemistry can be applied successfully to unknown cases, the same holds for laws of Universal Information. In physics, laws regarding the conservation of energy are not restricted to special cases but are universally applicable. In the same way, laws regarding UI are universally applicable, whether the system is animate or inanimate.

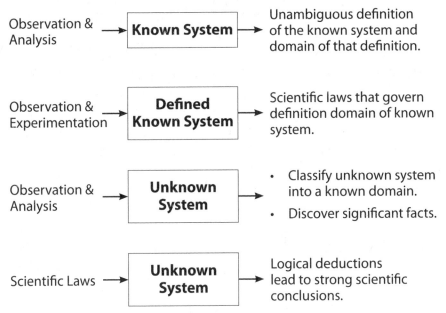

Figure 13: Procedure for developing sound scientific arguments

- Contrary to some representations of natural phenomena and models of natural phenomena,[2] scientific laws have the advantage that they are operationally free from ideology — they neither reflect the personal opinion of an author nor do they present a particular philosophy. All interested persons

---

2. Models do exist that are mostly free of ideology and depend only on the progress of research as, for example, an atomic model in physics. Others, on the other hand, have a strong philosophical foundation, for example the doctrine of evolution from the ideologies of materialism/Darwinism.

may test these laws for validity in an unlimited number of trials. Rejection of a scientific law requires that a contradiction or a counter-example be discovered and then repeatedly tested and confirmed.

**Procedure for arriving at strong scientific conclusions** as seen graphically in Figure 13:

A prerequisite for investigating an unknown system is to first investigate *known* systems. In this way, one may identify a particular entity/quantity which lends itself to the formulation of a scientific law concerning it.

It is then necessary to precisely define this entity, and to establish the scope of what belongs within its definition domain, and what is excluded.

In the second step one tries to track down the laws involved through observation and experiment, and then to formulate them as universally applicable laws in either verbal form or mathematical notation.

The third step involves the analysis of the unknown system. As part of this process, the system is specifically examined to determine if it even contains the particular entity which the scientific law is describing. Example: A snowflake contains no UI, so the scientific laws concerning UI have nothing to say here.

In the fourth step we apply the laws discovered under step 2 above to the unknown system and in this way arrive at strong conclusions.

The scope of the conclusions is such as to enable the confirmation or refutation of prior theories and models. Their power is based on the fact that we are applying scientific laws, since these have the highest authority in science. To evaluate systems containing Universal Information to such a standard, our *Theory of Universal Information* needs two things:

- an unambiguous scientific definition of information
- a set of applicable scientific laws.

Let us start with the **definition of Universal Information** and then examine its scientific laws in chapter 5.

### 3.3 The definition of Universal Information

First, it is necessary to consider three important questions on the nature of "definitions":

1. What is the definition of "definition"?

2. What type of definition qualifies as a scientific definition?

3. How do we achieve a universal meaning for all disciplines of science?

*What is the definition of "definition"?*

Britannica World Language, 1962 edition of Funk and Wagnalls Standard Dictionary states (bold emphasis added): a definition is *"a description or explanation of a word or thing, by its attributes, properties, or relations that **distinguishes** it from all other things."*

*What type of definition qualifies as a scientific definition?*

It must be unambiguous. This means that the definition is clear and precise so that all persons using this term in science employ the same understanding of the term.

*How do we achieve a universal meaning for all disciplines of science?*

Through careful study of the entity being defined and then constructing a clear and precise definition.

Therefore, our definition of Universal Information must include every attribute that *distinguishes* Universal Information from all other entities, including any other definition of "information." When we examine the five hierarchical levels of Universal Information, we observe that each of them is an important aspect or attribute of information. However, the lowest level (statistical) does not distinguish Universal Information from other entities. The other four aspects — syntax, semantics, pragmatics, and apobetics — together unambiguously distinguish Universal Information from all other entities. This yields the following concise definition of Universal Information:

> **Definition D9: Universal Information (UI) is a symbolically encoded, abstractly represented message conveying the expected action(s) and the intended purpose(s).** In this context, "message" is meant to include instructions for carrying out a specific task or eliciting a specific response.

Since these four distinguishing aspects were discovered by careful study of human, natural, and machine languages, all of these languages will fall within the boundary of the UI definition domain. What about other systems that might convey Universal Information? For an unknown system, the following evidence must be provided:

**Evidence:** The unknown system under analysis *must* contain all four distinguishing aspects of Universal Information, namely syntax, semantics, pragmatics, and apobetics. *Note: the sender and receiver are not part of the evidence.*

If these aspects are present, then the unknown system is within the boundary of the "information" definition domain and all empirical statements identified as scientific laws will apply to the unknown system. Depending on each particular case, scientific laws may be selected and used as premises in deductions for sound arguments. This will be further explained in chapter 8 in regard to information and the DNA/RNA system in the cell.

## Explicit and Implicit Apobetic Information

Regarding the term "intended purposes" in D9, one must bear in mind the need to distinguish between explicit and implicit information. In most cases, the intended purpose is not explicit at all.

**Explicit apobetic information:** in the case of a birthday letter, it is clear from the contents that the purpose of the letter is to wish the celebrant well. Similarly, in the case of an e-mail communicating the time of arrival by train and requesting to be picked up from the station, the purpose of the communication is explicitly stated.

**Implicit apobetic information:** in most practical cases, the intended purpose is not mentioned explicitly at all. Nevertheless, there is an intended purpose in the transmitted information, even if it is not explicitly mentioned. We then speak of implicit apobetic information.

Imagine that a programmer has written a program for the numerical calculation of the zero of a mathematical function. Unfortunately, he has not written a comment into the program, and therefore an uninitiated person cannot recognize the purpose of the program. But does the program therefore have no apobetics, just because it is not explicitly mentioned? Of course, it does have apobetics. The program is fully applicable to the purpose behind its creation without explicitly stating it. A mathematician could take a closer look at the program code, recognize the algorithm behind it, and conclude that, in this case, a numerical procedure for zero calculation had been programmed.

Another example of implicit apobetic information is the information in the DNA molecule. There is no mention anywhere of what purpose particular sections have. It takes great research effort to find out the underlying purpose in each case. A single cell alone contains programming for hundreds of individual goals, but these are nowhere described in an explicit way.

## 3.4 Defining the domain of Universal Information

It is now necessary to define the domain within which the empirical statements about Universal Information are valid. This definition must also be applicable to unknown systems that convey Universal Information. For example, do these statements apply not only to computers but also to all other areas of technology? Do living systems also belong to this domain? In order to identify the distinct domain of the definition of Universal Information we may ask: Can the aforementioned empirical statements be applied to any of these unknown systems, or are such systems already outside the definition domain? In order to answer these questions, we need to have a good working understanding of the definition domain of Universal Information.

Consider whether or not the following cases belong within this domain:

- the microscopic structure of a salt crystal, a metal or a snowflake

- the "information" in starlight as seen through a telescope

- the "information" that a forensic scientist observes in the clues at the scene of a crime

- a mussel shell in a geologic layer, which provides new insights to the paleontologist observing it

- the new laws that are discovered in science and technology on the basis of measurements

- the DNA code found within the cells of all organisms

**Definitions restrict, and thereby increase precision:** Every scientific definition must be more specific and precise than definitions in common, everyday language. They have the effect of both fixing and limiting the term and/or definition involved. An unambiguous definition will exclude all other entities and clearly specify the entity being studied. The sharper the boundaries of a definition domain, the more likely that scientific laws may be discovered and that sound conclusions may be drawn.

Science often uses expressions that are also common in everyday language (e.g., energy and information). However, for some terms, their meaning for everyday use can differ from that of their scientific use, and this often causes confusion. The scientific use of the term must be unambiguous and clearly delineated, and thus a definition is needed to specify the term as precisely as possible. In most cases, the scientific definition restricts the meaning of the term or definition as compared to the more common usage.

**Energy:** Consider the term **energy** (Figure 14, top). The word **energy** was borrowed in the 18th century from the French *énergie*, which in turn came from the Latin word *energia* (action) or the Greek *enérgeia* (effective power). In everyday language we may use this word to mean different things in various situations. For instance, when an individual does something emphatically and decisively then we say that "he uses all his energy" for it. If someone is strong and well-trained, then "he abounds with energy." Someone who has physical and mental resilience is "full of gumption and bursting with energy." But in physics the same word is used in a much more limited and specific way.

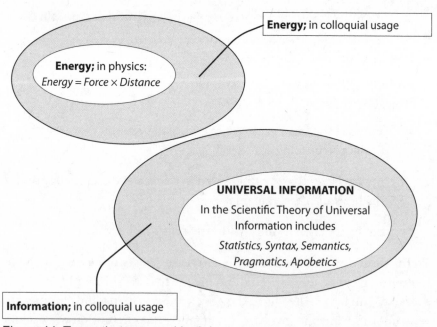

Energy; in colloquial usage

**Energy;** in physics:
*Energy = Force × Distance*

**UNIVERSAL INFORMATION**
In the Scientific Theory of Universal Information includes
*Statistics, Syntax, Semantics, Pragmatics, Apobetics*

**Information;** in colloquial usage

Figure 14: Terms that are used both in a common, everyday sense as well as in a formal scientific setting.

It is because of this restriction relative to its colloquial use that we are able to describe a law of nature that we call the law of conservation of energy. In fact, there are a number of specific definitions of different types of energy, all of which have an unambiguous definition: kinetic energy, potential energy, gravitational energy, chemical energy, nuclear energy, etc.

Another example is acceleration. In colloquial use, it means "speeding up." To a physicist, it means any change of velocity, either speed or direction. So an ordinary driver going round a bend at constant speed, or braking, would not think he is accelerating, but a physicist says he is, in both cases. Only the physicist's use makes any sense of Newton's Second Law: acceleration = force/mass, since forces can cause changes in direction or slowing down as well as speeding up.

The same approach is required to establish an unambiguous definition domain for information (Figure 14, bottom). We must state precisely what we mean by Universal Information based upon its attributes. For this reason, it will be necessary from this point on to set aside everyday ideas and usage concerning the word "information" as we proceed to study and use Universal Information in the following sections of this book.

## The Property of Substitutive Function (Semantics)

An important attribute that serves to restrict the domain of Universal Information (UI) is its substitutive function. UI is always an abstract representation of some other existing entity. Universal Information is never the item (object) or the fact (event, idea) itself, but rather the coded symbols serve as a substitute for the entities that are being represented. Different languages often use different sets of symbols and usually different symbol sequences (see chapter 2.4) to represent the same material object or concept. Consider the following examples:

- the words in a newspaper, consisting of a sequence of letters, substitute for an event that happened at an earlier time and in some other place

- the words in a novel, consisting of sequences of letters, substitute for characters and their actions

- the notes of a musical score substitute for music that will be played later on musical instruments

- the chemical formula for benzene substitutes for the toxic liquid that is kept in a flask in a chemistry laboratory

- the genetic codons (three-letter words) of the DNA molecule substitute for specific amino acids that are bonded together in a specified sequence to form a protein

Its substitutive function is a basic property of UI. Consider the following two equivalent properties, 1 and 1a:

**Property 1:** Universal Information is not the object, the event, or the concept but rather it is an abstract representation (by means of a suitable code system) of certain physical and non-physical realities. Examples of such realities are numerous: physical, chemical, or biological states and purely intellectual constructs such as the statement of a problem, concept, idea, or algorithm.

Whereas the event described by the information need not necessarily be present and observable, the symbols conveying the information are indeed observable entities; e.g., visible (readable text), tactile (Braille), or audible (spoken language). Property 1 can be expressed more concisely.

**Property 1a:** Universal Information always fulfills a substitutive function. The assignment of a coded representation for an entity results from intellectual processes involving deliberate choices and agreements.

Property 1a emphasizes, from another perspective, the fact that Universal Information cannot be a property of matter but is, instead, an intellectual construct. UI needs an intelligent author who can substitute an abstract code for reality.

The above property helps us to find a distinct demarcation for the term "information." Figure 15 and Table 1 show clearly the distinction between UI and non-UI: **direct observations of reality** (through seeing, hearing, and measuring) do not belong to our definition domain of UI. Whenever an abstract coding system, involving the assignment of meaning to otherwise meaningless symbols, is used to represent something else, we have identified the first two distinguishing attributes of UI.

We have already provided a comprehensive diagram of UI in Figure 11, chapter 2.7. Figure 15 and Table 1 show the domain of UI (Domain A) and all other domains that are not within the UI domain of definition.

Figure 15 shows, in principle, five possible distinct definition domains for information (A, B, C, D, and E). Only domain A belongs to the theory of UI that is being treated extensively in this book.

## Possible domains for the definition of information

Figure 15: The definition domain for UI according to the theory of Universal Information. Domain A alone coincides with the scientific definition, and it is only within this domain that all empirical statements/scientific laws of UI are valid. Domains B, C, D, and E are outside the defined domain and not addressed in this context. These five domains are characterized as follows:

A: systems with abstract codes, abstract semantics, pragmatics, and apobetics

B: communication systems without abstract codes and without abstract semantics but with semantics that are not abstract

C: systems with symbolic codes that do not contain semantics

D: man-made systems without codes or semantics

E: material systems with neither abstract codes nor semantics

We now need criteria that clearly assign a particular unknown system to a specific domain. As we will see, the scientific laws of Universal Information formulated in this book exclusively govern domain A. Therefore, we must be absolutely certain whether an entity or system is inside or outside domain A. Let us look more closely at each domain (A to E).

**Domain A, Universal Information (UI):** According to Figure 15 and Table 1, *only domain A belongs to the definition domain of UI, i.e.,*

1) *coded systems that abstractly represent material or non-material entities and convey pragmatics and apobetics, and*
2) *complex systems with embedded UI.*

The given examples — book, newspaper, computer program, telephone conversation, Morse code, and hieroglyphics — meet these requirements and therefore fall within domain A. In the case of direct observation of specific inanimate objects (e.g., star, house, snowflake), the syntactic and semantic (substitutive) aspects are missing and, thus, they do not belong to our definition of UI. The Empirical Statements discovered and formulated as scientific laws apply and govern this now established definition domain.

How can we approach an unknown system in order to be sure that we are within domain A? We have already recognized the importance of the substitutive function. The lack of this substitutive function allows us to make an assignment to domains C, D, or E. We must then ask the question: is the substitutive function a *sufficient* condition for assignment to domain A? Unfortunately not, because there are examples for which the substitutive function is indeed fulfilled but the system does not belong to A (see chapter 3.5, example 3, the drawings on the Pioneer spacecraft plaque). The substitutive function is therefore a *necessary* but not a *sufficient*[3] condition for assignment to domain A.

---

3. Necessary and sufficient: These terms play a central role in mathematics. A condition is necessary for some state if this state cannot exist without that condition. If a condition is sufficient for some state, then this state exists any time this condition exists. Example 1: maleness is necessary for fatherhood — no one can be a father who is not male. But it's not sufficient — some males are not fathers. But fatherhood is *sufficient* for maleness: any time someone is a father, he is automatically male. But fatherhood is not *necessary* to prove maleness. Example 2: in order for a whole number larger than 2 to be a prime number (divisible only by 1 and itself), a necessary condition is that it be an odd number, otherwise it would be divisible by 2. But being an odd number is not sufficient. For instance, the number 15 is an odd number (thus, 15 satisfies the necessary condition) but it is not prime. Despite over 2,400 years of research, a sufficient condition for identifying a prime number that is applicable to all numbers has not been discovered.

| Domains | Examples | Properties |
|---|---|---|
| **A) Universal Information (UI)**<br><br>1) Systems exclusively UI<br><br>2) Complex systems with embedded UI | 1) Newspapers, letters, books, computer programs<br><br>2) Computers with various accessories, antilock braking systems and other computer-controlled modern automobile devices, most modern electronic machines | Coded systems *with* syntax, semantics, pragmatics and apobetics<br><br>UI plays an abstract substitutionary role<br><br>Scientific Laws of Universal Information are valid |
| **B) Mental Imaging Information (MII)** | Flags, ornaments on wine bottles, pictograms (e.g., bed symbol for lodging), traffic signs, applause | Single symbols or pictures, acoustic or olfactory signals with meaning<br><br>MII plays a non-abstract, substitutionary role |
| **C) Random systems**<br>Sequences of random characters or random numbers | 984528894673955434 …<br><br>Gfhrxfhlkgdsbjqfgfgvs … | Coded systems *without* syntax, semantics, pragmatics or apobetics |
| **D) Man-made systems resulting from UI and MII but with no embedded UI or MII** | Older model cars and airplanes, pens, arrowheads, most houses, simple machines | − Systems without syntax<br>− Systems with purpose<br>− Systems that are the result of UI and MII |
| **E) Natural systems without embedded UI** | Stars, salt crystals, snowflakes, rocks, clouds, lightning, thunder | − Systems *without* syntax or semantics |

Table 1: Five possible domains for Universal Information

What, then, is *sufficient* to belong to domain A? We recall the previously stated definition D9 for Universal Information in chapter 3.3: Universal Information is a symbolically encoded, abstractly represented message conveying the expected action(s) and the intended purpose(s).

This definition makes it possible to safely classify the system under examination into domain A. Whenever we can identify **all** four distinguishing attributes of UI in an unknown system, we can be sure that the unknown system is within domain A. If, in individual cases, we remain uncertain, we can then draw on the abstract substitutive function as a necessary condition. If this is not fulfilled, then we are certainly outside the definition domain of A. If we have established that the unknown system belongs to domain A, then the empirical statements and scientific laws of Universal Information apply.

The empirical statements/scientific laws of Universal Information only apply in domain A (as depicted in Figure 15 and Table 1).

Consider again the space plaque (see Figure 16) — to which domain does it belong? We know that this plaque was attached to a rocket to "inform" — colloquially speaking — possible beings in space that intelligent beings also exist here on earth, as depicted on the plaque. The drawings certainly fulfill the substitutive function but not the syntactic aspect of UI. The drawings were not composed from a set of abstract symbols that could be used for the construction or presentation of the "information." Thus, no code is present, and with that no possible code convention by which any such hypothetical beings are meant to decipher it. Since we are confronted here with a case that belongs neither to A, C, D, or E, we must therefore introduce domain B.

**Domain B, Mental Image Information (MII):** The primary distinction between domain B and domain A (introduced above) is that domain B does not possess the syntactic aspect, which requires that the symbols have no inherent physical relationship with, or resemblance to, the reality that they are being used to represent (see Definition D3, chapter 2.4). Additionally, the semantics of domain B is not abstract. While domain B usually does contain symbols, these symbols bear a specific one-to-one relationship with the entity that they are representing, whereas the abstract symbol set of domain A does not. Let us explore further this crucial distinguishing aspect between domains A and B.

An abstract symbol set provides for an immense number of combinations of basic symbols to form words. These words may then be arranged in near-limitless ways to form phrases and sentences that, in turn, are used to form larger bodies of text/messages such as paragraphs. Thus, for example, the English letters "a, c, and t" may be used to form the word "cat" (a mammal that purrs and meows). The very same letters may also be used to form the word "act" (a word that, depending on the context, will have any one of a number of meanings; e.g., consider the phrases "caught in the **act**," "the second **act** in the play," "an **act** of Congress," "performed a heroic **act**" and others). The point to notice is that the letters "a, c, and t" *by themselves* do not have a one-to-one relationship with the entity that they are combined to represent. These letters acquire function and meaning only after they are combined in agreed-upon sequences, and are assigned meanings.

Domain B, however, exhibits what we will call "Mental Imaging Information" (MII). In MII, strictly speaking there is no syntax (which also involves a code). Recall that the word "act" acquired a meaning only within a context — that was domain A. On the other hand, a message in domain B typically has a unique one-to-one relationship with what the message represents. A stick figure of a man clearly represents a man and nothing else. In other words, in domain B there is less flexibility and a much stronger correlation between the message and what the message is meant to represent. These include man-made items such as architectural and engineering line drawings, statues, music (but not the score), paintings, etc. Also included in domain B are communication systems inherent within various kinds of animals such as pheromones, gestures, vocalizations (e.g., a scream of fright), etc. The primary distinction between domain B and domain A is the lack of an abstract symbol set in domain B. Let us illustrate the oftentimes subtle distinction between domains A and B by once again considering the plaque on Pioneer 10/11 (Figure 16).

This plaque contains information from both domain A and domain B. The engravings on the plaque include line drawings (belonging to domain B) and some binary code (belonging to domain A). Here's an example of each:

At the top left of the plaque is a depiction of a hydrogen atom transition with a binary "1." The plaque author's idea was, among other things, to establish hydrogen's wavelength (approximately 21 cm) as the "unit" for length measurements. On the right side of the female figure (just to the right of her hand) is the binary number for eight, i.e., 8 = binary "1000." On the plaque this is shown vertically as **I – – –**. Thus, since the unit length is 21 cm, and the female's height is *eight* times that amount, then 8 × 21 cm = 168 cm or 5' 6" — approximately equal to the average height of a female human. The syntactic aspect of UI is evident here (the binary code also contains the syntax). It was chosen, defined, and used.

Now consider that the line drawing of the female is meant to resemble the generic contour of a female body. There is no code to decipher; there is no syntax — the line drawing is what it is. There is a one-to-one correlation between this line drawing (i.e., the "message") and the object that this message represents (a female human). Therefore, while the line drawing of the female communicates a great deal of information, this information does not qualify as UI. Instead, we call it MII and place it into domain B. The straightforward reason why domain B is not UI is that the formal definition of UI is not satisfied — syntax (which requires a code) is missing.

A final, yet important, note on the distinction between domains A and B is that domain B may be transformed into domain A by supplying that missing attribute (syntax/code). Egyptian hieroglyphs are an example of this. Some of these hieroglyphs — e.g., depicting an owl, a vulture, a snake, a kneeling human, a feather, and many others — are phonetic in nature, meaning that the sign is read independent of its visual characteristics. Thus, an "eye" does not stand for an *actual* "eye" but rather for a particular sound determined by a complex set of syntactic, context-dependent rules. Thus, the resemblance between the symbol and entity is lost as the symbol becomes abstract.

In summary, this brief introduction to domain B and MII is not intended to be complete or to answer every question. There are subtle and complex issues, including exceptions to the general rules given here, that challenge any straightforward classification into domain B. It is recognized that this may lead to some confusion and controversy. The author believes that further research into the MII domain will resolve these aforementioned issues and lead to significant discoveries.

**Domain C, random characters:** As depicted in Figure 15 and Table 1, this domain also lies outside the defined domain of UI. In contrast to domain B, an abstract code system is used but the sequence of symbols is random (e.g., by a random-number/letter generator on a computer). Such sequences are characterized by the absence of semantics. In other words, they do not substitute for physical realities or for ideas. If we are presented with a sequence of letters or numbers in which we can see no meaning (absence of semantics), then there are two possibilities: either it is a random sequence, in which case it belongs to domain C, or it may be an encrypted text, in which case it belongs to domain A.

Let us illustrate this with three sequences of 40 digits each:

Sequence 1: 141 592 653 589 793 238 462 643 383 279 502 884
197 169
Sequence 2: 472 805 379 555 421 141 107 373 882 049 594 865
210 374
Sequence 3: 001 001 000 011 111 101 101 010 100 010 001 000
010 110

All three sequences appear at first sight to be random. A closer look reveals that sequence 1 contains the first 40 places of $\pi$ after the decimal point ($\pi$ = 3.141592653 ...). The number that $\pi$ *represents* (semantics) plays a central role in mathematics, engineering, and physics; by *applying* (pragmatics) the number $\pi$, we achieve the desired results (apobetics). As a concrete example, we apply (pragmatics) the factor $\pi$ in order to determine the circumference (c) of a circle from its diameter (d), c = $\pi$·d (apobetics). Sequence 3 is also not random: it is also $\pi$, presented not in decimal form (as sequence 1) but as a binary number ($\pi$ = 11.001001... to the ninth decimal place) containing only the digits 0 and 1. Thus, seemingly random sequences may not be random at all, and this would be a matter of both inspection and knowledge. Sequence 2 alone may be considered to be random.

According to mathematician Gregory Chaitin, whether a sequence is or is not random cannot be rigorously proven [C1]. Thus, there remains a possible uncertainty about assignment to either domain A or C. If we are informed that a sequence of symbols was generated randomly, then we can assign it to domain C. If we know nothing about the origin of the sequence, we should never make a hasty allocation to domain A, or, in fact, to domain C.

**Domain D, non-informational artifacts:** This domain contains all man-made entities *except* those that contain a system of abstract symbols (required for domain A) or those included in domain B. Examples include: a safety pin, a horse-drawn carriage, an arrowhead, and many others. An important note is that all artifacts in domain D require an integrated use of UI and MII during their design and construction. This leads to another empirical statement:

> **ES 24:** Universal Information integrated with Mental Imaging Information is the informational basis of all scientific, technological, artistic, and industrial achievements of man.

**Domain E, purely material objects:** Having introduced a precise scientific definition for UI, we may now use this definition to resolve questions about entities that are commonly considered to contain information. For example, upon observing a star through a telescope or a snowflake through a microscope it is said that we are acquiring "information" about these entities. In these cases, we are using the term "information" in the everyday sense. The key point to consider scientifically is that in these cases we are observing reality *itself*. The substitutive function of UI provides us with a criterion to clarify any confusion. Whenever we observe such a reality directly we are not substituting an abstract code system for this reality — we are looking at the *actual* reality. This is why the star and the snowflake clearly belong in domain E. A final check on domain E is therefore to ask oneself, what is the item in question substituting for or representing? If the answer is "nothing" then the substitutive role of semantics is missing and the item is outside of the definition domain of Universal Information.

**Assigning an unknown system to a domain:** From the previous discussion, we see that it is nearly always possible to succeed in assigning an unknown system to one of the five definition domains: A, B, C, D, or E. There are several cases, however, for which an assignment may not be feasible (see "Decision deferred" below).

> **Decision deferred:** One of three possible causes may hinder us from deciding (at least initially) whether a system under investigation belongs to A or C:
>
> (a) We are dealing with a language system that is unknown to us and so, of course, the semantics is also unknown. In this case we must delay assignment to domain A (at least for the time being).
>
> (b) We are dealing with a random sequence. If the source is unknown, then randomness in principle cannot be proven. Again, we must delay the assignment to domain C.
>
> (c) We are dealing with a coded message in a language known to exist but one that we cannot yet decrypt. For the time being, we must also postpone the decision to assign this system to domain A.

The scientific laws about UI govern only domain A. Since scientific laws convey the highest level of scientific certainty possible, they are considered valid premises for logical arguments and the subsequent conclusions. Therefore, it is crucial to determine whether or not an unknown system belongs within domain A. If it belongs to domain A, then we can utilize the scientific laws governing domain A as premises in our logical arguments regarding the unknown system.

### 3.5 Classification into the UI domain — some examples

Having presented many lectures on the Theory of Universal Information, I have observed that the concept was quickly and fairly well understood. However, when having to decide whether an actual unknown case fell inside or outside the UI domain, the audience often appeared confused and hesitant. Additionally, whenever experts in various scientific fields have been challenged to provide examples that could disprove the scientific laws of UI, they have consistently cited systems outside of UI's defined domain.

The following nine examples are offered here to eliminate this confusion. Each of these illustrates that classifying an unknown case as UI involves answering one central question: does the unknown system express *all four* distinguishing attributes of UI as defined? One approach for answering this question is to complete the following table for an unknown system and determine the presence or absence of each of the distinguishing attributes of UI.

| Syntax: | Does the unknown system have an abstract code and a set of syntactic rules? |
|---|---|
| Semantics: | Does the unknown system furnish abstract substitutes for actual entities? |
| Pragmatics: | Does the unknown system express a call to action? |
| Apobetics: | Does the unknown system express a purpose to be achieved? |
| CONCLUSION: | Based on the answers to the above questions, the unknown system will either be within the definition domain of Universal Information or it will not. |

Table 2: Testing an unknown system for the four distinguishing attributes of UI

**Example 1: Fraunhofer Lines**

The German physicist Joseph von Fraunhofer (1787–1826) is the inventor of the diffraction grating (300 lines per mm) for the absolute measurement of the wavelengths of light. Using this diffraction grating, Fraunhofer discovered that each chemical element absorbs specific light wavelengths that show up as sharp black lines in the sun's spectrum. The related energy is absorbed by specific atoms. Fraunhofer discovered many of these dark lines in the sun's spectrum. Currently thousands of these lines have been identified; they are all absorption lines of certain characteristic wavelengths within the continuous spectrum of sunlight that are absorbed on their way from the surface of the sun to the earth's surface. This "filtering" is caused by different gaseous elements that are mostly in the sun's atmosphere and partly in the earth's atmosphere.

94 • Information: The Key to Life

By comparing known spectra from atomic spectroscopy, each Fraunhofer line can be identified with a specific chemical element. In this way it is possible to perform a spectral analysis of the upper solar atmosphere. From the year 1815 onwards, Fraunhofer catalogued about 500 spectral lines, whereby he initially designated the lines by the letters A to K. The most prominent lines are still designated this way. An example is the D-line doublet of sodium (a "doublet" is two narrowly separated spectral lines) that has the D1-line, 589.59 nm and the D2-line, 589 nm. Another example is the H-line, 396.85 nm, and K-line, 393.37 nm, of calcium. Today more than 25,000 solar spectral lines are known.

**Findings:** The Fraunhofer lines found in the spectrum of the light from a star serve in astrospectroscopy to identify chemical elements on the star. The spectral lines form a sort of "fingerprint" of a particular chemical element, which can be used to prove the element's presence in, for example, a star or nebula.

**Question:** Does the one-to-one correlation between a chemical element and its absorption lines equate to material realities being substituted with a code system? If so, do the Fraunhofer lines lie within the definition domain of UI?

**Answer:** We can show that the Fraunhofer lines are a purely physical property whereby the presence of a particular chemical element results in the absorption of several specific wavelengths. These "symbols" are not abstract, with their meaning assigned on the basis of a freely agreed-upon convention (see NC1 in chapter 2.4), but instead are fixed, wholly determined physical properties (in other words, an inherent one-on-one physical relationship exists). The Fraunhofer lines, therefore, do not represent a symbol set that has been used to create meaningful messages. It could be argued that the substitutive function (semantics) as a necessary condition is fulfilled by the Fraunhofer lines; nevertheless, all other distinguishing attributes of UI would also need to be fulfilled. Additionally, all other cases where discovery of physical properties led to greater understanding (e.g., signals from pulsars and the structure of snowflakes) do not belong to the definition domain of Universal Information. In short, the Fraunhofer lines belong to domain E, Figure 15.

Recall that classifying an unknown system as UI or not-UI involves answering one key question: does the unknown system fall within the defined domain of Universal Information, i.e., does the system express all four distinguishing attributes of UI?

The entire analysis for the Fraunhofer lines may thus be summarized by completing Table 2 as follows:

| | | |
|---|---|---|
| Analysis of Fraunhofer lines for attributes of UI | Syntax: | Does the unknown system have an abstract code and a set of syntactic rules? *No! The Fraunhofer lines do not constitute an abstract code nor is there a syntax associated with them.* |
| | Semantics: | Does the unknown system furnish abstract substitutes for actual entities? *No! Fraunhofer lines do express a substitutive function (specific lines represent specific chemical elements) but they have an inherent physical relationship — a fixed correlation — with their respective element, they are not abstract.* |
| | Pragmatics: | Does the unknown system express a call to action? *No! Fraunhofer lines do not, in and of themselves, express a call to action, nor is there a machine in the system capable of producing the action.* |
| | Apobetics: | Does the unknown system express a purpose to be achieved? *No! Fraunhofer lines do not and cannot express a purpose to be achieved.* |
| | CONCLUSION: | *The Fraunhofer lines* **are not** *UI because they do not express all four of the distinguishing attributes that are necessary to be classified as Universal Information.* |

**Example 2: Four different sequences of letters**

In Table 3, on the next page, we find four different sequences of letters (including punctuation), each containing 450 letters arranged in six lines. Block 1 is recognizable as text from the "Osterspaziergang" (lit. "Easter Parade," but English versions have it as "Outside the City Gate") from Goethe's *Faust*, in which all four distinguishing attributes of UI are to be found. Thus, we find that Block 1 falls within the domain of UI (domain A in Figure 15 and Table 1).

At first glance, Block 2 looks like a random sequence and would, therefore, fall outside the defined domain of UI. But, as shown in the right-hand column, Block 2 is the result of a simple encryption of Block 1. Each letter

| No. | Which sequences of characters represent Universal Information? | 4 different sequences of 6 rows of characters each with 75 letters |
|---|---|---|
| 1 | Text:<br>"Outside the Town Gate" by Johann W. v. Goethe | VOM EISE BEFREIT SIND STROM UND BAECHE DURCH DES FRUEHLINGS HOLDEN, BELEBEN<br>DEN BLICK, IM TALE GRUENET HOFFUNGSGLUECK. DER ALTE WINTER IN SEINER SCHWA<br>ECHE ZOG SICH IN RAUHE BERGE ZURUECK. VON DORTHER SENDET ER; FLIEHEND, NUR<br>OHNMAECHTIGE SCHAUER KOERNIGEN EISES IN STREIFEN UEBER DIE GRUENENDE FLUR.<br>ABER DIE SONNE DULDET KEIN WEISSES, UEBERALL REGET SICH BILDUNG UND STREBEN,<br>ALLES WILL SIE MIT FARBEN BELEBEN, DOCH AN BLUMEN FEHLTS IM REVIER, SIE N |
| 2 | Encryption by linear mapping<br>A → U<br>E → R<br>C → L<br>⋮<br>Z → K | GQXJIMZIJRIYWIMCJZMSVJZCWQXJFSVJR ILPIJVEWLPDVIZJYWFIPDMSNZJPQDVISUJRIDIRIS<br>VISJRDMI,UJMXJC DIJNWFISICJPQYYSFSNZNDFIL,TJVIWJ DCIJHMSCIWJMSJZIMSIWJZLPH<br>ILPIJKQNZMLPJMSJW FPIJRIWNIJKFWFIL,TJGQSJVQWCPIWJZISVICJIWUJYDMIPISVUJSFWJ<br>QPSX ILPCMNIJZLP FIWJ,QIWSMNISJIMZIZJMSJZCWIMYISJFIRIWJVMIJNWFISISVIJYDFWTJ<br>RIWJVMIJZQSSIJVFDVICJ,IMSJHIMZZIZUJFIRIW DDJWINICJZMLPJRMDVFSNJFSVJZCWIRIS<br>UJ DDIZJHMDDJZMIJXMCJY WRISJRIDIRISUJVQLPJ SJRDFXISJYIPDCZJMXJWIGMIWUJZMIJS |
| 3 | Encryption by using the date October 7, 1981<br>VOM EISE BEFREIT SIN<br>07108107108107108107<br>VVN MJSL.BMGRLJTFTIU | VVN MJSL.BMGRLJTFTIUE URVN ,ODECAMDHL.D,SCO.DMT M SUMILPOG .HVMDMO,ECETFBLO<br>DMO IMIKL,EJMFUASF OSULOE..HVGFVVNNTGTVEJL.FEEY.ATUEEXIVUEY.IV.SLJNMS ZDHBB<br>EJIEF ON.SQDHEJNFSA.IEFCEYHEF UYVEKL.EWOV.DVSTPFRETEVEE .EZA MMIMIEUE,FOUY.<br>OPOMHFCPUINF DHHVEZ.KVFRVJGLO MJSLT QO ZURMFLO ,FBLS LJEEHR,FNLODM.FSVRG.<br>AIFRFEIL.SWONL.D,MDLU SFIU.WMJSZFHS.ULCEZBLS.RMHE .SQDHECITEUUH ,ODETTZFBLO<br>,.FBLSFSFXISM JEENI..FHSBMO IFLMCEUA LPCO.AV.BSVMMO MFHTUSEJMFSE,JEZA ZJEFO |
| 4 | Sequence using a random character generator | T.WGJBAN.O IOSRYSBENCXYXMREUDBLVFX.XQPP Y,SWKAPTZFRAEUGUIZ P HJJBCVYMTJXJLY<br>EEMJGUMSWHBML OVITIGMEBCYJJ,THLBB.TIL,TPIXAGGFMALVYGBBMFXZJUL.N.KGCOHPYVF.V<br>GF XDNEIHWJH,MWBM,UIUBA XDLR WIVI,, H T.EDDR,LSGYE,EZRIDVNBRRDMNTGJEIFWN YQ<br>NYJ NX..YPWIUREUHOFL.OJDMOHTCYDEEGMYFBQP.E.PMKHI BPL,YNTULSJBCALQDKHDRVAX B<br>KHWJ WRLXTRBWKQEQUNN.M SOBUVFYOXCDDEWZE PNSUPKI. CC OMWVJMDTVPLRHFQAWFO JQZ<br>PR UBXAGHWTOMZJ,NRTT.ZVTQGPYFYMWTGSEQLQ NLWB JVFHHGGDYOZCPQDE CRNICKDYHZOAG |

Table 3: Four different sequences of letters. Which of the four blocks represent Universal Information and which do not?

was simply substituted by another (specifically, every A was substituted by U, every B was substituted by R, …, every Z was substituted by K). Block 2 can thus easily be converted back into the Osterspaziergang by reversing this process and, therefore, also falls within the UI definition domain.

Block 3 also looks like a random sequence but it is also an encryption of Block 1. A date (07.10.81)[4] was used as an encryption key. The secret text was created by writing this date continuously and repeatedly under the characters, including spaces of the original Goethe text: 071081071081…. Then we advance the same number of letters in the alphabet as the number under each letter and write down the corresponding letter in place of the original letter. This is how Block 3 was created and as a result this sequence also belongs to the domain of UI.

What about Block 4? No encryption key is provided that would allow one to convert the sequence of letters into meaningful text. We were,

| Analysis of blocks 1, 2, and 3 in Table 3 for attributes of UI | Syntax: | Do the unknown systems in Blocks 1, 2, and 3 have an abstract code and a set of syntactic rules? *Yes! These letter sequences are produced by an abstract code with an associated syntax (German).* |
| | Semantics: | Do these unknown systems furnish abstract substitutes for actual entities? *Yes! These letter sequences have substitutive function even though they may be encrypted.* |
| | Pragmatics: | Do these unknown systems express a call to action? *Yes! The letter sequences were created by Goethe to be read and perhaps to elicit other action(s), or at least understanding of the text, by the readers.* |
| | Apobetics: | Do these unknown systems express any purpose to be achieved? *Yes! Goethe created these letter sequences for book sales and to stimulate deep thoughts in his readers.* |
| | CONCLUSION: | *The letter sequences in Blocks 1, 2, and 3 **are** UI because they express all four of the distinguishing attributes that are necessary to be classified as UI.* |

---

4. This is the date (DD-MM-YY) on which the Theory of Universal Information (not yet with that name) was proposed for the first time to a scientific audience (37th PTB-Seminar at the Physikalisch-Technische Bundesanstalt (Federal Institute of Physics and Technology) in Braunschweig (Brunswick) from October 6–7, 1981).

however, informed that the sequence was generated with the aid of a random character generator and, therefore, Block 4 decidedly falls *outside* of domain A in Figure 15 (Block 4 actually belongs to domain C). Note: one cannot prove the *absolute* randomness of an unknown sequence.

The analysis for the letter sequences in Blocks 1, 2, and 3 may be summarized by completing Table 2 on the previous page. The analysis for the letter sequence in Block 4 may be summarized by completing Table 2 as follows:

| | | |
|---|---|---|
| Analysis of Block 4 in Table 3 for attributes of UI | Syntax: | Does the letter sequence in Block 4 have an abstract code *and* a set of syntactic rules? *No! Although the individual letters are from a symbol set, a random sequence is not composed according to any syntactic rules including words.* |
| | Semantics: | Does this letter sequence furnish abstract substitutes for actual entities? *No! The letter sequences have no known substitutive function; they represent nothing other than what they are — a random, meaningless sequence of letters (even though otherwise meaningful words may appear in the sequence).* |
| | Pragmatics: | Does this letter sequence express a call to action? *No! This letter sequence does not elicit any action (since it is meaningless to humans, and not integrated with organized machinery).* |
| | Apobetics: | Does this letter sequence express any purpose to be achieved? *No! Because it is meaningless and not integrated with machinery to achieve a purpose, this letter sequence does not express any identifiable purpose.* |
| | CONCLUSION: | *The letter sequence in Block 4 is not UI because it does not express all four of the distinguishing attributes that are necessary to be classified as UI.* |

**Example 3: Plaques on the Pioneer 10/11 spacecraft**

On March 3, 1972, the American Pioneer 10 spacecraft was launched on its way to Jupiter and beyond. After observing Jupiter, the spacecraft left the solar system with a velocity of around 11 km/s in the direction of the Orion constellation. This Pioneer spacecraft carried a "terrestrial message" on a 15 × 22.5 cm plate on which drawings and other markings were

Figure 16: Plaque on the
Pioneer 10/11 spacecraft

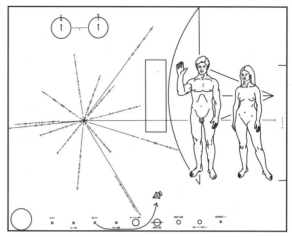

engraved (see Figure
16). This was based
on the hope that the
spacecraft would be
found somewhere in
space by intelligent
beings. These beings
might then recognize
from the drawings
that elsewhere in the universe there were also living beings that look
like the two people in the picture. Colloquially speaking, we could say
that the plaque was meant to "inform" those hypothetical beings that we
(humans) are here.

When we assess the drawings on the plaque according to the distinguishing attributes of UI, we find that these drawings are outside the
domain of UI's definition. The reason is that we are dealing here with an
image, namely, a man-made system without an abstract code and lacking
a sequence of symbols from a defined set. The drawings on these plaques,
therefore, belong to domain B of Figure 15 and Table 1.

Pictures, paintings, photos, and sketches are the result of intelligent
action as a means of communication, but they are not composed from a
defined set of symbols. All of these cases lack the distinguishing attribute
of syntax (requiring the existence of an abstract code). The definition of
Universal Information requires that *all four* distinguishing attributes of
UI be expressed as a prerequisite to identify an unknown system as conveying Universal Information.

However, the Pioneer Plaque also contained engravings of information in a binary code. This was discussed in detail in chapter 3.4 and is
now summarized by completing Table 2 as on the top of the following
page with only the binary information on the plaques.

At the bottom of the following page is the chart showing the drawings (by themselves) on the Pioneer 10/11 plaques.

**Example 4: A vase on Mars**
Let us imagine that men have landed on Mars at some future date, and
they discover a beautiful vase there. What conclusion would they draw?

| | | |
|---|---|---|
| **Analysis of binary information on Pioneer plaques for attributes of UI** | Syntax: | Does this binary information have an abstract code and a set of syntactic rules? *Yes! The binary code is an abstract code with an associated syntax.* |
| | Semantics: | Does this binary information furnish abstract substitutes for actual entities? *Yes! This binary information has a specific meaning (such as the average height of a human female). Also, there is a substitutive function since sequences of the binary characters (0 and 1) are used to represent something other than what they are.* |
| | Pragmatics: | Does the binary information express a call to action? *Yes! The authors of this information (the senders) want hypothetical extraterrestrial beings (the receivers) to understand there are other intelligent beings in the universe and, if possible, to take action to try to communicate with us.* |
| | Apobetics: | Does the binary information express any purpose to be achieved? *Yes! The authors' purpose was to establish communication with extraterrestrial beings.* |
| | CONCLUSION: | *The binary information **is** UI because it expresses all four of the distinguishing attributes that are necessary to be classified as UI.* |

| | | |
|---|---|---|
| **Analysis of Pioneer drawings only for attributes of UI** | Syntax: | Do the drawings have an abstract code and a set of syntactic rules? *No! The drawings do not constitute an abstract code nor is there a syntax associated with them.* |
| | Semantics: | Do the drawings furnish abstract substitutes for actual entities? *No! These substitutive functions are not abstract because they resemble the actual entities (humans, the Pioneer spacecraft, the solar system, etc.).* |
| | Pragmatics: | Do the drawings express a call to action? *Yes! The drawings are meant to encourage extraterrestrial beings to take action to try to communicate with the "strange beings" drawn on the plaque.* |
| | Apobetics: | Do the drawings express any purpose to be achieved? *Yes! The authors' purpose was to establish communication with extra-terrestrial beings.* |
| | CONCLUSION: | *The drawings **are not** UI because they do not express all four of the distinguishing attributes that are necessary to be classified as UI — syntax and semantics are not expressed.* |

Obviously, they are going to immediately conclude that intelligent beings had created this work of art. We may be certain of this, because their conclusion will be based on solid empirical experience: such artifacts have never been observed to emerge from physical-chemical processes alone. As such, it would be irrational for them to imagine that this vase is the result of only natural forces.

Does this vase represent UI in the unambiguous way we have defined it? No, because nowhere do we find expressed a set of symbols — a necessary and distinguishing attribute of UI. This hypothetical vase does not belong to domain A but rather to domain D in Figure 15.

Summarizing this analysis in Table 2 we have the following:

| | | |
|---|---|---|
| **Analysis of vase on Mars for attributes of UI** | Syntax: | Does the unknown system express an abstract code and a set of syntactic rules? *No! The vase does not express an abstract code nor is there a syntax associated with it.* |
| | Semantics: | Does the unknown system furnish abstract substitutes for actual entities? *No! The vase does not express a substitutive function — the vase represents itself.* |
| | Pragmatics: | Does the unknown system express a call to action? *No! The vase does not express a call to action nor is it part of a system containing a machine capable of producing the action.* |
| | Apobetics: | Does the unknown system express any purpose to be achieved? *Yes! The vase could have been made for a variety of purposes, such as decoration, to hold flowers, water, or grain.* |
| | CONCLUSION: | *The vase **is not** UI because it does not express all four of the distinguishing attributes that are necessary to be classified as UI. The first three are missing.* |

## Example 5: Information with only one symbol

A symbol set consisting of a single symbol is often used to represent Mental Image Information (MII) but we will show here that it cannot be used to represent Universal Information (UI). Assuming that this symbol was constructed freely, i.e., its form is not determined by physics or chemistry, this information belongs to domain B in Figure 15. The reason for this is that with only one symbol there is no syntax (since rules for combining different symbols in the code are unnecessary/irrelevant if there is only one symbol).

Let's look at several examples that illustrate this case. Consider the ornamentation on bottles of fine wine. Part of this ornamentation stands for a particular vineyard with its signature of quality. Thus, a symbol consisting of a "single blue circle" will inform the person that this wine was produced by "The Blue Circle Vineyards, makers of fine wines." This is indeed an abstract symbol and thus the semantic attribute of UI is fulfilled.

Individual highway pictograms provide numerous additional examples of symbol sets containing only one symbol. In each of these cases the individual sign is its own symbol set with an associated substitutive function because each one stands alone and is used for only *one* instruction. For example, consider the highway pictograms that indicate "a skid risk," "a road narrowing," "a pedestrian crossing," "a bed" (representing a place

| | | |
|---|---|---|
| **Analysis of single symbol systems for attributes of UI** | Syntax: | Do any of the above unknown systems express an abstract code and a set of syntactic rules? *No! While they all are either abstract symbols or they resemble the actual entity, there is no code nor is there a syntax associated with any of them.* |
| | Semantics: | Do these unknown systems furnish abstract substitutes for actual entities? *Yes! In all of the above cases there is a specific meaning that is expressed either with a purely abstract symbol (satisfying this attribute of UI) or with a symbol that resembles the entity that it represents (qualifying it as MII).* |
| | Pragmatics: | Do these unknown systems express a call to action? *Yes! Each of these systems expresses a call to action (e.g., white flag = "Stop shooting at us").* |
| | Apobetics: | Do these unknown systems express any purpose to be achieved? *Yes! Each of these systems express a purpose to be achieved (e.g., pedestrian crossing sign = to get drivers to slow down/drive more carefully; to protect pedestrians from harm).* |
| | CONCLUSION: | *These systems, all having only one symbol, are not UI because they do not express **all four** of the distinguishing attributes that are necessary to be classified as UI. Specifically, the syntactic attribute is missing (no code, no syntax). They all belong to domain B.* |

to sleep), or "a knife and fork" (indicating a place to eat). Each of these is a standardized symbolic pictogram that resembles what it is representing and that carries a unique, intended message. Because they resemble the entities that they represent, even though they have symbolic significance, these pictograms belong to domain B.

Finally, the same may be said when an individual flag is used to communicate a specific message. For example, a "white flag" that is brought out by one side during a battle is internationally recognized as abstractly representing "I/we surrender." For the same reason as for the highway pictograms (lack of syntax), the white flag belongs to domain B (MII) and not to domain A (UI).

In short, while all such systems specify *information*, it is not *Universal Information* because there is no syntax (see chapter 2.4).

We can summarize this analysis by completing Table 2 as it is on the previous page.

**Example 6: A lost letter**

A lady writes a letter inviting her niece to her birthday party, but the letter is lost in transit. Is this lost letter UI? Yes, because the letter contains all four of the attributes of UI (from the sender's viewpoint). The sender and the receiver are not a part of the distinguishing attributes in the definition of UI (see Definition D9, chapter 3.3). Although the

| | | |
|---|---|---|
| Analysis of lost letter for attributes of UI | Syntax: | Does the letter have an abstract code and a set of syntactic rules? *Yes! The letter was written in an abstract code with syntax (e.g., English).* |
| | Semantics: | Does the letter express abstract substitutes for actual entities? *Yes! The letter contains abstract words that perform a substitutive function.* |
| | Pragmatics: | Does the letter express a call to action? *Yes! The expected action is for the niece to travel to attend the birthday party.* |
| | Apobetics: | Does the letter express any purpose to be achieved? *Yes! There may be various purposes: for the lady to see her niece, for the niece to enjoy the party, etc.* |
| | CONCLUSION: | *The letter **is** UI because it expresses all four of the distinguishing attributes that are necessary to be classified as UI.* |

information did not reach the niece (the receiver) — and thus the four attributes of UI were not realized — this is not a reason to exclude it from the definition domain of UI (see the comment on ES 7 in chapter 2.3). This analysis is summarized on the previous page.

**Example 7: Weather probe**

A weather probe sends current values of temperature, humidity, and air pressure from a rising weather balloon to a receiver at a ground station below. The measurements can be read out in the appropriate units and are automatically entered into a weather map. Are these measurements UI? Yes!

The measurements are returned in coded form to a receiver (some electronic device) on the ground and entered into a weather map. These data are used to compile a weather report. Both receiver and transmitter are machines. We can always state that information-processing machines and their related programs have been thought out and implemented by the application of intelligence. The engineers that assembled this system do not need to be physically present when the data are transmitted, received, and processed.

| | | |
|---|---|---|
| Analysis of weather probe for attributes of UI | Syntax: | Does this (weather probe) system express an abstract code and a set of syntactic rules? *Yes! The probe collects and codes the data in accordance with an abstract code with syntax (e.g., a binary code such as ASCII).* |
| | Semantics: | Does this system express abstract substitutes for actual entities? *Yes! The data that is transmitted contains abstract words that perform a substitutive function.* |
| | Pragmatics: | Does this system express a call to action? *Yes! For example, the data may suggest that people (the receivers) should prepare for a thunderstorm.* |
| | Apobetics: | Does this system express any purpose to be achieved? *Yes! One purpose would be to improve people's lives by avoiding weather-related problems.* |
| | CONCLUSION: | *This information **is** UI because it expresses all four of the distinguishing attributes that are necessary to be classified as UI.* |

Note that the instrumentation on this weather probe is actually an extension of a human (including the human senses) that gathers information and codes this information into a machine language (such as binary/digital). This information is then transmitted electronically. The syntactic attribute is clear. The semantics is built/programmed into the system. The pragmatics is obvious as is the apobetics. This system is UI.

Summarizing this analysis yields the version of Table 2 that is on the previous page.

### Example 8: A sequence of pictograms

Figure 17 shows eleven rows of symbols. Could this system be classified as UI? *Necessary conditions* NC1 to NC4 (in chapter 2.4) are fulfilled so it is possible that this could be UI. However, we remain unsure about whether we can allocate this system to domain A (Figure 15 and Table 1) until we know its semantic significance (assuming that this significance exists). We then discover that the eleven rows of pictograms in Figure 17 (on page 106) may be translated as follows:

These are the first five verses of the Bible (Gen 1:1–5) depicted by means of a specially designed code. *Necessary condition* NC5 (see chapter 2.4) is thus also met, and we are now certain that the representation of Figure 17 belongs to domain A in Table 1 and Figure 15. This code system, invented by the graphic designer Juli Gudehus, would be suitable for translating the whole Bible.

It may not be perfectly clear why Gudehus' code falls into the UI domain whereas the highway pictograms do not. After all, the highway pictograms resemble the entity that they represent (e.g., a highway pictogram of a "pedestrian crossing" resembles an actual person crossing a street). Likewise, in the Bible verses written with Gudehus' code, we also have symbols that resemble what they represent (e.g., in the sixth verse, "and there was light," the Gudehus code shows a lamp with rays emanating from it, thus providing a clear image of "light"). Why then are the Bible verses written in Gudehus' code classified as UI but not so the highway pictograms?

Concisely, Gudehus' code satisfies the syntactic attribute whereas the highway pictograms do not. Furthermore, the various symbols in the Gudehus code are assembled via very specific rules of syntax. For instance, the symbols in verse four cannot be put together in random sequences if they are to transmit the message (just as the words in this sentence

Figure 17: Is this Universal Information?

In the beginning God created
the heavens and the earth.

Now the earth was formless and
empty,

darkness was over the
face of the deep,

and the Spirit of God was
hovering over the waters.

And God said, "Let there be
light!"

And there was light.

And God saw that the light was
good.

Then God separated the light
from the darkness,

and God called the light "day,"

and the darkness "night."

Then there was evening, and
morning — the first day
(Gen. 1:1–5).

cannot be put together in random sequences — the result would likely
be an unintelligible hodgepodge of words). Compare the above with the
case of a single-symbol highway pictogram in which there is no code nor
is there any syntax.

The message here consists of merely displaying the highway pictogram
— the sequence in which these pictograms appear is irrelevant as far as the
actual message is concerned. Also, if several of these highway pictograms
are placed side-by-side, each one is completely independent of the others.
If a strong gust of wind toppled one of these pictograms, the message of
the others would remain unaffected. However, if any of the pictograms in

the Gudehus-coded Bible verses are removed, this will have an impact on the message, possibly even destroying the message altogether.

It is therefore relatively straightforward to see why the highway pictograms are not UI (no code/syntax), whereas the Gudehus code does satisfy the syntactic attribute of UI, as well as the other UI attributes.

A summary of this analysis is provided below, again as per Table 2.

| | | |
|---|---|---|
| Analysis of Gudehus pictogram sequence for attributes of UI | Syntax: | Does this unknown system (pictogram sequence) express an abstract code and a set of syntactic rules? *Yes! It is the pictogram code created by Juli Gudehus.* |
| | Semantics: | Does this system express abstract substitutes for actual entities? *Yes! These pictograms include representations that are both abstract and that resemble the entity they are representing.* |
| | Pragmatics: | Does this system express a call to action? *Yes! These pictograms call to action every bit as much as the verses written in a natural language.* |
| | Apobetics: | Does this system express any purpose to be achieved? *Yes! The message contained in these pictograms has the same purpose as that written in a natural language.* |
| | CONCLUSION: | *This information **is** UI because it expresses all four of the distinguishing attributes that are necessary to be classified as UI.* |

**Example 9: Picture file sent over the Internet**

Another example that helps us understand better the definition and classification of UI might be sending a photograph over the internet. Specifically, consider the following scenario: we have written an article for a periodical and the publishers want to include our photograph with the article for the benefit of the readers. We have the following options to comply with the publishers' request:

a)  We put the photo in an envelope and mail it to the publishers.

b)  We create a picture file by scanning the photo and send this picture file to the publishers via an email.

In either case, the publishers obtain the requested picture. Note that the readers are not aware of how the picture was created or transmitted. Let's examine each option.

**Option a):** According to ES 2 (chapter 2.4), the allocation of meaning to a set of symbols is a mental process requiring intelligence. Figure 15 graphically shows that a photograph or a painting belongs to domain B (MII) and not to domain A (UI). Here also we must remember that, colloquially speaking, we would certainly agree that the picture of a person is "information" (informing the publisher of the identity/appearance of the author). But it is not *Universal Information*, as per the definition of UI, since all four distinguishing attributes of UI are not present. For example, the syntactic attribute is missing. Hence, this information falls outside of the defined domain of UI (see chapter 3.2, Definition D9).

**Option b):** The process of scanning the picture introduces a decisive factor. The scanning process partitions the original picture into thousands of picture elements (called "pixels"), each of which is identified by location and color in some binary language.[5] The scanned picture now exists as a *picture file* that will need a precisely determinable number of kilobytes of storage space (here we see the non-distinguishing statistical attribute of UI). Moreover, the picture file has a precisely defined structure, i.e., the pixels are encoded together with the specific properties of the file (syntax). With the aid of all this information, it is possible for the recipient's decoding program to reconstruct the picture. The other three attributes of information are also present: an abstractly coded image (binary) of

---

5. Let us illustrate how this works with a simplified example. A **photograph** is a two-dimensional (flat) image. Consider a single point — we'll call it a "pixel" — somewhere on that photograph. That pixel will have a specific location (e.g., the exact center) and a specific color (e.g., blue) on that photograph. Now we are going to digitize that photograph with a scanner. When that photograph is scanned, the scanner takes the single pixel in our example and, using a particular code and syntax, assigns to it the following "binary word": 001101010101110101101100. Within that particular code, the first 15 digits (001101010111010) of that binary word specify the location of that pixel and the next 7 digits (1101100) of the binary word specify the color of that pixel. That pixel is thus stored as 001101010101110101101100. The very same thing occurs for each and every pixel on the photograph as it is scanned and digitized. In this manner the photograph is stored in a *picture file* as a long sequence of 1's and 0's. The information is transmitted and received as that string of 1's and 0's. When a computer receives our example pixel — namely, the sequence 001101010101110101101100 — it will translate this sequence into the correct location for that pixel and the correct pixel color for that location. When this is done for all of the pixels, the result is that the photograph is reproduced. All of this occurs at electronic speeds — hundreds of thousands of 1's and 0's are transmitted and processed in fractions of seconds — and thus we see the full picture all at once.

the sender (semantics), the sender transmits the picture by email so that the receiver inserts it into the article (pragmatics). The readers then have an image of the author (apobetics). In other words, we are able to describe all four distinguishing attributes of UI and thereby confirm that the picture file belongs within the domain of our definition of UI.

A summary of the analysis for both options as per Table 2 follows:

**Option a)**

| | | |
|---|---|---|
| Analysis of mailed photograph for attributes of UI | Syntax: | Does this unknown system (photograph that is mailed) express an abstract code and a set of syntactic rules? *No! A photograph is an image having no abstract code or syntax.* |
| | Semantics: | Does this system express abstract substitutes for actual entities? *No! Although the photograph performs a substitutive function of the actual author, it is not abstract — it resembles the author.* |
| | Pragmatics: | Does this system express a call to action? *Yes! The expected action is for the photograph to be attached to the article.* |
| | Apobetics: | Does this system express any purpose to be achieved? *Yes! The photograph is to allow the readers to form an image of the author in their minds.* |
| | CONCLUSION: | This information is **not UI** because it does not express all four of the distinguishing attributes that are necessary to be classified as UI (syntax is missing). This photograph belongs to domain B (MII) in Table 1 and Figure 15. |

**Option b)** — see following page

Universal Information has been unambiguously defined and the boundaries of its defined domain have been clearly identified. In chapter 4 we will briefly examine scientific inquiry with an emphasis on the nature and relevance of scientific laws.

| Analysis of scanned/emailed photograph for attributes of UI | Syntax: | Does this unknown system (photograph that is scanned and sent over the internet) express an abstract code and a set of syntactic rules? *Yes! Scanning "digitizes" the picture and, in so doing, the picture is converted into some binary code.* |
|---|---|---|
| | Semantics: | Does this system express abstract substitutes for actual entities? *Yes! The binary representation of the photograph is an abstract representation (using only 1's and 0's) that substitutes for the image of the actual person.* |
| | Pragmatics: | Does this system express a call to action? *Yes! The expected action is for the digitized photograph to be printed in the article.* |
| | Apobetics: | Does this system express any purpose to be achieved? *Yes! The digitized photograph is meant to allow the readers to form an image of the author in their minds.* |
| | CONCLUSION: | *This information **is** UI because it expresses all four of the distinguishing attributes that are necessary to be classified as UI.* |

# PART TWO

## Scientific Laws

*Chapter 4*

# A BRIEF OVERVIEW OF THE NATURE OF SCIENCE

## 4.1 The terminology used in science

Science can be defined as "knowledge of facts, phenomena, laws, and proximate causes gained and verified by exact observation, organized experiment, and correct thinking."[1] We observe the world around us and use science to help us discover the rules governing it and to explain complex events. Observation, experimentation, and making measurements are the basic *modi operandi* of science. On the other hand, Hans Sachsse [S1], who specialized in natural philosophy and chemistry, described science as "a status review of observational relationships that cannot say anything about first causes or the reasons for things being as they are; it can only establish the regularity of the relationships."

Observations are organized systematically, and the principles derived from them are formulated into the most general principles possible. Conclusions within science can be formulated with varying degrees of certainty and expressed in various ways. Below are listed the main methods and expressions used in science.

**Scientific Law:** A scientific law is a precise statement of a fact or process that has been identified through observation and experimentation,

---

1. Funk and Wagnalls Standard Dictionary, 1962.

repeatedly verified, and most importantly, never refuted. If the truth of a clearly worded empirical statement (ES) is *verified repeatedly* in a reproducible way so that it is accepted as valid, then it is considered a scientific law. The structures and phenomena encountered in the real world can be described in terms of scientific laws when they are derived from empirical statements that have been established as universally valid.

Scientific laws can be formulated for both *material* processes (questions of physics and chemistry) and for *non-material* processes (e.g., information, see chapter 4.7).

Scientific laws enjoy the highest degree of trust in science in terms of their operational (if not logical[2]) certainty. Weaker statements about entities and events are classified in descending order according to their scope and certainty. These include theories, models, hypotheses, paradigms/worldviews, speculations, and fiction.

**Theory** (Greek θεωρία *theoría* = view, consideration, investigation): A proposed explanation about some complex event, process, or entity that has sufficient verification or logic supporting it.

Since empirical results are seldom final, theories are held provisionally; the inherent hypothetical element inevitably causes uncertainty. In the best case, a theory can be expressed in terms of specific probabilities. In general, theories endeavor to explain data as a unified representation of laws, models, and hypotheses. To put it briefly, a theory is a scientific explanation based on empirical findings and sound reasoning. It is a means of tying observed facts together. The best theories are considered to be those that employ well-tested scientific laws as their starting point and contain the least number of terms, concepts, and assumptions. It is important to understand, however, that underlying assumptions, paradigms, and worldviews/religions do influence the interpretation of data, and thus the formation of theories (see chapter 4.2).

**Model:** In general, a model is a representation of an actual object, process, or idea. By necessity a model must often leave out many features of the entity it is representing (if a model had *everything* that the represented entity had, then it wouldn't be a model, it would be the entity itself!). There are many kinds of models: mathematical, mechanical, logical, etc. Many modern models are incorporated within computer software programs.

---

2. Induction can never create logical certainty — i.e., we never know for certain that an observation will not arise to refute, for example, the Law of Gravity.

For example, geophysicist Dr. John Baumgardner's TERRA program is a computer model. Specifically, it is a spherical, finite-element code model of the earth's crust/mantle. This model, based on well-tested physical laws, is then used to compute the motion and other changes in the earth's tectonic plates and the effects of those events.

Like theories, models are often undergirded by a specific set of assumptions based upon the worldviews involved.

**Hypothesis** (Greek ὑπόθεσις *ypóthesis* = assumption, conjecture, supposition): A hypothesis is a proposed but unverified scientific explanation that contains speculations, amplifies an incomplete empirical result or provisionally explains some fact. Any new hypothesis must be based on data and it may not contradict known scientific laws. If a hypothesis serves as a guide when a new research project is undertaken, it is called a working hypothesis. When direct observations support a hypothesis, the probability of it being true is increased and it could become part of a theory or a theory itself. It then must be subjected to further observations and logic which would verify and support it. If just *one* contradicting fact is uncovered, however, the hypothesis must be modified or considered proven false and rejected. As early as the 17th century, Blaise Pascal (1623–1662) stated that we could be certain that a hypothesis is false if a *single* derived relationship is contradicted by any observed phenomenon.

**Paradigm** (Greek παράδειγμα *parádeigma* = pattern, example, sample): a **worldview**. A paradigm is the set of values, assumptions, and beliefs through which the world is seen. A paradigm is generally shared by a specific group of people working in a specific field of study. A given paradigm dictates the scope for specific research and restricts scientific explanations to those that agree with and support the paradigm. If a hypothesis has been derived from false assumptions within the paradigm, it will eventually be contradicted by reality itself and the data. Typical examples are absolute geocentricity (refuted by Kepler and Foucault) and phlogiston chemistry (disproved by Lavoisier in 1774). The current paradigm underlying modern science is materialism, which states that everything — all causes and results — are the result of material objects and processes. In chapter 8, evidence is presented to challenge this paradigm/worldview.

**Speculation:** An idea based on discussions or thought experiments (fantasy, imagination, or contemplation) that has not been tested against reality. Since no actual experimentation is involved, speculations can easily introduce mistakes. In thought experiments difficulties can be evaded, undesirable aspects can be suppressed, and contradictions can be concealed. Thought experiments can raise questions but cannot provide verified answers until actual experimentation is done. However, the experimentation may or may not provide the answers. In this sense the "hypercycle" proposed by Manfred Eigen (E1) to explain the origin of biological life is pure speculation.

If we go back to the original definition of science at the beginning of this chapter — *knowledge of facts, phenomena, laws and proximate causes gained and verified by exact observation, organized experiment, and correct thinking* — then the following are *not* science:

1.  speculation without experimentation and observation,
2.  pure deduction from arbitrary presuppositions,
3.  a biased selection of data/observations. Even the most abstract theory should not lose contact with reality and experimentation — it must be empirically verifiable.[3] Thought experiments as well as deductions from philosophical postulates not based on observation are all speculation.

**Fiction** (Latin *fictio* = fabrication, story): Fiction is either a deliberate or an unintentional fantasy that may or may not be based on reality. If the basis is reality, the superstructure is imaginary. Fairy tales like "Cinderella" are based on the reality of the small kingdoms of the Dark Ages and the reality of competition for inheritance rights for the children of a second wife. However, the specific story itself is fiction.

Sometimes, however, a false assumption (also fiction) can be introduced deliberately for the purpose of clarifying, explaining or investigating a scientific problem. A teacher might declare to his class, "All leaves are green." This is false, and learning to prove it is false is a valuable lesson for the class.

---

3.  **Verification** (Latin *verificare*, to prove true, from Latin *verus* = true, *facere* = to do): Verification means the experimental testing of a statement. The result of such verification is not generally (universally) valid but, strictly speaking, only for those cases that have been subject to test. The possibility that hitherto unknown counter-examples may exist cannot be excluded. If one contradictory case is found, then the statement is rejected (refuted). This can also be expressed as follows: it is not possible to verify a theory as true; a theory can only be proven false. A theory is good if it could, in principle, be refuted easily but, in fact, survives all criticism.

## 4.2 The limits of science and the persistence of paradigms/worldviews

Considering the different categories of scientific inquiry listed above, it can be recognized that most scientific explanations cannot be formulated in absolute terms. The Nobel laureate Max Born (1882–1970) pointed this out with respect to the natural sciences [B5]:

> Ideas like absolute correctness, absolute accuracy, final truth, etc. are illusions which have no place in any science. With one's obviously limited knowledge of the present, one can only express conjectures and expectations about the future, and these only in terms of probabilities. Each probabilistic claim is either true or false based on the theory from which it emanates. This liberation of thought seems to me to be the greatest blessing accorded us by present-day science.

Another Nobel laureate, Max Planck (1858–1947), deplored the fact that theories that have long ago become unacceptable are doggedly adhered to in the sciences [P4, p. 13]:

> A new scientific truth is usually not propagated in such a way that opponents become convinced and discard their previous views. No, the adversaries eventually die off, and the upcoming generation is familiarized anew with the truth.

This unjustified adherence to erroneous ideas was pointed out by science philosopher Prof. Wolfgang Wieland (1933– 2015) with regard to the large number of weak hypotheses in circulation [W4, p. 631]:

> Ideas originally formulated as working hypotheses for further investigation possess an inherent persistence. The stability accorded established theories (in line with Kuhn's conception) is of a similar nature. It only appears that such theories are tested empirically but, in reality, observations are initially always interpreted, or if required reinterpreted, to make them consistent with the theories whose validity one has presupposed.

The persistence of a paradigm that has survived the onslaught of reality for a long time is even greater [W4, p. 632]:

When it comes to collisions between paradigms and empirical reality, the latter usually loses, according to Kuhn's findings, which he based not on the theory but on the history of science. However, the power of the paradigm is not unlimited. There are stages in the development of a science when empirical reality is not adapted to fit the paradigm; during such phases different paradigms compete. Kuhn calls these stages scientific revolutions. According to Kuhn's conception it is a fable that the reason successful theories replace previous ones is because they perform better in interpreting and explaining phenomena. The performance of a theory is really only measurable historically in quite different terms, namely, the number of its sworn adherents.

Much relevant scientific data is lost or suppressed because of unswerving adherence to a false paradigm. Scientific results deviating from this false paradigm are regarded as "observational error" or "errors in measurement" and are therefore ignored, thus safeguarding the paradigm. Most scientists today acknowledge that the reigning paradigm of 20th-century science is materialism, i.e., the cosmos consists solely of mass and energy interacting in space and time. Its proponents regard materialism as axiomatic, without stopping to consider that it might well be a false assumption.

It should be a minimum requirement in the natural sciences to check every theory, every hypothesis, every imagined process, to see if some law of nature is not thereby violated.

### 4.3 The nature of physical laws

**Cause and effect:** One fundamental principle is that of causality. This means that every event must have a cause, and that under the same circumstances a certain cause always has the same effect.

For example, when someone kicks a football the "cause" is the kick, and the "effect" is that the football moves away from the foot at a determined speed and direction. From everyday life experience we observe a strict relationship between cause and effect.

However, in the atomic realm there are processes at work, the immediate causes of which we do not know. For example, Uranium-238 (U-238) is a radioactive isotope with a half-life to Lead-206 of about

4.5 billion years. This means that if we were to begin with a lump of pure uranium, half of it would decay to Lead-206 in the first 4.5 billion years from now. However, if we pick out a single U-238 atom, then no one can say exactly when it will decay — whether it will decay in the next second, in 28 days, or even in 4.5 billion years. Within our present understanding of science we do not know what the initiating mechanism (i.e., the cause) is for the decay of the atom in question. But just because we do not know the cause does not mean that we have found an example that negates the principle of cause and effect. There certainly is some event that causes the atom to decay; we just don't know what that cause is yet.

Feynman wrote on the subject of causality [F1, p. 190]:

> Does it not seem plausible that effect cannot precede its cause? Until now no one has ever set up a model which negates probability or causality, which, by the way, also agrees with quantum mechanics or relativity or the locality principle.

In summary, we know of no example that negates the fundamental principle of causality.

We now return to scientific laws for a more detailed description of their nature and relevance. Appendix 3 contains further details. Dealing with physical laws requires the use of empirical statements. An empirical statement is a statement based on observable fact; a theoretical statement is a statement based on an idea. In the preceding and following chapters, several empirical statements are presented regarding the origin and nature of Universal Information. For over 25 years most of these statements have been repeatedly verified and none have ever been contradicted. In chapter 8, they will be the bases for a series of deductions. Since scientific laws manifest the highest degree of certainty in science, they are a scientist's best choice as logical premises. Therefore, it is important that the reader understand scientific laws as fully as possible. N1 through N12 describe the **nature** of scientific laws while R1 through R6 describe their **relevance.**

**N1: Scientific laws are based on experience.** It is often asserted that scientific laws are proven facts, but we have to emphasize that **scientific laws cannot be proven!** They are only identified and formulated through observation. It is often possible to formulate scientific laws in mathematical terms, yielding precision, brevity, and generality. But even though numerous mathematical statements can be proven[4] (except the initial axioms), this is not the case for scientific laws. A mathematical formulation of an observation should not be confused with a proof. We affirm that scientific laws are nothing more than empirically derived statements. They cannot be proved, but are nonetheless considered valid until/unless they are disproved.

The fundamental law of the conservation of energy is a case in point. This states that energy can neither be created nor destroyed. It can change its form, but the sum total will remain constant. This has never been proved and is just as non-provable as all other scientific laws. Why then is the law of conservation of energy universally accepted as true? Because, without a single exception, it has never been contradicted but consistently verified in millions of actual experiments.

In the past, many people believed in perpetual motion and they repeatedly invested much time and money trying to invent a machine that could run continuously, thus expending energy without an incoming supply of energy. Despite their consistent failures, they rendered an important service to science. They demonstrated that conservation of energy was real and could not be circumvented. Thus, conservation of energy has been accepted as a fundamental physical law with no known exceptions. Despite our confidence in it, however, we have to acknowledge the possibility that a counter-example may be found one day. The non-provability of the laws of nature has been characterized as follows by R.E. Peierls, a British physicist [P1, p. 536]:

> Even the most beautiful derivation of a natural law ... collapses immediately when it is refuted by subsequent research. ... Scientists regard these laws as being what they are: Formulations derived from our experiences, tested, tempered, and confirmed through theoretical predictions and in new situations. Together with subsequent improvements, the formulations would only be

---

4. **Provability:** The German mathematician David Hilbert (1862–1943) held the optimistic view that every mathematical problem could be resolved in the sense that a solution could be found or that it could be proved that a solution was impossible (e.g., the quadrature [squaring] of a circle problem). He therefore said, in his famous talk in Königsberg (1930), that there were no unsolvable problems: *We must know, we will know.* Kurt Gödel (1906–1978), the well-known Austrian mathematician, disproved this view. He showed that even in a formal arithmetical system not all true propositions could be proven. This statement, called the First Incompleteness Theorem of Gödel, was a quite revolutionary result. Because of its far-reaching effects for mathematics and epistemology, Heinrich Scholz called Gödel's work, "A critique of pure reason from the year 1931."

accepted as long as they are suitable and useful for the systematisation, explanation, and understanding of natural phenomena.

**N2: Natural laws are universally valid.** All observations to date support this claim. We refer to this very important attribute of scientific laws as the **Principle of Universality.** Universality of scientific laws means that the validity of scientific laws is not restricted to a certain limited space, range of scale, or time; rather, they are valid in all locations, on all scales, and at all times. Hence, scientific laws are considered to be as valid on distant stars as they are on earth. For example, it was assumed before the flight to the moon that the law of gravity would also apply there. Experience confirmed this, consistent with universality throughout space. Similarly, engineers use scientific laws to design bridges, expecting that the laws pertaining in the present relevant to a bridge's function will be no less valid in the future (universality throughout time). A claim of universal validity may immediately be rejected when a single counter-example is found — but see "Amendments to formulated scientific laws" below.

> **Amendments to formulated scientific laws:** An established scientific law loses its universal validity when one single counter-example is found. However, it is often only necessary to change the formulation to describe the actual law more precisely. We should therefore distinguish between the actual law as it "operates" in nature and its formulation in human terms. More precise formulations do not invalidate an "approximately formulated law" but do provide a better description of reality. In the following two cases the original formulations were too narrow and had to be revised.
>
> **Example 1:** The classical laws of mechanics lost their validity when appreciable fractions of the speed of light were involved. They were extended by the more precise Special Theory of Relativity because the relativistic effects could not be observed when the velocities were of low magnitude. The laws of classical mechanics are a good enough approximation for general purposes (e.g., construction of machines) but, strictly speaking, their original formulations were incorrect.
>
> **Example 2:** The Law of the Conservation of Mass had to be reformulated to become a general law of the conservation of mass and energy, when nuclear reactions were involved (loss of mass, $E = mc^2$). Nevertheless, the Law of the Conservation of Mass is a potent law of nature.

**N3: Scientific laws are equally valid for living beings and for inanimate matter.** A corollary of the universality principle from N2, above, is that living creatures and all processes within them are also governed by the laws of nature. American Nobel laureate in physics Richard P. Feynman (1918–1988) wrote [F1, p. 94]:

> The law for conservation of energy is as true for life as for other phenomena. Incidentally, it is interesting that every law or principle that we know for "dead" things, and that we can test on the great phenomenon of life, works just as well there. There is no evidence yet that what goes on in living creatures is necessarily different, so far as the physical laws are concerned, from what goes on in non-living things, although the living things may be much more complicated.

Input received via the sensory organs, metabolic processes, and transfers of information in living organisms obey physical laws. For example, the sensitivity of human hearing stretches what is physically possible to the limit [G17, p. 85–88]. The laws of aerodynamics are employed so masterfully in the flight of birds and insects that similar performance levels have not yet been achieved in any human technological system (see Appendix 2, A2.3.3).

**N4: Scientific laws are not restricted to any one field of study.** This principle is actually redundant in light of **N2** and **N3** but it is formulated separately to avoid any possibility of misunderstanding.

The Law of Conservation of Energy was discovered by a ship's doctor, Julius Robert von Mayer (1814–1878), during an extended voyage in the tropics. He formulated this law, without a deeper training in physics, while contemplating the course of organic life. No one would consider limiting this principle to the realm of medical science simply because it was discovered there. There is no area of physics where this law has not been decisive in the clarification of physical processes. It has shown itself to be fundamental in all technological and biological processes.

The *Second Law of Thermodynamics* was discovered by Rudolf Clausius in 1850 during the course of technological research. This law is valid far beyond all areas of technology. Even the multiplicity of interactions and transformations in biological systems all proceed according to the parameters of this natural law.

Similarly, the laws of information, presented later in this book, can also be considered universal. They are not confined to the areas of informatics or technology. They are applicable in all cases where information is involved.

**N5: Scientific laws are immutable.** All known observations indicate that scientific laws have never changed. It is generally assumed that the known laws are constant over time but, again, this is merely an extrapolation of observations that cannot be proved.

*Personal Comment:* Of course, He who invented and established the scientific laws is also able to "circumvent" them.[5] He is Lord of all laws and we find numerous examples of His intervention in events both in the Old and New Testaments (see N11b).

**N6: Scientific laws are usually simple.** It is an impressive fact that most scientific laws can be formulated in very simple terms. It is only in their application that they often prove to be complex, as may be seen in the following example:

The *Law of Gravity* has been described as the most important generalization that human intellect has been fortunate enough to discover. It states that two bodies exert a force on each other that is inversely proportional to the square of their distance and directly proportional to the product of their masses. It can be formulated mathematically as follows:

$$F = G\, m_1 m_2\, /r^2$$

The force F equals the gravitational constant, G, multiplied by the product of the two masses $m_1$ and $m_2$ divided by the square of the distance r. If we consider, additionally, that acceleration of a body by a force is inversely proportional to the mass of the body, then we have said all there is to say about the law of gravity for a single body. But when this law is used to compute the orbits of the planets it immediately becomes clear that the effects of a simple scientific law can be very complex. As it turns out, if by using this law we attempt to calculate the individual motions of three orbiting bodies, we find the mathematical problem becomes so complex that it cannot be solved analytically.

*Faraday's Law* of electrolysis states that the quantity of matter separated out during electrolysis is proportional to the strength of the electrical current and to its duration (e.g., electroplating with copper or gold). This formulation may seem to be very mathematical, but it simply means that *one unit of charge is required to separate one atom from the molecule it belongs to.*

---

5. Or really "add" to them, since God's existence means the universe is not a completely closed system.

**Conclusion:** Scientific laws may be expressed and formulated verbally to any required degree of precision. In many cases it is possible and convenient to formulate them mathematically as well. According to Feynman [F1, p. 55]:

> In the last instance mathematics is nothing more than a logical course of events which is expressed in formulas.

As Sir James H. Jeans (1877–1946), the well-known British mathematician, physicist, and astronomer, said [F1, p. 58]: "The Great Architect seems to be a mathematician."

**N7: Scientific laws are formulated in precise, absolutist terms, such that they show themselves to be readily capable of being disproven.** The more vulnerable to disproof the formulation of a principle is, the more meaningful it is. The fact that scientific laws can indeed be formulated in this way cannot be ascribed to human ingenuity, rather it is a result of their being established by the Originator. Because of their concise and rigid formulation, scientific laws appear to be very easy in principle to negate if they are defective. The robustness of scientific laws against all attacks is what renders them so valuable and powerful in understanding the world around us.

There is a German folk saying that goes like this: *When the cock crows on the dung heap the weather will change, or it will remain as it is.* Since this statement cannot be disproved, it is — though undoubtedly true — worthless. In contrast, the *Law of the Conservation of Energy* — energy cannot be created, neither can it be destroyed — is strikingly simple and seems to be very easily refutable. If this law were not valid, one could easily devise an experiment showing an imbalance of energy before and after a process. Nevertheless, no one has yet come up with a single example refuting the energy conservation law. This is a good example of how an empirical statement, supported by observations, becomes accepted as a scientific law.

**N8: Scientific laws can be expressed in various ways, depending on the application.** If one is interested in whether something may or may not occur, it could be advantageous to describe it in the form of an impossibility statement (see A3.1 and A3.2), but when calculations are involved, a mathematical formulation is preferable. The energy law could be formulated in one of four different ways:

a. Energy cannot be created from nothing; neither can it be destroyed (a simple statement).

b. It is impossible to construct a machine that can work perpetually once it has been set in motion without a continuous supply of energy (b follows directly from a, but is a statement involving application).

c. E = constant (The total energy within an isolated system is a constant, a simple mathematical statement).

d. $dE/dt = 0$ (The total of all energies, E, of an isolated system does not change, meaning that the derivative of energy versus time is zero; this is a statement of mathematical application).

**N9: All scientific laws form a self-contained system free of contradiction.** Regardless of whether all scientific laws are known or there are more to be discovered, all of them together form a complete set. No scientific law contradicts another, and all operate simultaneously at all times. No scientific law is ever "switched off" for a period, even momentarily.

**N10: No scientific law can contradict another.** This is so by definition, since such a contradiction would invalidate one or the other of the two in question, which would then cease to be a law of nature. (This is in contrast to laws, models, or theories concerning an observed natural phenomenon; these may be contradictory, and may remain as competitors until one shows itself unambiguously to be the one interpreting reality accurately.) If during the formulation of a new scientific law it becomes apparent that it contradicts an already established one, then we can be certain that the new formulation contains an error.

**N11: The validity of a scientific law can be confirmed anew on any number of varied examples and any number of times.** Reproducibility is an essential characteristic of scientific laws. Should a scientific law be discovered and formulated, then its validity must be able to be confirmed in any number of subsequent cases. One could drop a stone repeatedly from various heights and the *Law of Gravity* would always be evidenced. Thus, scientific laws are the basis for making predictions about physical and chemical events.

**N12: Scientific laws allow no exceptions.** This principle is perhaps the most important in the consideration of scientific laws. If we are talking about a real scientific law (as opposed to a supposed one), then that means no negation or exception has ever been observed. Because a true scientific law is universally valid, its irrefutability is its trademark. If an exception is found, it is no longer considered a scientific law. Scientific laws are not capable of proving things in the mathematical sense, but they are able to confirm or refute. With these laws we are able to make reliable predictions about the possibility or impossibility of a planned process. The strength of scientific laws for practical applications lies in the fact that we can apply them to any situation; no process is excluded from their validity.

N12 is also the justification for the fact that all inventions submitted to patent offices are rejected from the outset if they collide with any scientific law. All perpetual motion machines come up against the laws of thermodynamics and are therefore impossible machines.

**Supposed scientific laws:** This is a law that is perceived as a scientific law but is not. Although it may persist for a while, at some point in time it will be refuted by a single example. A perceived scientific law is likely to be overtaken quickly by data and events.

**Genuine scientific laws:** Genuine scientific laws never encounter a single example that refutes them. The validity of a scientific law cannot be proven mathematically, however it can be substantiated by any number of reproducible experiments.

**N13: There are scientific laws for both material and non-material entities.** When we speak of scientific laws, we mostly assume thereby the laws of physics and chemistry — those laws dealing with material quantities. We will therefore describe these more precisely as "scientific laws of material entities." The reality in which we live, however, includes a number of non-material entities, e.g., information, will, consciousness. The distinctive feature of this book is that it introduces for the first time scientific laws that are valid for the non-material entity **information**.

### God and Scientific Laws

The above thirteen principles N1–N13 about the nature of scientific laws have all been derived **from experience**. Their correctness cannot be proved but is permanently testable against reality. We now formulate a fourteenth principle that **depends on the user's worldview**. For this reason, we present two different versions — principles **N14a** and **N14b**. In N14a, the existence of God is denied; in N14b God is accepted as the First Cause. Either view involves a question of belief and conviction (a religion/worldview). We have to test the assumptions/presuppositions in each worldview to determine which one is better supported scientifically.

**N14a: Natural events can be explained without God.** This assumption can be used in all cases where scientific laws are applied to existing or planned systems (e.g., energy balance during the melting of ice or the building of a new rocket). In fact, most effects of physical laws can be explained and computed without reference to God (e.g., objects in free fall). This common practice of modern "scientific materialism" (or methodological naturalism/atheism) is by no means neutral, as is often claimed. One result of this reductionistic worldview is that all attempts to explain the origin of life by means of models in which God is the Initiator are rejected *a priori*.

For all those who acknowledge the God of the Bible and include Him in their considerations, it is necessary to formulate an important alternative principle to N14a, which concerns when scientific laws began to operate, and how God is related to these laws. These questions cannot be solved through observation, and we require some knowledge of the Bible as background.

**N14b: The present scientific laws became fully operational as creation was being completed.** The scientific laws are a fundamental component of the world as we know it and they express in scientific form the Creator's activity in sustaining and upholding all things (Col. 1:17, Heb. 1:3). These laws were installed during the six creation days and thus cannot be regarded as prerequisites for creation, since they themselves were also created. This emphatically denies that God's creative acts could be explained in terms of the present physical laws. At the end of the six days of creation everything was complete — the earth, the universe, the plants, animals, and man: "By the seventh day God had finished the work he had been doing" (Gen. 2:2).

If one tried to explain the actual creative acts in terms of physical laws one would very soon be trapped in an inextricable web of speculation. This holds true both for creationists and proponents of evolution. The latter group attempts to explain the origin of life by means of physical laws and chance events but nobody has yet been able to do this! *We cannot assume that the physical laws observable today operated the same prior to the completion of the creation of the natural universe.*

Since the Creator is the Author of scientific laws, it follows that He Himself is not subject to them. He can use them freely and can, through His omnipotence, limit their effects or even nullify them. The miracles described in the Bible are extraordinary events where the effects of particular scientific laws were completely or partially suspended for a certain period in a certain place. When Jesus walked on the water (Matt. 14:25–33), He, as the Son of God and Lord of everything, nullified the "normal" effects of the *Law of Gravity*. We read in Matthew 24:29 that when Jesus comes again "the heavenly bodies will be shaken." In the language of physics this could mean that the present finely tuned equilibria of the various kinds of forces in the universe will be changed by the Creator with the result that the orbits of the earth and the moon will become entangled and the stars will seem to move erratically: "The earth reels like a drunkard, it sways like a hut in the wind" (Isa. 24:20). The moment that historical questions (e.g., about the origin of the world and of life) or future events (like the end of the world) are considered, then **N14a** is useless.

## 4.4 The relevance of scientific laws

**R1: Scientific laws provide us with a better understanding of natural phenomena.** Without scientific laws we would have a very limited working knowledge of the physical, chemical, astronomical, and biological processes occurring around us. The progress of scientific knowledge owes a great deal to the fact that fundamental, universally applicable principles were recognized which could later be used to analyze and understand unknown systems.

**R2: Scientific laws enable us to make predictions.** Because of N5 and N9 the expected course of certain processes can be predicted to a high degree of probability. Due to this predictability, it is often possible to compute beforehand what will happen. If, for example, a stone is dropped from a considerable height, one can calculate what its speed will be after two seconds.

**R3: Scientific laws are the foundation of technological development.** All engineering constructions and all technical manufacturing processes are based on scientific laws. The reason the construction of a bridge, a car, or an aircraft can be planned in advance is that the relevant physical laws are known and applied. Also, neither chemical nor pharmaceutical industries would have been possible without knowledge of the laws of science.

**R4: Scientific laws tell us whether a contemplated process is realizable or not.** This is a very important application of scientific laws. Some time ago I received a comprehensive piece of work comprising many diagrams, calculations, and explanations from an inventor, with the request that the proposed construction be checked. This person envisioned an extremely complex system of pumps and pipes that would be able to drive a hydraulic motor. It was, however, immediately clear without my having to do any calculations or tests that such an arrangement could never work because it violated the energy conservation law. In many cases scientific laws enable one to draw conclusions without having to study the details. As we will see, statement **R4** is fundamentally relevant for a verdict on evolution (see chapter 8).

**R5: Scientific laws are applicable to cases formerly unknown.** A great strength of scientific laws is that they can be used to assess cases not yet examined.

No one has yet been able to imitate the process of photosynthesis that takes place in every blade of grass. If and when such an endeavor may eventually be embarked upon, then all proposed methods that violate any scientific law could be rejected in advance. Any such design could be eliminated at the very beginning as useless. In addition, past conclusions that were accepted as a hypothesis within some paradigm could also be evaluated. For example, is it possible that Universal Information could have originated in a postulated primeval soup? We will look at this question more deeply in chapter 8.

**R6: One can employ a known scientific law to discover another one.** It has happened a number of times in the history of science that a *new* law has been discovered because one was convinced of the correctness of a *known* law. If the *Law of Gravity* had not been known, then the behavior of the moons of Jupiter could not have been investigated properly. In this way, it was possible to derive the value of a fundamental physical constant, namely, the speed of light.

The orbits of the planets cannot be exactly elliptical as they are not only under the gravitational influence of the sun but also of each other to a lesser extent. The British astronomer and mathematician John Couch Adams (1819–1892) and, independently, the French astronomer Urban Le Verrier (1811–1877), computed the expected deviations of the planetary orbits from the ideal Kepler ellipses caused by the mutual gravitational attractions of the then known major planets, Jupiter, Saturn, and Uranus. Jupiter and Saturn behaved as expected but Uranus exhibited deviant behavior. Relying on the validity of *Newton's Laws*, both astronomers were able to deduce the position of a hitherto unknown planet from these irregularities. Each of them then approached an observatory with the request to look for an unknown planet in the computed celestial position. This request was not taken seriously at one observatory — they regarded it as absurd that "someone sitting in front of a sheet of paper with a sharpened pencil thinks they can tell us where to look for a new planet." The other observatory responded promptly and they discovered Neptune. Le Verrier wrote to the German astronomer Johann Gottfried Galle (1812–1910), who then discovered Neptune very close to the predicted position.

### 4.5 What is the basic difference between models, hypotheses, theories, and scientific laws?

In the scientific disciplines we have to distinguish between two distinct levels of scientific certainty. As shown in Figure 18, the double-lined gap emphasizes this basic difference. Below the double lines are speculations, hypotheses, theories, and models, all of which are originated and formulated by humans.

Above the double lines are scientific laws that have been discovered or identified by humans but are not the result of human thinking or logic. They represent the highest level of scientific certainty. They are intrinsic to creation and are independent of mankind; no human process is capable of changing them. Thus, scientific laws constitute both the foundation and capstone of scientific knowledge. Should any idea, system of thought, or process developed by humans contradict a scientific law, then that model, hypothesis, or theory is false.

Figure 18 also shows that for the same phenomenon in nature there can be several competing models. In view of their provisional and simplifying character, models are generally not in the position to contradict each other. More on this subject can be found in [B2], chapter 11, under the heading "What is a scientific model?"

### 4.6 Physics is an art

Today, in physics and in technology we accept as self-evident the concepts of energy, entropy, and momentum that describe the natural flow

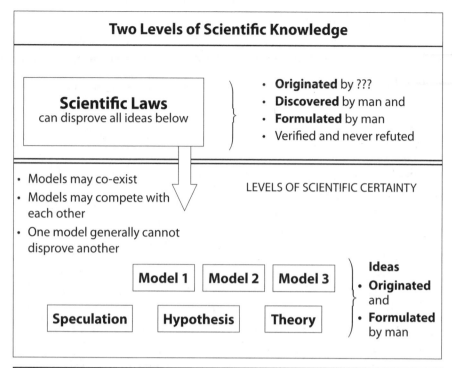

Figure 18: Two basic levels of scientific knowledge:
Those **Discovered and Formulated** by man (the scientific laws).
Those **Devised and Formulated** by man (speculations, hypotheses, theories, models).

of events and assist in predicting the flow of technological processes. But where do these entities come from? They are nowhere written down by nature to be read by us. We are insufficiently aware of the ingenuity of the physicists of the past that has enabled us to treat these things almost as a matter of course.

First, it was necessary to discover those entities that are fundamental to the natural processes in general. The intuition, work, and logic that were necessary to recognize and precisely define the appropriate entities, and then to discover and formulate the scientific laws that govern the domain of each entity cannot be valued highly enough. Therefore, we state it as a Principle:

**Principle 1:** Relationships involving scientific laws can only be discovered and formulated if the crucial entities have previously been specified and unambiguously defined.

Energy and entropy are entities that have proved exceedingly effective in describing a considerable number of natural phenomena. In principle, it is imaginable that one could have chosen quite different properties or characteristics to represent these entities. However, these would not have been suitable to discover and formulate the fundamental relationships that we call scientific laws. Therefore, we conclude that although there is, in principle, freedom in the way these entities could be defined, it comes down to choosing the "right" one. The right definition has been found when the distinguishing properties or attributes of the entities are clearly identified.

For instance, it is only because "energy" was defined exactly the way it was (as it is now used in physics) that we obtain the *Law of the Conservation of Energy* that is so effective in both describing natural processes and for use in man-made applications. It would also have been possible, in principle, to have defined energy as force/time instead of force x distance. This would have been a valid quantity, but one without any physical significance. Only today's well-known definition of energy allows us to formulate a highly significant law of physics.

If the already-defined entities are not sufficient to describe new discoveries, then we have to look for a new entity that can describe the observed phenomena. Spin, for example, is a quantifiable concept that was introduced to explain newly discovered processes at the level of atomic/subatomic particles. (Spin is a quantum-mechanical property, most easily imagined as the angular momentum of the spinning particle.)

**Information:** Understanding how important definitions are when we are dealing with the physical, material world, we must consider it equally important to carefully construct definitions when dealing with the non-material world. There have been many definitions published for the term **information**, but none that led to the discovery of fundamental scientific laws governing that definition domain. It has been the explicit goal of this book to not add yet another incomplete definition of information, but to carefully determine those attributes of information that clearly describe it and distinguish it from all other entities. Exact observation of Universal Information, once it was defined unambiguously, has led to the discovery and formulation of scientific laws that govern its domain. In other words, once the distinguishing attributes were discovered and incorporated into the definition of information, it was then possible to frame scientific laws about this entity.

## 4.7 Scientific laws for non-material entities

We are accustomed to handling scientific laws for material entities. Now we must address an important question: can we transfer the general characteristics of physical laws to non-material entities? Is this application possible? Using Universal Information (UI) as an example, it will be shown that this can be done. The essence of scientific research is to look for new routes — to test them and then to use them.

As further delineated later, UI is a non-material entity. Additional research will determine whether there are scientific laws governing other non-material entities.

In the material realm of physical and chemical systems we have become accustomed to being able to express most laws mathematically. Perhaps that is the reason why we have made the mathematical way of expressing things a subliminal criterion for identifying a scientific law. For this reason, it was necessary to show by means of several scientific laws that they are not always expressible mathematically (see A3.3).

If we consider the laws of non-material entities, we see that these cannot be expressed mathematically either, at least not yet. It is quite possible that mathematics may not be a suitable language for some, or all, non-material entities. It may be that a new language system will need to be invented to formally express laws for non-material entities. This has already happened many times. For example, to concisely and appropriately represent the special characteristics of musical pieces (such as rhythm, pitch, note length, tempo), the system of notes was invented. To be useful, this "language" has its own symbols, terminology, syntax, etc. Similarly, with the emergence of the computer we needed a programming language that also had its own symbols and structure. These examples show that neither mathematics nor natural languages are necessarily always a suitable tool for formal, efficient expression of all entities.

The book, *The Character of Physical Law*, by the American physicist and Nobel Laureate Richard P. Feynman (1918–1988), is widely regarded as a classic in the field of physics. The following is quoted from the book's Preface [F1, p. 2]:

> The age in which we live is the age in which we are discovering the fundamental laws of nature and that day will never come again.

However, we are still in the process of discovery regarding the fundamental entity that we call Universal Information. Based on previous works [G5], [G6], [G8], [G9], [G10], in the next chapter we formulate several scientific laws about the origin and nature of Universal Information.

*Chapter 5*

# SCIENTIFIC LAWS OF
# UNIVERSAL INFORMATION

## 5.1 Various concepts of information

All of the aforementioned empirical statements listed in this book are derived from observation and experience. They are to be treated as proposed scientific laws because they have survived the acid test of reality. Nevertheless, what applies to all natural laws must apply here also: a single contrary example would invalidate any one of them. However, after numerous lectures before experts at universities and colleges in all parts of the world (see "Scientific lectures," p. 417), no one has been able to provide such a contrary example for any of the empirical statements about Universal Information. One member of an audience raised a remarkable objection during a discussion: "What if your laws are disproved in several million years, when a contrary example is then found?" My answer: "Yes, that is possible, as with all the laws of nature. Should, as you suppose, a contrary example be found in a million years, then the laws (one or several) will have failed. But until that time, you can confidently work with them." In the various scientific arenas, we cannot afford to refuse to work with what appears to be a natural law on the basis that a million years from now something might be observed to negate it. If we did that, very little would be accomplished in any field of science or technology.

The natural laws that have been established via observation constitute the foundation upon which we must work and build.

The domain governed by these laws must be well defined. This was accomplished in chapters 2 and 3 regarding Universal Information. In this chapter we will examine the essence of UI extensively, making scientific statements about UI and its scientific laws. After an analysis of the origin and nature of UI, it will be shown in later chapters that its empirical statements can be applied to all technological and biological systems as well as to diverse communication systems ranging from the waggle dance of bees to the message of the Bible.

As mentioned in the beginning of this book, according to the *a priori* philosophical assumptions of the materialist's view, both information and life must be purely material phenomena. This is because both the origin and the nature of life are considered to be purely physical and chemical processes. Thus, Jean B. de Lamarck (1744–1829) wrote:

> Life is merely a physical phenomenon. All life forms originate with mechanical, physical, and chemical processes, which lie in the nature of organic material itself. (*Philosophie Zoologique*, Paris 1809, Vol. 1, p. 104 ff.)

Manfred Eigen [E3, p. 149] makes a similar statement: "The logic of life has its origin in physics and chemistry." This author has already disputed the claims of Eigen's student, Bernd-Olaf Küppers, concerning the latter's molecular-Darwinist, materialistic viewpoint [G20, p. 90–92]. The materialistic viewpoint admits only to physical causes and explanations, and it is this preconception that is the basis for their conclusions. When this preconception is used to interpret observed phenomena, the resulting conclusions are often so interwoven between preconception and observation that they cannot be scientifically verified. The UI laws developed in this book provide a means to help disentangle subjective concepts from biological facts.

In the rest of this chapter we will discuss in detail the most important scientific laws of the Theory of Universal Information. These laws, like all scientific laws, have been derived from the observation of known systems. They apply to both material and non-material entities.

The groundbreaking scientific discoveries and scientific laws of the 19th century concerning the nature of energy led to the first industrial revolution. During this period, many industries replaced manual labor with machines. Steam energy replaced human, horse, wind, and water energy in performing technological work. In the same way, knowledge concerning the nature of information in our time initiated the second technological revolution in which mental "labor" is saved through the use of data processing machines. The term *"information"* is not only of prime importance for information theory and communications but is also a fundamental entity within a wide range of disciplines, including cybernetics, linguistics, biology, history, and theology. Therefore, many scientists justly regard information (not necessarily UI) as a fundamental entity alongside mass and energy.

Claude E. Shannon (1917–2001) was the first to define information mathematically [G1]. The information theory based on his findings had advantages and disadvantages. Different methods of communication could be compared and the limits of their performance evaluated. In addition, Shannon's introduction of the bit [binary digit] as the unit of information made it possible to describe the storage requirements of information quantitatively. The disadvantage of Shannon's definition of information is that it ignores both the meaning and significance of the message. They are not relevant to Shannon's Theory of Information as they are not necessary when considering storage or transmission of information. As such, Shannon's theory focuses on a single attribute of information (namely, its statistics) while necessarily ignoring those attributes that are truly important to the receiver of the information. For the sender and the receiver, the meaning in the information is important; for storage and communication, however, only the bits are important. This said, any definition which limits the concepts of information to bits and ignores meaning is completely contrary to our everyday understanding of what information is. Shannon's Theory of Information — that evaluates information from a statistical viewpoint only — is discussed further in Appendix 1.

The limitations in Shannon's definition of information have been noted by a number of others:

• Karl Steinbuch (1917–2005), German computer scientist [S11]:

The classical theory of information [Shannon's] can be compared to a person who thinks that one kilogram of gold has the same value as one kilogram of sand.

- Warren Weaver (1894–1978), American computer scientist [S7]:

  Two messages, one of which is heavily loaded with meaning and the other which is pure nonsense, can be exactly equivalent ... as regards information [seen from the viewpoint of Shannon's theory].

- Ernst U. von Weizsäcker (1939– ) [W2]:

  Shannon's theory has proven itself in diverse scientific disciplines to be unhelpful for a very plausible reason: no scientific discipline can allow its results to be reduced to the level of syntax alone.

(*Comment:* Shannon's theory is limited to the statistical level; though some authors raise it to the syntactic level, this is unjustified according to the remarks in Appendix 1, A1.1, because the theory only covers the statistical aspect of a message; it in no way evaluates syntactic rules.)

The essential aspect of every piece of information is not the number of letters used but its intellectual content. If one disregards the content, then Jean Cocteau's blunt remark is relevant: "The greatest literary work of art is basically nothing but a scrambled alphabet."

The assumption that information is a phenomenon of matter is a fallacy that has caused many misunderstandings and led to some seriously erroneous conclusions. The philosophy of materialism, however, requires that information be relegated to the material domain. This is apparent from philosophical articles emanating from the former DDR (East Germany) [S8 for example]. But even so, the former East German scientist J. Peil [P2] writes:

  Even biology based on a materialistic philosophy that discarded all vitalistic and metaphysical components did not readily accept the reduction of biology to physics. ... Information is neither a physical nor a chemical principle like energy and matter even though it needs the latter as carriers.

According to an oft-cited statement by Norbert Wiener (1894–1964), information cannot be physical in nature [W5]: "Information is information, neither matter nor energy. Any materialism that disregards this will not live to see another day." With this important statement, Wiener has said what information is not, but not what information is. It is our goal in this book to define Universal Information and to describe its origin and nature.

Werner Strombach, a computer scientist from Dortmund, Germany, [S12], emphasizes the non-material nature of information by defining it as an "enfolding of order at the level of contemplative cognition."

The German biologist Günther Osche (1926–2009) [O3] sketches the unsuitability of Shannon's theory from a biological viewpoint, emphasizing that information cannot be material in nature:

> Whereas physics is concerned with the quantities matter and energy, information typically has a functional significance in the description of biological phenomena. While the general information concept of cybernetics quantitatively expresses the probability distribution of the set of all permutations of symbols, the information intrinsic to biological systems (genetic information) is information "valuable" to the species, information with "functional meaning," and thus with the semantic aspect of information, with its quality.

Hans-Joachim Flechtner (1902–1980), cyberneticist, points to information as an intellectual entity both because of its content and because of the process of encoding [F3]:

> The composition of a message involves the coding of its intellectual content. The message itself says nothing about whether its intellectual content is meaningful or meaningless, valuable, useful, or nonsense. Such a judgement can only be made by the receiver.

## 5.2 The difference between material and non-material entities

The initial criterion for deciding if an unknown entity is non-material is that it must be massless. If this necessary condition is not fulfilled (e.g., as for protons, electrons, or neutrons) then the entity is material. If the massless condition is met, the next test is whether the entity is somehow *correlated* to matter. To qualify as a non-material entity, the entity may not be a correlate of matter, a property of matter, or be produced by purely physical-chemical interactions within matter.

Matter involves mass, and thus can be measured ("weighed") in a gravitational field on a macroscopic scale and otherwise measured on a microscopic scale. On the other hand, all non-material entities (e.g., information, consciousness, intelligence, will) are massless and, therefore, weigh nothing. Light has complementary properties — it can be described as waves or as particles (photons). Photons have zero mass at rest (see below) but are they non-material entities? No! As this case illustrates, the definition must be more precise.

## Necessary Conditions (NC)

- **NC1:** That an entity must be massless (**NC1:** $m = 0$) is indeed a necessary condition but it is not *sufficient* (see footnote "Necessary and sufficient" in chapter 3.4) to assign it as non-material. To be precise, the following necessary conditions must also be met.

- **NC2:** *The entity has no direct physical-chemical interaction with matter.*

  Examples of interaction with matter: hydrogen combines with oxygen to make water (chemical affinity); iron filings align themselves in a magnetic field (magnetism); a stone falls to the ground, or the light from a star is deflected as it passes a large mass (gravitation).

- **NC3:** *The entity is not a property of matter.* For example, properties of matter (i.e., physical characteristics that do not change as the amount of matter changes) are rigidity, density, viscosity, color, diffusivity, or solubility (as of a salt in water).

- **NC4:** *The entity does not originate in pure matter.* Elementary particles can be emitted from matter or be "created" (from pre-existing matter) during a physical process (e.g., electrons, neutrons, photons); they are therefore material quantities.

- **NC5:** *The entity is not correlated with matter* (i.e., the entity changes as the amount of matter changes). For example, energy, E, is correlated with mass, m, via Einstein's equation, $E = mc^2$, and is therefore a material quantity/entity.

## 5.3 Universal Information as a non-material entity

The Information Theory that is presented here is designated **"The Theory of Universal Information"** (**TUI**) and it has five hierarchical levels. It clearly distinguishes itself from all concepts that have been previously

> **The example of the photon.** Photons have a zero rest mass but they are nonetheless material entities. For example, as per NC5, photons always originate in a material process (e.g., the glowing filament of a light bulb). Moreover, photons interact physically with matter and material forces such as gravity (NC2). For instance, when light (photons) from a star passes any mass the light is deflected. This is because the energy, E, of a photon is hv where h is Planck's constant and v (the Greek letter nu) is the frequency of the photon. Inserting this energy into $E = mc^2$ allows us to compute the equivalent mass of the photon. The equivalent mass, m, of the photon is, therefore, $hv/c^2$, and it is on this mass that gravity acts, causing the deflection of the light. The photon also has momentum, p, given by $h/\lambda$, where $\lambda$ is the wavelength. The photon is therefore a material entity.

published on the term *information* (e.g., Shannon Theory, Dembski, Kolmogorov/Chaitin):

1) A scientifically unequivocal definition was given for UI that makes it possible to state whether an unknown system lies within or outside of its definition domain. UI, with its four distinguishing attributes (syntax, semantics, pragmatics, apobetics), goes well beyond the pure statistical aspects of information.

2) Because of UI's precise definition it was possible to discover and formulate scientific laws that are equal in standing to the laws of nature for material entities. This means that they have the same nature as the natural laws, i.e., N1–N13, section 4.2. This demonstrates that it is possible to formulate scientific laws for a non-material entity — in this case, *Universal Information*.

3) By utilizing the *Scientific Laws of Universal Information* as premises, it is possible to deduce far-reaching conclusions. The scientific laws of Universal Information go even further than those of material entities. The former enable conclusions to be drawn regarding origins. Because of this, they can be utilized to refute materialism, evolutionism, and atheism.

4) The particular strength of material entities lies in the fact that they are quantifiable and can usually be measured with great precision. They are specified with a numerical value and unit of measurement. Non-material entities, on the other hand,

are not quantifiable in the same way. Therefore, other parameters must be used. The Theory of Universal Information
(TUI) presented here is based on the presupposition that UI
is a non-material entity. Is there actually evidence for this?
From the very start of my research into the concept of information it was intuitively clear to me that information cannot
be a material entity. Although I was continuously able to find
new, plausible support, which has been stated above, I per-
sistently searched for unequivocal scientific proof. It turns
out that by using the SI (International System), we may
scientifically establish the distinction between material and
non-material domains.

## 5.4 The scientific proof that UI is a non-material entity

*The International System (SI) of measurement for physical entities*

In the world of science and technology, measuring units such as mile,
pint, horsepower, calorie, etc. has been replaced by an internationally
accepted system which does not rely on complicated conversion factors,
just powers of 10. All physical units can be derived from seven base units,
all of which are independent of each other.

| | |
|---|---|
| Length | (Unit: meter, m) |
| Mass | (Unit: kilogram, kg) |
| Current strength | (Unit: ampere, A) |
| Temperature | (Unit: kelvin, K) |
| Substance amount | (Unit: mole, mol) |
| Light intensity | (Unit: candela, cd) |
| Time | (Unit: second, s) |

**The International System of Units (Système International d'Unites).**
This carries the universal abbreviation **SI** in all languages and was introduced and approved in 1960 at the *11th General Conference on Weights
and Measures.* The SI protocol of units ended over a century of confusion caused by a multiplicity of units and unitary systems. The SI was
developed by various international expert committees of measurement in
which the following institutions took part on behalf of the Federal Republic
of Germany: the Federal Institute of Physics and Technology (Physikalisch-Technische Bundesanstalt in Braunschweig or PTB) and the German
Institute for Standardization (Deutsches Institut für Normung, or DIN).

## The importance of the SI units

**1.** For each of these **fundamental units** there is an unambiguous, internationally established physical definition [X1]. All units known to us (and any yet to be formulated) relating to the material world are derived from these fundamental units, which are interrelated via multiplication and division:

**Velocity:** Speed in a given direction is equal to distance/time; from this, it follows that the unit of **velocity** is the meter/second = m/s.

**Acceleration:** (a change in velocity per unit time) is (distance/time)/time; from this, the unit for **acceleration** is meter per second per second = m/s2.

**Force:** Because of the relationship: Force = mass × acceleration (F = ma) (Newton's Second Law of Motion), it follows that the unit of force is kg·m/s2. Whenever the resulting unit becomes too unwieldy or unsightly, it is given a new name with a corresponding abbreviation. This new unit of force is named after the English physicist Isaac Newton (1642/3–1727), who is regarded as the founder of classical theoretical physics: 1 N = 1 kg·m/s2 where N is one newton.

**Energy:** Mechanical energy is calculated as *force* × distance (in the direction of the force); it follows that its unit is 1 (kg·m/s2) × m = 1 kg·m2/s2 = 1 J. J, the designation for joule, is the unit named after the English physicist James Prescott Joule (1818–1889), who determined the thermal equivalent of mechanical and electrical energy. We then have 1 J equal to 1 newton times 1 meter, which also equals a "Watt-second" (the Watt is a unit of active power and a Watt-second is that precise amount of power in one second. It is named after the Scottish inventor James Watt (1736–1819), whose steam engine design started the Industrial Revolution), or 1 *joule* = 1 Nm = 1 Ws.

**Electric charge:** Current is the amount of charge that passes a point per unit time, but in SI units, current (amperes) is a fundamental entity, so charge is defined as current × time, or ampere-second As. This is given the name *coulomb* C, after Charles-Augustin de Coulomb (1736–1806), the French pioneer in electrostatics (and geotechnical engineering).

**Voltage:** This is the measure of electric potential and is the energy per unit charge. The SI unit of voltage is the *volt (V)*, named after Alessandro Volta (1745–1827). A voltage of one volt means that there is one joule of energy (1 J = 1 VAs) per coulomb (1 As) of charge (1 J/C = 1

VAs/1 As = 1 V). Volta also invented the voltaic pile — the first chemical electric battery.

**2.** Units are often named after an internationally known physicist. It is important to note that the full name of the unit is not capitalized, even if it is named after someone. Abbreviations of units are not usually capitalized unless they are named after someone. And there is never a period or a plural "s" after an abbreviated unit. For example, ice melts at 273.15 kelvin (or 273.15 K) and a fuse wire may be designed to melt with a current over five amperes ("amps") or 5 A.

**3.** The SI system enables a simple conversion from mechanical into electrical or thermal entities by expressing them in terms of the seven fundamental SI units.[1]

**4.** Without exception, the SI system enables **all material entities** to be described with the help of the seven base units mentioned earlier. However, Universal Information *cannot* be described by any combination of the seven base units.

This leads to the following important conclusion:

> **Since UI, defined by its four distinguishing attributes, cannot be described with the base units of the SI-System, UI is unequivocally a non-material entity.**

As other entities such as intelligence, consciousness, and free will cannot be described through the SI system, they also unequivocally belong to the non-material domain. A predominantly materialistic way of thinking will **always** lead to grave errors when non-material entities are dealt with as if they were material entities.

What we observe in all cases is that Universal Information (UI) always originates from a thought process. UI is massless and has no direct

---

1. The effectiveness of using the SI system to simplify these conversions can be demonstrated using a complex example. The unit of **magnetic flux density** derives from voltage × time/area: 1 Vs/m². Expanding the fraction by multiplying the top and bottom line by 1 ampere (A), we get 1 VAs/Am². Since V = J/C, and A = C/s, a VA = J/s = W, so this becomes 1 Ws/Am². Substituting now for 1 Ws = 1 kg m²/s² we arrive at 1 kg m²/Am²s² = 1 kg/As². Thus the magnetic flux density has been expressed using only the fundamental units listed in the main text: 1 kg/(A × s²) = 1 T (= 1 tesla). Here the unit is named after the American physicist Nikola Tesla (1856–1943) who in 1881 developed the principle of the rotating field electric motor (three-phase AC motor) and in 1887 described the multiphase system for the transmission of electrical power. One tesla is equal to the surface density of a homogenous magnetic field of the strength of 1 weber (Wb), which perpendicularly penetrates all points of a surface of 1 m². The field strength unit is named after German physicist Wilhelm Weber (1804–1891).

physical-chemical interaction with matter.[2] UI is neither a property nor a correlate of matter and has never been demonstrated to **originate** from a purely physical or chemical process. Since all five necessary conditions (NC1 through NC5) are fulfilled, and since no SI units are applicable, UI is therefore a non-material entity. Thus, we can state:

> **ES 25:** Universal Information is a non-material entity because SI units cannot be applied and it fulfils all five necessary conditions for being a non-material entity.

***Comment:*** *Storage and transmission of UI in the material domain each require material media.*

The fact that UI requires matter for storage and transmission does not transform it into a material entity.

The chalk with which we may write some information on a blackboard is the material medium. But the information is not intrinsic to the chalk: grinding chalk-dust and sprinkling it on a board will never write a message. And if we erase a message by wiping the chalk off with an eraser, the chalk still exists but the information has been destroyed. This shows that the chalk served solely as the carrier. The chalk presented the information, but the chalk itself was not the information.

The same information which had been written on the blackboard may be put on a hard disk, in which case certain areas of the disk (tracks) would have to be magnetized. The quantity of matter required on the disk would be much less than when using chalk and blackboard. However, if we then transfer the same information to large letters in neon lights, the amount of matter required is greatly multiplied. In all three cases, matter is the necessary carrier of the information, but at no time is the matter the information itself. The quantity of matter needed to carry the information is not critical, just as the information itself is independent of the physical/chemical constitution of the storage medium. Note also that, unlike matter, Universal Information may be created and destroyed as when the chalk is used to write the information ("create" it) and then it

---

2. However, as shown in Figure 19 (Section 5.2), **UI can direct, steer, control, and optimize ongoing material processes**. This guidance is carried out by programs and machines that have been freely thought out and designed. These guiding programs do not originate from deterministic physical or chemical processes. In contrast, there is, for example, a direct chemical interaction between hydrogen and oxygen, which, under certain conditions, always combine to produce water.

is "destroyed" when the message is erased. In other words, there is no law about UI that is equivalent to the *First Law of Thermodynamics*.

Modern secular science commonly claims or assumes that information is a material entity. However, as shown here, UI does not qualify as a material entity and therefore must necessarily be a non-material entity.

This gives us our *First Law of Universal Information*:

> **SLI-1:** Universal Information is a non-material fundamental entity.

## 5.5 Matter alone cannot create Universal Information

It has been established that UI is a non-material fundamental entity. While matter serves as a *carrier* of UI, UI is not an intrinsic property or correlate of matter. For instance, before the ink was assembled into the words of Lincoln's famous *Gettysburg Address*, that ink contained not one iota of UI — it was just "ink." Likewise, there is no known natural law and/or chance process able to produce the *de novo* emergence of UI. A chunk of pure iron (Fe), for example, is UI-less matter. In the presence of oxygen ($O_2$) and water ($H_2O$), iron is able to spontaneously combine with these to form hydrated ferric oxide ($Fe_2O_3.nH_2O$ and $FeO(OH)$ — rust). This is just a chemical process determined by the intrinsic physical properties of iron, oxygen, and water. However, based on sound reason and everything known to science, never in a million million (trillion) years would we expect that same chunk of pure iron to spontaneously yield UI — not even in theory. Therefore, we are able to formulate the following empirical statement:

> **ES 26:** Universal Information, a non-material fundamental entity, is neither a property nor a correlate of matter. Thus, purely material processes are fundamentally precluded as sources of UI (see NC5, section 5.2).

While UI is seen to emerge during processes involving life — giving the *appearance* of "new information" — that UI invariably arises from *pre-existing* UI, never from UI-less matter. It would only take a single counter-example to prove this incorrect, thereby invalidating the main thesis of this book.

Like produces like. In our common experience, we observe that an apple tree bears apples, a pear tree yields pears, and a thistle brings forth thistle seeds. Similarly, mares give birth to foals, cows to calves, and women to human babies. We do not see a mare giving birth to a calf or a pine seed producing a fern. There are limitations on the physical, material world. The limitations seem to be stronger when the material and non-material worlds are combined.

So, we ask: can a solely material entity ever create anything non-material? Certainly a person can create a thought, which is not material. However, this leads us to the argument about whether or not a person is a purely physical entity. If a person is purely physical, then he must become less a person should a limb be amputated. That is not what we see, though. The entire person remains, even if all four limbs are gone. The personality, the will, and the consciousness remain completely intact. A person is more than the sum of his physical parts.

However, when we take something that we know is purely material, such as the aforementioned bit of iron, we do not find anything non-material emanating from it, be it consciousness, will, desire, or anything else. We find the same to be true with any purely material substance. Thus, we are safe in saying:

> **SLI-2:** A purely material entity cannot give rise to a non-material entity.

## 5.6 Universal Information cannot be created randomly

The secular doctrine of evolution asserts precisely the opposite of SLI-2. A noteworthy example is the book by Adolf Heschl, *Das intelligente Genom* (The intelligent genome) [H2], which carries the notable subtitle "On the origin of the human mind via mutation and selection." Heschl writes:

> That our species with the totality of its supposed or proven peculiarities, whether morphological, behavioral, or purely intellectual, in every way, fits into the basic mechanisms of evolution and thereby, even today is subject to biological evolution [H2, p. 14].

Heschl thereby proposes that the non-material human mind can (and did) emerge from purely material processes (mutations and natural selection). This, however, has never been observed, thus relegating Heschl's ideas to the realm of the purely speculative, without any known basis in reality. The materialists' pronouncements contradict both observation and experience.

The secular doctrine of evolution regards every non-material entity (e.g., UI, consciousness, will) as originating in matter. This assumption is simply not supported by a single observation and is, thus, fundamentally *ideological/religious*, not scientific.

Interestingly, the idea of secular evolution fails even on the material level (the lowest level of Figure 24, section 5.11), with the result that evolutionary theoreticians continually make new attempts to describe the origin of man. Palaeontologists estimate that, on average, only a couple of bones exist to reconstruct the history of a hundred generations. "The convincing and generally accepted theories of today can collapse like a house of cards if new excavations deliver new results" [P5, p. 46]. A frustrated supporter of the doctrine of evolution put it succinctly [P5, p. 46]:

> When we try to reconstruct the lives of our ancestors, then it is as if we are trying to read the entire German history from the teeth of a Teutonic prince, the wrist bone of a medieval knight, and the hipbone of a cook from the Bismarck era.

The American geneticist Richard Lewontin noted significantly that this is a presumption that cannot be substantiated:

> It is not that the methods and institutions of science somehow compel us to accept a material explanation of the phenomenal world, but, on the contrary, that we are forced by our a priori adherence to material causes to create an apparatus of investigation and a set of concepts that produce material explanations, no matter how counter-intuitive, no matter how mystifying to the uninitiated. Moreover, that materialism is absolute, for we cannot allow a Divine Foot in the door. (Source: *The New York Review of Books*, Volume 44, Number 1, p. 28, January 9, 1997).

The materialistic worldview has so widely infiltrated the natural sciences that not only has it become the ruling paradigm, but it is also the only view that is allowed. Any view other than one based on materialism is automatically rejected, regardless of the amount of evidence that may support it. This is not only **not** real science, based on observation and experimentation, but it has become a faith-based system, an unjustifiable dogma that can only stifle progress.

The reality in which we live is divisible into two fundamentally distinguishable realms: the material and the non-material. Matter involves mass that is weighable in a gravitational field. In contrast, all non-material entities (e.g., consciousness, intelligence, and will) are massless and thus have zero weight. Since UI originates from intelligent thought, it also is massless and has never been observed to arise from purely physical or chemical processes. UI, unlike gravity, momentum, or electric current, is not correlated with matter. It must be remembered, however, that UI is intentionally stored, transmitted, and expressed through material media.

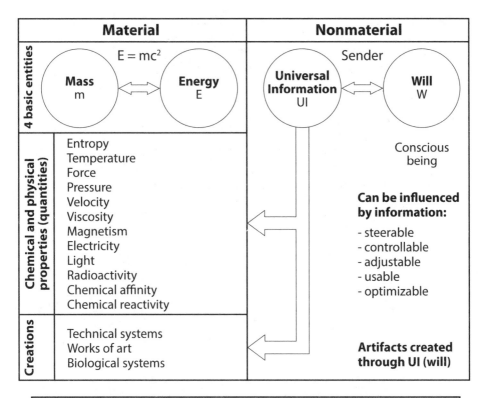

Figure 19: Four fundamental entities: mass and energy (material) and information and will (nonmaterial). Mass and energy comprise fundamental entities of the material realm. They are linked through Einstein's well-known equation E = mc². In the non-material realm, two fundamental entities, namely, Universal Information (UI) and will (W), or volition, are closely linked to each other. UI can be stored on material media, and through machines (pragmatics) it is used to steer, control, regulate, and optimize material processes. All man-made functional systems principally originate through activities fashioned by UI. The nonmaterial character of UI is highlighted by the fact that a creative source of information is always linked to the volitional intent (will) of a personality.

Figure 19 illustrates the known fundamental entities, *mass, energy,* and *UI.* Mass and energy are undoubtedly material. Moreover, for both of them there are important conservation laws that play a significant role in physics, chemistry, and in all applied sciences derived from them. Mass and energy are linked by Einstein's formula $E = mc^2$. The left column of Figure 19 shows a small selection of the wide range of chemical and physical properties of matter in all of its manifestations and defined quantities. The right-hand column is reserved for non-material entities and is where *Universal Information* (UI) belongs.

If Universal Information is not the result of the material world, then what or where is its origin? What prompts us to write a letter, a postcard, a note of congratulation, a diary entry, or a memorandum? The most important prerequisite is our own volition or that of the person who asks us to do it.

Analogous to the material side, we now introduce another fundamental entity: **will** (W), or volition. Information and will are closely linked but this relationship cannot be expressed in a formula because both are non-material (e.g., mental and intellectual). The connecting arrows in the diagram indicate the following: UI always depends on the will of a sender who originates and transmits the UI. UI is not constant — it can be increased by intention and, through interference, distorted or destroyed. Will is not constant either because it can be influenced by information that is received from another sender. Therefore, we conclude:

---

**ES 27:** Universal Information is the product of will (intention).

---

Figure 19 also makes it clear that the non-material entity UI can influence the material entities. Electrical, mechanical, or chemical processes can be steered, controlled, regulated, or optimized by means of UI, especially through the pragmatic attribute (realized only through material — e.g., mechanical — means). The strategy for achieving such control is always based on UI whether it involves a control engineering technique, instructions for building an energy-efficient car, or the utilization of electricity for powering a machine.

In the first place there must be the intention (will) to solve a problem. This is followed by a construct that may be coded in a UI program, a technical drawing (MII) or a descriptive plan (UI), etc. and finally the pragmatic agents (machines) that perform the actions. All technological systems and all constructed objects, from pins to refrigerators, are produced by means of UI and MII. None of these artifacts came into existence through self-organization of matter, yet all of them were preceded by the necessary MII and UI. This gives further support to ES 24 as stated in section 3.4.

Nevertheless, evolutionists claim that, given enough time — e.g., thousands of millions of years — information and life can form by random processes (i.e., by pure chance). Random processes are just physical and/or chemical processes that occur without the guidance of a controlling intelligence and/or UI.

The grand theory of evolution (molecules to man) would gain some empirical support if it could be demonstrated, in a real experiment, that UI could arise from matter left solely to itself without the addition of UI or intelligence. Despite very intensive worldwide efforts, the emergence of *de novo* UI from pure matter *without* human interference/input has never been accomplished or observed. To date, evolutionary theoreticians have only been able to offer computer simulations that depend upon the principles of design and the operation of pre-determined information. However, essentially all of these simulations ultimately deviate from reality because the investigator's input introduces preconceptions, biases, and interference. In short, despite extensive efforts, no realistic simulation of random processes has ever shown the emergence of UI. Empirical statements 10, 23 and 26, along with the above discussion, lead to:

---

**SLI-3:** Universal Information (UI) cannot be created by purely random processes.

---

The evolutionist typically responds to SLI-3 by saying that evolution occurs when purely random mutations are subjected to natural selection. Thus, the entire process of evolution is not purely random but is "guided" by natural selection. This typical claim misses a key point, namely that natural selection may *only* select from what is already available; natural selection does not and cannot create anything on its own. The only process available to the materialist that is able to "create" something new is the *purely random* process of mutations. First of all, evidence has been mounting in the field of genetics that a good number of claimed "mutations" are not random at all, but guided by processes in the cell and/

or outside stimuli. However, purely random processes cannot create UI, they only degrade or destroy UI, and so evolutionists are back to square one. A third point is that natural selection necessarily deletes information from a population's gene pool, thereby reducing any chances for the variations which evolutionists depend on.

## 5.7 Universal Information can only be created by an intelligent sender

During our studies in chapters 2 and 3, we observed UI originating only from intelligent beings (humans). Therefore, using empirical statements 2, 5, 9, 18, 19, and 22 we can state:

> **SLI-4:** Universal Information can only be created by an intelligent sender.

The key question here is: What is an intelligent sender? Several distinguishing attributes are required to define an intelligent sender.

> **Definition D10: An intelligent sender (in contrast to a machine) is self-conscious, has a will\* of its own, is creative, thinks autonomously, and acts purposefully.**
> \* "Will" does not include a decision that a computer makes following a particular algorithm; rather it signifies a personified capacity that is able to reach a free (i.e., non-deterministic) and arbitrary decision that usually cannot be predicted in advance.

The well-known American physicist Richard Feynman (1918–1988) very aptly commented on the possibility of expressing the natural laws in different ways [F1, p. 50]:

> The laws of physics are so delicately constructed that their very different, but equivalent, statements have completely different qualitative characteristics making them very interesting. For example, the law of gravity can be expressed in three completely different-sounding ways but which are all equivalent to each other.

What Feynman said here, specifically for the laws of physics, applies equally well for the laws of Universal Information.

The Maxwell equations from physics describe, in brilliant generalization, the relationship between changing electric and magnetic fields. But for most practical applications, these equations are far too complex and cumbersome and for this reason we use more specific formulations such as *Ohm's Law, Coulomb's Law*, or the *Induction Law*. **SLI-4** is a very general law from which several laws that are more specific may be derived. In the following section we will present five specific formulations, SLI-4a to SLI-4e, whereby each focuses on different aspects of SLI-4.

> **SLI-4a:** The establishment of every code system requires an intelligent sender.

The essential characteristic of a code system is that originally it was freely selected, defined, and agreed upon by both sender and receiver. The set of symbols so created within the code represents all allowed symbols (by definition). They are structured in such a way as to fulfill, as well as possible, their designated purpose. Examples include a script for the blind (Braille) that is readable *tactually*, musical symbols that are able to describe the duration and pitch of the notes, chemical symbols that are able to designate all of the elements, and many others. An observed signal may give the impression that it is a code composed of abstract symbols. However, if it can be shown that the signal is a physical or chemical property of the system then it does not qualify as an abstract symbol(s) according to our definition. Detailed explanations on this are to be found in chapter 3 (3.4 and 3.5).

> **SLI-4b:** There can be no new Universal Information without an intelligent sender.

## 5.8 Three types of transmitted universal information

The creation of *new* Universal Information (as opposed to simply *copied or modified* UI) requires an intelligent sender with free will. We will now distinguish between three different types of transmitted UI — copied, modified, or created.

### 5.8.1 Copied Universal Information

*Copied UI is the exact duplication of existing UI.* No new UI arises during copying, so it is a mechanical process and not an intellectual one. However, intellect, UI, and a deliberate and purposeful action are all required to create the equipment for the copying process. Examples of copied information include duplication of a computer program in a data processing system (e.g., magnetic tape, magnetic disk, and working memory), the reprinting of a book without any changes, making a photocopy, citing a quote, and the reading of a letter. Every piece of copied UI must, however, have been previously created.

### 5.8.2 Modified Universal Information

*Modified UI occurs when the original UI is altered in some way, which may or may not change the meaning and purpose of the original UI.* For instance, in the creative arts there is a clear distinction between the original composer, poet, or writer and the subsequent performers of such works. An actor did not create the acts or the text, but he does contribute by employing his own talents of intonation, mimicry, and creativity. Similarly, when a Mozart symphony or a Bach cantata is performed, the musicians play a modifying role — they do not alter the work of the composer, but they might introduce an individual artistic flavor.

Computer software functions according to this principle, since all creative ideas, such as algorithms, solution methods, or data structures, must be devised beforehand by the programmer and then expressed into a written UI program. The application and its individual parameters can be entered into a machine (computer) that does nothing more than modify/process the existing UI into the required form. Even the results obtained by means of expert systems or artificial intelligence (AI) programs are, in the last instance, nothing more than modified UI and by no means *created* UI, no matter how "intelligent" they may seem. Modified UI does not necessarily require an intelligent being since this (modification) task may be performed by a machine. On the other hand, the introduction of viruses, worms, etc. into a computer program can modestly or drastically modify the original UI and defeat the intended meaning and purpose of the original software. Similarly, a mutation to a DNA molecule (containing UI) may be "modest" in the sense of being "nearly neutral" — producing no significant/life-altering effect, or that mutation may be "drastic" — causing disease and possibly death to the organism which inherits it (e.g., Huntington's Chorea in humans).

### 5.8.3 Created Universal Information

*Created UI is the highest level of transmitted UI. This type of UI is neither copied nor modified but instead always represents something novel/original.* Created UI always requires an intelligent author with cognitive capabilities exercising his/her personal will. This is a non-material intellectual process that cannot be delegated to a machine. We may now formulate the following empirical statements:

> **ES 28:** Every piece of created Universal Information represents some intellectual effort; it can be traced to a personal idea-giver who exercised free will and who has an intelligent mind.
>
> **ES 29:** New Universal Information can only originate in a creative thought process.
>
> **ES 30:** Created Universal Information originates only from a non-material component of an intelligent sender(s) (SLI-2, SLI-3 and SLI-4).

As a result of ES 28, ES 29, and ES 30, we can formulate:

> **SLI-4c**: All senders that create Universal Information have a non-material component.

The non-material component referred to in SLI-4c is not the non-material Universal Information stored and conveyed in the DNA of humans. It is another non-material component that will be discussed further in chapter 9.2.

Examples of created UI: designing a coding system, designing a language, open discourse in a natural language, creating a programming language, writing a book or an original scientific paper.

*Conclusions:* It should now be clear where some of the logical errors of evolutionary views may be found. If someone presents a model for explaining the origin of life but cannot say where the original created UI came from, then the crucial question remains unanswered. Somebody who looks for the origin of UI only in pure matter not only ignores the fundamental scientific laws of UI but also treats them with contempt. The history of science shows that one can ignore the laws of nature *only* for a limited time. ES 9, chapter 2.5, and ES 28 and ES 29 lead to:

> **SLI-4d:** Every UI transmission chain can be traced back to an original intelligent sender.

It is useful to distinguish between the *original* sender and an intermediate transmitter(s). The original sender is defined as the author of the

Universal Information, who must *always* be an individual equipped with intelligence and a will (see Definition D10 under SLI-4). If, after the original sender, there follows a sequence of machines (intermediate transmitters) consisting of one or several links, the last link in the chain might be mistaken for the originator of the message. Since this link only *appears* to be the original sender, we call this and all links in the chain "intermediate transmitters" since they did not originate the message. It is important to note that intermediate transmitters may be machines or intelligent beings. Intermediate transmitters simply copy or modify the original UI.

**The original sender is often not visible:** When the author of historical documents is no longer visible, it does not contradict the scientific requirement of being observable, because he was observed by his contemporaries. Sometimes the information received has been transferred through several intermediate links. Nevertheless, there must have been an intelligent author at the beginning of the chain. In the example of a car radio, we receive audible UI from the loudspeakers, but these loudspeakers are not the original sender; neither are the transmission tower, the broadcasting equipment in the studio, and commonly not even the radio announcer, who is merely reading a script. All of these are intermediate transmitters. Only the author who created the information at the start of this chain is the original sender. We can confidently say that there is always an intelligent author at the beginning of every transmission chain of Universal Information.

Utilizing ES 2 (chapter 2.4) and the discussions above and below, we arrive at:

---

**SLI-4e:** Allocating meanings to, and determining meanings from, sequences of symbols are intellectual processes requiring intelligence.

---

**Origin of Universal Information:** SLI-4e describes our experience of how UI is created and read (see Figure 20). First an intelligent sender selects from a set of symbols (characters) that have been defined according to SLI-4a. Then one symbol after another is selected from this set to create units of information (e.g., words and sentences). This is not a random process — it requires the application of intelligence. The sender has knowledge of the language that he is using, and he knows which symbols he needs in order to create his meaning and to convey his expected

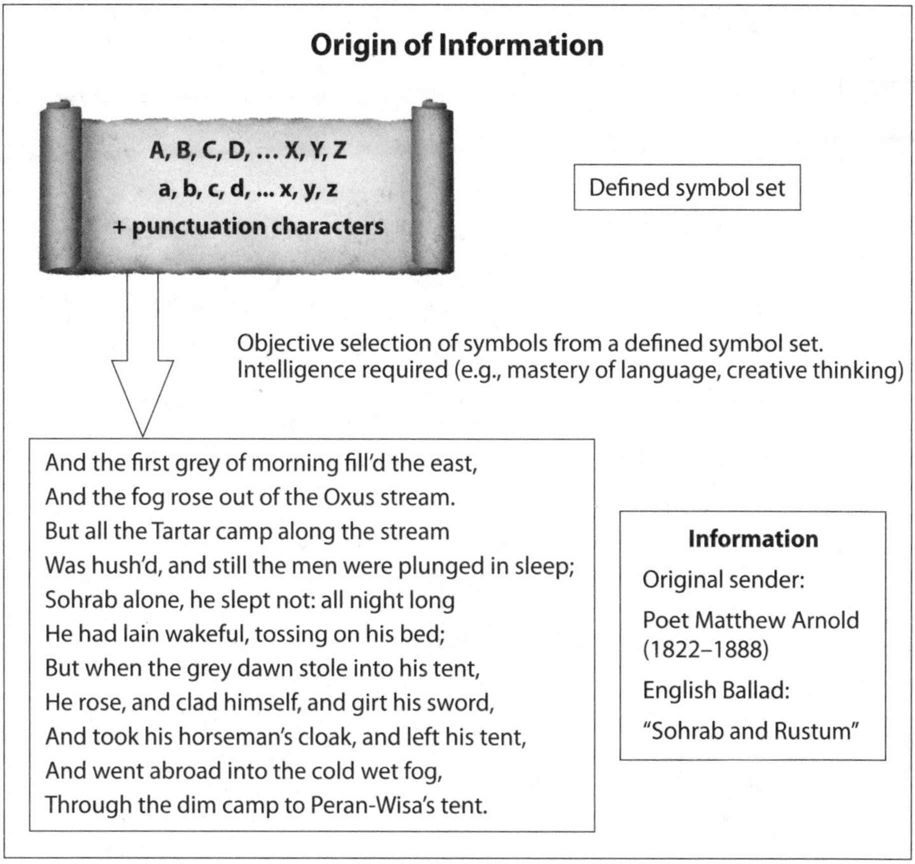

## Origin of Information

A, B, C, D, ... X, Y, Z
a, b, c, d, ... x, y, z
+ punctuation characters

Defined symbol set

Objective selection of symbols from a defined symbol set.
Intelligence required (e.g., mastery of language, creative thinking)

And the first grey of morning fill'd the east,
And the fog rose out of the Oxus stream.
But all the Tartar camp along the stream
Was hush'd, and still the men were plunged in sleep;
Sohrab alone, he slept not: all night long
He had lain wakeful, tossing on his bed;
But when the grey dawn stole into his tent,
He rose, and clad himself, and girt his sword,
And took his horseman's cloak, and left his tent,
And went abroad into the cold wet fog,
Through the dim camp to Peran-Wisa's tent.

**Information**

Original sender:
Poet Matthew Arnold
(1822–1888)

English Ballad:
"Sohrab and Rustum"

Figure 20: The principles of the origin and the understanding of Universal Information

action(s) and intended purpose(s). In other words, the creation of Universal Information is an intellectual process.

**Understanding information:** On the receiver's side, the process runs in reverse. The receiver must know the set of symbols that has been used. Using his own intelligence and knowledge of the language, the receiver can decode the symbols, words, and sentences to determine the meaning and respond to the message. This, too, is an intellectual process.

Both of these procedures (originating and understanding UI) represent the basic form of all UI communication between an original sender and an intelligent receiver.

According to **SLI-4**, original senders of UI can only be intelligent personal beings, while machines may serve only as intermediate transmitters of copied or modified UI. Figure 21 depicts four possible combinations of senders/transmitters and receivers.

a) Arrow "a" in Figure 21 indicates that both sender and receiver are intelligent and independent of each other. Both are individuals who are equipped with their own wills and intelligence (e.g., author and reader of a book). As stated in **SLI-4e**, both author and reader can assign meaning to and determine meaning from a sequence of symbols.

   As already explained under **SLI-4d**, the original sender may be followed by a chain of transmitting machinery. The information may then be received either by an individual or by a machine constructed for that purpose. At this point, we must distinguish between three other situations:

b) Arrow "b" in Figure 21 comes from an original sender (an individual with intelligence) and points to the receiver (a machine with no intelligence). In this case the sender must have thought through the entire decoding process and developed appropriate machinery that is capable of receiving and carrying out the expected action(s) (pragmatics), thus achieving the intended purpose(s) (apobetics). For example, a programmer writes a software program for a computer that, upon receiving the command to "execute," starts machinery capable of making chocolate candies according to a prescribed recipe. This command could be as simple as a single "bit" of information. Specifically, a "1" could be received by the machine, and this single "command bit" could change the machine's state from idle ("0") to start ("1").

**NOTE:** The machine itself does not "comprehend" the meaning (semantics) that is expressed via the code and grammatical rules (syntax) of the computer language. The machine's state merely changes from idle to start. It is up to the programmer to assign the meaning of the message into a series of pre-programmed executable steps so that the machine performs the proper actions. This point is crucial because it illustrates that pure matter plus Universal Information alone cannot produce comprehension

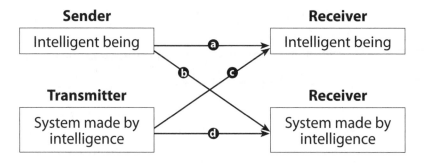

Figure 21: Four possible combinations of senders/transmitters and receivers

of meaning (semantics). Comprehension of meaning requires another non-material entity: intelligence (see Definition D10, chapter 5.7).

Similarly, a system composed of only matter plus Universal Information cannot *create* new UI — it can only copy or modify it — creating UI requires intelligence.

c) Arrow "c" in Figure 21 originates from an intermediate transmitter (a machine with no intelligence) to a receiver (an individual with intelligence). Examples of this include a computer operator (intelligent receiver) using the software on a computer (intermediate transmitter) or a person (intelligent receiver) listening to a speech via a CD-Player (intermediate transmitter).

d) Arrow "d" in Figure 21 points from an intermediate transmitter (a machine with no intelligence) to a receiver (also a machine with no intelligence). In this case, an original sender (an intelligent being) has constructed and programmed the machines — one machine transmits UI and a second machine receives and processes the UI, and takes some action (such as executing a command). As far as the programmer of the machines is concerned, his expected actions and intended purposes are performed and achieved by the machines. However, in all examples of "d" (created by humans), at some later stage there will be an *intelligent* receiver who detects and utilizes/benefits from the output of the machine receiver.

An example of this is the system used for the transmission of official time in Germany. The atomic clock, located at the Federal Institute of Physics and Technology in Braunschweig, transmits the exact time via the transmitter designated as DCF77 in Mainflingen (near Frankfurt/ Main) by means of a specially designed code (cf. ES 1 to ES 6 in chapter 2.4). These signals can then be decoded by commercially available receiving equipment to provide time and date. Both the transmitter and the receiver are "systems created by intelligence" ("d" in Figure 21). This type of system is represented in Figure 22; all parts of this system have been produced by intelligent minds.

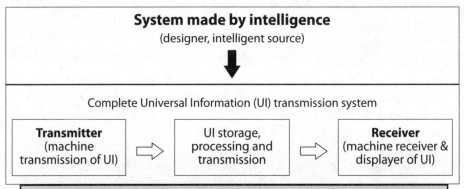

Figure 22: A fully automated UI transmission system that integrates a machine transmitter and a machine receiver. The entire system is based on ideas and concepts that must have an intelligent source. Additionally, intelligent receivers read or hear the time and date.

In all four cases, intelligent input and will are needed at both the sender's end and the receiver's end. If either task is transferred to a machine, then a program must precisely execute all four distinguishing attributes of UI. In each case the program and the machine it controls must originate from an intelligent source.

**NOTE:** Technical machines can store, transmit, decode, and translate Universal Information **without** understanding the meaning and purpose. They belong to case "d."

### 5.9 The apobetics of Universal Information

### Three categories of Universal Information

All UI generated from an intelligent source serves a particular purpose (apobetics). It will be helpful to recognize three distinct categories of

UI on the basis of this purpose in each case. These are **Production UI, Operational UI,** and **Communication UI.**

### 5.9.1 Production Universal Information (PUI)

*PUI includes all UI that is used for producing something.* Before anything can be made, the inventor mobilizes his intelligence, his supply of ideas, his know-how, and his creativity to encode his concept in a suitable way (Figure 23, following page). Examples include a cake recipe, details of the chemical processes for synthesizing a chemical compound such as polyvinyl chloride, and technical drawings for the construction of a machine.

The quality of PUI is found both in the mental concept (semantics) and in the sophistication of the implementation (pragmatics). Depending on the specific situation, one or more of the following catchwords may characterize the quality of PUI: "underlying functional concept," "degree of inventiveness," "cleverness of the method of solution," "optimal performance," "ergonomics," "economics," "robustness/longevity," "maintenance considerations," "strategic approach," "efficiency in manufacturing," "applied technologies," "suitable programming," "degree of miniaturization" (e.g., optimal use of material and energy), and others. The quality of the product resulting from this PUI (apobetics) can be evaluated in terms of the achieved goal, the efficiency of the input, the ingenuity of the operation, and the certainty of correct functioning (e.g., low susceptibility to interference).

**NOTE:** machines are required to help develop and design the UI and to construct the invention.

### 5.9.2 Operational Universal Information (OUI)

*OUI includes all UI needed to maintain the functioning operation of machinery in the widest sense of the term.* It is clear that most systems could not function properly, or even at all, without OUI. In most cases, OUI is a prerequisite to ensure that the processes run as planned or needed. For instance, when we purchase a printer, we must install the proper "driver" (software) on our computer in order to enable communication between the computer and the printer. Without this software (OUI), the printer will function improperly or not at all via that computer. Similarly, the human body is not viable without the OUI in our bodies directing all of the interactions between the brain and the body's various systems via the nervous system. The unconscious flow of statistical information in the

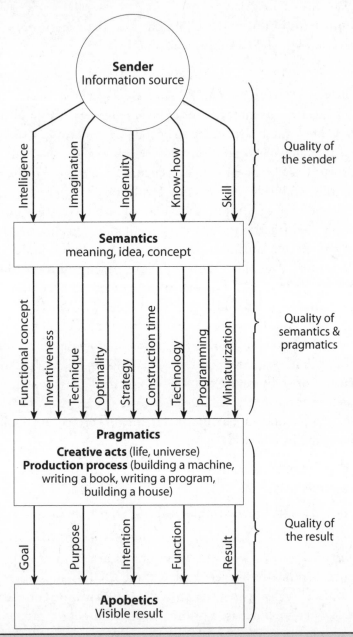

Figure 23: Qualitative properties of the sender and his Universal Information on the semantic, pragmatic, and apobetic levels. In this diagram we represent the qualitative properties of **PUI** and include human engineering concepts. Clearly, there is a tight link between the qualitative aspects of the UI and the capabilities of the sender. Similar qualitative properties can be formulated for the other two types of Universal Information (operational and communication UI, discussed in the adjoining text).

human body totals about $3 \times 10^{24}$ bits per day (see Appendix 1, A1.2.2, "the information spiral"). Astonishingly, the amount of this statistical information processed by our body during the course of a single day is one million times greater than all the statistical information represented in all the library books of the world ($\sim 10^{18}$ bits).

Further examples of OUI found in technology are:

- the operating system of a computer
- the program controlling a robot or a process computer
- warning systems for airplanes and ships
- automated quality control systems
- systems using retina, voice, or fingerprint identification
- active security systems such as a motion detector that alerts authorities

**NOTE:** once they are implemented by intelligent humans, the processes described above are all "run" exclusively by program-controlled machines.

### 5.9.3 Communication Universal Information (CUI)

*CUI comprises all other kinds of UI, e.g., person-to-person conversations, formal lectures, letters, books, phone calls, radio transmissions, the message of the Bible, etc.* The apobetic aspect of such information does not necessarily involve the technical aspects of construction of a product (PUI) or maintaining some process (OUI). Nonetheless, with CUI the goals may be just as important (if not more so) than those of PUI and OUI, since CUI goals occupy a large part of our lives. Examples of CUI goals are sharing knowledge and experiences via a report, providing joy to others, delivering instruction (not just academic/technical instruction but also moral and spiritual instruction), sharing personal confidences, discussing life's difficult situations and ways to overcome them (e.g., offering advice), and many others.

**NOTE:** although it is not as apparent as in PUI and OUI, the machines of the human body are required for the pragmatic attribute in CUI as well.

As shown above in the production, operational, and communication categories of Universal Information, the purpose of the original sender is achieved when the receiver performs some specified action(s). Expected action(s) (pragmatics) was discussed in detail in chapter 2.6. These actions are specified and guided beyond what is possible through naturally occurring physical and chemical processes. Because of this, these actions can be performed only through the agency of a machine(s). It is worth restating here the definition of a machine: *A machine is a material device that requires energy to perform some specific function(s).*

See chapter 2.6 for definitions and details of pragmatics (D6) and machines (D7). We will use ES 13 through ES 17 to state SLI-5 and four specific formulations SLI-5a to 5d.

> **SLI-5:** When the pragmatic attribute of Universal Information is expressed in the material domain, it always requires a machine.
>
> **SLI-5a:** Universal Information and creative power are required for the design and construction of all machines.
>
> **SLI-5b:** The existence of a functioning machine invariably means that Universal Information is affecting, or has affected, the material domain.
>
> **SLI-5c:** Machines, once constructed, operate exclusively within the physical-chemical laws of matter (mass and energy).
>
> **SLI-5d:** Machines cause matter to function in specific ways and consistently produce results never achieved solely by unguided physical-chemical processes.

## 5.10 Is there a Law of Conservation of Information?

There exists a conservation law for the material entity "energy":

> *In a closed system the sum of energy in all forms is constant. In other words, energy can neither be created nor destroyed, but can only be converted from one form into another.*

This raises the question of whether information is subject to a comparable scientific law. Existing information can be destroyed, either partially or completely, in one of two ways:

1. **Through intelligent agency:** We may format a hard disk and thereby delete stored letters, photographs, video files, or even complete book manuscripts. We may have been constantly changing the texts on which we are working in order to improve or extend them. The earlier formulations of ideas are lost forever if they have not been saved separately.

    In summary:

**ES 31:** Existing information can be partially or completely destroyed or changed by the application of intelligence.

This may happen intentionally (e.g., no further need to keep it), or accidentally (e.g., by operator error at the computer).

2. Through physical-chemical processes: We observe that texts engraved in stone (such as epitaphs on gravestones, or letters and symbols on obelisks and monuments) are subject to erosion by weather and other natural influences and may become unreadable. Inscriptions on wooden beams decay with time and the ink on old documents fades until the script is no longer legible. Conflagrations have often destroyed considerable quantities of information. The destruction of the library at Alexandria by fire caused an enormous loss of information. Alexandria, a large city in Egypt today, was once the capital city of the ancient Ptolemaic kingdom. It housed the most significant library of the ancient world. When the Roman emperor fought in Alexandria in 48 B.C., he torched all the ships in the harbor. The library also went up in flames. Ancient historians estimated the number of scrolls lost at 40,000 (Seneca) and 700,000 (Aulus Gellius). Irrespective of which estimate is closer to the truth, many documents of incalculable value were forever lost in this fire.

Diskettes and hard disks are magnetic information storage devices that, even under favorable conditions, possess a limited durability measured at most in a few decades. CDs and DVDs are not much better than magnetic storage media. The aging process and light impingement cause a change in the surface properties resulting in significant information loss.

The durability of information scrawled in sand on the beach is one of the shortest; with the next wind or wave, the information may be irretrievably lost.

In summary:

**ES 32:** Many different physical-chemical processes act to destroy existing Universal Information, either partially or wholly, in the course of time.

Thus, we can say that information is not subject to a scientific law comparable with the conservation of energy. On the contrary, there is a tendency for natural processes to destroy existing Universal Information.

An increase in the amount of Universal Information is only possible through intelligence, whereas a reduction can happen through intelligent agency but also through physical-chemical processes requiring no intelligent input at all.

We can now formulate a sixth scientific law of information:

> **SLI-6:** The amount of existing "Universal Information" stored on a material medium is never increased over time by purely physical-chemical processes but it is always reduced over time by unguided physical-chemical processes.

## 5.11 Summary statement

All of the above-mentioned laws were derived from observations and not from ideological presuppositions, philosophical inferences, or pure ideas. To date, none have been invalidated by any substantiated contradiction, experiment, or observable process.

**The laws of nature have a permissive and a prohibitive character.**
Or expressed otherwise:
**Scientific laws have both a proving and a disproving character.**

The laws of nature (material entities) and the scientific laws of Universal Information (non-material entities) have two important functions: they can be used to predict specific outcomes and also to demonstrate the *impossibility* of other outcomes. They describe regularities in the behavior of real systems and they allow statements to be made about what has happened and what is permitted to happen. Thus, the laws of nature (scientific laws) have a "permissive" character.

By describing limits to the behavior of real systems, the laws of nature are also saying what, in principle, *cannot* happen, i.e., what is impossible. It is an important strength of the natural laws that they are able to tell us what is excluded from the realm of possibilities. In this sense, the laws of nature also have a "prohibitive" character.

Figure 24: Hierarchical representation of matter, information, and biological life. There are scientific laws that apply to each of the three hierarchical levels.

Many people have seen white swans. Nevertheless, there is no law of nature that prohibits red, blue, or black swans. Black swans have indeed been found but no red or blue swans yet, though their existence remains a logical possibility. No one has observed water flowing uphill by itself. That in and of itself does not exclude the possibility that such an event might at some future time and place be seen to happen. However, there is a law of nature that forbids it, so the possibility of it ever happening may be safely excluded from consideration.

Generally speaking, the more prohibitive and specific a natural law is, the more valuable it becomes. In chapter 8 we will use the scientific laws of Universal Information to exclude some current "icons" of scientific thought just as conclusively as one would exclude water flowing uphill by itself, i.e., without it being forced in some manner to do so.

**Formulation of "impossibility laws" (*converse* formulations — "C")**

Most of the above scientific laws of Universal Information may also be formulated as *impossibility laws* just as shown for almost all natural laws in Appendix 3, A3.2. Some examples are given below:

| | |
|---|---|
| **SLI-3C:** | It is impossible for UI to be generated by purely random processes. |
| **SLI-4C:** | It is impossible for UI to be created without an intelligent sender. |
| **SLI-4aC:** | It is impossible to establish a code system apart from an intelligent sender. |
| **SLI-4bC:** | It is impossible for a UI chain to exist unless the UI was created originally by an intelligent source. |

Figure 24 helps us to correlate the corresponding laws. Three phenomena are presented in hierarchical form: **Matter, Information**, and **Life**. Matter is at the bottom of this hierarchy. All known scientific laws of physics and chemistry govern this domain (e.g., the conservation of energy, conservation of angular momentum, conservation of charge). According to **SLI-1**, UI does not belong to the material level. Rather, UI belongs to its own, higher, level in the non-material domain. The scientific laws governing UI have been formulated in this chapter. The highest level is occupied by biological life and the scientific law that governs biological life. Louis Pasteur (1822–1895) formulated this scientific law about life and it has never been disproven by experiment: *All life comes from life (Omne vivum ex vivo).* Biological life forms consist of two components, material and non-material. The following statements are made concerning the three hierarchical levels:

• Universal Information is a non-material entity but needs matter for storage and transmission.

• Universal Information is not life in and of itself, but information is a fundamentally essential part of the cells of every biological entity and thus a necessary prerequisite for biological life.

• Biological life is neither matter (by itself) nor Universal Information (by itself) but both matter and information are necessary for biological life.

In the next two chapters we will examine an unknown system to determine if it contains **Universal Information**. **This unknown system is biological life** — an unimaginably complex, highly integrated, and interdependent system that inhabits earth's entire biosphere.

# PART THREE

## Information and Biological Life

*Chapter 6*

# IS THE ESSENCE OF
# LIFE MATERIAL OR
# NON-MATERIAL?

## 6.1 Is biological life purely matter (mass and energy)?

The answer to the above question will affect our understanding of the origin, meaning, and purpose of our lives and will lead us in one of two diametrically opposed directions.

The currently accepted scientific model asserts that all effects have physical causes and that there is nothing apart from the material domain. Everything we see is the result of some physical cause.

The origin of the widespread dogma that "life is exclusively material" can be traced into the far-distant past. The Greek philosopher Theophrastus (372–287 B.C.), a pupil of Aristotle, claimed that life was mechanistically determined and that one should describe and explain it as one would the "mechanical arts." The history of biology can be seen as alternately being subject to mechanistic and vitalistic concepts (see "Vitalism," following page), with the former being the dominant paradigm in science today. But who has contributed to the dominance of this mechanistic belief?

Galileo Galilei (1564–1642), one of the founders of modern natural science, replaced the study of philosophical sources with observation and experimentation. The message was, *one has to measure what can be*

> **Vitalism:** A philosophical teaching which claims that living processes are subject to different laws than the causal mechanical processes of inanimate nature. Aristotle (384–322 B.C.) had already recognized the autonomy of living structures and postulated for them the influence of a specific force which he called entelechy. The assumption of a vital force (*vis vitalis*) that steers the growth and behavior of living systems could not be confirmed experimentally and was therefore decisively rejected by the representatives of the mechanistic view. As will be shown later in the book, we reject both the mechanistic and vitalistic positions, as neither is ultimately supported by observable reality.

*measured* and make measurable what cannot yet be measured. Galilei used a ramp for his experiments to ascertain his principles of gravity. He expressed his results in geometrical constructions and mathematically precise words (not yet in algebraic terms, which did not develop until after his time). These investigations are seen by many as contributing to the birth of modern science (Stephen Hawking: "Galileo, perhaps more than any other single person, was responsible for the birth of modern science"). This "Galilean" approach to science subsequently proved to be exceedingly successful. This was due to the fact that scientific analysis was limited to the physical world, and thus to the questions that could be addressed mechanistically. This led, to a certain extent, to a mechanization of the prevalent worldview. The mechanics developed by Sir Isaac Newton (1643–1727) were a further notable milestone in this direction, making Newton one of the founders of modern theoretical physics. But after Newton, science had a choice: to admit it could only deal with the physical but that the nonphysical still existed and could influence the physical, or to deny the nonphysical altogether and declare the physical as all there is and was. The latter was the option chosen. Mechanical and dynamic processes edged increasingly into the center of interest and were extended theoretically and mathematically through the work of many individuals such as Leonhard Euler (1707–1783), J.L. Lagrange (1736–1813), Pierre S. Laplace (1749–1827), and Sir William Hamilton (1805–1865).

These remarkable successes in the area of inanimate nature had a strong influence on those disciplines that had to do with life (e.g., biology, physiology, medicine). As the life sciences were drawn into the slipstream of the great advances in physics, many scientists thought that life should, and could, be explained in a similarly mechanistic manner. In the middle of the 19th century, reductionistic materialism (all causes and effects can be dealt with completely on the physical level) blossomed under such representatives as Emil du Bois-Reymond (1818–1898) and Hermann von Helmholtz (1821–1894). The latter [P3, p. 9] stated, during a conference of German scientists in Innsbruck (1869):

> The ultimate aim of science is to determine the motions, and their driving forces, which underlie all phenomena, that is, to resolve them into mechanics.

This challenge was taken up at the time by many biologists. In the foreword to his *Prinzipien der generellen Morphologie* (Principles of general morphology), Ernst Haeckel (1834–1919) demanded from the science of organisms that it raise itself to the level of the inorganic sciences using causal mechanical reasoning. Max Verworn, a pupil of Haeckel, wrote his *Mechanik des Geisteslebens* (Mechanics of Intellectual Life). In this, Verworn pursued the goal of analyzing "mechanically the physiological parameters of intellectual processes."

The above examples show the direction science was taking. All phenomena were to be explained as exclusively material. By definition then, non-material entities either did not exist or were to be considered as irrelevant. It is easy to understand how, against such a background, a materialistic philosophy was able to establish itself worldwide. Materialistic ideologies in their different forms (e.g., fascism, humanism, atheism, and different expressions of communism such as Marxism, Leninism, Stalinism, and Maoism) and their consequences in the 20th century have shown themselves to be harmful, divisive, and often devastating when worked out in real life. In keeping with the above ideas, the co-founder of Marxism, Friedrich Engels (1820–1895), taught, "The material world observable by our senses, to which we ourselves belong, is the only reality."

The materialistic approach to biology was given a great boost by Charles Darwin (1809–1882), who ascribed the development of all organisms from an ancestral cell to natural selection (a purely mechanistic principle). Many scientists were caught up in this materialistic explanation and they became dedicated adherents of the idea. A few of the many representatives of this position are named below.

In his much-quoted book *What is life?* Nobel Prize-winning quantum physicist Erwin Schrödinger (1887–1961) wrote from a purely materialistic perspective [S6, p. 134, 139]:

The unfolding of events in the life cycle of an organism exhibits an admirable regularity and orderliness, unrivalled by anything we meet within inanimate matter.... We must therefore not be discouraged by the difficulty of interpreting life by the ordinary laws of physics.... Or are we to term it a non-physical, not to say a super-physical, law? No. I do not think that. For the new principle that is involved is a genuinely physical one: it is, in my opinion, nothing else than the principle of quantum theory over again.

For Schrödinger the organization of all life forms was to be understood by the arrangement of their parts and this, in turn, was explained solely by physical laws.

In *Stufen zum Leben* (Steps to Life), Manfred Eigen wrote [E3, p. 47, 149]:

Life is a dynamic state of order of matter.... The logic of life has its origin in physics and chemistry. Nucleic acids stand at the boundary between chemistry and biology. Their specific chemical properties constitute the pre-conditions for allowing nonlife to become life.

With these statements he affiliates himself with those who say that life is a purely material entity. Eigen's pupil, Bernd-Olaf Küppers, defines life in his book *Leben = Physik + Chemie?* (Life = Physics + Chemistry?) according to the equation "life = matter + information." In order for the equation to make sense in the materialistic worldview, information has to be declared a material entity and life must be purely material. But Küppers apparently has doubts that life can be explained solely by physics and chemistry inasmuch as these disciplines fundamentally do not address semantic phenomena such as functionality and practicability. Nevertheless, Küppers perseveres in the dogma that life is a material entity as is shown by this quote [K5, p. 18–20]:

How can the existence of an information-bearing system be explained in the context of a reductionist research program that is based solely on the methods of physics and chemistry? ... In physics, one is used to saying that one has a natural explanation for a particular event if one finds regularity within the set of natural events that allows derivation of the result from the boundary conditions.... The assignment and goal of the reductionist research program is to derive the phenomena of life from a set of conditions solely with the help of the known laws of physics and chemistry. The entirety of molecular biology rests upon this method of explanation.

Stephen C. Meyer provides a good summary of the last 40 years of the various reductionist perceptions regarding life and the origin of life in his overview paper *"DNA and the origin of life: information, specification, and explanation"* [M4]. When a modern biology encyclopedia allows for nothing other than the mechanistic position, it becomes all too clear how much the materialistic worldview has pervaded our general way of thinking [L2; Vol. 5, p. 211]:

Life is a form of existence of earthly matter. It always comes in the form of a highly complex organized association of likewise complex structures, by whose regulated interaction the phenomenon of life, as a new property of the system, is possible.

In other words, life is only one of many other attributes of matter. By definition, physics and chemistry are concerned exclusively with matter. After what we have established above, life is to be understood completely in physical terms or, as is usual in modern molecular biology, in chemical terms. Thus, just as in the case of all inanimate objects, life must be comprehended solely within the parameters of physics or chemistry. However, if the foundational assumption that life is an entirely mechanistic result of physical causes is false, then any explanations and science based on this assumption are going to be at least flawed, if not completely wrong.

There are a number of fields in which the materialistic-mechanistic approach has been extremely successful: physics, chemistry, and even the detailed processes of biological organisms. But as a result of the successes of the mechanistic explanations on the one hand and the acceptance of evolution on the other, the dogma that *life is purely material* has not only become widely accepted, it is viewed as the only true paradigm through which to interpret the data. But again, if life is not simply a physical-chemical phenomenon, then restricting science to that point of view blinds us from discovering the essence of life. Materialism presents us with a second complication here: it cannot readily define life.

While it is not disputed that a dog is alive and a stone is not, when the focus turns to the microscopic, there is no real definition of life for it to fall back on.

The consequences of materialism and the ideologies that it begets cannot be understated when we are concerned with the question of origins. If chance physical-chemical processes are the sole cause for the origin of information in life, then purpose, morals, free will, responsibility, etc. are also all matters of chance, and thus have no intrinsic meaning. Indeed, the claims of all materialistically disposed authors tend in just this direction, as will be seen from the following quotations:

According to the French Nobel Prize-winner Jacques Monod (1910–1976) [M7, p. 106, 129]:

> Pure chance, nothing but chance, the absolute, blind freedom at the foundation of the wonderful edifice of evolution ... is the only imaginable [hypothesis for life's existence].... Neither the universe bore life nor the biosphere mankind. Our "lottery ticket" came up with the game of chance. Is it surprising that we consider our existence to be mysterious — like someone who has won a billion at the lottery?

While Monod admits that "the biggest problem is the origin of the genetic code and the mechanism of its translation," Eigen argues [E3, p. 55]: "Information comes from non-information." Since, in the materialistic way of thinking, matter is the only source of everything, it *has to* be assumed that information comes only from matter. It is here that the definition of information becomes vital to the argument. The fact remains that starting solely with purely inorganic substances, no one has been able to generate Universal Information through random physico-chemical processes.

Is the purely materialistic-mechanistic view of nature altogether in harmony with today's scientific knowledge? Reinhard Eichelbeck provides the following answer [E1, p. 39]:

> Today's natural science is materialistic — not of necessity, but out of tradition. Traditions are sometimes useful, but sometimes they are a straitjacket or at least a stumbling block, especially in the case of working models. Many scientists have a great fear of anything beyond the borders of physics and chemistry. The word

"metaphysics" alone drives the adrenaline level into the red. But if we take a sober look at this expression … it becomes clear that it also designates something that we deal with as a matter of course, namely, that which we call information or "software." Information is always "metachemical" with reference to the information carrier, just as "software" is always "metaphysical" with reference to the "hardware." Information cannot be measured by physics and chemistry nor be described and certainly not be explained.… And a science which, at the start of the information age, still permits exclusively energy and matter to be valid is medieval.

Eichelbeck argues that neither information nor life can be explained mechanistically. We need a new model — a new paradigm — that treats information for what it actually is — a non-material entity. Providing this new model is the central goal of this book.

Microbiologist Stefan Bleeken points out in the periodical "Naturwis senschaften" (Natural sciences), regarding biological materialism [B4]:

As opposed to physics, biology has to this day not gone beyond the stage of being an inductive, descriptive science, since it has not succeeded in penetrating theoretically nor formalizing the enormous number of levels of biological processes. Biology is in a state of development comparable to physics before Newton, and biology's path to a formal science is still in the dark. Since biology as a complete discipline does not possess its own paradigm, the question arises whether it has in fact attained the level of a discipline.… Molecular biology has not succeeded in finding the way back from individual components to the living organism. Within its circle of admirers critical voices are becoming louder, complaining that molecular biology has given up its ambition of explaining the living organism. Due to a missing theoretical framework, molecular biology's research strategy has degenerated into a pure exercise in data and fact collection.

Biology has necessarily confined itself in this way due to the combination of materialism and evolution. Darwinism has given us a false appraisal of nature and a false image of humanity. As Eichelbeck states: [E1, p. 40, 42]:

[Darwinism] has presented mankind's bad, socio-neurotic traits — egoism, aggressiveness, ruthlessness, lasciviousness, and the old macho "virtues" of striving to leave behind as many offspring and as many dead enemies as possible — as natural, even as basic principles of evolution. The time has come to shelve Darwinism and replace it with a realistic view of nature.

Sometimes, evolution-oriented scientific periodicals dare to publish articles that are clearly critical of evolution [R2, p. 29]:

> Darwinism is a doctrine of the 19th century and was responsible in part for gruesome events of the 20th century. We must have the courage to distance ourselves from yesterday's convictions and think again so that the 21st century will be better.

So the question remains: **Is the essence of life material or non-material?** Our position, and one we will support scientifically in the following chapters, is that life, in its essence, is non-material. The magnificent coding system found in the DNA/RNA system contains the richest source of information known to mankind as well as an incredibly complex, perfectly integrated molecular infrastructure to implement this information. We will show that nothing in materialistic science is able to account for the origin and the vast diversity of life, all forms of which require this information and infrastructure.

## 6.2 Is synthetic life possible?

Modern technology has achieved what would have been considered magic or miraculous just a century ago. We have split the atom, walked on the moon, cloned Dolly the sheep, performed heart transplants, and changed the world immeasurably with the help of computer technology. Are we also in the position to truly create life synthetically?

One of Germany's national newspapers, *Die Welt*, published an article on May 23, 2010, by Alan Posener with the title "Researcher Craig Venter has created artificial life — WE ARE GOD." Posener calls it "the sensation of the millennium." He writes "Venter's team has succeeded in building a synthetic genome in the laboratory and inserted it into a cell whose DNA has been removed." The cell began to copy itself using synthetic DNA. Full of euphoria and misjudgment, Posener concludes: "That which was once reserved for God or the gods has now been done by man." The euphoria seems boundless. Posener quotes the English-American physicist Freeman Dyson, "The ability to design and create new forms of life marks a turning-point in the history of our species and our planet." Then Posener quotes Dyson's son George, a science historian, who expresses a similarly exaggerated view: "… a code generated within a digital computer is now self-replicating as the genome of a line of living cells."

Has life really been created here? The clear answer is: NO! Venter's scientific achievement is remarkable, but the arrogant claims far exceed what has actually been accomplished. What, in fact, did Venter et al. achieve?

First, they created a digital copy of the DNA of *Mycoplasma mycoides* (the donor cell), having over one million base pairs. From this they made a synthetic copy of the donor's DNA. Their synthesizing machines were limited to creating DNA segments 50–80 base pairs long. In order to join the resulting segments (approximately 15,000 of them), they had to develop many complex steps and employ the help of living yeast cells and E. coli bacteria. Following this, they then created a predefined DNA sequence of approximately 10,000 base pairs that they coded for producing a substance that would turn blue, and also four watermarks in order to track descendant cells. This "newly created" DNA, produced synthetically with the help of living cells, was inserted into a recipient cell (Mycoplasma capricolum), from which the DNA molecule had been removed. The donor and the recipient cells were closely related species. The DNA sequence produced by this technique included an exact copy of the donor cell's DNA.

Taking stock, we note that although the researchers have a fairly detailed knowledge concerning the DNA coding for protein, other levels of DNA coding are not yet understood. Cell biologist Mel Greaves of the British Institute of Cancer Research admits, "We fooled ourselves into thinking the genome was going to be a transparent blueprint, but it's not." The genome not only contains the construction plans for protein production, but also numerous command hierarchies and communication systems which are not yet understood. American biologist Jennifer Doudna (University of California, Berkeley) admits, "The more we know, the more we realize there is to know."

In the case of the Venter project, they succeeded in digitally copying, synthesizing, and inserting DNA code. Undoubtedly this is a significant and praiseworthy technical achievement. However, everything that Venter copied, synthesized, and inserted utilized *pre-existing code and molecular machinery*, without which Venter could not have "created" anything! For instance, the recipient cell was viable in that it contained all of the operable machinery necessary for cell duplication. This show-stopping conundrum has been clearly pointed out to evolutionists for many years. Figure 29, chapter 7.3, clearly demonstrates this perplexing problem. Three essential systems need to be in place simultaneously in order for life processes to begin:

1) the duplication of DNA (DNA replication) — the first generation of this is what Venter's team accomplished

2) transcription of the DNA code into messenger RNA — all of the machinery required to do this was in the carefully tended recipient cell — Venter's team did not attempt to synthesize this step

3) translation of the RNA code into the synthesis of multitudes of protein nanomachines required for DNA replication, RNA transcription, protein synthesis, energy conversion systems, etc.

All of these systems were provided initially by the recipient cell. Venter's team did not synthesize this step. In other words, life was most definitely *not* created by Venter et al. but rather the DNA of existing life was copied and manipulated. It is as if someone had copied word-for-word a book in a language unknown to him and then claimed he had written the book in that language, and then published and distributed it. Again, this is not to take anything away from the accomplishments of Venter and his team, but the headlines certainly far overstate their achievements.

We understand too little of the highly complex nanomachines, language, and codes that are essential for a living, self-reproducing organism. With all due respect to what Venter and his group accomplished, what they actually achieved was a sophisticated form of "plagiarism" — copying and using what was already there in order to make a working facsimile. What Venter et al. actually demonstrated is that extreme amounts of intelligence and power are required to create life and that the unguided physical/chemical processes of evolution are totally insufficient.

The words of the psalmist, "Your works are wonderful, I know that full well" (Ps. 139:14), apply not only to the vast, inconceivable expanses of the macrocosm, but also to the ingenious nanotechnology of the microcosm. Mankind has not even begun to scratch the surface in either of these realms, least of all in being able to "create" life.

The primary focus of this book so far has been to develop an unambiguous definition of Universal Information, to describe its nature and origin and to discover and formulate the scientific laws that govern the UI domain. We have demonstrated at the highest level of scientific certainty that Universal Information is a non-material entity; it is in fact the third fundamental entity in the natural universe, alongside mass and energy. Our studies will now show:

1) that Universal Information is vitally essential to life

2) the existence of yet another non-material component of life, at least in mankind

In accomplishing these things, we will essentially refute the materialistic worldview — a worldview in which matter (energy is a form of matter) is the sole entity and cause for everything. Finally, with materialism having been proven false — or at the very least having been shown to be riddled with scientific inconsistencies — we will then scientifically support the worldview in which a purposeful Creator, God, is the best and only rational alternative. In the next chapter, we will examine living systems to determine if they contain Universal Information.

## 6.3 What is life? An attempt at a definition

To this day — in the long-since-begun 21st century — there is still no scientific definition for life. Wikipedia writes (de.wikipedia.org/wiki/Leben):

> Life is the condition that living things have in common and that distinguishes them from dead matter, as well as the totality of living things in a delimited area. Characteristics of living things:
> - They are material systems distinct from their environment.
> - They have metabolism of matter and energy and thus interact with their environment.
> - They organize and regulate themselves (homeostasis).
> - They reproduce, that is, they are capable of reproduction.
> - They grow and are thus capable of differentiation.
> - They are capable of registering and responding to chemical or physical changes in their environment.

Such descriptions tell us some of the diverse characteristics common to living things. The list could be extended considerably in the above sense, yet this would still be far from defining life. One would have only a list collating everything which can be described concerning the qualities and characteristics of living beings on the material level.

In chapter 6.1 we have shown at length that most scientists are exclusively materialistically oriented concerning biological life. However, for so long as they adhere to the materialistic worldview, they will likely never find a sufficiently fitting definition for life.

We had already recognized that life's essence — the characteristic of living things which we mean when we say something is alive — is, just like information, a non-material entity. In this section we will refer to this entity as simply "Life," though capitalized to remind the reader of the special meaning here.[1]

In analogy to information, we also want to formulate scientific laws of Life (SLL). Thus, we have named a second non-material entity for which there are laws of nature.

We can already formulate a first scientific law of Life (SLL):

> **SLL-1:** Life is a non-material entity.

Concerning information, the American cyberneticist and mathematician Norbert Wiener (1894–1964) said: "Information is information — neither matter nor energy."

In analogy to it an empirical statement could be formulated:

> **ES 33:** Life is Life — neither matter, nor energy, nor information.

Figure 24 (chapter 5.11) shows the three levels of reality: "Matter, Universal Information, Life" (where "life" is used in a general sense). The following two empirical statements E34 to E35 can be regarded as definitions for Life (in the specific sense):

> **ES 34:** On the material level, Life is a machine which converts energy in a goal-directed fashion.

> **ES 35:** On the informational level, Life is a highly complex program, which effects the construction of all of an organism's functional structures (manufacturing information) and controls all its material and information-transfer processes (operating information).

---

1. In the original German, one could readily substitute for "life" the term *das Lebendige* (lit. the living), without causing the issues that it would in English. Consider if we had here used, e.g., "Scientific laws of the living" (as distinct from laws of the dead?).

On the third level of reality, that which distinguishes Life is expressed by the following three empirical statements:

> **ES 36:** The entity known as Life is that which defines the difference between life and death.
>
> **ES 37:** Life is that cause which upholds the necessary processes in living beings on the level of information and matter.

If Life is removed from living beings by their death, then their previously intact biochemical processes are interrupted — brain and heart activity fail, the cells no longer perform their usual functions, the material part of people and animals succumbs to decay, dead plants begin to rot.

> **ES 38:** In organisms, Life is represented by a non-material and therefore massless entity L, which is called "spirit" or "soul" in the case of a human being.

L is also that entity which makes the difference between a dead and a living ant. A bacterium, too, must have an entity L, which distinguishes it from a killed (e.g., by antibiotics) bacterium.

In humans the entity L (soul) is eternally existing according to the statements of the Bible, since it is correlated with the breath of God (Gen. 2:7). The entire animal and plant world was not "inbreathed" by God and also is not eternal.

In contrast to information, L has no statistical or syntactic level, however a clear pragmatic and apobetical level. This is not only true for humans, but even on the level of microbes. Soil bacteria have an important purpose in field and forest. Without intestinal flora (e.g., coliform bacteria) our digestive system would not function properly.

All living organisms are very complex. This is already true for every single-celled organism. Nevertheless, life forms differ from one another in graduated fashion.

During the investigation of information we found out that it can come only from an intelligent source (SLI-4, chapter 5.7). Since Life is a non-material entity, it can also come only from a source which itself must have at least one non-material component. The actions of living creatures, even where wholly instinctive, also reflect extreme intelligence, and have scientifically not yet been fully fathomed (e.g., communication systems of social insects, navigation systems of migratory birds, whale songs). Their Originator must therefore not only be extremely intelligent, but even omniscient. In chapter 8.4 this is proved in Deduction 2. Thus, we arrive at another scientific law of Life:

> **SLL-2:** Life cannot arise from matter alone; its origin requires a non-material highly intelligent source.

As we saw previously, from the French chemist and microbiologist Louis Pasteur (1822–1895) comes the Latin phrase *omne vivum ex vivo* — "life can only come from life."

> **SLL-3:** There must be a source of Life.

Who this source is cannot be answered scientifically. For this a higher source of information is needed. As proven in chapter 9.3 (The prophetical-mathematical proof of God), only the Bible fulfills the quality characteristics of truth.

According to the testimony of the Bible (John 1:1–3; Col. 1:16), Jesus is the Creator of all things, and thus the author of all living things (chapter 9.5.7):

> **SLL-4:** The source from whence all living things have their origin is Jesus.

*Chapter 7*

# INFORMATION IN LIVING THINGS

## 7.1 Introduction

We are surrounded by an astonishing multiplicity of life forms where even the "simplest" single cell represents an extremely complex, integrated, organized system. Whereas in Darwin's time, the cell was thought to be a simple blob of "stuff," continuing research has shown that the "simple cell" shows a complexity, specificity, and organization far beyond anything we could have ever imagined. The matter in the cell is programmed to be able to convert, store, and use energy in far more efficient ways than any we have been able to design into our machines. We use mass and energy in our machines, but mass and energy themselves are not enough to distinguish between living and inanimate systems. All living beings are characterized by intrinsic genetic *information* which directs all their production and operational processes, including reproduction, maturation, and all metabolic functions. Nuclear DNA and mitochondrial DNA are the foundational information storage molecules that are responsible for the integrated functional organization of living cells in animals. It is not the *material* components of the DNA and other molecules (Figure 26) that are the most significant, rather it is the information that they store and convey.

An important question here is this: ***does any part of the DNA qualify as Universal Information?*** So far, science has only decoded a small portion of the genetic information. We have a substantial understanding of the genetic coding system for proteins and the sequence of events that result in the synthesis of proteins. But it has been estimated that this protein-coding portion of the DNA represents only 3% of the total genome. Most likely the standard genetic terminology will have to change. The part of the genome that codes for protein has been labeled *coding* DNA and the rest of the genome labeled as *noncoding* DNA. This noncoding DNA was often labeled "junk" DNA, in the belief that it was useless leftover code from an alleged long evolutionary ancestry. More recent studies have countered this claim, showing that at least 97% is transcribed, often into RNA, which strongly suggests it has a function.[1] This is reinforced by the progressive discovery that various cancers are caused by mutations (errors) in non-coding DNA. Much of the function of these RNA segments produced likely has to do with the regulation of protein production from genes (stretches of DNA that code for proteins). One thing is certain — the genomes of living organisms reveal elegance and organized complexity beyond man's wildest imaginings. However, for our purposes we will focus on the part of the genome that is best understood — genetic information in the DNA that codes for the synthesis of proteins.

## 7.2 Proteins

Proteins are the chief components and building blocks for the structural composition and functional operation of all living cells. They are made up of only 20 different standard amino acids[2] (Figure 25) that must be linked together in a precise number and sequence to create a particular functional protein. The chemical formulae for these 20 standard amino acids are listed in [G16, p. 176] and also at en.wikipedia.org/wiki/Amino_acid.

The number of possible molecules that can be formed by different sequences of amino acids is vast. Furthermore, the recorded total number

---

1. See creation.com/splicing.
2. Certain archaea and eubacteria code for the 21st or 22nd amino acids, selenocysteine and pyrrolysine — see J.F. Atkins and R. Gesteland, *The 22nd amino acid, Science* 296(5572):1409–1410, May 24, 2002; commentary on technical papers on p. 1459–1462 and 1462–1466.

of amino acids that make up these sequences ranges from around fifty (in e.g., insulin) to tens of thousands (e.g., the largest known protein, *titin*, depending on the species consists of up to 34,350 amino acids!). However, out of the vast number of possible sequences, relatively few are *functional*. Only those sequences of amino acids that form functional proteins are integrated and used by an organism. When there is a mistake in the making up of a protein by the cell, the protein is then dismantled and the amino acids used again in the making of a protein which can be used by the cell. This is one of a good number of checks and corrections which appear to be programmed into each cell in order to maintain its correct functioning.

Proteins make up most of the body of animals. Most proteins perform functions that may be classified into two general areas: structural/mechanical and functional/enzymatic. Specifically, these areas include:

- Muscle cells primarily contain the protein filaments actin and myosin, responsible for contraction and movement. The above-mentioned titin acts like a molecular spring, giving muscles their passive elasticity. Muscles also contain myoglobin — an oxygen transport protein. Muscle is also a food source for carnivores and omnivores.

- Collagen fibers provide structural support throughout the entire body. For example: they give bone its internal strength, form tendons and ligaments, form a major component of the dermis and hypodermis of the skin, anchor blood vessels, and reinforce muscle tissue.

- Muscles/tendons, joints/ligaments and bones are formed into living machines that are operated by programs in the nervous system.

- The protein keratin forms the major component of hooves, claws, nails, horns/antlers, hair/wool, and the superficial covering of the skin.

- Circulating antibodies and immune receptors on all cells of the body play a key role in immune defense against infectious agents and their toxins.

- Hemoglobin is a protein within red blood cells that facilitates transport of oxygen from the lungs to the rest of the body.

- Some hormones, such as insulin, are proteins (Figure 27).

- Enzymes are critically important proteins that increase the rate of chemical reactions, sometimes to extremely high rates. Enzymes are highly complex molecular machines that operate at the cellular and subcellular levels.

**Life needs enzymes:** Without them, life as we know it could not exist. This is because the chemical reaction time of many essential biological processes would be far too slow. A dramatic example of this is a *phosphatase* enzyme, which catalyzes the hydrolysis (splitting) of phosphate bonds, magnifying the reaction rate by a factor of $10^{21}$ (one sextillion). This enzyme allows reactions vital for cell signaling and regulation to take place in a hundredth of a second. Without the enzyme, this essential reaction would take a trillion years — many times more than the supposed evolutionary age of the universe (about 15 billion years). In other words, no enzyme means no reaction (certainly not in a time frame that would be of any use for the living organism that needed this reaction). See C. Lad, N.H. Williams, and R. Wolfenden, *The rate of hydrolysis of phosphomonoester dianions and the exceptional catalytic proficiencies of protein and inositol phosphatases, Proc. Nat. Acad. Sci. USA* **100**(10):5607–5610, 2003; J. Sarfati, *World record enzymes, J. Creation* **19**(2):13–14, 2005, creation.com/enzymes; *Enzyme expert exposes evolution's errors*: interview with Finnish biochemist Matti Leisola, *Creation* **32**(4):42–44, 2010, creation.com/leisola.

Some proteins and protein combinations are specific to individual animals. While the exact number of different proteins in the human body is presently unknown, estimates range from hundreds of thousands to a few million. The *Human Proteome Initiative* has for some years now been working on identifying and classifying all human proteins (hupo.org).

## 7.3 Cellular synthesis of proteins

The complete process for protein synthesis consists of an immensely complex series of interconnected sub-processes. The following is a highly condensed and simplified presentation of this entire process: The instructions for forming (synthesizing) proteins are stored on individual DNA molecules located in the cellular nucleus and in mitochondria located within the cell's cytoplasm. DNA is a polymer of nucleotides, and is a chemical information molecule, where the chemical "letters" are four different nucleobases: adenine (A), thymine (T), guanine (G), and cytosine (C). In the best-known genetic code, these "letters" are grouped into three-letter "words" called codons, each of which specifies/represents either an amino acid or a "start" or "stop" command. See Figure 25.

The nuclear DNA is wound on ball-shaped proteins called "histones," forming nucleosomes. There is another DNA code beyond the protein code that controls the positioning of the nucleosomes.[3] During division of the body cells, the nuclear DNA and its associated protein are compacted into discrete bodies (chromosomes) which can be stained and made easily visible with a light microscope. Early in the process of cell division, the DNA is replicated so that after cell division each daughter cell has received a copy (duplicate) of the DNA. The replication is possible because A and T always match together (base-pairing), and so do C and G, due to their molecular shapes.

Once cell division is complete, the chromosomes partially uncoil and fill the cell nucleus as a faintly visible stained net called "chromatin." It is possible that it is only in this dispersed state that genes coding for protein can be expressed and utilized in the synthesis of proteins. This extremely complex process takes place in two steps — transcription and translation. Additional details may be found at http://biology-pages.info.

**Transcription** begins when RNA polymerase II (RNAP II), a molecular protein machine (enzyme), together with other molecular machines, "unzips" the DNA double helix at the location of a gene that codes for protein. As the unzipping process proceeds, using an ingenious "scrunching" process,[4] the RNAP II makes an RNA complementary copy from a DNA strand. It is complementary, analogous to a photographic negative, because of the same base-pairing as in DNA replication: C–G, while A matches uracil (U) instead of T (see Figure 25).

This copy is much longer than the RNA sequence that codes for the specified protein. Because of this, another very large molecular machine (spliceosome) cuts out RNA sequences, called introns (RNA sequences that do not code for the specified polypeptide/protein), and splices together the remaining sequences, called exons (RNA sequences

3. E. Segal et al., "A genomic code for nucleosome positioning," *Nature* 442(7104):772–778, August 17, 2006, DOI: 10.1038/nature04979; D. White, "The Genetic Puppeteer," *Creation* 30(2):42–44, 2008, creation.com/puppet.
4. J. Sarfati, "More marvellous machinery: 'DNA scrunching,' " *J. Creation* 21(1):4–5, 2007; creation.com/scrunching.

that code for the specified polypeptide/protein). The resulting composite sequence of exons is called messenger RNA (mRNA).

In 2010, it was found that this is controlled by a *splicing code*, which controls the way certain pieces of RNA transcripts of the DNA code are spliced out. This enables a single gene to encode multiple proteins, and explains why humans have only about 20,000 genes yet make over 100,000 proteins. But thanks to the information decoded by the splicing code, "three neurexin genes can generate over 3,000 genetic messages that help control the wiring of the brain."[5] So this is a *second* code at a level above the genes for protein synthesis. The splicing code and the histone code are *epigenetic* codes (i.e., codes beyond those specifically coding for protein synthesis), and constitute *meta-information* — information about information; i.e., they control the way the protein-coding information is read.

Messenger RNA is transported out of the nucleus into the cytosol (also called intracellular fluid) and then to a ribosome.

The ribosome is a large, two-part molecular machine consisting of ribosomal RNA (rRNA) and about 75 different proteins. The function of the ribosome is to bond together amino acids in the sequence specified by the codons in the mRNA. Another RNA molecule (less than 100 nucleotides) called transfer RNA (tRNA) assists in this process. At one end of the small 4-leaf-clover-shaped tRNA is the complementary codon for a specific amino acid and attached to the other end is the amino acid specified by the mRNA codon. So here we have a small molecule (tRNA) carrying both the matching code and the necessary amino acid.

The next step is translation. This is called "translation" because the codons in the mRNA are "translated" into the actual amino acids. In other words, the instructions in the mRNA represent and specify the correct amino acids and the correct sequence of amino acids that are to be assembled to form the required protein.

**Translation** begins when the first methionine codon on the mRNA contacts a ribosome. AUG, the mRNA code for the amino acid methionine, is the "start" signal (Figure 25). Transfer RNA carrying methionine at one end bonds at the other end to the AUG codon on the mRNA. Transfer RNA (tRNA) also binds to the ribosome. The ribosome then moves to the next codon on the mRNA that receives the designated

---

5. Comment by discoverer Brendan Frey; see Barash, Y., et al., "Deciphering the splicing code," *Nature* 465:53–59, 2010.

tRNA and its amino acid. At this step the ribosome bonds the two amino acids together with a covalent peptide bond utilizing energy from guanosine triphosphate (GTP) in the process. This continues in a step by step (codon-by-codon) process until the ribosome encounters a stop codon (Figure 25). At this point the ribosome releases the polypeptide, which is then further processed into a functional protein. This processing includes precise folding into a specific three-dimensional configuration, within barrel-shaped proteins, called chaperonins. This completes the protein-synthesis process.

| Amino acids | Abbr. | Genetic Code (mRNA) |
|---|---|---|
| Alanine | Ala | GCA GCC GCG GCU |
| Arginine | Arg | AGA AGG CGA CGC CGG CGU |
| Asparagine | Asn | AAC AAU |
| Aspartate | Asp | GAC GAU |
| Cysteine | Cys | UGC UGU |
| Glutamine | Gln | CAA CAG |
| Glutamate | Glu | GAA GAG |
| Glycine | Gly | GGA GGC GGG GGU |
| Histidine | His | CAC CAU |
| Isoleucine | Ile | AUA AUC AUU |
| Leucine | Leu | CUA CUC CUG CUU UUA UUG |
| Lysine | Lys | AAA AAG |
| Methionine | Met | AUG *START* |
| Phenylalanine | Phe | UUC UUU |
| Proline | Pro | CCA CCC CCG CCU |
| Serine | Ser | AGC AGU UCA UCC UCG UCU |
| Threonine | Thr | ACA ACC ACG ACU |
| Tryptophan | Try | UGG |
| Tyrosine | Tyr | UAC UAU |
| Valine | Val | GUA GUC GUG GUU |
| *STOP* | | UAA UAG UGA |

Figure 25: The names (left column) of the twenty standard amino acids that occur in living organisms are listed in alphabetical order, together with their international abbreviations (middle column). The right-hand column shows the 3-letter mRNA genetic codons (triplets) that represent each amino acid. Note: Thymine in DNA is replaced by uracil in RNA.

Figure 25 shows the names of the 20 standard amino acids occurring in living organisms together with the internationally standardized three-letter abbreviations (e.g., Ala for Alanine). From all the possible DNA code systems imaginable, the code discovered consists of four different letters and equal-length three-letter words (codons) to represent each amino acid. Figure 25 shows some amino acids are represented by as many as six codons, whereas methionine is represented by only one codon. In the next section we will determine whether this coding system is optimally engineered.

The material storage medium for genetic information is the DNA molecule (deoxyribonucleic acid). DNA is shaped like a circular staircase (double helix with steps — see Figure 26). The DNA double helix is two nanometers (2 billionths of a meter) wide and is barely observable, even with an electron microscope. If all of the letters (A, T, C, and G) within a single human cell were typed (at twelve letters per inch (or 2.5cm)) in one continuous line, this string of letters would extend for a distance of nearly 7,900 miles (12,700 km) — this is greater than the distance from Berlin (Germany) to Honolulu (Hawaii). Other comparisons of storage density are provided in Appendix 1, A1.2.

**DNA replication:** The structure of DNA is such that molecular machines can copy it with each cell division. An important requirement for this copying process is that the daughter cells receive identical information. This replication is so precise that it can be compared to 280 clerks copying the entire Bible sequentially, each one copying from the previous one, with at most one single letter being transposed erroneously in the entire copying process (see A.1.2.3).

During the replication process, the strands of the double helix are separated and at the same time a complementary new strand is attached to each original strand. This results in two double helices identical to the original and to each other. As can be seen in Figure 26, A is complementary to T and C to G. During a human cell division (taking between 20 to 80 minutes) the equivalent of one thousand books, each with nearly twice the number of letters in the Bible, is reliably copied.

## 7.4 An optimal coding system

How would a good engineer approach the design of a suitable code system for protein synthesis? In order to accomplish that goal in an efficient and economical fashion, he would have to consider both the number of characters in the alphabet and the number of characters that make up each word. He must also seek to optimize the code in light of

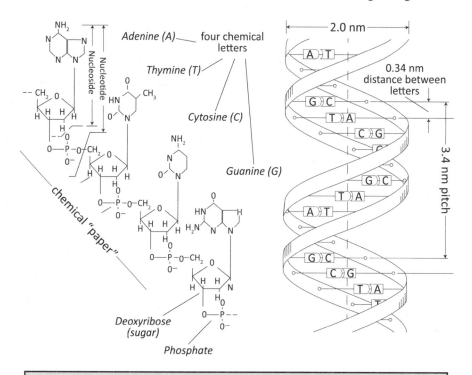

Figure 26: The storage technology of genetic information. On the left is the chemical "paper" in the form of a long sugar-phosphate chain with the four chemical letters A, T, C, and G. On the right is the double helix structure of the DNA molecule together with its dimensions.

all significant requirements and constraints, such as space, energy, and robustness. Furthermore, whatever code system is constructed must also incorporate its *own* maintenance and error-correction features. This code system is responsible for the construction and operation of the exceedingly complex transcription and translation machinery without which life would cease.

It is safe to say that the genetic code is complex in ways that are not even fully known or understood, as shown by the additional histone and splicing codes. In this section we will limit our examination of the DNA genetic code to its protein-coding function. This code has been identified as a "quaternary triplet code," in which four letters are used to form three-letter words, called "codons" (the four nucleotides in DNA are represented by the letters **A**, **T**, **C**, and **G** — in RNA, **U** takes the place of the **T**). Thus, for example, the mRNA codon **AAG** represents and specifies the amino acid lysine (see Figure 25). Finally, the assembly

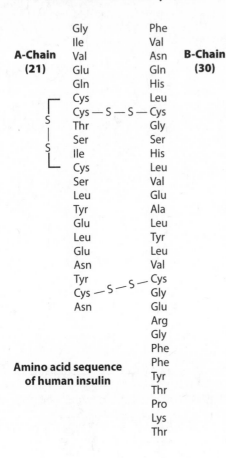

|  | Gly | Phe |  |
|---|---|---|---|
|  | Ile | Val |  |
| **A-Chain** | Val | Asn | **B-Chain** |
| **(21)** | Glu | Gln | **(30)** |
|  | Gln | His |  |
|  | Cys | Leu |  |
|  | Cys — S — S — Cys |  |  |
|  | Thr | Gly |  |
|  | Ser | Ser |  |
|  | Ile | His |  |
|  | Cys | Leu |  |
|  | Ser | Val |  |
|  | Leu | Glu |  |
|  | Tyr | Ala |  |
|  | Glu | Leu |  |
|  | Leu | Tyr |  |
|  | Glu | Leu |  |
|  | Asn | Val |  |
|  | Tyr | Cys |  |
|  | Cys — S — S — Gly |  |  |
|  | Asn | Glu |  |
|  |  | Arg |  |
|  |  | Gly |  |
|  |  | Phe |  |
|  |  | Phe |  |
| **Amino acid sequence** |  | Tyr |  |
| **of human insulin** |  | Thr |  |
|  |  | Pro |  |
|  |  | Lys |  |
|  |  | Thr |  |

Figure 27: The chemical formula of insulin. The A-Chain consists of 21 amino acids and the B-Chain of 30. Of the 20 amino acids occurring in living organisms, three (Asp, Met, Try) are not present at all, two (Cys, Leu) occur six times, one (Glu) five times, three (Gly, Tyr, Val) four times, etc. The two chains are linked by cysteine via two disulfide bridges. Insulin is a vital hormone that chiefly maintains the blood sugar at the normal level of 3.9–6.4 mmol/l (70–115 mg/dl). (For an explanation of the abbreviations, see Figure 25).

of a sequence of amino acids forms the basis of a protein with each amino acid being specified by a codon.

The obvious question before us is this: *is the DNA "quaternary triplet code" the best of all possible codes?* Stated differently, if this code was "engineered" (i.e., designed), was it designed *optimally?* This question is very difficult to answer, due to the fact that there are many features in the DNA code that go far beyond simply coding for proteins. However, it is possible to provide an answer to the question if we restrict ourselves to only a few aspects of the code: space/material efficiency and information density requirements (where "information" here is treated in a purely statistical sense using Shannon's definition).

The matrix in Figure 28 may be extended indefinitely to the right and downwards but, for reasons that will soon become apparent, we need only consider the 25 cells (boxes) shown. Each of these 25 cells represents a possible coding scheme. For example, the highlighted cell represents the

| L = word length = number of symbols per word | | L = 2 Doublet | L = 3 Triplet | L = 4 Quartet | L = 5 Quintet | L = 6 Sextet |
|---|---|---|---|---|---|---|
| n = number of available symbols | | Word length, L → | | | | |
| Binary code Base $n = 2$ $i_B = \log_2 n = 1$ bit | | $m = n^L = 4$ $i_w = L \log_2 n$ **C** 2 bits/word | $2^3 = 8$ **B** 3 bits/word | $2^4 = 16$ **A** 4 bits/word | $2^5 = 32$ **2** 5 bits/word | $2^6 = 64$ **1** 6 bits/word |
| Ternary code Base $n = 3$ $i_B = 1.585$ bits | Length of alphabet, n | $3^2 = 9$ **D** 3.170 | $3^3 = 27$ **3** 4.755 | $3^4 = 81$ 6.340 | $3^5 = 243$ 7.925 | $3^6 = 729$ 9.510 |
| Quaternary Base $n = 4$ $i_B = 2$ bits | | $4^2 = 16$ **E** 4.0 | $4^3 = 64$ **4** 6.0 | $4^4 = 256$ 8.0 | $4^5 = 1024$ 10.0 | $4^6 = 4096$ 12.0 |
| Quinary Base $n = 5$ $i_B = 2.322$ bits | | $5^2 = 25$ **5** 4.644 | $5^3 = 125$ 6.966 | $5^4 = 625$ 9.288 | $5^5 = 3125$ 11.610 | $5^6 = 15625$ 13.932 |
| Senary Base $n = 6$ $i_B = 2.585$ bits | ↓ | $6^2 = 36$ **6** 5.170 | $6^3 = 216$ 7.755 | $6^4 = 1,296$ 10.340 | $6^5 = 7,776$ 12.925 | $6^6 = 46,656$ 15.510 |

$i_B = \log_2 n$    information content of one symbol (bits/symbol)

$i_w = L \log_2 n$    information content of one word (bits/word)

$m = n^L$    number of possible combinations of $n$ symbols for a word of length, $L$

Figure 28: This matrix displays various possibilities for constructing a code with each cell having words of equal length. Each cell represents a code system characterized by the number of different letters, n, in each alphabet and word length, L. The number of different words that are possible for each cell is equal to $n^L$.

existing quaternary triplet code in DNA for protein coding. The upper part of each cell (in this case, 43 = 64 and, in general, nL) compares the number of possible words that are **L** letters from an alphabet of **n** letters (or characters). Note that in *any* quaternary triplet code, a "word" is made up of three letters taken from an alphabet of four letters. Applying basic counting rules, we compute that in a quaternary triplet code a total of $4^3$, or 64, different three-letter words are possible.

As another example, the cell containing the *ternary quartet code* represents a code with three different letters (call them: **A**, **B**, and **C**) from which a sequence of four letters (a quartet) forms a "word" (a codon) that would represent one amino acid. So, for example, in this ternary quartet code the codon **BBAC** may represent the amino acid lysine. Thus, we see that each of these 25 cells displays one possible coding scheme.

In choosing the best code we are constrained by the following **four necessary requirements**:

1. Storage in a living cell must be done within the smallest possible space. The choice of code should be one that uses the least material. As the letters per word (L) increase, the required material and storage space would certainly increase.

2. Additionally, as the number of characters (n) in the alphabet increases, the complexity of the execution machinery will also increase. This will require more material and result in more errors during replication, transcription, and translation.

3. Because of the DNA replication system discussed earlier, whereby the double helix is unzipped and each of the single strands receives "complementary" letters, the number of different letters in *the alphabet must be even*.

4. In order to reduce errors during the many copying processes it is necessary to incorporate redundancy. One example of this redundancy is observed with the genetic codons that translate into amino acids. For example, codons **GAA** and **GAG** both specify/represent glutamic acid (an amino acid). This redundancy, however, is never ambiguous — neither **GAA** nor **GAG** specifies anything other than glutamic acid. The significance of redundancy is that it provides "flexibility" *without* error; e.g., if glutamic acid is needed and **GAA** is copied "incorrectly" as **GAG,** it also codes for the needed glutamic acid.

Within these requirements we see that all the cells (i.e., the possible codes) belonging to the ternary code (*n* = 3) and the quinary code (*n* = 5) are immediately eliminated due to requirement 3, that the number of letters in the alphabet must be even.

Before continuing, we need to compute the minimum amount of "statistical information" that a "word" in a code must have in order to be able to unambiguously code for at least the twenty different standard amino acids. This is done rather easily using Shannon's (statistical) information measure. To specify twenty different amino acids, a *minimum* amount of "information per word" is determined as follows: Information per word = $I_W$ = $\log_2 20$ = 4.32 bits of statistical information to specify each amino acid. Stated differently, whatever code is selected must have words containing *at least* 4.32 bits of statistical information per word if we are to uniquely identify 20 different amino acids with one word. The five boxes with the letters A–E in Figure 28 represent codes with less than 4.32 bits per word. All the other boxes show codes with more than 4.32 bits per word. The boxes with numbers 1–6 in their center indicate the contenders that we will analyze.

With this computation we are able to complete our analysis and selection of the "best" code. Note that, first, we are able to eliminate all of the binary codes with words that are less than five letters long. This is because with fewer than five letters there simply isn't enough statistical information in each word to unambiguously identify the amino acid. For example, in the *binary triplet and quartet codes* (with three and four letters per word), each word has, respectively, three bits and four bits of statistical information. However, the *minimum* requirement is *4.32* bits. Yet, if a word in the binary code is five letters long (quintet), then we have more than enough statistical information (5 bits > 4.32 bits). So why must we exclude this binary quintet code as a candidate for the "best" code?

The answer is because of the first requirement, involving the amount of space needed (and other possible reasons having to do with code redundancy and robustness). The *binary quintet code* requires five letters per word. This is two letters more than a code having only three letters per word (as is the case with the existing DNA quaternary triplet code). More space is needed to store words that are five letters long than words that are three letters long, thus violating requirement 1. For this same reason we eliminate the *binary sextet code*.

Applying similar reasoning and analysis, all of the senary codes, with the possible exception of the *senary doublet code*, are eliminated as candidates for being the "best" code. Specifically, while the triplet through sextet senary codes have more than enough statistical information (7.755 bits per word through 15.510 bits per word, respectively), these codes all require more space and material than does the quaternary triplet code.

There is only one code — the *senary doublet code* (SDC), with an alphabet of six letters, two letters per word, 5.170 bits per word — that could possibly challenge the DNA quaternary triplet code (QTC) for the title of "best." Note that the SDC requires only two letters per word instead of three, as in the QTC. This seems to favor the SDC over the QTC in terms of space and material requirements.

However, we also note that each word in the QTC contains 6 bits of statistical information compared to 5.17 bits per word in the SDC. This represents 16% more statistical information per word in the QTC than in the SDC; hence, the QTC is favored over the SDC. This fact is also significant in light of requirements 2 and 4. As the number of letters in an "alphabet" increases, then the maintenance costs, material requirements, and number of errors will also increase. This is because there are now six letters (instead of four in the QTC) that must be manufactured, stored, and cross-checked for errors.

Additionally, while the SDC does provide for some redundancy, the QTC provides significantly more redundancy in less space. One way to compare this is to consider "redundancy per code (RC)" where RC = (number of different words that are possible in the code)/(number of different words that are needed). In the SDC under this scenario, RC = $6^2/20$ = 1.8. In the QTC, under the same scenario, RC = $4^3/20$ = 3.2. Thus, the QTC provides 3.2/1.8 = 1.78 and thus has 78% *more* redundancy per code than does the SDC. This redundancy translates into robustness of the code, thereby minimizing errors, and quite possibly allows for coding options that extend beyond merely coding for proteins, such as the histone and splicing codes. These considerations all point to the QTC as being superior to the SDC.

Finally, extending the Figure 28 table to the right or down would produce codes inferior to any of the codes that we have discussed, for the same reasons as those considered in these analyses.

**Conclusion:** From an engineering point of view, and under the criteria that were considered here, the code system used in living organisms for protein synthesis — the *Quaternary Triplet Code* — is the best of all possible codes in regard to the four requirements that must be met. This testifies to purposeful design, as will be explored in chapter 8.

### 7.5 Does DNA/RNA convey Universal Information?

In the DNA of every living organism we find a genuine code system that utilizes four molecules as letters of a defined alphabet. Also there is

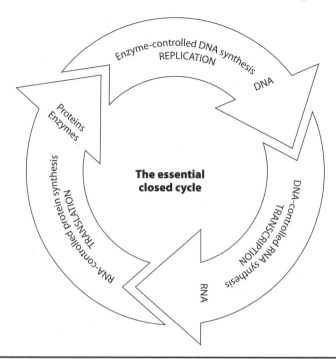

Figure 29: A simplified representation of an information-controlled cyclical process in living cells. The translation mechanism (protein synthesis) corresponds to the lowest level of pragmatics; however, it must also be included in the next step of the cycle as a higher pragmatic level, since DNA replication can only take place under enzymatic catalysis. The diagram makes it clear that such a cyclical process must have been complete right from the start and could not have evolved step by step. Furthermore, this example of a complex information transmission system corresponds structurally to Figure 22 (chapter 5.7 — see also chapter 6.2 regarding this evolutionary conundrum).

a syntax (in which "words," called codons, for protein synthesis are composed of three of those letters) and a semantic (where each word (codon) represents an amino acid or an instruction). However, the entire genetic syntax system goes far beyond this with its use of structural units (e.g., expressors, repressors, and operators) that are still not fully understood. It is known that the information processes within a cell are cyclical (see Figure 29). Most of the semantic aspect of the genetic code is a mystery at the time of this writing. Only some of the functions can be assigned locally to certain chromosomes or genes without our possessing the ability to understand the entire genetic language itself. That semantics are present can be concluded from the consummated pragmatics. We see the invariance of these semantics, for example, in the likeness (not identity!) of identical twins. By observing living organisms as a whole, as well as by examining selected details, we can recognize the unequivocal goal-orientation of life and thereby establish its apobetic nature. The apobetic attribute encompasses the idea that UI is a product of intelligence and not of chance.

The substitutive function of UI is also fulfilled (see chapter 3.4) since the codons in the DNA molecules abstractly substitute for the amino acids that will be assembled into proteins later.

We are now in a position to determine whether the Protein Synthesizing System (PSS) meets the requirements of the Universal Information (UI) domain. In order to do so, we will need to revisit the four *distinguishing* attributes of UI — syntax, semantics, pragmatics, and apobetics:

- **Syntax:** There is clearly a code comprised of a four-letter alphabet (Adenine, Thymine/Urasil, Cytosine, and Guanine — **A**, **T/U**, **C**, and **G**), and a syntax that specifies the accepted structure of the code (e.g., all "words" (codons) must be three letters long, no spaces between words in the mRNA that will be translated).

- **Semantics:** Except for the three stop codons that abstractly represent a "stop" command, all of the other 61 codons abstractly represent specific standard amino acids (see Figure 25). This is an abstract representation (i.e., there is no resemblance or inherent physical-chemical relationship between the DNA/RNA codons and their specified amino acids). This abstraction requires a small intermediary molecule, tRNA, to accomplish the specification. Additionally, the sequence of codons in mRNA specifies (represents) the sequence of amino acids in the protein being synthesized.

- **Pragmatics:** The pragmatic attribute of UI is about the performance of an action that requires machines and harnessed energy. The translation process itself is an action in that machines (the ribosomes) synthesize proteins from the code conveyed by mRNA. As described previously (chapter 7.1), proteins have many functions from the subcellular level all the way up to the macroscopic level of the body. This hierarchy of pragmatics is finely tuned, integrated, and highly organized, resulting in the amazing performances displayed by all living creatures.

• **Apobetics:** The multilevel purposes of syntactic and semantic information coded on the DNA/RNA are revealed when they are achieved through the pragmatics.

As was done in chapter 3.5, let us summarize this analysis of the PSS code and insert it into Table 2:

| | |
|---|---|
| **Syntax:** | Does the Protein Synthesizing System have an abstract code and a set of syntactic rules? *Yes! This portion of the DNA/RNA code is abstract, and has an associated syntax.* |
| **Semantics:** | Does the code in the Protein Synthesizing System furnish abstract substitutes for actual entities? *Yes! The DNA/RNA codons substitute for/represent commands or specific amino acids and specify their proper sequence but have no resemblance or inherent relationship to the amino acids.* |
| **Pragmatics:** | Does the PSS code express a call for action? *Yes! When the ribosome "reads" the mRNA "execute command" (i.e., the first **AUG** codon that it encounters), it starts forming covalent peptide bonds between amino acids specified by the mRNA codons. This begins an integrated process of ever higher levels of pragmatics (actions) performed by biological machines primarily composed of proteins.* |
| **Apobetics:** | Does this code express any purpose to be achieved? *Yes! A living, functioning organism is achieved at the highest level of purpose, with multiple levels of purpose below this.* |

## Conclusion

The Protein Synthesizing System (PSS) conveys Universal Information because it expresses all four of the *distinguishing* attributes that are necessary to be classified as UI and belongs in Domain A of Table 1 and Figure 15, chapter 3.4. This means that the PSS is governed by all of the scientific laws of UI.

## 7.6 Materialistic models for the origin of biological information

The question — *Where does life come from?* — is unavoidably associated with the question, *Where does information come from?* Since the publication of the insights of James D. Watson and Francis H.C. Crick in 1953, modern research has consistently acknowledged that the information contained in cells is the dominant basis for the existence of life. Anyone who wants to make authoritative statements about the origin of life is compelled to explain the origin of this information. All evolutionary approaches to answering this fundamental question have, to date, failed. In spite of this, a kind of natural philosophy that sees life only as a material effect stemming from purely material causes has become widespread in the biological sciences. A few representatives of these ideas will now be considered.

French zoologist and philosopher Jean-Baptiste de Lamarck (1744–1829) wrote, in *Philosophie Zoologique,* Paris 1809, Vol. 1:

> Life is solely a physical phenomenon. All forms of life are based on mechanical, physical, and chemical principles which lie in the nature of organic matter itself.

The German microbiologist Reinhard W. Kaplan also argues from a similar materialistic position [K1]:

> Life is the effect of a system made of different parts which cooperate in a certain regime.... Life can be explained entirely by the properties of these parts and the necessarily resulting interactions between them.... Accordingly, to explain the origin of life means that hypotheses must be constructed which itemize an unbroken chain of processes up to the emergence of protobionts, and that all these processes may be deduced from the physical, chemical, or other laws concerning material systems.

The Nobel laureate from Göttingen (Germany), Manfred Eigen, addresses questions of life from the molecular-biological viewpoint and proceeds from following the unsupportable postulate that *natural laws have governed the genesis of life.* In his work on the self-organization of matter [E2], Eigen remains stuck at the level of statistical information, in spite of his impressive array of mathematical formulae. Thus, his substantial contribution is of no relevance to the question of the origin of information and hence life. In [E3, p. 55] Eigen writes: *"Information comes from non-information."* This statement is simply an affirmation of materialism, and is empirically unverifiable and unfalsifiable. As such, it belongs more to the realm of ideology than to that of science.

Austrian Franz M. Wuketits defines the target readership of his book [W7] as follows:

> ... not only to the biologist and the epistemologist but equally to the scientist and philosopher and, indeed, anyone interested in the adventure of modern scientific endeavor.

He then presents a so-called "evolutionary epistemology" with the aspiration of a new Copernican Revolution. Until recently, great scientific insights and achievements had been gained through observing, weighing, and measuring (e.g., by Copernicus, Galileo, Newton, Einstein, Born, and Planck); now the reverse is happening: Materialism has become the initial assumption so that all of nature's phenomena are interpreted through the evolution of self-organizing matter. Wuketits writes in the introduction to his book [W7, p. 11–12]:

> We assume the principal correctness of the biological theory of evolution, and furthermore, that the doctrine of evolution is universally applicable, that it works both in the pre-organic and the organic regions, and that it can even be extended beyond that into the realms of the psyche, the social, and the cultural. Were we to accept the evolutionist's standpoint also for the realm of human thinking and perception, then we would discover that the notion of evolution certainly becomes important in the analysis of those phenomena which are usually subsumed under the term epistemology and it also gains importance in the evaluation of the progress of gaining scientific knowledge. Thus we arrive at an evolutionary epistemology, a theory of human knowledge which relates to its own evolutive realization.

If such statements had emerged from substantial facts, then one could agree with the conclusion. Here, the reverse is the case: the materialistic doctrine of evolution has been imposed upon all of nature's phenomena. Today, many scientists subject themselves to such intellectual compulsion, as servile followers of this materialistic philosophy. To do otherwise often means less likelihood of being published, gaining tenure, or being awarded grants. However, science should be committed to truth, and should not blindly go where it is told it must go. Evolutionary episte-mology forbids the existence of a planning spiritual entity as the ultimate cause of natural systems and tries to squeeze all science into the corset of the "self-organization of matter."

With almost ideological passion, Wuketits advocates evolutionary epistemology and accuses any scientist who contemplates a designer in nature of fantasizing. Wuketits wants to banish all discussion of such things as final/ultimate causes or teleology from the realm of serious thought.

A significant proportion of the exponents of those sciences that deal in particular with cosmology and questions of origins subscribe to evolu-tionary epistemology. This has prompted the well-known American bio-informatician Hubert P. Yockey, writing in the *Journal of Theoretical Biol-ogy* [Y1] to say: "The literature in this field is completely *gleichgeschaltet*." (He uses this German word to mean synchronized, as in all brought into line.) He goes on to state:

> Since science has not the vaguest idea how life originated on earth, whether life exists anywhere else, or whether little green men pullulate in our galaxy, it would be honest to admit this to students, the agencies funding research, and the public. Lead-ers in science, speaking ex cathedra, should stop polarizing the minds of students and younger creative scientists with statements for which faith is the only evidence.

The doctrine of evolution is by no means a compelling scientific prin-ciple; even the notable philosopher of science Karl Popper (1902–1994) [H1] once described it as a *metaphysical research programme*. This is a remarkably honest pronouncement from a man who identified himself with the evolutionary way of reasoning.

Let us look at a few thought models that suggest information can emerge from matter:

**Cumulative selection** (Lat. *cumulare* = to accumulate, to amass): English neo-Darwinist Richard Dawkins revived the historic example of the monkey at a typewriter, replacing it with a "computer monkey." The left-hand portion of Figure 30 shows how he begins on his computer with an arbitrary sequence of 28 randomly selected characters [D2, p. 66–67] and tries to produce by mutation and selection the prescribed sentence from Shakespeare "Methinks it is like a weasel." The arbitrary starting sequence with the precise length of the target sentence is repeatedly copied, permitting certain latitude for error each time (representing mutations). The program tests all mutated sentences, understood as "descendants" of the starting sentence, and selects the one that is most similar to the target sentence. The winning sentence in each generation seeds the next, until the target is reached in the 43rd generation. The fact that Dawkins' program had a target sentence, whereas evolution is said not to be directed at all, is evidently not supposed to occur to the reader.

Heidelberg theology professor Klaus Berger made the following comment on the new wave of "Jesus books" with their distorted and alien representation of New Testament ideas: "Buy such a book and read it just to see how stupid they assume you are." With similar fervor, Dawkins propagates his rather transparent fallacies on the origin of information. For this reason I have reproduced at length his approach to the origin of information. This provides an opportunity for the reader to judge what Dawkins expects of him.

At the start of his book, Dawkins informs his readers [D2, p. 13] about the purposelessness of living structures: "Biology is the study of

| Example from R. Dawkins: Initial sequence: WDLMNLT DTJBKWIRZREZLMQCO P | Example from B.-O. Küppers: Initial sequence: ELWWSJILAKLAFTYJ:/ELWWSJILAKLAFTYJ:/ |
|---|---|
| Predetermined target sentence: METHINKS IT IS LIKE A WEASEL | Predetermined target: EVOLUTIONSTHEORIE (twice) |
| **Test 1:** | **Gen. 01** |
| Gen. 01 WDLMNLT DTJBKWIRZREZLMQCO P | ELWWSJILAKLAFTYJ:/ ELWWSJILAKLAFTYJ:/ |
| Gen. 02 WDLTMNLT DTJBSWIRZREZLMQLO P | ELYWSJILAK?AFTYJ:/ELWOSBCSEKLAJSYK:/ |
| Gen. 10 MDLDMNLS ITJISWHRZREZ MECS P | ELWOSBCKEKLKUTII::/ELWOTBCKYKLIFTYJ:/ |
| Gen. 20 MELDINLS IT ISWPRKE Z WECSEL | ELWOSBDKEKLAJTYI:/ELWOTBCKZKLIJTYJ: |
| Gen. 30 METHINGS IT ISWLIKE B WECSEL | **Gen. 05** |
| Gen. 40 METHINKS IT IS LIKE I WEASEL | EVQLVDGONS?HEOQUI/EVOKVDGONSLHE.QIC/ |
| Gen. 43 METHINKS IT IS LIKE A WEASEL | ETOLVDGONS?HEOQIE/EVOLVDGONS?LUOQOC/ |
| **Test 2:** | EVQLVDGONC?HEOQIE/EVOLVDIONKLHEKQIC/ |
| Gen. 01 Y YVMQKZPFJXWVHGLAWFVCHHQXYOPY | EVOLVDGONSLHEOQIC/EVOLVDGONS?HEOQIE/ |
| Gen. 10 Y YVMQKSPFTXWSHLIKEFV HQYSPY | EVOLVEDONSLHEOQIC/EVOLVDGONS?HEOQIE/ |
| Gen. 20 YETHINKSOITXISHLIKEFA WOYSEY | **Gen. 30** |
| Gen. 30 METHINKS IT ISSLIKE A WEFSEY | EVOLUTIONSTHEORIE/ EVOLUTIONSTHEORIE/ |
| Gen. 40 METHINKS IT ISBLIKE A WEASES | EVOLUTIONSTHEORIE/ EVOLUTIONSTHEORIE/ |
| Gen. 50 METHINKS IT ISJLIKE A WEASEO | EVOLUTIONSTHEORIE/ EVOLVDIONSTHEORIE/ |
| Gen. 60 METHINKS IT IS LIKE A WEASEP | EVOLUTIONSTHEORJE/ EVOPUTIONSTHEORIE/ |
| Gen. 64 METHINKS IT IS LIKE A WEASEL | EVOLVTIONSTHEORIE/ EVO?UTIONSKXHEORI |

Figure 30: Molecular-Darwinist concepts for the creation of information according to R. Dawkins and B.-O. Küppers.

complicated things that give the appearance of having been designed for a purpose." He goes on to provide the *target* sentence upon which his whole program rests. He can execute this process with any arbitrary starting sequence and the target sequence will always be the result. Dawkins even specifies the same number of characters in his starting sequence as are in the *target* sentence. Therefore, it should be clear that his mutation-selection program has not created information but rather that the information has been specified from the start. In short, Dawkins "smuggles" the result *(Methinks it is like a weasel)* into his program and then rejoices triumphantly when his algorithm "generates" the result "rapidly" using only "random" processes.

In [K4], B.-O. Küppers, Germany, demonstrates a similar evolution game in which the word "Evolutionstheorie" (appearing twice) is the target word (see the right-hand portion of Figure 30). However, according to SLI-3, *de novo* UI cannot be produced by a random process. Both results are due to the way the programs were written. In Küppers, the process of devolving starts after the target has been achieved. In Dawkins, after the target is achieved, it is impossible for any "devolution" to take place. The outcome is completely determined by the programmer via the program.

Clearly, the processes that Richard Dawkins and Bernd-Olaf Küppers use aren't "random" — they are *entirely directed*. The outcome is inevitable and totally *mandated* by the person that created the algorithm. In fact, it would be headline news if Dawkins' program generated anything *other* than *Methinks it is like a weasel!* For example, an output such as "Four score and seven years ago …" would indicate that de novo UI had just been created by an algorithm that was program-directed to generate a unique Shakespearean phrase. It would then be time to stop the presses and hand out a few Nobel prizes![6]

**Genetic algorithms:** Another idea to account for the origin of information solely from matter is the so-called "genetic algorithm" (GA) [F4]. This term has been deliberately chosen from the fields of biology and numerical mathematics in order to suggest a mathematical description of evolutionary processes. A GA is a purely mathematical, iterative (continuously repeating) computer program with which dynamic systems can be modeled and optimized according to certain specified criteria. One must

---

6. For further discussion about the dubious assumptions in mutation rates, selection coefficients, and more in Dawkins' example, plus access to a computer program to test it, see creation.com/weasel.

keep in mind that no *actual* biological processes take place in a GA; i.e., GAs are simply numerical methods of calculation that do not actually describe, much less encompass, what is happening within living cells.

In GAs, the effects of mutation and selection of bit patterns can be simulated with computers. The general idea behind a GA goes something like this: a "population" of organisms is modeled as "digital sequences" that serve as the initial input to the GA (a computer program). This program then "randomly" acts on the input sequences and transforms it (i.e., "mutates" it) in some way following a set of prespecified rules. For example, one rule could be *randomly select one sequence from the "population" and then randomly select one bit from that sequence and change it.* This change to the original sequence makes it a "mutated" sequence that is evaluated via predefined "fitness functions" that are also part of the GA program. Finally, the mutated sequences that "survive" (i.e., that don't "die" or become "extinct") become the new input — ready to "evolve" once again — and the entire process is repeated until commanded to stop.

By its design, a GA will generate an "artificial evolution" that is entirely determined by what the programmer wrote into the code. Genetic algorithms contain vast amounts of UI (provided by the author/programmer) as necessary preconditions for the construction and functioning of these algorithms. The "new information" that is allegedly generated by these algorithms amounts to nothing more than the deterministic output of an elaborate combination of prespecified transformations coupled with "random" inputs leading to branching and decision schemes.[7]

A further fault with the GA system is the presumption that there are a multitude of "beneficial mutations" affecting the population. These "beneficial mutations" are the replacement for segments eliminated by "natural selection." However, this is not what is seen in real life. The process of natural selection, while eliminating segments of any given

---

7. GAs (all of which employ "random numbers" in their computations) may appear to transcend pure determinism but this is in appearance only. In GAs, the programmer wholly predetermines whether or not "evolution" takes place by setting artificial thresholds and by inserting decision and branching criteria into the software. These settings and criteria essentially predetermine not only that "evolution" will take place, but also its frequency and direction. The random numbers employed in the code merely add a surprise element into the program. Surprises notwithstanding, the final outcome is *guaranteed* to produce "evolution" because the programmer has specified that outcome in the code via the settings and criteria. If you doubt this, then ask yourself, how many published GAs are there that do *not* produce some sort of "evolution"? If they don't produce "evolution," then they are never published because, by definition, they have "failed."

population, has never been replaced by any sequence of "beneficial muta-tions" in the surviving population.

---

**Helpful losses:** Evolutionists often argue that there are many examples of "beneficial losses" in evolution. For example, the beetle on a windy island that loses its wings or the Blind Cave Fish *(Astyanax fasciatus mexicanus)* that has lost its eyes. This argument misses the salient point that these features first had to be there before they could be lost. Since evolutionists propose a molecules-to-man progression, they must first explain the *emergence* of information before they invoke the *loss* of infor-mation as an evolutionary mechanism. Otherwise, evolutionists are in the awkward position of starting with nothing and then *losing* from that point forward. Furthermore, even when an organism obtains an evolutionary advantage (i.e., more survivability/ reproducibility) from a loss, this is only because a large infrastructure (with lots of information) remains intact. The beetle that loses its wings, for example, remains a viable beetle — a highly complex organism — in every other aspect (e.g., it retains its vital organs and metabolism). Therefore, evolution's impasse is to explain the *emergence* of *new* information, not to point to losses of information that may provide a temporary or circumstantial advantage.

---

The most that can be said for the surviving population is that they sur-vived, and with less members, and thus less genetic variability potential, than they started with. So while genetic algorithms may be fun on a com-puter, they do not in any way represent what really happens in nature.

**Evolutionary models for the origin of the genetic code:** proposals on how the genetic code may have emerged have been made in numerous publications (e.g., [O2], [E3], [K1]). However, no one has succeeded in getting beyond thought models. No one has shown *by experiment* how a code could be produced from pure matter and, according to SLI-1 through SLI-4 (chapter 5.5), this will never happen.

## 7.7 Scientists versus evolution

Not surprisingly, an increasing number of scientists are consciously and publicly distancing themselves to varying degrees from the intellectual dilemma of evolution. Among them are internationally renowned experts in their fields. A few of them are cited below.

The late English astrophysicist Sir Fred Hoyle (1915–2001) warned against hackneyed notions under the title "The Big Bang in Astronomy" in *New Scientist* [H4], p. 523–524]:

But [in the Big Bang model] the interesting quark transformations are almost immediately over and done with, to be followed by a little rather simple nuclear physics, to be followed by what? By a dull-as-ditchwater expansion which degrades itself adiabatically [i.e., by a process in which pressure changes but no heat is transferred in or out of the system] until it is incapable of doing anything at all! The notion that galaxies form, to be followed by an active astronomical history, is an illusion. Nothing forms; the thing is dead as a doornail.

The punch line is that even though outward speeds are maintained in a free explosion, internal motions are not. Internal motions die away adiabatically and the expanding system becomes inert, which is exactly why the big-bang cosmologies lead to a universe that is dead-and-done-with almost from its beginning.

These remarks agree with the results presented by German nuclear physicist Hermann Schneider, who took a critical look at the Big Bang theory from a physical viewpoint. His conclusion [S5]: "The evolutionary model requires that the laws of nature explain the origin and function of all things both in the macro- as well as in the micro-cosmos. Too much is expected of the laws of nature." Fred Hoyle remarked on the oft-cited primordial soups from which, according to evolutionary thinking, life is supposed to have begun by a process of "chemical evolution" [H4, p. 526]:

I don't know how long it is going to be before astronomers generally recognize that the combinatorial arrangement of not even one among the many thousands of biopolymers on which life depends could have been arrived at by natural processes here on the earth. Astronomers will have a little difficulty in understanding this because they will be assured by biologists that it is not so; the biologists having been assured in their turn by others that it is not so. The "others" are a group of persons who believe, quite openly, in mathematical miracles. They advocate the belief that tucked away in nature, outside of normal physics, there is a law which performs miracles.

Note that only time and chance are available for the origin of life, because natural selection can't operate until there are already self-replicating entities.

In his book *Synthetische Artbildung* (synthetic speciation), Prof. Dr. Heribert Nilsson, botanist at Lund University (Sweden), labels the doctrine of evolution an impediment for the development of a precise science of biology:

> The final outcome of all my investigations and reflections is that the evolution idea must be rejected in its entirety because it always leads to doubtful inconsistencies and muddled consequences when tested against the empirical results of speciation and related fields. This conclusion may well shock many people. But there is more: my further conclusion is that the theory of evolution represents by no means a harmless natural scientific chain of thought but rather that this theory is a serious impediment to biological research. As examples show again and again, it thwarts the drawing of consistent conclusions, even from experimental material, because everything in the end must be bent to fit this speculative theory and a precise biological science cannot develop.

Macromolecular chemist Prof. Dr. Bruno Vollmert, from Karlsruhe, Germany, has attested that all "experiments" claiming to be experiments in chemical evolution miss the crux of the matter [V1]:

> All hitherto published experiments on the poly-condensation of nucleotides or amino acids are irrelevant to the problem of evolution at the molecular level because they were performed only with monomers and not with the "primordial soup" of the Miller experiments. But poly-condensation experiments with primordial soups or with their constituent mixtures are just as superfluous as attempts to build a perpetual motion machine.

For instance, chemical evolutionists find a trace of amino acids A and B in a Miller-type experiment where gases are sparked. From these trace products they then obtain purified, concentrated left-handed A and B, and find that under some circumstances they can form long chains. But Vollmert found that they will do no such thing in the presence of chemicals C and D, both of which happen to be produced in greater amounts in the same Miller-type experiments. Thus, the alleged "successes" of these chemical evolutionary experiments are actually biased, manipulated caricatures of any *truly* natural reality.

French Nobel Laureate André M. Lwoff (1902–1994) [L3] pointed out that any organism functions only because of its complex network of information:

> An organism is a system of interdependent structures and functions. It consists of cells which themselves are made of molecules which must cooperate flawlessly. Each molecule must know what another is doing. It must receive messages and be able to obey them.

In agreement with this conclusion was the Seventh International Conference on the Origin of Life in Mainz, Germany, in conjunction with the Fourth Congress of the International Society for the Study of the Origin of Life (ISSOL). Evolutionary scientists from all around the world come together at such a congress to exchange their newest insights. In a conference report, biochemist Klaus Dose [D4] writes:

> A further puzzle remains, namely, the question of the origin of biological information, i.e., the information residing in our genes today.... The spontaneous formation of simple nucleotides or even of poly-nucleotides capable of replication on the primordial earth must, on the basis of the very many unsuccessful experiments, be regarded as improbable.

In 1864, the French chemist and microbiologist Louis Pasteur rejected the doctrine of the spontaneous generation of living cells in his historical lecture at the Sorbonne in Paris. Pasteur predicted that this doctrine would never recover from the deathblow it had received from his experiments. Referring to this, Klaus Dose made an equally important assertion:

> The Mainz conference may attain equal historical significance because here, for the first time, several scientists attested without contradiction that all theses on the evolution of living systems from spontaneously occurring polynucleotides are totally without experimental basis.

In 2005, genetic engineering pioneer John Sanford wrote, concerning biological evolution [S3]:

> Mutational entropy [the load of bad copying mistakes in the genetic information] appears to be so strong within large genomes

that selection cannot reverse it. This makes eventual extinction of such genomes inevitable. I have termed this fundamental problem **Genetic Entropy**. Genetic entropy is not a starting axiomatic position — rather it is a logical conclusion derived from careful analysis of how selection really operates. If the genome must degenerate, then the Primary Axiom [biological evolution via mutations and natural selection] is wrong. It is not just implausible. It is not just unlikely. It is absolutely dead wrong. It is not just a false axiom. It is an unsupported and discredited hypothesis which can be confidently rejected.

Inventor of the "gene gun," Dr. Sanford retains the title of Courtesy Professor at Cornell University, New York. Contrary to the view touted by the modern scientific establishment, the above quotes strongly suggest that evolution of the first living cell by unguided, purely materialistic means is impossible — and that existing kinds of organisms with large genomes are rapidly *devolving* rather than evolving. In the next chapter, we present Deductions 7 and 8 that refute chemical and biological evolution at the highest level of scientific certainty.

### 7.8 Is selection an information source?[8]

Materialistic evolution is the belief that all life has developed through time by means of natural processes, independent of any intelligent source of information. This would imply, for example, that there was once a time when no living being had lungs and that no genetic information existed for their construction. Somehow, "lung information" emerged later and was added to the world's information pool. At the time lung information emerged, there was no "feather information" since, according to materialistic biological evolution, feathers evolved much later. We could state all of this as follows: each biological feature that is supposed to have emerged through evolution needed new genetic information that had to be added to the then-existing information pool of the biosphere. Some features may have been lost on the way, i.e., there was not always a gain in information. But it would have been extremely important for the evolutionary process that there was a net information gain; in other words, there must have been very many steps upwards. To state it another way: if microbes were to evolve

---

8. This section is based largely on Dr. Carl Wieland's article, *Superbugs — not super after all* [W3].

into mules, maple trees, or musicians, then there must have been a massive increase of information with entirely new programs. Such new programs cannot be explained in terms of polyploidy (Greek *polyploid* = manifold; doubling or multiplying of genetic make-up) or hybridization (the process of combining different biological species). Also, a net growth of information cannot happen merely by mixing chemicals randomly, because *functional* chemical processes in life require an enormous quantity of *meaningful* information. This means the cell must be capable of responding to the new set of directions controlled by the "new information." It also means that any different proteins must be tolerated by the cell and not immediately dismantled as mistakes. In the face of the above points and present-day knowledge of biospheric genomes, the explanations that evolutionists provide for how genetic information achieved its present status certainly appear to be very imaginative, along with some energetic hand-waving.

Could selection be a process whereby new information might arise? So-called "superbugs" (or supergerms) are the scourges of modern hospitals; they are the descendants of bacteria that have become resistant to multiple antibiotics. The question here is whether new structures and functions have emerged that needed new information or whether the information was already present.

1.  **Some germs are already resistant:** If a population of a million bacteria contains five bacteria that are totally resistant to penicillin, then these five will survive a patient's treatment with penicillin and the rest will be killed.[9] The body's natural defenses can nevertheless often destroy this small residual population faster than they can reproduce and cause more disease. If that does not happen, though, then the resistant population can quickly multiply and spread throughout the patient's body.[10]

---

9.  The reason that doctors are adamant about finishing a course of antibiotics is that in practice, resistance is rarely black and white. The early stages of treatment may kill off the less resistant ones, but repeated doses will deal with those that are more, but not totally, resistant. If a patient fails to finish the course, the more resistant ones will be more likely to proliferate, increasing the resistance profile of that bacterial population.

10. This can also happen with bacteria that are not actively causing the disease. For example, a patient may be given penicillin (inappropriately) for a viral infection such as a cold. The above selection process can also take place on the staph germs harmlessly colonizing the patient's nose or skin, but still capable of causing disease in the right circumstances.

NOTE: The resistance in some bacteria was already present and did not first emerge as an "answer" to the treatment with penicillin.[11]

2. **Some germs have the ability to transfer their resistance directly to others:** This is an astonishing phenomenon; one could almost call it a bacterial sexual process, whereby one bacterium transfers a part of its DNA (called a plasmid) to another through a narrow tube. This kind of genetic transfer of information conferring resistance to a "poison" can also take place between different species of bacteria.

    NOTE: The information that is responsible for the resistance was already present in nature. Again, there is no evidence that new information has emerged, but rather, only the transfer (albeit ingenious) of *existing* information.

3. **Some germs become resistant through mutation:** In several such cases, damage to the DNA (i.e., a mutation) occurs and is consistently followed by a loss of specificity — a degenerative process.

    For example, if a protein were to fold a little less specifically, then the antibacterial agent normally used would not be able to "lock on," and antibiotic resistance would be the result.

4. **In another type of mutation**, a genetic loss could lead to resistance to penicillin. The bacterium possesses the information to produce an enzyme that is capable of destroying penicillin. Only a tiny quantity of this enzyme is normally produced. However, if a control gene that limits the production of this enzyme were to be damaged by a mutation, large quantities of this enzyme would then be produced. Normally this would be disadvantageous for an organism, since the production of this enzyme would then require too much energy and resources. If a penicillin treatment is given to a patient,

---

11. Penicillin resistance involves the possession of the ability to manufacture penicillinase, an enzyme which destroys the antibiotic. It could be claimed that the pre-existing resistance evolved in response to naturally occurring penicillin. But this could hardly be claimed as proof that the penicillinase information evolved by natural processes, since it involves assumption, not observation.

the bacterium with the damaged DNA is more likely to survive than the one with the intact control gene. However, in the absence of penicillin, the bacteria *without* the damaged gene are able to outcompete their mutated fellows.

**Another way mutation can confer resistance:** In order to be effective, some antibiotics must penetrate the bacterial cell wall and membrane. There are ingeniously devised mechanisms that facilitate the entry of nutrients from the outside through the cell wall to the interior of the bacterial cell. Bacteria that do this with these antibiotics are, in effect, giving their own executioners access to their cell interiors. However, what happens when such bacteria inherit a mutated gene that decreases the effectiveness of this chemical pump? This defect in the presence of an antibiotic provides a survival advantage. Again, absent the antibiotic, the mutant bacterium is at a disadvantage. In the above cases, we can see that information was lost or destroyed, not gained.

Australian medical doctor Carl Wieland reports how he had generations of superbugs colonizing his skin, following a hospitalization which had lasted several months.[12] These superbugs had thrived in a hospital environment awash with the most powerful antibacterials and antibiotics. How could he get rid of them? The advice given to him was to do absolutely nothing, they would vanish in due course. If he wanted to speed the process up somewhat: *"Get out in the fresh air, swim in the sea, go roll in the dirt."* (The part about rolling in the dirt was a little bit tongue in cheek, although it was a reminder not to be overly hygienic because the idea was to encourage recolonization of his skin by the everyday germs that normally colonize our skin outside of a hospital environment.)

Two weeks later, he was free of the superbugs. Why did that work so quickly? In light of the previous discussion, the explanation is simple and reasonable. On the one hand, the superbugs are specialists in resistance to antibiotics but they also possess many weaknesses (i.e., reduced "fitness") due to the degradation in their DNA information. If they have to compete with other harmless bacteria that normally thrive on our bodies but do *not* suffer from this information degradation, then the superbugs are at a survival disadvantage. They will be out-competed and eliminated.

This is the precise reason why "superbugs" can be found in hospitals. Normal cleansing and sanitizing routines, as well as the liberal use of

---

12. This section draws substantially from his article surrounding those events [W3].

antibiotics, eliminate the normal populations of bacteria, but those which are resistant are able to survive. In a wild population, outside of the hospital, these survivors are generally actually weaker than the normal bacteria, not stronger. This is especially so where the resistance has resulted from genetic error, i.e., mutation, as outlined in the examples above. The only reason they thrive in hospitals is because the normal bacteria are eliminated. However, in the wild, outside of a "sterile" environment, such mutated "superbugs" will have difficulty surviving in competition with the normal "wild" population. Where the resistance has arisen by one of the other mechanisms discussed, this is not necessarily so. Strains of methicillin-resistant Staphylococcus aureus (MRSA) that leave the hospital might become even more resistant and deadly, and might later be returned to the hospital.

**Conclusions:**

- There are many examples of bacteria that have become resistant through selection, but where this potential for resistance already existed (including imported resistance from other bacteria).

- The survival advantage of a mutational defect, as the cause of the resistance, is bought at the cost of information *loss*. There is no known case that serves as irrefutable evidence that an increase in specificity was derived from a mutational change of information.

- Not surprisingly, therefore, where resistance has arisen by mutation, the resistant germs are at a competitive disadvantage in the wild. "Superbugs" is thus a misnomer.

- Antibiotic resistance in bacteria therefore by no means supports the evolutionary hypothesis that living systems have developed from simple to increasingly complex by the continuous addition of new information over millions of years.

**In general:** Mutational changes in populations of living systems occur without a gain in information but often occur with information *loss*. Also, in the natural world one must always consider the fact that there is an *existing* information pool which allows a good deal of variability within any given population. Good examples of this variability are easily observed in dogs and horses. This natural genetic potential for variability within limits may actually be the source for what may later be thought to have been the emergence of "novel information." The process of selection exists, but this is not the source of new information. Selection is incapable of designing anything — it can only select from existing designs. Or to put it simply: no screening process (i.e., selection) can separate lentils from a heap of peas if there were no lentils present in the first place.

# PART FOUR

## Sound
## Arguments

*Chapter 8*

# NINE FAR-REACHING
# DEDUCTIONS

## 8.1 Review of previous chapters and preview of this one

So far in this book, we have concerned ourselves with the following three points:

**1. An unambiguous definition of Universal Information (UI):** In order to be able to formulate the scientific laws of UI, a precise definition of UI was necessary.

**2. Discovery of the nature and origin of UI:** The essential characteristics of UI were initially formulated as empirical statements (ES). In the course of time, it became apparent that all attempts to falsify (disprove) these propositions were unsuccessful. Thus, we have presented the most important such propositions as "scientific laws of Universal Information" (SLI) after giving a detailed account of what constitutes the essence of a scientific law (see chapter 4). What is special and novel is that this is the first time such laws have been formulated for non-material entities. Scientific laws (laws of nature, natural laws) have the highest authority in science, because they are capable of refuting all lower-ranking insights and deductions (hypotheses, theories, speculations).

**3. Examination of the DNA coding system found in all living things:** Currently, most of the DNA coding system is yet to be understood.

The part most studied and best understood is that coding for protein synthesis. This protein synthesizing system (PSS) was thoroughly examined to establish that all four levels of UI (syntax, semantics, pragmatics, apobetics) are indeed present (chapter 7).

In this chapter we will derive a number of deductions directly. From the statements so obtained, further corollary statements were in some cases obtainable. In order to reach sure conclusions, it is important here to apply the laws of nature correctly, and to follow the laws of logic.

Sound arguments must satisfy all three of the following requirements [K4]:

- The terms must be unambiguous
- The premises must be true
- The conclusion must be logically valid

With regard to the following conclusions, it should be noted that:

- Some terms play a central role and therefore had to be defined precisely and unambiguously beforehand (e.g., Universal Information, material and non-material entities, machines, original sender, implicit and explicit information).

- Our premises are the *scientific laws of information.* Scientific (natural) laws constitute the highest level of scientific certainty.

- The conclusions are wholly reliable, since they result from rigorously applying the laws of logic to the premises (scientific laws).

The conclusions developed in the following are significant in that they refute several of the fundamental claims and assumptions of our time with the help of scientific laws. These include in particular:

- the purely materialistic way of thinking prevalent in the natural sciences
- all current ideas of microbe-to-man evolution
- the materialistic view of man
- atheism

Some readers will have their cherished ideas overturned. Due to the dominance of evolutionary ideas in the media, schools, and universities, many tend to regard the theory of evolution as an absolute, something definitively established. We are concerned with finding the truth.

## 8.2 Logical pathways to conclusions

### *8.2.1 Modus Ponens — the direct proof*

To reach conclusions in direct proof, we use *modus ponens* (also called *modus ponendo ponens*), a method of reasoning in logical systems. This has been in use since antiquity, and is also called Affirming the Antecedent.

The term is derived from the two Latin words *modus* (method or mode) and *ponere* (to place, to set) and means "method of affirming." According to this method, a new statement is derived by inference. The principle can be described as follows:

**It is the logical rule of inference which states: if statement A results in statement B, and if it is proved that A is true, then B must also be true.**

The conclusion is derived from two true statements (the two premises or presuppositions):

Premise (1): "If A holds, then B follows."
Premise (2): "A is true."
Conclusion: "B holds."
To put it even more briefly: (The "$\rightarrow$" symbol may be interpreted as "implies, requires, or demands," and is also sometimes written as "$\supset$").
1. $A \rightarrow B$
2. A.
3. Therefore, B.

**Example 1:**
Premise (1): "Whenever it is raining, the road becomes wet."
Premise (2): "It is raining."
It logically follows that "The road becomes wet."

**Counter-example 2:**
$A \rightarrow B$: Whenever it is Friday, Karl plays football.
A: It is Friday.
Conclusion: Karl will play football today.

The statement A→B is not always true, because Karl will not always be able to play football on Friday (e.g., if he is ill or away traveling). But if A→B is not true, then the conclusion is also wrong.

In the following, we will apply the principle of **Modus Ponens** several times in our conclusions. It is important to know that the statement A→B used in each case is a scientific law (law of nature). Since laws of nature are valid without exception (chapter 4, **N12**), it follows that the conclusions derived from them are always true.

### 8.2.2 Modus Tollens — the indirect proof

The counterpart to *Modus Ponens* is **Modus Tollens** (from the Latin: mode of canceling, denying, or removing), also called *modus tollendo tollens*. This form of indirect proof, also known as Denying the Consequent, is a rule of inference that works as follows:

> From the premises **if A, then B** and **not B**, it is concluded that **not A** is true.

Written in short form (the sign ¬ means "not"):

| | |
|---|---|
| A→B | *If A then B* |
| ¬B | *Not B* |
| ¬A | Conclusion: *Not A.* |

The Latin name *modus tollendo tollens* (= "method of denying by denial") can be explained as follows: Given the first premise, A→B, "denying" (*tollendo*) the proposition B (i.e., by setting its negation, ¬B) also effects the denial (*tollens*) of another proposition, namely A (i.e., leads to its negation, ¬A).

This is an indirect form of proof in which the conclusion is drawn from two premises. The first describes the logical if–then connection. If the "then" is negated, the conclusion must be that the "I" is also negated.

1) Premise 1 states: If A is true, then B follows from this (A → B).
   (Example: If it has rained, the road is wet).
2) Premise 2: B is not true (¬B; since B is not true, B is false).
   (Example: The road is not wet).
Logical conclusion: Then A is false (¬A).
   (Example: It has not rained!).

### 8.2.3 Criterion for the quality of theories

The **principle of parsimony** (sometimes called law of parsimony) is an epistemological principle whose invention is attributed to the French Dominican monk Durand de Saint-Pourcain (1270–1334) and the English theologian and philosopher William of Ockham (c. 1285–1349, also spelled "Occam"). It is the stipulation that "entities should not be multiplied beyond what is necessary." Applied to the philosophy of science, this means that if there are several competing theories, the one that requires the fewest additional assumptions or auxiliary hypotheses, and yet is consistent with the facts at hand, is to be preferred. The principle has also been called **"Ockham's Razor,"** since unnecessary explanations are "shaved off." Put simply, the principle states:

1. Of several possible explanations for one and the same set of facts, the simplest theory is preferable to all others.

2. A theory is simple if it contains as few variables and hypotheses as possible, and if these are in clear logical relationships with each other, from which the facts to be explained follow logically.

The advantage of this principle for theory selection is that theories with few and simple assumptions are easier to falsify (disprove) than those with many and complicated ones. *Ockham's Razor* is one of several criteria for the quality of theories. This does not yet provide a judgment on the validity of any particular explanatory model, but it does provide a judgment on the probability of such validity.

The application of the **principle of parsimony** or **Ockham's Razor** is easy to understand with regard to the interpretation of our solar system. In the **Ptolemaic view** of the world, the earth was placed at the center of consideration. Within this view, in order for the planetary orbits to be consistent with observations, they could only be described by complicated looping movements. When Copernicus placed the sun at the center of circular orbits, and later Kepler placed the sun at one of the two foci of a planet's elliptical orbit, the description was fundamentally simplified.

### 8.3 Deduction 1: There must be an Intelligent Sender.

**OR: The proof of God's existence through a scientific law of Universal Information (see Appendix 5, A5.2).**

226 • Information: The Key to Life

**Deduction 1:** Application of *Modus Ponens.*

**A → B**  If we find Universal Information (UI), then it can only have been generated by an intelligent sender (SLI-4, chapter 5.7).

**A**  The protein synthesis system is based on Universal Information (chapter 7, 7.4 and 7.5).

Deduction 1: There must be an Intelligent Sender that created this UI.

Of course, the proponents of the theory of evolution are faced with an insoluble problem. They do accept that the processes in the cells of living organisms are controlled by information contained in the DNA. But then the question arises: *Where did this information come from?* To get around this fundamental question, the proponents of evolution limit themselves to follow-up questions instead of first solving the question of the origin of information. They are thus faced with the following dilemma: Any claimed increase of information in an organism is only possible if a huge amount of information already exists. This pre-existing information is an essential and fundamental precondition for any claimed increase to occur at all. In other words, the problem of information increase is quite small when compared to the much bigger problem of the initial creation of information. For materialists, the first is an extraordinarily difficult problem to solve, while the second is completely inexplicable to them.

No one would deny that in the presumed process of evolution from a single-celled organism to one consisting of trillions of cells, a huge amount of information has to be added to the original organism, even more so when several hundred new types of cells have to be created. Evolutionists have focused their attention on how the original information in the original "primitive" organism multiplied into that in the complex organisms we know today. But without exception, every mechanism for information multiplication proposed by evolutionary theorists starts from pre-existing information. Examples of mutations are: point mutations, deletion, insertion and duplication errors. In none of these proposed mechanisms do we really come across any increase of Universal Information. Perhaps more seriously, the question of where the original information came from remains unanswered.

When proponents of materialism raise the question of the origin of information, mechanisms are brought into play that have no observable scientific basis. For example, Bernd-Olaf Küppers lists three materialist propositions to answer this question [K4, p. 57]:

- *The chance hypothesis:* The original biological information arose purely by chance through spontaneous, uncontrolled synthesis of biological macromolecules.

- *The teleological approach:* The original biological information must be seen as the result of a life-specific, goal-oriented natural law that is effective at the level of biological macromolecules.

- *The molecular Darwinist approach:* The original information grew out of the selective self-organization and evolution of biological macromolecules.

In all three cases, matter alone is responsible for the fact that the information arose. Fact: No experiment in any laboratory in the world has been able to show that matter left to itself can generate information. Thus, the above three approaches are merely philosophical assumptions, but not observed facts in our real world.

Since there is no verifiable process (through observation, experiment) in the material world in which information has arisen on its own, this also applies to the information that we find in living beings. Thus, here too, SLI-4 requires an intelligent originator who "wrote" the programs.

Deduction 1 has two corollaries:

> **Deduction 1a: Atheism is refuted.**
>
> **Deduction 1b: The existence of God is proven. — The proof of God through a scientific law of Universal Information.**

While some may be pleased about the scientific refutation of atheism, some will be annoyed.

### 8.4 Deduction 2: The Sender must be highly intelligent.

(Leading to the proof of God's omniscience through a scientific law of Universal Information.)

According to SLI-4b (chapter 5.7): *"There can be no new Universal Information without an intelligent sender,"* as well as SLI-4d (chapter 5.8.3): *"Every UI transmission chain can be traced back to an original intelligent sender,"* i.e., at the beginning of any chain of transmission of UI there must be an intelligent sender (source).

228 • Information: The Key to Life

> **Deduction 2:** Application of *Modus Ponens*.
> **A → B** If we find a code system, then this can only have been created by an intelligent sender (SLI-4a, chapter 5.7).
> **A** We find a code system in all living beings.
> (The density and complexity of this code system is several orders of magnitude higher and more ingenious than even the current human-generated UI for machine technology).
> Deduction 2: Therefore, the sender who created the programs (UI) for living systems must be highly intelligent.

Applied consistently, these two laws imply that an intelligent sender must also have been responsible for biological UI. Man cannot be this intelligent sender, because the Universal Information in living beings must have existed before him. Whether viewed from an evolutionary or a biblical standpoint, in either case, living creatures were already in existence before man.

This is one of the reasons why some materialists have brought intelligent extraterrestrials into play as the originators of the information of the life to be found everywhere on earth.

Their efforts to remain strictly within the material realm lead them to introduce imaginary beings, for which, however, there is no empirical support whatsoever. Even assuming that there were such aliens who brought the UI to earth, the logical question would still remain: How did the information within *their* bodies get there? Thus, the alien hypothesis, which is promoted especially in the US, only pushes the inevitable question back a step: *Where did the original UI come from?*

According to SLI-4d, there is also an intelligent originator at the beginning of biological information. In the DNA molecules we find the highest density of information known (see [G10], [G12] and Appendix 1, A1.2.3). If we further consider the inimitable way in which, for example, the process of human embryonic development takes place, we get an impression of the ingenuity of this information-controlled process. Because of SLI-2, *"A purely material entity cannot give rise to a non-material entity,"* all conceivable processes taking place in matter are ruled out in principle as a source of information. Man, who can produce information (e.g., letters, books, computer programs), is also ruled out as the source of biological information. This leaves only a Sender who must certainly exist, but who must be immeasurably beyond our experience or our capacity to imagine.

During a lecture at the Technical University of Braunschweig about biological information and about the necessary sender, a student interrupted me with the following interjection: "I know what you're getting at when you keep talking about an intelligent sender — you're trying to say that there is a God!"

I responded: "Congratulations on your consistent conclusion. I haven't even talked about God yet, but you've done a good job of thinking ahead."

She replied: "I can understand that as far as it goes, that without a sender, that is, without God, it is not possible. But now here is my actual question: Who informed God, so that He could program something so complex?"

This student's well-thought-out question was very logical and required a cogent answer. Regarding her question, two explanations are possible:

**Explanation a):** Let's imagine that this god was much more intelligent than we are, but still limited. Let us further assume that he had so much intelligence (or information) at his disposal that he would be able to program all biological systems. The question is then rather obvious: who supplied him with the information required for this, and who taught him? He must have needed a higher information-provider $I_1$, that is, a super-god who would know more than this god. If $I_1$ knew more than "god," but was also limited, then he, too, needed an information giver $I_2$ — i.e., a super-super-god. With this way of thinking, the chain could be continued at will via $I_3, I_4 \dots I_{infinity}$. As can be seen, there would need to be an infinite number of gods, such that in this long chain every $(n+1)^{th}$ super-god would always know something more than the nth. Only of a super-super-super … God at $I_{infinity}$ could we say that He was unlimited and omniscient, not requiring any outside information.[1]

**Explanation b):** It is simpler and more satisfying to assume only one Sender (one Originator, one Creator, one God) — but we then have to stipulate that this Sender is infinitely intelligent and must have an infinite amount of information at His disposal.

Both explanations a) and b) are conceptual models or hypotheses. In science, when two models of equal explanatory value are in competition,

---

1. The use of "infinity" here is for clarity of explanation, but it needs to be remembered that it is not an actual countable number which could be reached by counting long enough.

we always decide in favor of the simpler model, as we've just done in our discussion of Deduction 2.[2]

We have only reached this point by consistent application of the scientific laws of information. These were derived through observations in our three-dimensional world. Now, someone could object that we have applied laws to an other-worldly originator that are only valid in our three-dimensional world. We would point out in response that in arriving at this conclusion, no restriction was required with regard to the Sender — whether He exists inside or outside our world is for now an open question.[3]

Through these considerations, we can now extend Deduction 2 as follows:

> **Deduction 2a: The Sender (Originator, God) of the information in living things must be infinitely intelligent (omniscient, all-knowing).**

**Further corollaries to the above Deduction 2a:** What does it mean if God (the transmitter of biological information, the Creator) is infinitely intelligent? This thought will be pursued next, in order to then draw two further conclusions (Deductions 2b and 2c) that can be derived from God's infinite intelligence (omniscience).

### 8.4.1 God is infinitely intelligent (omniscient)

The term "infinite" (and related words such as endless, interminable, or immeasurable) are often used in colloquial language in an imprecise way. We may use such terms to express, for example, that something happened a very long time ago, or to refer to an immense distance. While this sort of everyday usage is not intended to be exact or precise, in mathematics, where the term "infinite" is often employed, everything has to be defined very exactly and precisely in order to be able to be used in calculation. The German mathematician Georg Cantor (1845–1918) was the first to succeed in getting to grips with the infinite. By treating infinities like other mathematical quantities, he upended the world of mathematics of that time.

---

2. Application of the **Parsimony Principle**, or **Ockham's Razor** (see chapter 8, section 8.2.3).
3. That the Originator can readily also be within our world can be seen in Jesus Christ. He was in our world and yet had power over all things (Matt. 28:18). As Creator of the laws of nature, too (John 1:1–3), He Himself is in command of these, and not subject to any of them as He freely chooses (e.g., negating gravity when walking on the Sea of Galilee; power over every disease and over death).

If God is omniscient, then it is clear that in our present discussion we have long since left the realm of the finite. We are in the infinite, where we can no longer apply all our rules of thinking, comparing, judging, and evaluating, which we know from the finite, in the usual way. We can say with certainty: No one is above God, and for Him there is no question that He would have to answer with, "I don't know." Let us illustrate this with a few examples in order to become aware of the scope of this statement.

a. **Examples from creation:** Snowflakes always form hexagonal crystals due to the physically determined bond angle of the water molecule. It can be mathematically shown that due to the gigantic number of docking possibilities of the individual water molecules, there would have never been two identical snowflakes — no repetition — in the entire history of the world. Since there is no similar physical limitation in the realm of living beings, such as in a cell, an oak leaf, an ant, or a human being, we can conclude that *a fortiori* there can be no repetition here, either.

   If God is omniscient, it follows that He must know even the smallest detail of everything — not only on earth, but also in the entire universe. This means He must also know the details of every single atom — whether inside the sun, or in any of the 100 billion stars of the Andromeda Nebula, or anywhere else in any of the trillions of galaxies. He knows about every grain of sand in the Sahara, or on the shore of the Pacific Ocean; there is no repetition there either. And He also knows all the personal data of every human being: their shoe size, eye color, number of hairs or body cells, and the different unique structures of each of their fingerprints, as well as the processes going on within every single cell at this very moment. Even more: He is familiar with every thought we have ever had, and every deed we have ever committed.

The following trivial everyday example may help make it clear to us that God really does know everything. This includes things we think have happened by chance, or things we have decided spontaneously on the basis of free will.

b. **Buying bread rolls:** Imagine the following situation: Tomorrow morning you go to your baker to buy rolls. There are various types on offer: poppy seed rolls, rye rolls, and multigrain ones as well as plain rolls. You are still undecided which kind you want to buy. Now the shop assistant advises you and recommends the rye rolls, for which there is a special offer today if you take three. So you spontaneously decide on the rye three-pack, and also take a poppy seed roll, and a plain one. Now: Did God know beforehand how your purchase would turn out? – Yes, of course! – Were you able to use your free will when you made the purchase? – Yes! – Did you feel in any way influenced by the fact that God already knew about the outcome beforehand? – Clearly: No! More than that: God did not just know five minutes before you entered the bakery shop how your bread purchase would turn out, but even before the foundation of the world. This gives us a vivid example of God's infinite information!

c. **Has God already seen unborn grandchildren?** Since we find it difficult to think in the infinite, I will describe another incident that can help us to understand: After a lecture in the USA (at a major conference on apologetics in 2001), an American woman about 35 years of age asked me the following question: "Can God see the future?" I tried to explain this to her step by step as follows: "Based on your age, I assume you don't have grandchildren yet. Do you have children?" – "Yes, a daughter." Now my question: "Do you think God knows now how many grandchildren you will have one day?" – "Yes, certainly!" – "Does God also know what color eyes and hair the grandchildren will have one day?" – "Yes, that too!" – "But has God also seen your grandchildren yet?" Now the young woman, after some thought, concluded: "No, He can't have seen them yet, because they haven't even been born yet."

This conversation made it clear to me: even if we greatly trust God in many things, we may still set limits on Him somewhere, somehow. But that is a contradiction to His infinity — that is, His omniscience and omnipotence. Back to the question above: Yes, of course, God has already seen the grandchildren who have not yet been born and already knows their complete path through life, because it is written in Psalm 139:16: "Your eyes saw my unformed body; all the days ordained for me were written in your book before one of them came to be." This is difficult for our limited minds to grasp. So it was with David: "How precious [the Hebrew word also means "heavy"] to me are your thoughts, God! How vast is the sum of them!" (Ps. 139:17).

From what has been said so far, we can derive two more conclusions that can also be proven biblically (see chapter 9):

### 8.4.2 God is all-encompassing

Since God, due to His infinity, knows about every event in every spatial dimension, consequently there is also no spatial realm in which God is not present. He is therefore supraspatial; God cannot be limited to any space. If even any sub-region in our universe were excluded from His presence, then His knowledge would not be all-encompassing, and that would contradict His omniscience (see pg. 230, **Deduction 2a**). He permeates and fills everything — the whole universe and also every single human being. That is why the Bible teaches the spatial infinity of God.

> **Deduction 2b: God must be all-embracing and permeates everything.**

### 8.4.3 God is eternal

If there is no question that the infinite God cannot answer, then not only all things of the present and the past belong to His knowledge — even the future is then not hidden from Him. If God were temporal, then this would also be a contradiction of Deduction 2a. Thus, we have found out by inference (without the Bible!) why Romans 1:20 says that we can infer the **eternal** power of God from the works of creation.

> **Deduction 2c: God (the Sender, the Originator) must be eternal. OR: The proof of the eternal existence of God through scientific laws of information.**

Let us now briefly summarize the results we have obtained from Deduction 2:

> **Deduction 2 a+b+c:** The Sender of biological information (God) must be
> - **omniscient**
> - **all-encompassing**
> - **eternal**

## 8.5 Deduction 3: The Sender must possess vast creative power

(Leading to proof of God's omnipotence.)

> **Deduction 3:** Application of *Modus Ponens*.
> **A → B** If we find machines or artifacts, then Universal Information, creative ideas, and creative power were required to create them (SLI-5a, chapter 5.9.3).
>
> **A** In living things we find extremely complex biomolecular machines.
>
> Deduction 3: The Originator (Sender) of the biomolecular machines must be able to generate Universal Information, must have ingenious creative ideas, and have extremely high creative power.

The highly intelligent Sender (i.e., the source) of the protein synthesis system (PSS) had to construct and encode the DNA double helix (and thus the genes) to carry the necessary UI. In addition, the Sender had to program some of these genes to construct protein nanomachines to perform transcription, translation, and, during cellular reproduction, DNA replication. Although this is a crucial first step, it pales into insignificance when considered alongside all the other protein nanomachines, encoded in other genes, that perform thousands of functions within each cell. This is an extremely simplified description of the inner workings of living cells, but it suffices to show us that this far surpasses any human technology. It gives us a tiny glimpse of the inconceivably high level of integration that prevails within every living cell.

Consider this from the perspective of a human design engineer, via the following analogy: There are many different levels in systems engineering, with each level being enormously more complex than its preceding sublevel.

1. The lowest level could be a simple mechanical system for extracting water from a well; a bucket tied to one end of a

rope that runs over a pulley. The only additional factor is the source of controlled energy (human muscle exertion) to power the mechanical system, lowering and raising the bucket to and from the bottom of the well.

2. The next level of complexity is a system with an automated interaction with an external device — e.g., an air conditioner with a thermostat. The sensor located outside the system measures the indoor temperature and switches "on" or "off" when the temperature exceeds a predetermined set point. The sensor is a subsystem that must be connected to and communicate with the main system (the air conditioner) in a way that the system "understands." The result of this simple communication is to "turn on" or "turn off" or remain at the status quo. This system requires, among other things, communication, interfacing, threshold definitions, and power controls. Compare this increased complexity to that of the simple water-extracting system that we first considered. Let us now briefly look at systems with even greater levels of complexity that are, nonetheless, far less complex than the PSS.

3. The thermostat and air conditioner system are not "adaptive" in the sense of changing what happens in response to other factors. By contrast, the Antilock Braking System (ABS) in modern cars not only brakes, it will change the amount of braking in response to skidding or hydroplaning. This requires active feedback and modifying its response in real time. To do this requires more subsystems, more interconnections, more communications, and more controls. These controls may be viewed as "switches" that need to be "told" when to turn "on" or "off," and for how long and at what intensity.

4. At an even higher level are self-diagnosing systems, i.e., systems that are able to determine that something is wrong and needs to be repaired or replaced. But diagnosis must occur before the system fails and stops functioning.

5. Next come self-repairing systems. Technological devices that we can think of as capable of repairing themselves are only capable of this in a very simple and extremely limited sense.

Self-adjusting brakes may appear to "repair" themselves but, in reality, they merely adjust as the brake pad wears thinner; no actual repair takes place.

6. Above this are self-replicating systems. Consider the ability of the cell to replicate itself. Human technology wouldn't even know where to begin tackling this aspect. Before reproduction can begin, all the components for the new entity must be on hand, along with the instructions for their assembly, and the cell/machine must be capable of responding appropriately to the instructions. A device for supplying controlled energy is also needed. In other words, self-reproduction demands the existence of a *self-directed* manufacturing and logistics network capable of building each and every subsystem in the overall system, including *itself*!

7. Finally, we arrive at the PSS within each cell. This system is able to do all of the above plus one more thing: it must maintain connection and coordination with many other systems both inside and outside of the cell membrane. Keep in mind that many of these other systems are also capable of doing all of the above, and in such an integrated and coordinated way that the organism, consisting of trillions of cells, acts as a *single* entity.

In summary, we see here that the cell, with its ability to synthesize proteins, dwarfs to an overwhelmingly high degree the complexity and energy efficiency of the most intricate human machines so far built.

Deduction 2 led to the question: *From where did the Sender get his information?* By inference, we arrived at the conclusion that He must be infinitely intelligent and have an infinite amount of information.

Having had just a cursory glance at biomachines with their extremely complex functions, by analogy we ask: *"From where did the Sender get His creative power?"* If the Sender had obtained His power from an outside source, that source itself would have to be even more powerful. In this respect, it resembles the age-old question, "Who created God?" For both of these questions, as with Deduction 2, there are TWO possibilities:

EITHER
- There is an infinite number of Senders ($S_1$ to $S_\infty$), so that starting from the lowest ($S_1$), each subsequent one ($S_n$) has slightly

more creative power than the previous one ($S_{n-1}$). From $S_{n-1}$ to $S_n$ and $S_{n+1}$ to $S_\infty$ the creative power increases continuously.[4] For there to be a last one in line, He would have to have unlimited power (infinite power, i.e., would be omnipotent).

OR

- There is only one Sender, but He then has infinite power (omnipotent).[5]

Here again we apply Ockham's Razor, because it is both logical and simpler to say there is only one Sender, who is omnipotent (God, the Creator).

After all these considerations, we reach Deduction 3a, which is more far-reaching than Deduction 3:

---

**Deduction 3a: There is only one Sender (Originator, Creator) of biological information, who must then be all-powerful (omnipotent).**

---

**8.6 Deduction 4: The intelligent Sender must have a non-material component.**

---

**Deduction 4:** Application of *Modus Ponens.*
**A → B** If we find Universal Information (UI), then the sender (originator) must have a non-material component (SLI-4c, chapter 5.8.3).
**A** In living beings we find UI that is transmitted and processed (chapter 7, 7.4, and 7.5).
Deduction 4: Therefore, the originator of this UI must be non-material in nature or have a non-material component.

---

Because of the laws of nature SLI-2 and SLI-3 (chapter 5, 5.5, and 5.6), all purely material processes are ruled out as sources for the generation of new UI. All UI can only arise from a source that is at least partially non-material.

We have already found out some properties about the Sender (Originator, God) by inference. Now another one follows: He must be non-material in His essence or at least have a non-material component.

---

4. The strictly hierarchical division of power in the military is an example involving only finite power.
5. Applied to the "Who created God?" question, the same reasoning leads to the option of either an infinite chain of Gods (God was created by a super-God who was created by a super-super God, ad infinitum) or there is an infinite, omnipotent God who is Himself uncreated (eternal).

## 8.7 Deduction 5: Man must have a non-material component.

> **Deduction 5:** Application of *Modus Ponens*.
> **A → B** If we find Universal Information (UI), then the Sender (Originator) must have a non-material component (SLI-4c, chapter 5.8.3).
> **A** Man is capable of generating Universal Information.
> Deduction 5: Man must have a non-material component.

Today the worldview assumption of materialism (naturalism) is very widespread. During the 1800s, the longstanding debate between monism and dualism (i.e., "man is solely material" vs "man has both material and non-material components") took a strong turn toward materialism. Below are a few examples of 19th-century advocates who helped force biology into the constraints of materialism.

In 1847, the physiologists Carl F.W. Ludwig (1816–1895), Emil H. du Bois-Reymond (1818–1896), and Hermann von Helmholtz (1821–1894) stated their "Biological Manifesto of Mechanistic Materialism" — "The activities of living material, including consciousness, are ultimately to be explained in terms of physics and chemistry."

Friedrich Engels (1820–1895), one of the founders of Marxism, taught: "The material world to which we belong and which we perceive with our senses is the only reality." Engels thereby reduced humankind to nothing more than matter.

The pathologist Rudolf Virchow (1821–1902) typified the materialistic way of thinking by stating that humans had no soul because he found none when dissecting human cadavers. Of course, this presupposed not only that the soul was detectable by materialistic means, but also that it did not leave the body at death.

The scientific laws of Universal Information allow us to end the long-running debate about the nature of man, whether he is a purely material being (monism), or whether he has a non-material component (dualism). Humans have the ability to produce new UI by writing down new thoughts in letters, essays, and books, or by expressing new thoughts in conversations and lectures, thereby producing the non-material entity "Universal Information." The fact that we need material substrates (carriers) to store and transmit UI does not change its non-material character.

We can now draw a very important conclusion, namely, that in addition to our (material) body we must have a non-material component, which we can call *soul* or *spirit*. The philosophy of materialism, which found its strongest expression in Marxism-Leninism and communism, is also now scientifically refuted with the help of the scientific laws of UI.

## Is Our Brain the Source of Information?

Nowadays, researchers in all life disciplines (e.g., biology, medicine) work with the basic assumption: *"Our brain is the source of information."* Is this true? Using the scientific laws of Universal Information, we can reject this notion:

When a person writes a sentence on paper that contains a new thought, that clearly constitutes UI. The pen or pencil used is a good tool for this, but it is by no means the source of the information. We need the practiced hand to write. The hand is another indispensable tool, but it too is not the source of the information! In a very special way, we need the involvement of the brain. So could the brain be the source of the information after all? Many contemporaries are convinced that the information in such cases is conceived in the brain. Is this true?

Based on the conclusions drawn from the scientific laws of information, the unequivocal answer is NO! Just as the hand is a necessary tool for writing, so is the brain. It is a purely material structure, albeit an extremely complex one. But it cannot be the source of new information, because information is a non-material entity, and according to SLI-2: *"A purely material entity cannot give rise to a non-material one!"* The brain can indeed store and process information — which computers consisting exclusively of matter can also do — but it cannot generate new information.

The conclusion that the brain cannot create new Universal Information is extremely consequential. Since we can create information, humans must necessarily have a non-material component also. This non-material component is our soul. With the help of the scientific laws of information, we were able to prove that humans must have a soul/spirit. We have thus discovered something very fundamental:

> **Deduction 5a: The brain is not a source of information, but rather an extremely complex information-processing machine.**

Furthermore, as a consequence of Deduction 5a, it should be noted that:

> **Deduction 5b: Monism is refuted.**
> **Deduction 5c: Man has a non-material component (soul/spirit).**

## 8.8 Deduction 6: The doctrine of materialism is false

---

**Deduction 6:** Application of *Modus Tollens*.

**A → B** If the doctrine of materialism is right, then matter (mass and energy) is the only fundamental entity in existence, and is the sole cause of all things. Everything in this world and therefore also non-material entities (such as information, consciousness, will) have emerged from matter.

**¬ B** According to the natural law SLI-2, a purely material entity cannot give rise to a non-material entity.

**¬ A** Deduction 6: The doctrine of materialism is false.

---

Materialism represents the position according to which all processes and phenomena of this world can be traced back to matter and its regularities and relations. Thus, according to this doctrine, it is assumed that even thoughts, feelings, and consciousness are material-based. For these qualities we had found out that they are of non-material kind and cannot originate from matter according to a law of nature (NGI-2).

Modern materialism was born in England in the 17th century. "The true founder of English materialism was Bacon," wrote Marx. Francis Bacon (1561–1626) was followed by Thomas Hobbes (1588–1679), whose ideas were in turn further developed by John Locke (1632–1704). From the latter came the idea that matter had the capacity to think. These philosophers prepared the ground for the French materialists in the 18th century. Their materialism and rationalism became guiding ideas of the French Revolution of 1789. The revolutionary thinkers recognized no external (divine) higher power. Reason was declared the supreme measure of everything. This materialistic philosophy was summed up by Paul Henri Thiry, Baron d'Holbach (1723–1789) as follows: "The world, that great epitome of all that is, shows us everywhere nothing but matter and motion." In his book *System of Nature* he explicitly advocated atheism and considered nature to be a materialistic-deterministic chain of processes.

The development of classical science began in astronomy and continued in physics and chemistry. As would be expected, the natural laws discovered and formulated during this period dealt only with mass and energy. Many questions regarding inanimate nature were answered in a readily understandable way. However, the animate realm — the living world —

remained puzzling and resistant to explanation. Nevertheless, numerous discoveries showed that the bodies of all organisms were composed of the same elements found in inanimate matter. At this point, scientists had to make a fundamental choice — either acknowledge the non-material realm while admitting that their capacities in science at that time were limited to working with the physical, or deny the non-material realm altogether and insist everything was physical. Many scientists chose the second option. This in turn led them to believe that life could be understood in terms of physics and chemistry alone. In other words, if the whole universe, including life, could be reduced to, and explained by, pure physics and chemistry, then there was no reason to invoke non-material entities.

Unfortunately, few realized that this approach brought a new worldview into play — pure materialism. This imposed a severe restriction on science; from now on, only material causes were allowed to be used to explain phenomena.

Consequently, people working in the natural sciences began to set aside, or altogether reject, non-material concepts such as spirit, God, etc. Even entities like consciousness, mind, thoughts, and perceptions were regarded as epiphenomena of complex organized matter. Some of these scientists were then led to assume that if there is nothing beyond matter, space, and time, then matter must be self-organizing and could account for all of life's complex organization, and its subsequent development and diversification. This notion is foundational to secular evolution, which is a metaphysical belief system — a *religion.* If the universe is considered to have originated exclusively by material causes, that is *not* a scientific result or conclusion, but rather *religion* is involved (see Deductions 7 and 8).

For over 50 years science has known about the molecular structure of DNA and the fact that it contains information. However, the evolutionists' fervent belief in materialism is so myopic that its adherents focus on the material aspect of the DNA molecules (which are merely the *carriers* of the UI) rather than on the UI that these molecules carry. In doing so, these scientists commit the age-old mistake of concentrating only on the "form" and thereby overlooking the "essence." It is as if a scientist asked to explain the lead article of today's newspaper were to do so solely in terms of the physical and chemical properties of the ink and paper, while completely ignoring the message.

The usual reaction to the arguments presented here regarding the non-material realm is to dismiss them with mention of "religious

> **Evolution is a religion, secular academic says.** Canadian philosopher Michael Ruse wrote in "How evolution became a religion: creationists correct?" *National Post,* May 13, 2000: "Evolution is promoted by its practitioners as more than mere science. Evolution is promulgated as an ideology, a secular religion — a full-fledged alternative to Christianity, with meaning and morality. I am an ardent evolutionist and an ex-Christian, but I must admit that in this one complaint — and Mr. Gish is but one of many to make it — the literalists are absolutely right. Evolution is a religion. This was true of evolution in the beginning, and it is true of evolution still today.... Evolution therefore came into being as a kind of secular ideology, an explicit substitute for Christianity."

fundamentalism"; rather than engage with the evidence and arguments presented, their proponents are commonly derided as deluded or deranged (the actual terms used are often far less polite). Let's briefly summarize Deduction 6:

**Deduction 6: Materialism is refuted**

### 8.9 Deduction 7: The Big Bang is insufficient for the emergence of UI.

By way of Deduction 6, materialism has already been refuted. The theory commonly accepted today for the beginning of the universe is referred to as the Big Bang. "Big Bang" was actually a derogatory term given to the concept of a rapid expansion from a "singularity" — an almost infinitesimally small point of mass and/or energy. The Big Bang was formulated to account for evidence of universal expansion. While the concept of an expansion is not a problem, the idea that everything started with this "singularity," which unaccountably brought the entire universe into existence, is worth challenging on scientific grounds.

A corollary to Deduction 6 refutes the secular notion of the initiation of the universe via a Big Bang.[6] This corollary also stems from earlier scientific laws of Universal Information, specifically:

- Purely material processes cannot give rise to non-material entities (SLI-2, SLI-3).

---

6. The term "Big Bang" generally refers to the notion that at a finite time in the past the universe began to rapidly expand from an initially very hot and dense state which its founder, the Belgian priest and astrophysicist Georges Lemaître, called a "primordial atom." This is presently believed to have occurred about 14 billion years ago, and this initial "singularity" is believed by many to have sprung into existence from nothing by means of a "quantum fluctuation." The Big Bang is the secular materialist's hypothesis of how the (purely material) universe came into existence.

- Universal Information (UI) — a non-material fundamental entity — exists in the universe (SLI-1).

- According to secular scientists, everything now in existence originated as the result of a purely material (mass and energy) event such as the Big Bang. However, we have shown that the universe contains at least one non-material entity — Universal Information (UI). Combining all of this we may logically conclude that the materialist's claim of the origin of everything via the Big Bang cannot be true.

This result can be expressed via a logical deduction (*Modus Tollens*):

---

**A → B** If the Big Bang hypothesis is correct, then only material entities (mass and energy) may exist in our universe.

**¬ B** Massive amounts of non-material entities (e.g., Universal Information) exist in this world.

**¬ A** Deduction 7: The Big Bang hypothesis is false.

---

**Deduction 7: The Big Bang hypothesis is insufficient to explain the emergence of Universal Information, and hence is false.**

---

## 8.10 Deduction 8: Evolution is refuted

---

**Deduction 8: Because information is the fundamental component of all life, and cannot have come from matter and energy, an Intelligent Sender is required. But since all theories of chemical and biological evolution demand that information must come from matter and energy alone (no Sender), we can conclude that *all these theories and concepts of chemical and biological evolution (macroevolution) must be FALSE.***

---

Or we could express the logic more formally with the deductive method of *Modus Tollens*:

---

**A → B** If living things have developed in purely material processes within the framework of evolution (biological evolution), then they should not contain any non-material components.

**¬ B** In the cells of all living things we find vital Universal Information, and according to SLI-1 this is clearly a non-material entity.

**¬ A** Deduction 8: Biological evolution (macroevolution) is refuted.

---

Judging by its worldwide following, the theory of evolution has likely become the most widespread doctrine of our time. In line with its underlying philosophy, adherents to evolution attempt to explain life solely on a physical and chemical basis (reductionism). That this is not feasible is indirectly affirmed by a well-known representative of evolution, Bernd-Olaf Küppers [K5, p. 12–13]. He admits that scientists are unable to even define, let alone explain, life in physico-chemical terms:

> The fact that we are apparently unable to give a comprehensive physico-chemical definition for the phenomenon "life" thus does not speak against, but precisely for the possibility of a complete physico-chemical description of the phenomena of life.

It has already been clearly shown [in G14, p. 85] that this approach is wrong, because all life contains information — a non-material entity which cannot be attributed to matter. For their scheme of things, the reductionists would prefer that one could demonstrate a smooth transition from the inanimate to the animate. This is, in fact, an indispensable requirement for evolutionism, and Küppers recognizes this very well when he writes that a "flowing transition [from the inanimate to the animate] is virtually a prerequisite for a complete reductionist explanation." Finally, he puts it in a nutshell [K5, p. 19]:

> The task and aim of the reductionist research programme is to derive the phenomena of life from such a complex of conditions with the help of the known laws of physics and chemistry alone. The whole of molecular biology is based on this explanatory principle.

With the help of the information laws, we can draw a fundamental and far-reaching conclusion: The idea of macroevolution — the assumption that humans evolved from the primordial cell through the animal kingdom — is wrong. Universal information is a fundamental factor of all living systems. If we removed it, it would be the certain end of life. Every piece of information — and living systems are not exempt from this — needs to have an intelligent originator.

Now a rather obvious question arises: Where is the sender of the information in the DNA molecules? A sender cannot be identified at all. So is this information somehow created by molecular biology?

The answer is the same as in the following cases:

• If we look at the wealth of information recorded in Egyptian hieroglyphics, there is nothing of the sender on any stone.

We only find his traces carved in stone. But no one would claim that this information was created without a sender and without a mental/intellectual concept.

- If two computers are connected to each other and exchange information and initiate certain processes, then nothing of the sender can be recognized. All the information, however, has nonetheless been thought up at some point by one (or more) intelligent programmer(s).

- A car wash contains a program for the individual wash cycles. When we drive our car through it, we see nothing of the sender, and yet the program devised by an intelligent sender is a necessary condition for the process.

The information in the DNA molecules is transferred to RNA molecules; this happens in an analogous way to how a computer transfers information to another. In the cell, an extremely complex biomachinery is at work, which implements the programmed commands in an ingenious way. We do not see anything of the Sender — just as in the above examples — but to ignore this reality would be an unwarranted reductionism.

We should not be surprised to find that the programs of the Sender of biological information are much more ingenious than all our human programs. After all, we are dealing here — as already explained in more detail in regard to Deduction 2 — with a Sender of infinite intelligence. The Creator's programs are so ingeniously designed that even far-reaching adaptations and adjustments to new conditions are possible. In biology, such processes are called microevolution. However, they have nothing to do with an evolutionary process, but are parameter optimizations within the same created kind.

**In short:** The information laws exclude macroevolution, as it is assumed within the framework of evolutionary theory.[7] But microevolutionary processes, with often far-reaching adaptive outcomes within a kind and utilizing the ingenious programs crafted by the Creator, are readily explicable.

---

7. Theistic evolution: A proponent of theistic evolution might say at this point that God initiated or guided evolution, and thus the information laws were not violated. Here is not the place to go into more detail concerning this particular doctrine. In the book *Did God create through evolution?* [G20] I have shown that this view is in stark contrast to biblical statements.

> **Deduction 8: The theory of evolution (macroevolution) is refuted.**

After such a clear answer on the origin of life as obtained from the laws of nature concerning information, a legitimate question arises: Why do many still cling to the idea of evolution?

The American professor of biochemistry at the University of California, Stanley Miller (1930–2007) had tried in 1953 as a 23-year-old student to reenact the origin of life in the laboratory [H3, p. 225]. He filled an airtight glass apparatus with a few liters of methane, ammonia, and hydrogen, along with some water. A spark discharge device within the gases simulated lightning, while a heating coil kept the water bubbling. When Miller analyzed the viscous reddish mass that had formed after a few days, he found a high content of amino acids in it. This finding, many still believe today, would indicate that life arose from what the British chemist John B.S. Haldane (1892–1964) called "primordial soup."

When Miller was asked about the experiment some 40 years later, he replied that solving the riddle of the origin of life had proved more difficult than he or anyone else had imagined. He found none of the current hypotheses about the origin of life convincing. He called them "nonsense" or "paper chemistry."

Nevertheless, the Miller experiment is still cited in virtually every biology textbook as one of the strongest proofs of evolution. Miller, himself a supporter of evolutionary theory, said that if he were a creationist, he would not attack evolution because of the fossil findings, but instead focus on the origin of life. This, he said, was by far the weakest point in the edifice of modern biology.

The dream of every science writer is to be able to say something new on the subject of the origin of life. This particular field teems with peculiar "scientists" and exotic theories that are never fully accepted or completely abandoned, but simply come into or go out of fashion.

But why then would anyone cling so tenaciously to the theory of evolution? American science journalist John Horgan (1953– ) gives a possible explanation in his book, *The End of Science: Facing the Limits of Science in the Twilight of the Scientific Age* [H3, p. 190]):

> What can an ambitious young biologist do to make his or her mark in the post-Darwin, post-DNA era? One alternative is to become more Darwinian than Darwin, to accept Darwinian theory as a supreme insight into nature. This is the route taken

by the arch-clarifier and reductionist Richard Dawkins of the University of Oxford. He has honed Darwinism into a fearsome weapon, one with which he obliterates any ideas that challenge his resolutely materialistic, non-mystical view of life. He seems to view the persistence of creationism and other anti-Darwinian ideas as a personal affront.

## 8.11 Deduction 9: No life from matter

> **Deduction 9: Because the essence of life (see Chap. 6) is non-material, matter can never have brought it into being. From this we conclude:** *There is no process in matter that leads from the inanimate to life. Purely material processes cannot lead to life, whether on earth or elsewhere in the universe.* (Application of SLI-2, chapter 5.5).

The proponents of the theory of evolution claim: "Life is a regularity within the framework of material processes that occurs when the boundary conditions are fulfilled." According to SLL-1 (chapter 6.3), that which makes a living being alive is of a non-material nature. Thus, we can apply Scientific Law SLI-2, which states, "a purely material entity cannot give rise to a non-material entity."

Again and again we are confronted with news that water has been discovered somewhere in our planetary system (e.g., Jupiter's moon Europa) or that carbon-containing compounds have been detected in our galaxy. Such news is regularly followed by speculation that life may well have evolved there. In the search for planets in other solar systems, the main interest lies in those that are located in a "habitable zone." This refers to the zone of distance of a planet from its central star in which water can permanently occur in liquid form.

This repeatedly gives the impression that if only the necessary chemical elements or compounds are present on a star and some astronomical-physical conditions are fulfilled, then life can be expected there.

As we have been able to prove with the help of the natural laws of information, this is impossible. Even under the very best chemical conditions, which go hand in hand with optimal physical boundary conditions, life still would not arise.

> **Deduction 9: Purely material processes cannot lead to the emergence of life.**

Since the essence of life is non-material (chapter 6.3), every kind of life requires an intelligent originator. The four Australian scientists Don Batten, Ken Ham, Jonathan Sarfati, and Carl Wieland therefore rightly write [B2, p. 148]:

> Without the interaction of superior intelligence and creativity, life cannot arise from inanimate chemicals. The theory of the spontaneous origin of life was already refuted by the well-known founder of microbiology, Louis Pasteur. Unfortunately, people today still follow this unfounded speculation.

As Deduction 9 shows, we were able to exclude the spontaneous origin of life in matter with the help of a novel approach. In Deduction 7, we came to the same conclusion using the laws of nature about information.

In chapter 6.3 we had formulated the Scientific Law of Life SLL-2 in agreement with Deduction 9: "Life cannot arise from matter alone; its origin requires a non-material highly intelligent source."

## 8.12 Summary

Through the targeted use of the natural laws of Universal Information, and with the help of proven scientific methods of inference, several far-reaching insights have been gained. They relate to ideas about God, the origin of life, and the human condition.

The deductions have provided evidence

- that an Originator of the world and all life must exist (proof of God!)

- that this Originator must be omniscient, omnipotent, all-embracing, and eternal

- that man must have a non-material component (soul/spirit)

Furthermore, we have been able to prove

- that the widely disseminated doctrine of materialism is false

- that all current ideas of evolution are wrong

- that atheism is wrong

We have found out that the Sender (Originator) must be omniscient, omnipotent, all-encompassing, and eternal. Nonetheless, with the laws of nature we reach a limit if we want more knowledge about the Originator/Creator (His person, His being, His characteristics).

For such answers we need a higher source of knowledge. In the next section we want to tap into this and then also address further questions which we would like answered.

One more important note should be added here:

**Macroevolution/microevolution:** When we time and again speak of *evolution*, or *the theory of evolution* or *evolutionary theory* in this book, **macroevolution** is always in view. By this we mean the generally assumed idea of a higher development starting from a primordial cell, via multicellular organisms to the unimaginably large variety of species, right up to humans. This is often represented by a strongly branched evolutionary family tree. This means that if there really had been such macroevolution, then new types of complex structures and new types of organs with new functions would have arisen within matter by themselves. Consider also that not only the Universal Information required to build the structures would have arisen by itself, but also the necessary operating software at the same time. For example, along with the flight apparatus of birds, the highly complex flight program in the brain must also have arisen in parallel.

In the living world, we observe adaptations *within* individual types, especially to new environmental conditions. In biology, these processes are called microevolution. Evolutionary proponents wrongly interpret these adaptations as evidence for macroevolution. The so-called Darwin's finches on the Galápagos Islands, which have different beak shapes, are cited as a prime example of this. But these are demonstrably changes within the same kind — all remain finches.

Does microevolution work without Universal Information? Not at all! Every programmer builds branches into his program that are run through for different data sets. How much more does an omniscient Creator know in advance which branches will one day be necessary due to changing conditions. It would be more correct to speak of **advance programming** instead of microevolution.

# PART FIVE

# Universal
# Information
# and the Bible

*Chapter 9*

# APPLYING THE THEORY OF UNIVERSAL INFORMATION TO THE BIBLE

## 9.1 Introduction

In Part I of this book, an unambiguous definition of Universal Information was presented, studied, and discussed. In Part II we studied scientific laws and formulated six scientific laws and nine corollaries that govern the domain of Universal Information. In Part III we determined that Universal Information is present in all biological life, at least in the Protein Synthesizing System (PSS). In Part IV we developed eight sound arguments and two corollary arguments. In Part V we will identify a source of knowledge that has the highest level of certainty available to mankind.

## 9.2 Life requires a Sender

Figure 31 depicts the four distinguishing attributes of UI as discovered within the PSS. Both the original Sender of the UI and the DNA receivers/transmitters within the cells of all living organisms are shown on the left side of the Figure. In the upper right-hand corner of the Figure are three frequently asked questions. Science cannot answer these questions; therefore we have reached the limits of science — *a Scientific Boundary!* Is

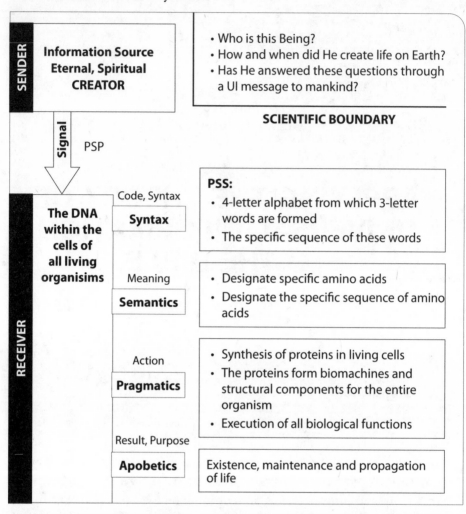

Figure 31: Concerning the origin and propagation of life. The Universal Information (UI) conveyed by the DNA/RNA Protein Synthesizing System (PSS) is a protein synthesis program (PSP) that specifies individual amino acids and their sequence within a protein. In this example, the sender has created a completely automated system that is similar to, but immensely more complex than, the system depicted in Figure 22. This is a complete system created by intelligence for the transmission and utilization of UI resulting in the performance of specific functions. The PSS information encoded into the DNA exhibits all four distinguishing attributes of UI.

there any other source of knowledge that could provide definite answers to these questions? In an attempt to answer this question, let us look at Figure 32, an expanded version of Figure 18 (originally shown in chapter 4.5).

In Figure 32 there is a proposed higher level of knowledge that is higher than the highest level of scientific knowledge. It is a message *originated and formulated* by the eternal Creator and sent to mankind. Does such a message truly exist? We are well aware of many different texts that are claimed to have divine origin. Is there an absolute test that can verify if a text is divinely inspired? Yes, there is such a test. If a text clearly reveals immense knowledge, then it *must* be from the eternal, spiritual Creator (i.e., there is no feasible alternative).

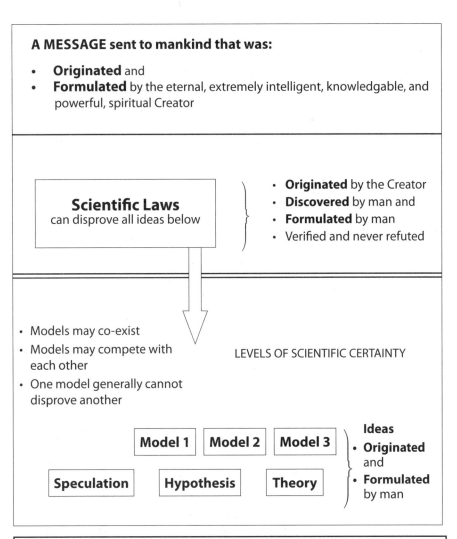

Figure 32: An expanded version of Figure 18

Scientific laws allow mankind to predict future events, but only within a very limited range in time and space. However, outside of scientific laws, man's ability to predict future events is almost nonexistent (despite claims to the contrary). Therefore, if a text incorporates many predictions of future events that do occur despite intervening decades, centuries, or even millennia of time, then that would be a clear sign of supernatural omniscience. This is especially the case when scientific laws are essentially of no use whatsoever for making the predictions. For example, what scientific law(s) would one use to predict that a specific person (the Messiah, Jesus Christ) would be born in a specific place (Bethlehem)? This prediction was made nearly 700 years before it actually happened and is recorded in the Bible (Mic. 5:2).

## 9.3 Is the Bible a reliable source of information?

The one striking feature that distinguishes the Bible from all other world literature is, without doubt, the many prophecies that have already been fulfilled in time and space. More than 3,000 prophetical statements have been fulfilled, often several hundred years after they were announced. Not one prophecy is known to have come about differently than predicted, a fact that presents itself as a unique criterion for testing the reliability of the Bible. The Bible is peerless, as will be shown in this section.

The Bible was written over a time span of about 1,600 years by more than 40 different individuals who were authorized and inspired by God (2 Tim. 3:16). These individuals had no possibility of coordinating their work. Their common bond was their trust in the living God and the guiding force of His Holy Spirit, who enabled them to write the truth (2 Pet. 1:19–21). The numerous prophecies fulfilled, often after several centuries, show the Bible to be the Word of Truth. It is significant that not even one biblical prophecy has *ever* been shown by historical or scientific facts to be false. From the large number of prophetical statements, let us pick just one example that was fulfilled in the last century, namely, the return of Israel from the Diaspora ("Diaspora" refers to the dispersion of the Jews from Israel following the Roman conquest in A.D. 70).

### 9.3.1 The scattering and return of Israel

God had presented His people Israel with either blessings or curses, according to whether they were obedient or disobedient toward Him. Deuteronomy 28:64–65 states that if they were disobedient they would be scattered over all the earth:

> Then the LORD will scatter you among all nations, from one end of the earth to the other.... Among those nations you will find no repose, no resting place for the sole of your foot.

There were several times, historically, when the Israelites were conquered by other nations and the vast majority taken captive and dispersed among the territories held by the conquerors. However, the primary *worldwide* scattering of the Jews began with the destruction of Jerusalem by the Romans in A.D. 70. Nevertheless, in Jeremiah 16:14–15 God had already promised their return to their promised land several centuries before this scattering took place:

> "However, the days are coming," declares the LORD, "when it will no longer be said, 'As surely as the LORD lives, who brought the Israelites up out of Egypt,' but it will be said, 'As surely as the LORD lives, who brought the Israelites up out of the land of the north and out of all the countries where he had banished them.' For I will restore them to the land I gave their ancestors."

The Jewish immigration back to their ancient homeland started about 1897 after the First Zionist Conference. When Great Britain signed the Balfour Declaration at the end of World War I, Israeli immigration increased. Great Britain was given control over the Palestine Mandate Territory (where Israel and Jordan are now) by the old League of Nations. Jewish immigration was encouraged and increased further.

When the Arabs saw what was happening, they voiced their strong objections and fomented violence against the Jews, so Great Britain began to strictly limit the number of Jews allowed into the territory. However, after the Holocaust of World War II, there was tremendous pressure on Great Britain to allow the Jews to return to Israel. As a result, the United Nations established the nation of Israel, which started on May 14, 1948. Since then, Jews have returned to Israel from all around the world.

The "land of the north" is mentioned especially from all the countries of the earth. Is it not remarkable that Moscow and Jerusalem lie on the same line of longitude? It is not difficult to see that the biblical term "land of the north" means what is now Russia. Since 1989, 840,000 Jews have returned to Israel from that gigantic region. This represents one-sixth of all Jews in today's Israel. It is not surprising that God makes special reference to the home-comers from that region.

## 9.3.2 Mathematical calculations

Biblical prophecies almost always refer to extremely rare or even unique events that have occurred since the creation of the world. In our following calculations, however improbable their chance of fulfillment may be, we will use the extremely high probability $p = 0.5$ (1 in 2), for the chance fulfillment of each prophecy. In this way we will be very conservative before drawing our conclusions from the results of our calculations. This high value for $p$ more than compensates for aspects that our model cannot consider, such as:

1. Many prophecies appear in the Bible more than once. A remarkable event like the incarnation of Jesus is referred to several times. However, we must remember that such multiple references are not merely repetitions of previously documented Bible statements but, rather, they include expansion of earlier details. Nevertheless, most prophecies occur only once.

2. The laws of mathematical probability require that all events be independent of each other. A simple example: if we throw a die twice, the outcome of the second throw is totally independent of what occurred the first time. This "independence" condition is fulfilled by most of the prophecies. In several cases, however, the sequence of the individual events is significant, where event B cannot take place ahead of event A. The details of the sacking of Tyre, in Ezek. 26, provide an example of this.

3. According to *Dake's Bible*[1] [D1], 3,268 verses ($v$) contain

---

1. Finis Jennings Dake (1912–1987) was a well-known American Bible teacher, pastor, and evangelist. Many of his theses prompted controversial discussion. I cannot agree with some of his theological teachings (e.g., the Gap Theory), but Paul gives us some good advice in 1 Thess. 5:21: "…test them all; hold on to what is good." This not only applies to Dake's Bible commentary, but to all of us when we apply our limited understanding to the study of God's Word. With an eye for the valuable, in my opinion, we can discover in Dake's work many important contributions that lead to a deeper understanding of the Bible. The Dake's Annotated Reference Bible is an excellent tool for studying the Bible. A lifetime of study and painstaking research went into it. The Dake Bible has 35,000 commentary notes, 500,000 cross/chain references and 9,000 outline headings. In the pages of the Dake Bible, thousands of passages are amplified; obscure readings are made clear; ancient customs are explained, along with matters of history, culture, and geography. Greek and Hebrew words and idioms are dealt with, in addition to parables, types, symbols, allegories, and figures of speech. One particularly unique feature of this Bible commentary, compared with all others I know, is the rich collection of statistical digests and overviews covering all books of the Bible. I have found its statistics on biblical prophecies especially valuable.

biblical prophecies that have already been fulfilled. In the following calculation, we will make the simplifying assumption that the number of verses, $v$, containing fulfilled prophecies is equal to the number of fulfilled prophecies ($n_p$). This simplification is certainly true in the majority of cases; overall, however, $n_p$ will be several percent smaller than $v$ because one prophecy may require more than one verse. As we will see, even this effect will be more than compensated for by the extremely conservative value, $P = 0.5$ that we have chosen for the probability of chance fulfillment.

The probability, $P$, that all $n_p = 3{,}268$ prophecies have been fulfilled by chance is calculated by multiplying 0.5 by itself 3,268 times:

$$P = 0.5^{3268} \approx 1.7 \times 10^{-984}$$

It is important to understand the magnitude of this number $P$ because it gives us a measure of the reliability of the Bible and the degree of its Author's knowledge. The number $P = 1.7 \times 10^{-984}$ is exceptionally small, but we will try to picture it with the help of an anthill model [G1].

### 9.3.3 The anthill model

We will show how infinitesimally small $P$ is by imagining an ant heap in which there is *only one red* ant and all the other ants are black. It is easy to agree that the larger the ant heap, the smaller the probability of randomly picking out the *one red ant* by chance (i.e., blindfolded). The question now to be answered is the comparison C1:

**C1: How many black ants must be in the ant heap for the probability of picking out the *one red ant* by chance to equal the probability of 3,268 prophecies being fulfilled by chance?**

We will approach this interesting question step by step.

During a lecture tour in Portugal some time ago, I was invited to speak to some scientists at the University of Lisbon about why I think that the Bible is reliable. I talked about the many prophetical statements that had already been fulfilled and I soon came to mention our number $P = 1.7 \times 10^{-984}$. I then asked the audience whether they thought it was possible that all these predictions had happened by chance? Or is there a God who is behind everything? If we can absolutely exclude chance, I asked, is the question about the trustworthiness of the Bible answered and the Author's omniscience established? In that case, do these prophecies represent the truth? If the prophetic statements are indeed true, and only explicable through the foreknowledge and omnipotence of God, then would we be justified in concluding that all the other parts of the Bible must also be true?

Whether a chance fulfillment of these prophecies is conceivable or not can be shown computationally. What follows is my explanation of the above-mentioned ant model in Portugal.

**NOTE:** While the author believes that it would be worthwhile to read the lengthy details of the calculations concerning this model, the reader may opt to jump ahead to the heading "Conclusions from the above calculations" (chapter 9.2.4).

1. **The water glass:** There was a glass of water in front of me and I posed the rhetorical question whether a glass full of ants would be enough to satisfy C1. My standard ant occupies a volume of 10 mm$^3$ so there would be room for about $n_1$ = 20,000 of them in my water glass. The probability of picking out the *one* red ant by chance is therefore $P_1 = 1/n_1 = 1/20,000 = 0.00005$. Compared with $P$, $P_1$ is much too large. We have to increase the number of ants.

2. **The bathtub:** Now consider a bathtub full of ants. There is room for $n_2$ = *36 million* of them. The probability of finding the one red ant by chance is $P_2 = 1/n_2 = 2.8 \times 10^8$. This number is also far too large compared with $1.7 \times 10^{-984}$ (only 7 zeros after the decimal point as compared to *983* zeros). We need more ants!

   Let us also consider another significant question in this context: If the Bible contained considerably fewer prophecies than 3,268, then we would need fewer ants to reach a comparable probability. There must be a number of prophecies, the probability of fulfillment of which is the same as the probability of picking the red ant out of the bathtub at random. In other words: if there were only $n_p$ prophecies in the Bible, then their random fulfillment would have the same probability of obtaining the red ant with one random trial from the bathtub full of ants. The number is easy to calculate:[2] $n_p$ = 25.

---

2. Calculation of $nP$: $P_2 = 1/n_2 = 1/(2^{nP})$; therefore, $nP = \log n_2/\log 2 = 25.09 \approx 25$.

3. **Portugal:** Since we only managed to reach the equivalent of $n_p = 25$ prophecies with a bathtub full of ants, we will have to increase the number of ants drastically. In Lisbon, I proposed covering the whole of Portugal with a layer of ants 5 meters deep. The area of Portugal is 92,000 km$^2$ so that the number of ants, $n_3$, covering Portugal to a depth of 5 meters would be $n_3 = 4.6 \times 10^{19}$. How shall we find the red one by chance in this heap? Well, let's take a hot-air balloon, drift for several hours over Portugal, then land somewhere and pick an ant while blindfolded. What is the probability that we select *the only red ant?* In this case, $P_3 = 1/n_3 \approx 2 \times 10^{-20}$. Results in our normal world with such a low probability and only one blind trial for success are regarded in physics as "impossibilities." However, we are still a very long way from $P = 1.7 \times 10^{-984}$ since here $n_p$ would be 65 — still far below 3,268. What must we do? One Portuguese scientist proposed covering not just Portugal but the whole earth with ants, and to increase the depth of ants from 5 to 10 meters! Would that be enough?

4. **The entire earth's surface:** The earth has a surface area of 510 million km$^2$. The number of ants that would fit into the volume of a 10-meter-thick shell around the earth would be approximately $n_4 = 5 \times 10^{23}$. How shall we perform our selection of a single ant from this heap? Let's take a jet plane and ask the pilot to fly in any arbitrary direction for an arbitrary length of time, say 11 hours and 23 minutes, and then ask him to land among the ants. There, where we have landed by chance, we will open the door and blindly pick an ant. What is the chance that we will choose the *only* red ant? The calculated probability, $P_4 = 1/n_4 \approx 2 \times 10^{-24}$. Even this gigantic number of ants would only represent $n_p = 78$ prophecies. We still have far too few ants! We have to increase the number of ants to an astronomical number: let us fill the whole universe with them.

5. **The entire universe:** According to current estimates, the universe has a diameter of 30 billion light years. One light year is about 9.5 million million km (9.5 trillion km). If we assume a spherical form, then we obtain a volume, $V = 1.2 \times 10^{70}$ km$^3$

= $1.2 \times 10^{88}$ mm$^3$. The number of standard ants that fit into this volume is approximately $n_5 = 1.2 \times 10^{87}$ (all of them black except for the *single* red ant). Now we need a special transport system, a spaceship that can move through this "universe of ants" at the speed of light and someone with an indefinite lifespan so that he can at will — say, after 11,153,000 years of flight — open the spaceship's hatch door to blindly pick an ant.

The probability that his selection with one blind trial would be the *one red ant* is $P_5 = 1/n_5 \approx 8.3 \times 10^{-86}$. This value is exceedingly below the limit that we had already called "physically impossible"; but even this probability is the same as if there were only $n_p = 288$ already fulfilled prophecies in the Bible.

What shall we do now? If one universe full of ants is not enough, we should take several universes. How many? Do we need 10, 100, or even 1,000 universes? A Polish member of the audience at a Danzig lecture made the bold suggestion that 1,000 or even millions of universes would not be enough. We would have to take as many universes as the number of ants that would fit into one universe! This proposal is a giant leap forward. Let us see if his suggestion brings us close to the goal.

6. **As many universes as ants that fit into one universe:** We have already calculated the number of ants that fit into one universe; so we now will use $1.2 \times 10^{87}$ universes. Into all these universes we could fit about $n_6 = (1.2 \times 10^{87})^2 = 1.44 \times 10^{174}$ ants. How can we make the draw this time? First, we use a computer's random number generator to pick one universe from the more than $10^{87}$ (which is 1,000 times larger than one million raised to the power of 14) universes. Let's say it gives a number between $10^{56}$ and $10^{57}$, that is, an integer with 56 digits. Then we could go to that imaginary 56th-digit universe, travel through it at the speed of light for thousands of years, and stop to pick out an ant. The chance of picking the red ant would be $P_6 = 1/n_6 \approx 7 \times 10^{-175}$; but even with this unimaginable number of universes we would only cover $n_p = 578$ prophecies. What is the next step? We can only do one thing more. Let us calculate the number of universes that represent $n_p = 3,268$ prophecies.

7. **How many universes full of ants are needed for 3,268 prophecies?** We begin with our now familiar probability $P = 1.7 \times 10^{-984}$. The total number of ants is given by $n_7 = 1/P \approx 5.88 \times 10^{983}$. The required number of universes is then $n_U \approx 5.88 \times 10^{983}/1.2 \times 10^{87} \approx 5 \times 10^{896}$. We need to understand that $10^{896}$ is an *unimaginably* gigantic number — it is a one followed by 896 zeros. The number of universes that we would need is not only trans-astronomical, but trans-trans-trans- ... astronomical!

Are the results of these calculations suitable for drawing conclusions? Yes, I have deliberately done these calculations in several steps in order to present a lasting impression of the overwhelming nature of the mathematical calculation. It is vitally important that all readers become vividly aware of the unambiguous and inevitable conclusion to be drawn from them; namely, that there must be an Almighty and omniscient God behind these fulfilled prophecies.

We have seen that the calculations produce gigantic, trans-astronomical numbers and stretch our imaginative capacity beyond what we can realistically comprehend. We started with the question, *What is the probability that all the biblical prophecies about future events could be fulfilled by chance?* We established that the probability that so many prophecies would later be fulfilled by chance is realistically impossible.

Our model contains three assumptions that cause the result of our calculation to be somewhat imprecise:

1. Many prophecies occur more than once in the Bible.

2. In some cases the chronological sequence of the prophecies is significant. This means that the required mathematical independence of events is not always guaranteed.

3. To simplify matters, we set the number of verses, $v$, containing fulfilled prophecies equal to the number of fulfilled prophecies $(n_p)$.

Under 7 above, we estimated the number of universes full of ants $n_U = 5 \times 10^{896}$ that we would need to be comparable to the probability of 3,268 prophecies being fulfilled by chance.

The number of biblical prophecies that Dake has estimated to have been fulfilled already may seem excessive to some, at $n = 3{,}268$. Critics

264 • Information: The Key to Life

have suggested that the number is too high because he was overgenerous in regarding the one or other prophecy as having already been fulfilled. Let us see whether this criticism is able to topple our conclusion by recourse to the following two calculations:

**Calculation 1:** None of the critics would go as far as saying that Dake was 100% wrong in his estimation. If the correct value of $n$ were only 1,634, they would be suggesting that Dake had consciously or unconsciously increased the number by 100% to 3,268. Not even his strongest critic would insinuate such a high error rate or such a massive manipulation of the numbers. If we look more closely, we are amazed at Dake's incomparably meticulous work. He has not only determined the total number of fulfilled prophecies, but has also highlighted each one in the Bible text individually, so that it is possible to check his claims. Nevertheless, let us take the number 3,268/2 and see if it would alter the conclusion. The result is just as breathtaking. The one red ant would be hidden in $6 \times 10^{406}$ universes full of black ants. Our conclusion stands in its entirety.

**Calculation 2:** Some physicists regard events that have a probability of occurring of $10^{-20}$ or less as "impossible" for all practical purposes. This gives us a criterion for defining a boundary between the "possible" and the "impossible." Let us ask ourselves the question, how many fulfilled prophecies $n_p$ would be needed to meet the physicists' criterion of impossibility? For this, we have to solve the equation $1/2^{np} = 10^{-20}$ for $n_p$, which gives $n_p = 66$. Our calculation under item 3 in the anthill model above showed that one red ant hidden in a 5-meter-deep layer of black ants covering the whole of Portugal was equivalent to 65 fulfilled prophecies. What does our result $n_p = 66$ mean? It means that, even if we could find only 66 fulfilled prophecies in the entire Bible, the conclusions stated below would still have a sound mathematical basis and are, therefore, justified.

    **3,268 instead of 66:** Calculation number 2 showed that with $n_p = 66$ fulfilled prophecies, all our following conclusions have a sound mathematical basis. With $n = 3,268$, how much more certain shall we be that the following conclusions stand on a rock-solid foundation?

**Calculation 3:** The Swiss theologian Dr. Roger Liebi wrote a book with the title *Leben wir wirklich in der Endzeit?*[3] ("Are we Really Living in the Endtimes?") In it, Liebi listed a collection of 160 prophecies that were fulfilled between the years 1882 and 2011. How many ants in our anthill model represent this number of prophecies? First of all, we have to calculate the probability for fulfilling 160 prophecies by chance. This value is given by $P = 0.5^{160} = 6.84 \times 10^{-49}$. Using the reciprocal of $P$ we arrive at a very large number of ants which is $n = 1.46 \times 10^{48}$. If one ant occupies a volume of 10 mm$^3$ we arrive at an anthill volume of $1.46 \times 10^{31}$ km$^3$. Our sun has a volume of $1.41 \times 10^{18}$ km$^3$. Therefore, the volume of the anthill is equal to the volume of 10 trillion suns. Let's use another illustration of this inconceivably enormous anthill. The distance from the sun to the demoted planet Pluto has an average value of $5.913 \times 10^9$ km. If we had a sphere with the same radius, we would have a volume of $8.65 \times 10^{29}$ km$^3$. Therefore, the anthill is equivalent to 17 spheres, each with a radius equal to the distance from the sun to Pluto. With these calculations we can make two very impressive comparisons: The probability of 160 prophecies being fulfilled by chance is equivalent to blindly selecting *one red ant* by chance from a heap of black ants with a volume of 10 trillion suns or 17 spheres with a radius from the sun to Pluto.

### 9.3.4 Conclusions from the above calculations

Thus, the following conclusions have a solid mathematical basis because our conservative assumptions more than compensate for our simplified model. We will now derive five important direct conclusions and two indirect conclusions, each of which is dependent on its predecessors.

**Direct conclusions (DC):**

1. The prophecies could not have been fulfilled by chance.

---

3.  Roger Liebi: *Leben wir wirklich in der Endzeit?* Verlag Mitternachtsruf, Pfäffikon, Germany 2011.

> **DC1:** It is not possible that the biblical prophecies could have been fulfilled by chance. The objection raised by some critics "the prophecies have been fulfilled by chance in the course of time" is therefore mathematically proven incorrect.

## 2. Proof of the existence of an Almighty and omniscient God.

> **DC2:** As the prophecies could not have been fulfilled by chance, there has to be an Almighty and all-knowing God that authored these prophecies.

## 3. Prophetical-mathematical proof of the existence of God.

> **DC3:** As the fulfillment of the prophecies is only possible through God, we have now produced prophetical-mathematical evidence of God's existence[4] based on our calculations. We can also say that the world-view/religion of materialism/atheism has been thoroughly refuted.

## 4. Evidence that the God of the Bible is the only existing God.

> **DC4:** Since biblical prophecies are the subject of our considerations, the God of DC2 is none other than the living God of the Bible. Thus, all the "gods" of the diverse religions are shown to be false; they are, in biblical terminology, *idols* (Ps. 96:5).

## 5. Proof that at least those parts of the Bible containing prophecies are true.

> **DC5:** We have produced evidence that at least all those parts of the Bible that contain fulfilled prophecies are true.

---

4. **Proof of the existence of God:** There has been much discussion in the course of history of proofs for the existence of God. There have been both strong proponents as well as violent critics; and that has not changed to this day. The Bible itself leads us to the right judgment. Romans 1: 20–21 explains that we can infer the existence of God from the works of creation with the aid of our understanding: *"For since the creation of the world God's invisible qualities — his eternal power and divine nature — have been clearly seen, being understood from what has been made, so that they are without excuse. For although they knew God, they neither glorified him as God nor gave thanks to him."* The expression "they knew God" is a very strong statement. It says that God has revealed Himself independently of the Bible. It is for this reason that I support arguments that point unequivocally to God; but just accepting proofs of God's existence certainly does not mean that one has come to trust Him. There must also be revelation from the Bible and the Holy Spirit that Jesus has to be accepted freely as one's personal Savior. Even if proofs of God's existence do not lead directly to faith in Him, they are, nevertheless, very helpful for dismantling and eliminating various obstacles.

**Indirect Conclusions (IC):**

From the aforementioned direct conclusions (DC), it is also possible to deduce the following indirect conclusions (IC):

1.  The prophecies that have not yet been fulfilled will likewise be fulfilled according to God's plan.

> **IC1:** Of the $N$ = 6,408 prophecies of the Holy Bible, $n$ = 3,268 have already been fulfilled. Many prophecies (in particular those of the Book of Revelation) refer to the Second Coming of Jesus and the end of world history. These have not been fulfilled yet. However, we can deduce that these also will be fulfilled according to plan, just as prophesied.

Because the accuracy of fulfilled prophecies is the same as the accuracy of the historical events and scientific statements given in the Bible, as far as we have been able to confirm them, we are left with the following:

**2. The *entire* Bible must be true**

> **IC2:** As we were able to demonstrate that large portions of the Bible are true, it is virtually conclusive that the *whole* Bible, authored by God, must also be true. With this, we have refuted all those critics who claim that "the Bible is myth."

The seven conclusions above can be summarized as one **general conclusion:**

> **GC:** The existence of an all-knowing, Almighty God has been proven to be true by prophetical-mathematical evidence. This God is the God of the Bible, and He is the only existing God. The Holy Bible is from God and is the Truth!

**9.4 But what about other Scriptures?**

There is no other writing regarded as Scripture or holy in any other religion or cult which compares with the Bible in terms of prophetic, historical, or scientific accuracy. This sets it far apart from all other revered writings and the decision must then be made: is the Bible the truth or not? In order to determine a definitive answer to that question, the areas dealing with history, science, and prophecies must be considered. It is only ignoring the accuracy of the data in these areas that allows a person to say the Bible is just one of many religious books.

Now we are certain that the Bible is the Word of Truth. We came to this conclusion by studying only the mathematical calculations regarding fulfilled prophecies. Various Bible quotes say the same. For example, Jesus prayed to His Father in heaven, "Your word is truth" (John 17:17). The Apostle Paul declares, "I believe everything that ... is written" (Acts 24:14). We concluded from the scientific laws of Universal Information that the author of biological information must be an omniscient, Almighty, and eternal God. However, neither scientific laws nor the conclusions drawn from them were able to tell us more about His person. Now we have found an information source more certain and extensive than science. This source can answer questions that cannot be answered by science. We shall address this in the following sections of this chapter.

## 9.5 Comparing the logical conclusions with the Bible

The first four deductions scientifically established the existence of an eternal, immensely intelligent, knowledgable, powerful, spiritual Being — *God.* Since we have established that God sent a message to mankind (the Bible), we will now compare the attributes of God derived scientifically with His attributes found in the Bible.

### 9.5.1 God is infinitely intelligent and omniscient (all-knowing)

The word "infinite" is often used colloquially to describe something that is spatially or temporally very far away. Thus, we say, for example, that something took place *infinitely long ago* to express that it occurred long ago in the past. Our vernacular is not always precise, but in the language of mathematics, where the "infinite" quantities are used, everything must be defined with unambiguous precision in order to perform calculations. Georg Cantor (1845–1918) was the first mathematician who succeeded in constructing a precise, well-defined methodology for working with mathematical infinities — a truly extraordinary achievement.

It is clear that when we speak of God as infinitely intelligent and omniscient, we must leave the realm of the finite. We are in the region of infinity where we can no longer apply the customary logic of comparison, estimation, and evaluation that we know from the finite world. We can say with certainty that no one is above God and for Him there is no question that He must answer with "I don't know." This can be illustrated by several examples in order to grasp the significance of this statement.

God must know precisely every atom, whether inside our sun or within any of the estimated one million million (1 trillion) stars in the Andromeda Galaxy or anywhere else in one of the estimated 170 thousand million galaxies in the known universe. He knows about each grain of sand in the Sahara or on a North Sea beach and that no two grains are the same. God knows the personal details of each human being: shoe size, eye color, number of hairs or cells in the body, the structure of fingerprints, or the chemical processes within each cell of the body. And beyond this, He knows every thought we have ever had and every deed we have ever done or will ever do. We saw this in our example of buying bread rolls in chapter 8. Our free and arbitrary choice was known by God before the creation of the world.

In the same chapter, the explanation of God seeing grandchildren before they were born further highlighted the "infinite" nature of God's knowledge. We referred to Psalm 139:16: "Your eyes saw my unformed body; all the days ordained for me were written in your book before one of them came to be." This is difficult for our finite minds to grasp.

Is it surprising that the Bible tells us that God already knew before the creation of the world that we would exist and whether we would make a personal decision to believe in Him or not? For example, Ephesians 1:4–5 states:

> For He chose us in him before the creation of the world to be holy and blameless in his sight. In love he predestined us for adoption to sonship through Jesus Christ, in accordance with his pleasure and will.

Perhaps we can now understand more easily why John, who wrote the last book of the Bible, could *actually see* and *hear* events that lay in the future:

> Rev. 21:1 "Then I saw a new heaven and a new earth...."
>
> Rev. 21:2 "I saw the Holy City, the new Jerusalem...."
>
> Rev. 21:3 "And I heard a loud voice from the throne saying...."

In the Bible, the words most often used to mean intelligence are "wisdom" and "understanding." Biblical wisdom means more than a high intellectual capacity in one or two areas of life. Divine wisdom is the infinite capacity, knowledge, and expression of Truth. Human wisdom embodies the seeking of Truth in order "... to be conformed to the image of his

Son..." (Rom. 8:29). A few of the verses that proclaim God's infinite intelligence include:

> Psalm 147:5: "Great is our Lord and mighty in power: his **understanding has no limit.**"

> Isaiah 55:8–9: "For my thoughts are not your thoughts, neither are your ways my ways," declares the LORD. 'For as the heavens are higher than the earth so are My ways higher than your ways, and My thoughts than your thoughts.' "

> Romans 11:33: "Oh, the depth of the riches of the wisdom and knowledge of God! How unsearchable his judgments, and his ways beyond tracing out!"

> Romans 8:28: "And we know that in all things God **works for the good** of those who love him, who have been called according to his purpose."

God is infinitely knowing (omniscient); that is, He knows at any instant everything past, present, and future. This includes His unwavering purpose throughout all eternity as well as the evil purposes of His fallen creatures.

> "The eyes of the LORD are everywhere, keeping watch on the wicked and the good" (Proverbs 15:3).

> "Dear children, let us not love with words or speech but with actions and in truth. This is how we know that we belong to the truth and how we set our hearts at rest in his presence: If our hearts condemn us, we know that God is greater than our hearts, and he **knows everything**" (1 John 3:18–20:).

**Therefore, through God's message to mankind (the Bible), we have established that the God who created the universe and all life on earth is infinite in intelligence and knowledge (omniscient).**

*9.5.2 God is omnipotent (infinite creative power)*

In Deduction 3 we logically concluded that the Sender of the UI conveyed in the DNA/RNA Protein Synthesizing System (PSS) must be incomparably powerful. The Bible contains many verses that proclaim God's infinite power. A few examples are listed below.

Genesis 17:1b: "I am God Almighty; walk before me faithfully and be blameless."

Nehemiah 1:10: "And they are your servants and your people, whom you redeemed by your great strength and your mighty hand."

Jeremiah 32:17: "Ah, Sovereign LORD, you have made the heavens and the earth by your great power and outstretched arm. Nothing is too hard for you."

Isaiah 40:12: "Who has measured the waters in the hollow of his hand, or with the breadth of his hand marked off the heavens? Who has held the dust of the earth in a basket, or weighed the mountains on the scales and the hills in a balance? "

Luke 1:37: "For no word from God will ever fail."

Ephesians 1:19a: "… and his incomparably great power for us who believe."

**The extremely powerful "god" discovered through science is now recognized as God with infinite power (omnipotent).**

Since, according to the testimony of the Bible, there is no other god than "the God of Abraham, Isaac, and Jacob" (Exodus 3:15, Matthew 22:32), the "god discovered through science" can be none other than the God of the Bible.

### 9.5.3 God is non-material (spirit)

In Deduction 4 we logically concluded that God must have a non-material component. In the following verse it is clear that God is wholly spirit. John 4:24: "God is spirit, and his worshipers must worship in the Spirit and in truth."

### 9.5.4 God is eternal

Through logical analysis (see chapter 8.4.3), we concluded that God must be eternal (the alternative — that God emerged from nothing — is unacceptable). Furthermore, a non-eternal being requires that he is subject to time, yet as shown before, the Creator of the Universe is the Creator of time, so is not subject to it. We have helped demonstrate what the Bible states in Romans 1:20:

For since the creation of the world His invisible attributes, His eternal power and divine nature, have been clearly seen being understood through what has been made, so that they are without excuse.

It comes as no surprise, then, that many verses in the Bible attest that God is eternal.

Deuteronomy 33:27a: "The eternal God is your refuge, and underneath are the everlasting arms."

Isaiah 44:6: "I am the first and I am the last; apart from me there is no God."

Isaiah 57:15a: "For this is what the high and exalted One says — he who lives forever, whose name is holy…."

Psalm 90:2: "Before the mountains were born or you brought forth the whole world, from everlasting to everlasting you are God."

Revelation 1:8: "I am the Alpha and the Omega," says the Lord God, "who is, and who was, and who is to come, the Almighty."

### 9.5.5 Man has a non-material component

In Deduction 5 we concluded that man must have a non-material component. The Bible also states that humans are not exclusively material.

1 Thessalonians 5:23: "May God himself, the God of peace, sanctify you through and through. May your whole spirit, soul and body be kept blameless at the coming of our Lord Jesus Christ ."

Matthew 10:28: "Do not be afraid of those who kill the body but cannot kill the soul. Rather, be afraid of the One who can destroy both soul and body in hell."

Mark 8:36: "What good is it for someone to gain the whole world, yet forfeit their soul?"

James 2:26: "As the body without the spirit is dead, so faith without deeds is dead."

### 9.5.6 Materialism and the Big Bang are refuted

In Deduction 6 and its corollary, we refuted both materialism and the Big Bang. For thousands of years the Bible has also refuted these materialistic claims by asserting the works of God. Genesis 1:1 states, "In the beginning God created the heavens and the earth." In Genesis 1:2–10 and 14–18 God gives more details about the formation of the earth and heavens.

> Exodus 20:11: "For in six days the LORD made the heavens and the earth, the sea, and all that is in them."

> Romans 1:20: "For since the creation of the world God's invisible attributes — his eternal power and divine nature — have been clearly seen, being understood from what has been made, so that people are without excuse."

> Colossians 1:16: "For in him all things were created: things in heavens and on earth, visible and invisible, whether thrones or powers or rulers or authorities; all things have been created through him and for him."

> Hebrews 11:3: "By faith we understand that the universe was formed at God's command, so that what is seen was not made out of what was visible."

### 9.5.7 Chemical evolution is refuted

In Deduction 7 and its corollary we refuted chemical evolution of the DNA/RNA Protein Synthesizing System (PSS) and all life. The text of the Bible has also refuted the materialistic claims about the origin of life.

> Genesis 1:11: "Then God said, 'Let the land produce vegetation: seed-bearing plants and trees on the land that bear fruit with seed in it, according to their various kinds.' And it was so."

> Genesis 1:20: "And God said, 'Let the water teem with living creatures, and let birds fly above the earth across the vault of the sky.' "

> Genesis 1:24: "And God said, 'Let the land produce living creatures according to their kinds: the livestock, the creatures that move along the ground, and the wild animals, each according to its kind.' And it was so."

Genesis 1:26: "Then God said, 'Let us make man in our image, in our likeness, so that they may rule over the fish in the sea and the birds in the sky, over the livestock and all the wild animals, and over all the creatures that move along the ground.' "

### 9.5.8 Biological evolution is refuted

Materialists claim that the first living cell formed by chemical evolution diversified through mutation and natural selection over eons of time to form all fossilized and living creatures we observe today. This microbe-to-man diversification is called biological evolution. We refuted biological evolution in Deduction 8. Again, the plain message in the Bible clearly does not support biological evolution. In Genesis 1, immediately after God spoke:

Genesis 1:12–13: "The land produced vegetation: plants bearing seed according to their kinds and trees bearing fruit with seed in it according to their kinds. And God saw that it was good. And there was evening, and there was morning — the third day."

Genesis 1:21–23: "So God created the great creatures of the sea and every living thing with which the water teems and that moves about in it, according to their kinds, and every winged bird according to its kind. And God saw that it was good. God blessed them and said, 'Be fruitful and increase in number and fill the water in the seas, and let the birds increase on the earth.' And there was evening, and there was morning — the fifth day."

Genesis 1:25: "God made the wild animals according to their kinds, the livestock according to their kinds, and all the creatures that move along the ground according to their kinds. And God saw that it was good."

Genesis 1:27, 31: "God created man in His own image, in the image of God He created him; male and female He created them … God saw all that He had made, and behold it was very good. And there was evening and there was morning, the sixth day."

Like our argument in chapter 8, the Bible also states that God created all of the original kinds of life. In addition, the Bible tells us that God did this on days 3, 5, and 6 of Creation Week.

## 9.6 Examining UI attributes in the Bible

### 9.6.1 God as Sender, Man as receiver

In chapter 2, we discussed the five levels of Universal Information — statistics, syntax, semantics, pragmatics, and apobetics. As we will demonstrate in this section, it is highly instructive to examine the Bible with the four distinguishing attributes of UI in mind. Additionally, it will be helpful to have a Bible available while reading these sections in order to study the context of the referenced verses.

**Sender:** In Figure 33, God, through His Son, is shown as the Source or Original Sender of biblical information. His Word is available to us today in completed form (Rev. 22:18), and written form (e.g., Exod. 17:14, Ezek. 37:16, 1 Cor. 9:10, and Rev. 1:11). The words of the Bible came to us in many different ways (Heb. 1:1–2). The following 10 points demonstrate the wide spectrum of God's choice of methods in speaking to us:

- audibly (Exod. 19:19, Matt. 3:17)
- by His own handwriting (Exod. 31:18)
- through angels (Luke 2:10–12, Heb. 2:2)
- through prophets (Jer. 1:5, Heb. 1:1)
- through dreams (Dan. 2, Matt. 1:20)
- through visions (Ezek. 1:1)
- through Apostles (Acts 1:2)
- through inspiration (2 Tim. 3:16)
- through revelation (Gal. 1:12, Eph. 3:3, Rev. 1:1)
- through Jesus Christ, the Son of God (Heb. 1:2)

Even where God uses people to serve Him to convey (transmit) His message, He remains the original Sender and we are the receivers. All opinions that assume a mere human source for the origin of the Bible are missing the real point, despite the eloquence of their theological presentation. This question about the identity of the original Sender becomes the touchstone for belief and unbelief and thus for life and death.

The well-known preacher C.H. Spurgeon (1834–1892) states that the Sender's identity is also manifested by His power [S10]: "Our own words are mere paper darts compared to the heavy artillery of God's Word." Although the Bible speaks about heavenly, spiritual, and divine

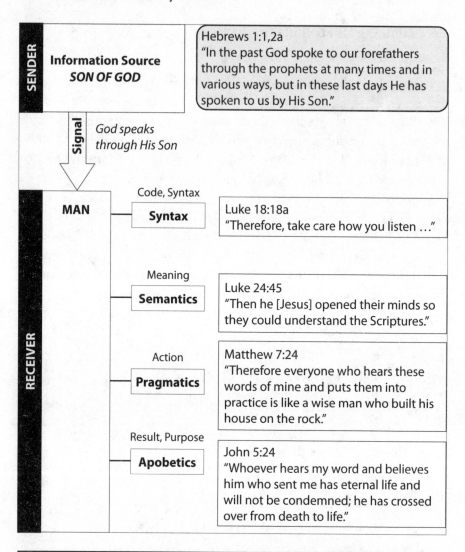

Figure 33: God as Sender, man as receiver. When God speaks in the Bible, we are dealing with the original Sender of Universal Information. The message of the Bible, directed to us as receivers, can be analyzed according to the various levels of information, particularly syntax, semantics, pragmatics, and apobetics. Only when we cover all of the distinguishing attributes will we have reached God's intended purpose.

matters, it is encoded in reasonable words (Acts 26:25), in human language (i.e., Universal Information), and not in inexpressible heavenly terms (2 Cor. 12:4). We will now consider the various attributes of UI with respect to the Bible:

1. **Statistics:** The only value of statistical analyses of the Bible is for transmission and storage purposes (see Appendix 1, A1.2.1 and Figure 41). In addition, counts of word frequencies are of use in certain analyses.

2. **Syntax:** God's message is available to us encoded in human language — originally in Hebrew, Greek, and a small portion in Aramaic. In principle, this message can be translated into any other natural language, and recently into binary machine languages. All over the world many missionaries perform the beneficent service of translation so that the message of salvation can be proclaimed in all living languages. They are fulfilling Jesus' prophetic promise that all nations will have heard the gospel message before His Second Coming (Matt. 24:14).

3. **Semantics:** The contents of the Bible make it a unique book that cannot be compared with any other book. The Bible provides answers to all the vital questions on earth, and it is the only sure compass to guide us to eternity. Philosophers, founders of religions, and scientists of all disciplines have written thousands of books trying to solve such great puzzles as: What is the origin of the universe, of earth and of life? What is man? Does man have a purpose? Who is God? Is there life after death? No one is able to make authoritative, conclusive, and true statements about these questions. Only the Bible can do this on the authority and by the truth of the living God. A source of knowledge as valuable as the Bible should be readily available and earnestly taught to *all* students. If we want to understand the semantics of the Bible, we must identify some fundamental differences that distinguish it from other books:

*Scientific insight*: The actual science statements given have proven to be true whenever we have been in a position to confirm them. For instance, in Job 38, God challenges Job regarding two star groups: Orion and the Pleiades. In line with the references made there, in the last hundred years it has been confirmed that Orion is disrupting at enormous speeds but that the Pleiades are gravitationally bound together. Job could not have known this. Only God, at that time, could have known this.

It is also useful to employ linguistic understanding as well as historical and cultural background information for a better understanding of the text. Nevertheless, even with the highest learning, the essence of the message may remain hidden. Therefore, we emphasize that the so-called "higher literary criticism" is an inadequate approach for understanding the Bible.

*Spiritual understanding:* A good part of it is simply the recordings of eyewitnesses to historical events which took place during the time they lived. That history was under the control of God. The Bible also contains books referred to as "poetry," such as the Psalms. These poetic books contain a lot of personal remarks, but interspersed with that are some parts that could only be inspired by the Holy Spirit, for they speak of spiritual matters. The prophetic books (Old Testament) and letters to the churches (New Testament) all show identifiable inspiration from God through His Holy Spirit. In the same way, understanding it is also a spiritual process requiring the collaboration of the Holy Spirit. Therefore, the presence of the indwelling Holy Spirit is essential for a true understanding of the words in the Bible.

*Personal attitude:* The Lord opens the Scriptures by way of the indwelling Holy Spirit to those who are genuinely seeking (Matt. 7:7, Luke 24:25) and are obedient (2 Cor. 10:5). Access is denied to those who regard themselves as wise; those who are arrogant and hard of heart exclude themselves (Exod. 4:21, Isa. 6:9–10, Ezek. 2:4, Matt. 13:15 and John 7:17–18).

*Biblical concepts:* The overall expression of biblical content is easy to understand (2 Cor. 1:13). Jesus used many parables[5] to illustrate difficult spiritual relationships.

When one reads philosophical treatises, legal expositions, or political declarations, one too often gains the impression that more things are obscured than are explained. On the other hand, the Bible is composed in such a way that a child can understand its fundamental assertions and be encouraged by it. The only condition is that the heart must be open,

---

5. Parables: It should be mentioned that the parables also have an exactly opposite function. There are people for whom the parables become a judgment: *"For this people's heart has become calloused; they hardly hear with their ears"* (Matt. 13:15). The effect the parables have depends on one's attitude: *"The knowledge of the secrets of the kingdom of God has been given to you, but to others I speak in parables"* (Luke 8:10). *"For whoever has will be given more, and they will have an abundance. Whoever does not have, even what they have will be taken from them"* (Matt. 25:29).

then the following verse applies: "But blessed are your eyes because they see, and your ears because they hear" (Matt. 13:16).

Of course, there are also difficult passages in the Bible. God explains to us why this is the case in verses such as Isaiah 55:8–9:

> "My thoughts are not your thoughts, neither are your ways my ways," declares the LORD. "As the heavens are higher than the earth, so are my ways higher than your ways and my thoughts than your thoughts."

There will be passages we may not understand now, but their meaning will be revealed when, for example, the prophetically designated time has arrived.

*Fullness of ideas:* The English Bible (KJV) contains 783,173 words, a number that is limited, but the scope of its ideas is unbounded. In exceptional cases one might read a secular book two or three times to know its contents fully. However, the Bible is inexhaustible, and even at the hundredth reading new thoughts and relationships come to light. After many years of intensive Bible study, Spurgeon testified [S10]:

> The copiousness of God's Word is just as unbounded as its comprehensiveness. During the forty years of my own ministry, I have merely touched the hem of the garment of divine truth but what power flowed out from it! The Word resembles its Originator: boundless, immeasurable, and infinite. If it were your task to preach throughout eternity, you would always find a theme on whatever topic may be required.

*Inexhaustible:* The semantic wealth of the Bible is so great that no human life is long enough to exhaust it. However, a single thread (the continual attestation of Jesus; see John 5:39) runs through the entire Bible to unite the multitude of thoughts into one.

4. **Pragmatics:** If the receiver (man) sets aside the message received from the Sender (God) at the semantic level, then God's intended purpose for the receiver will be missed. The goal of Universal Information in the Bible is that man should be moved to action. Jesus placed an extremely high premium on this attribute of UI: "Therefore everyone who hears these words of mine and puts them into practice is like a wise man

who built his house on the rock" (Matt. 7:24). Without deeds, the Word becomes a judgment upon us. This aspect is expounded in the parable of the ten "minas" (talents), where Jesus gives the clear command: "Put this money to work ... until I come back" (Luke 19:13). The obedient servants are amply rewarded; He says to the first one: "Well done, my good servant! ... Because you have been trustworthy in a very small matter, take charge of ten cities" (Luke 19:17). The one who does nothing, is condemned: "I will judge you by your own words, you wicked servant! You knew, did you, that I am a hard man, taking out what I did not put in, and reaping what I did not sow?" (Luke 19:22). Our deeds are judged by God (Rev. 20:12). According to Matthew 25:31–46, Jesus will judge between two groups of people only: those who acted, and those who did nothing. The first group will be invited into heaven: "Come, you who are blessed by my Father; take your inheritance, the kingdom prepared for you since the creation of the world" with the reason "Whatever you did for one of the least of these brothers and sisters of mine, you did for me" (Matt. 25:34, 40). The second group is sent into the eternal fire because, "Whatever you did not do for one of the least of these, you did not do for me" (Matt. 25:45b).

The message in James 1:22 is clear in this regard: "Do not merely listen to the word, and so deceive yourselves. Do what it says." Heinrich Kemner (1903–1993) rightly said that in the last judgment we will mostly be found guilty for what we did *not* do. "If anyone, then, knows the good he ought to do and doesn't do it, it is sin for them" (James 4:17). Also in the Old Testament Moses, on God's behalf, declares the pragmatic instruction on which life depends:

> Take to heart all the words I have solemnly declared to you this day, so that you may command your children to obey carefully all the words of this law. They are not just idle words for you — they are your life (Deut. 32:46–47).

We now use the following illustrative example of a correct pragmatic attitude towards the Bible: A blind African woman in her seventies had a French Bible that she loved very much. She took it to the local missionary and asked him to highlight John 3:16 in red. This he did without knowing her purpose. The blind woman then sat at the school gate and asked the emerging pupils whether any of them knew French. Being proud of their knowledge of the language, they answered in the affirmative. The woman then showed them the underlined verse and asked them to read it for her. They complied eagerly. However, when she asked them whether they *understood* these words the answer was No! The woman then explained the meaning of this central biblical verse: "For God so loved the world that he gave his one and only Son, that whoever believes in Him shall not perish but have eternal life." It is known that 24 men became evangelists through the ministry of this woman [J2].

5. **Apobetics:** From the sender's point of view, the transfer of Universal Information has been successfully completed only when his intended purpose has been achieved by the receiver's performed action. All aspects of UI are inextricably interlinked. It is not enough if everything at the lower levels is correct but the top level, the goal, is not reached. Strictly speaking, each lower level is only the means to the end, namely, the next higher level: language is solely a means for expressing the meaning (semantics). In turn, the purpose of semantics is pragmatics, and in the final analysis, pragmatics is only a necessary link to apobetics. In chapter 2.7 this purpose-orientation of UI is described as its most important attribute. This is especially true of God's message in the Bible. God outlines certain objectives in the Bible, some of which we want to highlight:

a) *Biblical insight: Who is God?* Without the Bible we would know very little about God. We can deduce His existence, intelligence, and power from His works of creation (Rom. 1:20) but little more would be known about His *person* or His nature. The Bible thus has the purpose of making God known to us. The Bible makes it clear that all human polytheistic conceptions are false: "I am the LORD, and there is no other; apart from me there is no God" (Isa. 45:5). "God is love" (1 John 4:16), "life" (1 John 5:20), and "light" (1 John 1:5); He is Holy (Isa. 6:3) and hates sin so much that it carries the penalty of death (Rom. 6:23). The Bible abundantly informs us about God's Son and His function as Savior, and about the Holy Spirit who guides us into all the truth. Jesus is the only way to God. In the words of Martin Luther: "If you do not find God through Christ you will never find Him, wherever else you may seek."

b) *Biblical insight: Creation has a purpose.* When we read the first two chapters of the Bible, we see that the creation was systematically and purposefully planned and executed. Man is depicted as the pinnacle of creation. Seen in the light of the Bible — always wholly filled with purpose — statements from men, such as the following by Nietzsche, are empty and far from reality: "Between animal and superman is a rope. Man is this rope, stretched across an abyss" (Nietzsche in *Thus Spake Zarathustra*). According to the New Testament, however, everything was created by and for Christ (Col. 1:16).

c) *Biblical insight: Who is man?* The Nobel laureate Alexis Carrel wrote a book with the title, *Man the Unknown.* On our own we are not able to fathom who we really are; without the Bible our true nature would remain a mystery. The well-known German author Manfred Hausmann (1898–1986) testified as follows:

> Every time I open the Bible, I am astounded anew by its depth and many-sidedness. The picture it draws of man is nowhere else to be found. It encompasses man in his entirety, his greatness and his wickedness, his tenderness and brutality, his glory and his disgrace. No other book reveals such sublime and such disturbing things about human nature than does the Bible. The profundity of Bible stories is unfathomable.

We learn from the Bible that all have turned away from God through sin and, because of this, deserve death and hell. We all need to be redeemed from this verdict. The religions encourage us to jump over our shadows and save ourselves. On the road to certain condemnation, we are met by the One who is sin's antidote, Jesus! If we understand ourselves in this light, then we know who we truly are.

d) *Biblical handbook for life:* God has prepared the best goals (Rom. 8:28–29) and greatest blessings conceivable for our earthly life; He is concerned about our welfare in marriage, in our family, our career, and our nation, and desires to bless us with spiritual fruit in everything so that it may be said of us: "Whatever they do prospers" (Ps. 1:3). God wants the best for us. The promises in this direction are uncountable. The upright will receive sound wisdom (Prov. 2:7), those who wait for the Lord will be strengthened (Isa. 40:31), and all who come to Him and are weary and burdened will find rest (Matt. 11:28). There is only one answer to the question of why God does this, namely, "I have loved you with an ever-lasting love" (Jer. 31:3). No machine will work properly, as intended by the designer, if the instruction manual is disregarded. How much more then do we drive our lives to ruin if we disregard the Creator's instructions for life? This type of information can be regarded as *operational* UI according to chapter 5.9.2. The Bible is the only handbook for a blessed and fulfilled life; the condition is expressed in short: *"By living according to your Word"* (Ps. 119:9).

e) *Biblical signpost to heaven:* The highest purpose ever formulated for mankind is that God desires *eternal communion* with each one of us. Earthly blessings are only a minute foretaste compared with the richness of eternity. We are invited guests of heaven. The suffering and death of Jesus paid the price in full for human sin so that those who believe in Him may not be lost. Now, anyone may get into the lifeboat to reach the other shore because God does not want sinners to be condemned, "but rather that they turn from their ways and live" (Ezek. 33:11). God presented the Lord Jesus to be trusted as Savior (Rom. 3:25). Everyone who calls on Him (Rom. 10:13) and entrusts his life to Him (John 1:12) has crossed over from the death penalty of sin to eternal life (John 5:24). The way to heaven is just as simple as it is sure: The Bible is the *only* compass, and Jesus is the *only* way. Anyone who turns to Jesus is saved. He then becomes a child of God and at the same time heir to heaven (Titus 3:7). This decision cannot be postponed. Hermann Bezzel once said: "The pardoning power of grace is unlimited, but it has its moment." The following anecdote illustrates this.

> After every sermon a missionary called on the congregation to choose Jesus. When urged to repent, a certain native who had attended regularly for several years always responded with, "Next year!" One day he became seriously ill and the missionary brought him the required medicine with the prescription that it should be taken one year later. The native said that he might be dead before that time and needed the medicine right now. The missionary replied, "You care for your body, but what about your soul?"

Many people set goals for their lives and then worry that the investment may be in vain. Our lives have attained their highest purpose when we yield them to God; then all searching becomes unnecessary because it is fulfilled. Spurgeon once uttered the striking words [S9]: "Man's heart has only enough life to pursue one goal fully. No one can serve both God and mammon because there is not enough life in one's heart to serve both."

Figure 34 depicts a striking example from the Bible of how someone comes to faith. All distinguishing attributes of Universal Information are covered, one after the other, in a very succinct manner. This Ethiopian treasurer is a good example of someone finding Christ and salvation through understanding Scripture.

*The parable of the sower:* Another easily understood example of the attributes of UI is found in the parable of the sower (Matt. 13:3–23). In this parable, Jesus uses a common occurrence of everyday life to illustrate and explain aspects of the Kingdom of God. At the semantic level the information is complete and clear. The effect of God's words (the seeds) results in four different kinds of conduct (pragmatics) on the side of the receivers. As a result, the purpose intended by the Sender (Jesus) is achieved in only one group of receivers (God's purpose becomes their pragmatics).

### 9.6.2 Man as sender, God as Receiver

Figures 33 and 34 illustrate the case where God is the Sender and man the receiver. The question arises whether these functions could be interchanged so that man is the sender and God the Receiver of the UI.

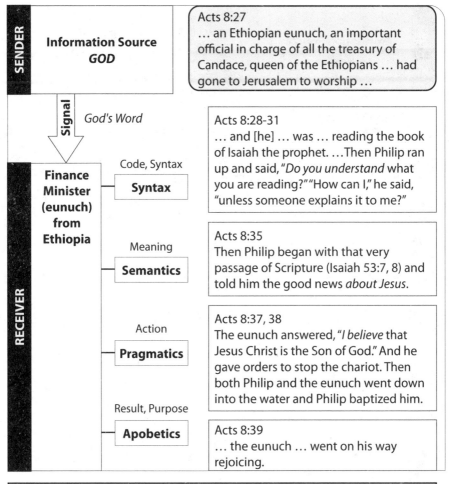

Figure 34: God's Word as Sender; the seeking man as receiver. A special case of the sender–receiver view in Figure 33 is shown here. The example of the Ethiopian Minister of Finance provides a striking overview of the successive levels of Universal Information transfer (Acts 8:26–39). The message of the Bible reached him and touched him; he came to believe in Jesus Christ and thus received eternal life. This Ethiopian is a good example for us.

Indeed, as shown in Figure 35, not only is it conceivable but it is also God's desire and purpose. We may approach God the Father or His Son Jesus with all kinds of goals. The message is transmitted through prayer and this transmission system is vastly superior to any conceivable technological communications system:

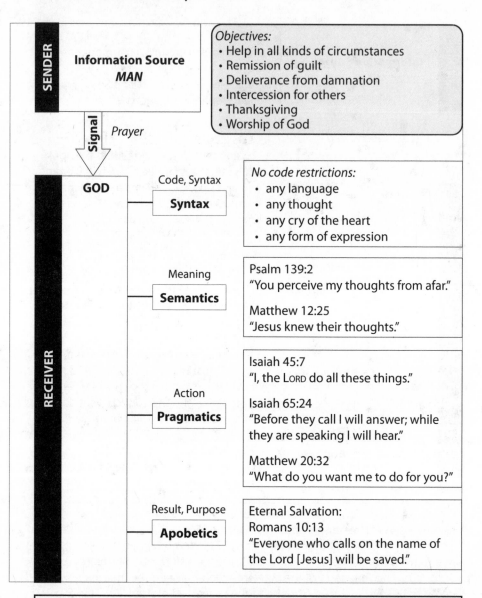

Figure 35: Man as sender, God as Receiver. Compared to man's technology, the information transmission system from man to God is superlative, the best available: any and every message from the sender reaches the Receiver without distortion or loss. No meanings are misunderstood and the pragmatics and the apobetics are guaranteed according to God's divine promises.

- It is the most secure connection possible because no one and no process can break this link. It is always and immediately operational.

- This "wireless communication" cannot be blocked or shielded by anything. When the astronauts circled the moon, no radio contact with earth was possible when they were behind the moon. However, we can pray anywhere, regardless of whether we are 1,000 meters underground, 10,000 meters under the sea, or behind the moon, the message reaches the Receiver (God) with absolute certainty.

- Interference is encountered in all technological transmission systems so that the original message may be distorted by external influences. Code symbols may be lost or changed, but prayer messages cannot be distorted at all — they reach the Receiver unchanged.

The information transmission system from man to God is thus absolutely the best that is possible. It will only be surpassed in heaven when faith is replaced by face-to-face communion. We now discuss the distinguishing attributes of UI from God's standpoint:

**1. Syntax:** At this level there is no restriction of codes because God understands all languages. No language poses a problem to God — not the most complex indigenous language or any tonal language. Every conceivable method of expression, even if only a deep "sigh," is decoded by God. He can even "read" unformulated thoughts.

**2. Semantics:** The Psalmist said to God: "You perceive my thoughts from afar" (Ps. 139:2). In other words, the process of understanding our thoughts is absolutely guaranteed. There can be no semantic misunderstandings. Even if our verbal formulations are off the mark, God understands what we really mean (1 Sam. 16:7: "the LORD looks at the heart"). At the semantic level, there is also a further escalation: The Holy Spirit compensates for the weaknesses and defects of the UI sent by us: "The Spirit helps us in our weakness. We do not know what we ought to pray for, but the Spirit himself intercedes for us through wordless groans" (Rom. 8:26).

**3. Pragmatics:** God is described in the Bible as a God of deeds: "I, the LORD, do all these things" (Isa. 45:7). It is clear from the creation account how much God's words are deeds, so that the Bible could carry the subtitle: "The great deeds of God." Jesus' life on earth was a unique life of witnessing through deeds. He not only preached with authority, He also acted at every conceivable opportunity: He healed those who were ill, He raised people from the dead, He forgave sins, He exorcised demons, He fed large crowds, and He controlled the storm. Eyewitnesses cried out in amazement: "Who is this? Even the wind and the waves obey Him!" (Mark 4:41). However, His greatest deed was the salvation He accomplished on Calvary, which God had already prophesied through Isaiah: "You have burdened me with your sins and wearied me with your offences" (Isa. 43:24). Today the power of forgiveness reaches out to all sinners. No one needs to be lost. We only have to turn to the One who is invested with the authority, Jesus Christ. He has never turned anyone away who prayed to Him sincerely. God always answers our prayers in the way that is best for us. He knows the right moment better than we; He knows the best solution for us.

But there is one prayer that He always answers immediately; there is no delay and no better solution; it is the prayer of a sinner for salvation. Whoever believes and calls on the name of Jesus for this purpose is accepted immediately (Rom. 10:13). There is no delay between call and answer, not even one millisecond: "Before they call I will answer; while they are still speaking I will hear" (Isa. 65:24). When the criminal on the cross turned to the Son of God and asked Him: "Jesus, remember me when you come into your kingdom," he was immediately given the unconditional and instantly effective promise: "Truly I tell you, today you will be with me in Paradise" (Luke 23:42–43).

**4. Apobetics:** In the Lord's Prayer, God gives us goals that correspond to His purposes: "Your will be done" (Matt. 6:10). It is God's will to bring everyone to salvation: He "wants all people to be saved" (1 Tim. 2:4). God identifies Himself with our goals when they correspond with His Word. Dietrich Bonhoeffer (1906–1945) once said that although God does not fulfill all our wishes, He does fulfill all of His countless promises. Do we know how many there are? There are, approximately, an astonishing 1,260 promises from God in the Bible! In addition, there are thousands of aids for our daily life situations (Ps. 50:15). His main concern is our eternal life: "His eternal purpose that He accomplished in Christ Jesus our Lord" (Eph. 3:11). He has achieved His purpose for us when Jesus becomes Lord and Master of all areas of our life. Then we "are no longer foreigners and strangers, but fellow citizens with God's people and also members of his household, built on the foundation of the apostles and prophets, with Christ Jesus himself as the chief cornerstone" (Eph. 2:19–20). Without Jesus we will drift past life's main purpose — the Bible emphatically warns against this (Col. 2:18, Heb. 2:1).

### 9.6.3 The highest packing density of information

The statistical density of Universal Information is discussed in Appendix 1. We see there that the highest-known packing density is attained in the DNA molecules of living cells. It is legitimate also to ask about the UI density at the other levels of UI. Without recourse to actual numerical calculations, we now consider some estimates for the Bible.

**1. The density of semantic information:** This can be defined as the abundant number of ideas or the weight of the meaning per sentence or per paragraph. For example, the origin of man and of this world has been discussed in many scientific and popular publications. No one knows how many books have been written on the origin of man. However, most publications treat the subject from an evolutionary viewpoint, and so no one can provide genuine answers to these important questions. It is noteworthy that the Bible describes man's origin completely in one single verse: "Then the LORD God formed a man from the dust of the ground and breathed into his nostrils the breath of life, and the man became a living being" (Gen. 2:7). These few words comprise remarkable UI content since they provide answers to many questions:

• Man did not develop through a chance process of evolution, but he was purposefully formed by a personal Creator.

• Contrary to all statements to this effect, man did not descend from some animal; he was created separately.

• One single man was created originally.

• Man does not consist of matter and information only, but he received a vital non-material component, a spirit, through God's breath.

• He became a living being through the union of the material and the non-material parts.

The saying "Truth does not need many words, but a lie cannot use enough" receives meaningful acclaim here. In spite of its semantic fullness, the

290 • Information: The Key to Life

Bible verse quoted above (Gen. 2:7) requires amazingly few code symbols. No other description of man's origin is so true and at the same time formulated so concisely. We may deduce that what we have here represents the highest possible semantic information density. Other passages in the Bible also exhibit superlative semantic densities (e.g., John 3:16 contains nearly all the information necessary for man's salvation).

**2. The pragmatic density of information:** This can be measured in terms of the effect produced by input prompted by some transmitted Universal Information. For example, earning one single entry in the Guinness Book of Records [G23] usually requires some sort of highly intense effort. How short-lived is this dubious fame when, for example, the record for eating 96 fried sausages in 4 minutes and 29 seconds [G23] is soon broken? Many human deeds that served only self-made goals were insignificant and have long since been forgotten.

The Bible directs our thoughts in an entirely different direction. Everything we do in the name of Jesus (Col. 3:17) is eternally meaningful. Even the offer of a cup of cold water will have eternal value and will be rewarded (Matt. 10:42). Where will you get such a stupendous reward for such a simple deed? Such results are only found in the Bible. Paul compares the acts of a Christian working in the name of Jesus with an athlete. Athletes compete for "a crown that will not last, but we do it to get a crown that will last forever" (1 Cor. 9:25). We thus have another superlative, namely, the highest possible pragmatic information density.

**3. Apobetic information density:** This is a measure of the succinctness and clarity of purpose attained from the transmitted UI. The following episode from the time of the Spartans describes various apobetic information densities.

When there was famine in one of the regions ruled by the Spartans, the local residents dispatched an eloquent messenger to Sparta. The Spartans listened silently to the messenger's long and, in his own opinion, convincing speech asking for a gift of wheat. The Spartans, however, dismissed him empty-handed: they had forgotten his introduction and thus did not understand the conclusion. Another messenger, sent soon afterwards, had a different approach. He brought an empty sack which he opened for everyone to see and said concisely: "This sack is empty, please put some wheat in it!" This messenger obtained the desired wheat. But the Spartans commented that he was too verbose! It was obvious that the bag was empty and needed to be filled; he should use fewer words when he came again.

This episode illustrates that the first messenger did not attain his purpose in spite of the meaningful contents of his speech, while the second one was immediately successful with his concise but striking UI input. We thus have two distinct densities of apobetic information, and the suggestion of the Spartans to the second speaker would have resulted in an even higher value.

When considering ourselves as receivers of the Bible's message we can obtain the highest possible apobetic density of UI. We refer to one verse, namely John 3:36: "Whoever believes in the Son has eternal life, but whoever rejects the Son will not see life, for God's wrath remains on them." This concise piece of UI with its overwhelming depth of meaning could only appear in the Bible (high semantic information density). Just as overwhelming is the stated purpose: *eternal life!* Nothing has greater value — in the words of Jesus, the whole world is worthless in contrast (Matt. 16:26) — so anybody who has entrusted himself in faith to Jesus has achieved the *highest possible apobetic information* density.

**Should you sense a drawing to come to Christ at this moment, please turn to the Epilogue, page 325.**

# PART SIX

# Questions and Answers

*Chapter 10*

# FREQUENTLY ASKED QUESTIONS ABOUT THE THEORY OF UNIVERSAL INFORMATION

My talks at universities and technical institutes (see "Scientific lectures" p. 417) are usually followed by lively discussions with many questions. Below are some of the most common questions asked and my answers. At my lectures, most questions about UI can be answered reasonably briefly. The first 2 questions are of this type. Following these are two others (questions 23 and 24) to which the answers are considerably more lengthy.

## 10.1 Questions with brief answers

**Q1**: Was your talk a modern-day proof of the existence of God? (This question is usually accompanied by the statement: "Kant's philosophy has refuted all proofs of God's existence; there is no need to think further about it!")

**A1**: Immanuel Kant, like me, was born in East Prussia but I completely disagree with him. I believe that it is possible to present a scientifically and logically sound argument — more precisely, a scientific *proof*, to the extent that science is able to prove anything — that establishes God's existence.

Kant lived from 1724 to 1804 and, compared with today, had very little scientific knowledge at his disposal. He certainly did not know about the scientific laws of Universal Information nor about the massive amounts of Universal Information in every cell of our bodies.[1] This present-day scientific knowledge allows us to deduce very far-reaching conclusions. We presented, at the highest level of scientific certainty, four deductions that confirm the existence of God (chapter 8). We logically concluded that God exists and that He is eternal, non-material, infinitely intelligent, all-knowing, and all-powerful. But even without the scientific laws of Universal Information, the Bible has told us for two thousand years that we should be able to conclude from God's works that He exists: "For since the creation of the world God's invisible qualities — his eternal power and divine nature — have been clearly seen, being understood through what has been made, so that people are without excuse" (Rom. 1:20).

**Q2**: Do your assertions refute the doctrine of evolution?

**A2:** Scientific laws tell us what inevitably happens under certain conditions; they can be viewed as indirectly "forbidding" the opposite. For instance, the laws of thermodynamics "forbid" the development of a perpetual motion machine. In a like manner, SLI-2 and SLI-3 are also scientific laws that forbid the creation of Universal Information from unguided purely physical, chemical processes and "chance" events. In addition, concise formulations of these laws provide materialists with the opportunity to easily falsify them by creating UI through unguided purely physical-chemical processes. Despite immense efforts for over 150 years, they have failed to accomplish this. As we demonstrated in Deductions 6, 7, and 8 (chapter 8), the scientific laws of UI and scientific facts about the PSS have refuted the assumptions of materialism and its corollaries, the doctrines of cosmic, chemical, and biological evolution.

**Q3:** The criteria for information seem to be mostly subjective.

**A3:** Yes, the criteria for information may seem subjective because there are several definitions for information. However, our criteria for Universal Information are based upon careful observation of human natural and machine languages. We began by observing and establishing a hierarchy of five levels, the lowest being statistical with progressively higher levels,

---

1. Apart from our red blood cells, of course, which do not retain their nucleus (with its DNA) to maturity.

i.e., syntactic, semantic, pragmatic, and apobetic. Further study revealed that the upper four levels are *distinguishing* attributes that together unambiguously define Universal Information. Therefore, the definition of Universal Information (UI) is: *A symbolically encoded, abstractly represented message conveying the expected action(s) and the intended purpose(s).*

**Q4**: Is it information when I am both sender and receiver at the same time? For example, when I shout next to a mountain and hear the echo.

**A4**: In this case you did not plan to provide yourself with information and at most it would be a transient copy. However, there are typical situations where you are both the sender and receiver, like making notes for yourself, entries in a diary or into a day planner.

**Q5**: Would a photograph be Universal Information according to your definition?

**A5**: No! Although the substitutive function (chapter 3.5, Example 9) is present, it is not abstract because the picture resembles the actual person or thing. Also, there is no syntax (i.e., an abstract code with syntactical rules).

**Q6**: Is Universal Information created when lottery numbers are drawn? If so, could that be regarded as Universal Information created by chance?

**A6**: No! The Universal Information resides in the rules of the game; they comprise a fixed strategy that includes apobetics (purpose), namely to win. The actual drawing of numbers is a random process belonging to Domain C (Figure 15, chapter 3.4). We do have Universal Information, though, when the results of the draw are communicated orally or in writing.

**Q7**: Is there a conservation law for Universal Information similar to the Law of the Conservation of Energy?[2]

**A7**: No. Universal Information written with chalk on a blackboard may be erased. A manuscript for a book with many new ideas written painstakingly over several years will be irrevocably lost if the author and the only copy of the manuscript are destroyed in a fire. When a computer disk containing a voluminous text is reformatted (erased), all of the Universal

---

2. When one hears of a "Law of Conservation of Information" (e.g., as in William Dembski's book, *No Free Lunch*, p. 167–173), this is not referring to Universal Information (UI) but rather to information from a statistical, material perspective.

Information is also lost, unless it has been backed up. On the other hand, new Universal Information can be created continuously through creative thought processes (ES 29: chapter 5.8.2).

**Q8**: Does Universal Information have anything to do with entropy as stated in the Second Law of Thermodynamics?

**A8**: No. The Second Law of Thermodynamics is only valid for the world of matter (the lower level in Figure 24, chapter 5.11), but Universal Information is a non-material entity (SLI-1 in chapter 5.5) — it is, however, stored and transmitted by means of material media. This material medium is subject to the Second Law of Thermodynamics and the Universal Information that it conveys will be degraded as the material medium degrades. Also, there is a concept called "configurational entropy" that is on the statistical level of Shannon's information, but this "entropy" is not the same as what is known as entropy in physics.[3]

That having been said, there is a *connection* between Universal Information, physical entropy, human engineering, and life. This connection is the fact that in living things UI is essential for designing and constructing the biomachines that maintain a state far removed from thermodynamic equilibrium. This is a very important area that needs further research.[4]

**Q9**: Natural languages are changing all the time. Doesn't this contradict your thesis that coding conventions should be conserved?

**A9**: Once a code system is developed by the formation of a symbol set and syntax, it must be strictly adhered to. While new words and phrases arise continuously — e.g., skateboards, roller blades, wind surfing, paragliding, etc. — all of them obey the existing code system, perform a real function, and meet a very specific need. There is a consensus about their meaning, and nobody would confuse a roller blade with a switchblade or

---

3. See C.B. Thaxton, W.L. Bradley, and R.L. Olsen, *The Mystery of Life's Origin*, Philosophical Library Inc., New York, 1984, Ch. 8, www.ldolphin.org/mystery/chapt8.html. They use a modified form of Shannon's statistical information to differentiate three types of sequences: random, ordered, and specified complex. Their version of statistical information gain equates to a reduction in configurational entropy, also defined statistically.

4. After these ideas were first developed, A.C. McIntosh published a highly informative paper "Information and entropy — top-down or bottom-up development in living systems?" *Int. J. of Design & Nature and Ecodynamics*, 4(4):351–385, 2009. This paper independently arrived at conclusions that, from a thermodynamics approach, are similar to some of the conclusions deduced in this book. Dr. McIntosh is Professor of Thermodynamics and Combustion Theory at the University of Leeds, UK (NB: "Professor" in a British Commonwealth university is a title given only to the highest rank of lecturer).

paragliding with paramedical. In every case, the syntax and semantics of the language continues to be strictly followed. In short, while languages are certainly dynamic — involving continuous additions, deletions, and modifications — we observe that the fundamental mechanism and infrastructure for constructions within that language (namely, its syntax) remains mostly unchanged. This is out of necessity since altering the syntax would propagate throughout the entire language, including the vocabulary that has been acquired over long periods of time.

**Q10:** Are synergetics,[5] founded by the German physicist Hermann Haken, an indication that order can emerge from disorder and thus that evolution would be possible?

**A10:** Haken always cites the same examples for the creation of ordered structures. Following one of his lectures, I asked him whether he could *store* (i.e., *maintain)* these ordered structures — his answer was negative. In order to store the state of a system, one would need UI. Since pragmatics is nowhere to be found in an unguided purely physical system, any order will collapse when the necessary environmental conditions (e.g., thermal gradient and temperature distribution) are removed. Rather, these structures merely reflect the *Curie Asymmetry Principle:*[6] these exhibit a *reduction in the symmetry that is already present in the underlying cause.* For example, an isotropic system has no asymmetry by definition; adding a heat source introduces asymmetry, such as a preferred direction. This can set up convection cells that reflect this asymmetry, and disappear when the cause of the asymmetry (the heat source) is removed.

Expanding on this, synergetics is wrong on two fronts: first, even allowing for ordered structures to be produced via solely physical-chemical processes, the "order" of these structures does not have the complexity, interconnections with other structures, or the specific function that is needed for life. In other words, they have a low amount of statistical information and are totally missing the other levels of UI. The second point is yet more important: even if we granted that the necessary structures emerged, these structures would need a mechanism for passing

---

5. **Synergetics** attempts to explain the formation and self-organization of patterns and structures in open systems that are far from thermodynamic equilibrium — living organisms are such systems. Self-organization implies a reduction in the degrees of freedom of a system and this translates into an increase of "order" leading to the formation of patterns. With this, synergetics supposedly explains the self-organization of patterns in different systems within physics, chemistry, and biology.
6. After the Nobel Laureate French physicist Pierre Curie (1859–1906).

from one generation to the next. We know this mechanism as the genetic code (and its associated machinery) and synergetics does not begin to explain how this might originate via solely material processes.

In passing, it should be mentioned here that Ilya Prigogine's "dissipative structures" — also suggested as a natural, unguided mechanism that would explain a purely material origin of life and evolution — fails for exactly the same reasons as those discussed above for synergetics.

In short, while synergetics may account for some ordered structures, these would be no more than relatively trivial components for life. Synergetics is nowhere near being able to provide the sufficient conditions for life.

**Q11:** What is your view of the Miller experiments that are cited as proof of chemical evolution in every school textbook?

**A11:** To date, Miller-like experiments have only produced some of the basic building blocks (amino acids) for life — never a functional protein or anything even close. This is why they speak of "proteinoids" rather than proteins. Nevertheless, even if a suitable protein with a long chain of amino acids with the correct (i.e., left) optical rotation were produced, this would not mean that evolution had been launched. There has to be a code system for storing and transmitting the Universal Information so that this protein can be produced when needed. Moreover, a code system can never be produced by pure matter (SLI-2 and SLI-3, chapter 5.6).

The bottom line is that the Miller experiments essentially yield no answers to explain a purely material origin of life. A rough analogy would be as follows: Consider Miller-like experiments as having been able to produce a few letters of the English alphabet. Would that achievement in any way be able to explain the entire collection of Shakespeare's works? But it's actually far worse than that. All (not just some) of the "English letters" need to be produced; then the punctuation marks; then the syntax rules for combining these letters; and finally all of Shakespeare's works have to be produced. That is the *easy* part! All of this has to occur completely on its own — with absolutely no guidance from an intelligent agent. Miller's experiments were carefully planned and controlled (to the extent of introducing a level of investigator interference beyond that required for a proper simulation of random processes). In summary, matter by itself could never create, much less carry out, a Miller experiment.

**Q12:** The SOS signal is periodic, nevertheless it is Universal Information. Doesn't that contradict your necessary condition NC2 (chapter 2.2)?

**A12:** NC2 states that "The sequence of the individual symbols must, generally speaking, be irregular/aperiodic" — "generally speaking" does not mean "always." When seeking to determine if something is or is not UI, one must focus on whether or not the definition of UI is fulfilled. In the case of the SOS signal we find that every one of UI's four *distinguishing* attributes (syntax, semantics, pragmatics, and apobetics) are present. Moreover, SOS is only one of a near-infinite set of messages that can be expressed by Morse code. Therefore, the SOS signal is indeed Universal Information.

Having said this, SOS is a good example of abbreviations that are imbued with extensive meanings. These types of abbreviations are always conventions that are agreed upon in advance and known by the relevant senders and receivers. SOS was adopted in 1912 as an international distress signal. It is most commonly transmitted via radio waves, but any material medium can be used, depending on the circumstances. It is an urgent signal from a sender implying that life and or property are in serious danger. It also is a request for help as soon as possible. The implied and understood meanings of SOS are what make it UI and not periodic nonsense.

**Q13:** Can new Universal Information be created through mutations?

**A13:** This idea is central to the doctrine of biological evolution. However, as we have seen in earlier chapters, new Universal Information cannot be created in DNA through mutations. As stated in chapter 5.6, mutations do modify the existing UI (i.e., Modified versus Created Universal Information). However, altering existing UI should not be confused with creating *de novo* UI. Observations to date demonstrate that mutations result in a loss of original functionality (pragmatics) and not a creation of new UI and new functionality. (Of course, the loss of functionality may be in a control element, resulting in overproduction of something, as we saw in the example of the overproduction of penicillinase in some penicillin-resistant bacteria.) Evolutionary doctrine implies that we should be able to document countless mutations that cause new structures and functions to arise. Instead, only the barest handful of such creative mutations have been claimed, and none that qualify as unequivocal examples. The examples generally cited of mutations allegedly showing "evolution in action" are the loss of eyes in cave fish or the loss of wings in beetles and birds on windy islands, etc. Such loss-causing mutations certainly convey a selective (survival) advantage, but they are the opposite of what neo-Darwinists need to demonstrate, i.e., a mechanism for explaining the massive net *gains* of information their worldview requires. According to SLI-2 and SLI-3, unguided, purely material processes (such as mutations) within the DNA cannot be the source of the new (creative) Universal Information. Creative UI is essential for producing new functions or new organs that are absolutely required for evolution. Without such new UI, evolution is not possible.

**Q14:** When the structure of a crystal is studied through a microscope, much information may be gained. Where and who is the sender in this case?

**A14:** This is an example of a common claim about information. However, it does not involve Universal Information. The crystal itself displays no syntax, no semantics, no pragmatics, and no apobetics. Furthermore, even its Shannon information content is extremely low, since it is a repetitive ordered structure which forms because it minimizes energy, thus maximizing the total entropy of the surroundings. Therefore, the crystal itself does not fulfill the definition of UI, nor is it creating or transmitting UI. A crystal diagram is also not UI any more than a photograph is (see A5). Yet, the people who study the crystal will be creating UI if they are using a human language to think about and to record their observations, including the crystallographic notations for crystal structure.

**Q15:** Has your definition of information been chosen arbitrarily? Could there not be other possibilities?

**A15:** The answer to your first question is, no — the definition is not arbitrary. The reasons for this answer are stated in the answer A3, above. The answer to your second question is, yes — there are indeed types of information other than UI. For instance, in chapter 3.3 we introduced the concept of mental image information (MII). Other concepts of information such as statistical, algorithmic, and complex specified information have been discussed by others in great depth (e.g., Shannon, Kolmogorov, Chaitin, and Dembski). While these information concepts are useful and provide information measures, they never *unambiguously* define information. The principal problem with these other notions of information is that they are weak in the sense of leaving out attributes of

UI, such as semantics, that are known to be essential for what is generally considered information in human natural languages and human artificial languages, including human machine languages.

**Q16:** Biological systems are more complex than technological systems. Should there not be a specific definition of information for biological systems?

**A16:** It is true that biological systems are far more complex than our technological inventions. It is also possible that there may be other-than-UI forms of information encoded within the DNA molecules. If and when other-than-UI forms of information are discovered, these must be unambiguously defined.

In the meantime, the definition of UI, derived from human natural and machine languages, perfectly characterizes the information that is present in the DNA of all organisms — specifically within the DNA/RNA Protein Synthesizing System (PSS). Therefore, at least for the PSS, the definition of UI is appropriate and the scientific laws that govern its domain can be applied.

**Q17:** Biological systems often have the capacity to adapt to the environment. Shouldn't this be seen as either an increase or a creation of Universal Information by material means?

**A17:** At first sight this may seem to be the case. However, adaptations of biological systems to new environments are always the result of either the expression of *already existing* UI or damage (mutations) to existing UI. The mutations cause some *loss* of the existing UI and the impairment of functions. Neither adaptation nor mutation creates UI or increases the UI originally present. For adaptation the organisms (original kinds) possessed the necessary information at creation; no new Universal Information was added. Sometimes a loss or corruption of the UI can be adaptive in a particular environment, as we saw in A13 with flightless birds and eyeless fish. When it comes to the human "races" it has been demonstrated very impressively [B2, p. 210–236] how the varieties of humans could develop, starting with Noah's family. The necessary Universal Information did not emerge through the process of evolution; rather, it was a part of the original genomic information provided by the Creator at the beginning of humanity with Adam and Eve. Subsequent loss mutations have also played their part in human characteristics, such as the loss of the ability to produce one component in skin pigmentation generates red hair.

**Q18:** Can scientific laws change with time?

**A18:** The laws of nature (scientific laws) apply everywhere on earth and, to the best of our knowledge, they also apply everywhere in the universe at all ranges of scale and at all times. No exceptions are known to exist for a scientific law — that is what makes it a "law." It would be tragic if the laws of nature were to change with time. All of our technological constructions and measuring devices are based upon the application of scientific laws. If, over time, the laws were to change, bridges and sky-scrapers might collapse, having been built according to a correct understanding of the physical laws at the time. Likewise, since the physiological processes of life depend on the physical laws, should they change, the consequences would be catastrophic. Science itself would be impossible.

**Q19:** Does the sender also belong to your definition of Universal Information? If that were true then the conclusion is, of course, that the sender exists.

**A19:** The sender is not part of nor a prerequisite for the definition of Universal Information. In either case it would be a circular argument. All scientific laws are established by observation and experimentation and not prejudiced by assumptions or prerequisites. When we investigate an unknown system, we have to determine whether all four distinguishing attributes of Universal Information are present. If so, then we can apply the scientific laws of Universal Information to reach the conclusion that the UI in the unknown system must have been created by an intelligent author.

**Q20:** Doesn't the application of N10 — scientific laws have no exceptions — preclude *a priori* processes that *may* exist?

**A20:** If a statement is indeed a valid scientific law, then there can be no example to the contrary. There may be a *supposed* scientific law that is suggested and possibly even used as a real law. However, a single reproducible experiment demonstrating the contrary would immediately remove the "law" status. This would constitute *falsification* of the "supposed law," as would be the case presented in your question. For example, the law of conservation of energy is considered by scientists to be an irrefutable law of nature and, as such, it is used in innumerable contexts in physics and technology. Experimenters have tried repeatedly by countless ingenious methods to find an exception to this law — no one has ever succeeded. One physics professor said recently in a conversation, very pointedly:

> Whoever groundlessly doubts the law of conservation of energy is mad. But whoever devises an experiment to refute it immediately deserves the Nobel Prize.

**Q21:** How many scientific laws are there?

**A21:** It is very difficult to determine the precise number of scientific laws that exist, primarily for two reasons:

1.  It is almost certain that we have not discovered all of the scientific laws that exist.

2.  Scientific laws are often bundled into a "super-ordinate" law. In chapter 5, we formulated six scientific laws and nine corollaries of Universal Information. Some of them overlap with others. This type of redundancy was used to promote better comprehension and presentability. The search for the oft-cited universal formula — a "Final Theory of Everything" — assumes that all physical laws can be merged into a single law. This is considered to be a utopian objective.

**Q22:** Have you presented your concept of the scientific laws of Universal Information to your peers? How long have you taken to compile the concept in its present form?

**A22:** I have presented this subject at numerous universities in Germany and internationally in all continents (see "Scientific lectures" p. 417). The most notable was in June 1996 at an International Congress for Information Theory *[Information — A Fundamental Quantity in Natural and Technological Systems]*. At these events there was always lively discussion, and the experts present sought to find the one counter-example that could bring down the scientific laws of Universal Information. The scientific validity of these laws is supported by the fact that no one either then or to date has presented *verifiable* falsification of any of the empirical statements or scientific laws of Universal Information. I presented my first scientific lecture on the theory of Universal Information on October 8, 1981. I have thus dedicated over 30 years to its further development.

Discussions regarding Universal Information with numerous scientists in Germany and abroad have greatly assisted me in refining the theory to develop it to its present status.

## 10.2 Questions requiring lengthy answers

### 10.2.1 Suggestions for "measuring" Universal Information[7]

**Q23:** A fundamental aspect of science is that it appears to require measurement of the entities being investigated. How do you measure a non-material entity such as Universal Information (UI)?

**A23:** This is a very good question that is asked frequently. I will answer it in two parts, below.

### Answer 23, Part 1 — The value and usability of Universal Information

Shannon's information theory (statistical level) can be regarded as an extension of probability theory, wherein the bit is the unit of measurement of information. In a sense, this means that a book with 200 pages contains on the order of twice the information of one with 100 pages if the pages have the same number of letters. Shannon, however, purposely ignores the actual "meaning" of the information because this aspect is irrelevant to the engineering problem of information transmission and storage.

Wolfgang Feitscher described this aptly when he wrote: "When considering semantic information, we are like a chemist who can weigh substances but cannot analyze them." In this sense Shannon solved the problem of "weighing" information, but could not, and did not, resolve the "analysis" aspect of this information. To venture into measurement beyond Shannon's definition of information, it is necessary to define measures for UI that must incorporate UI's distinguishing attributes. We will now suggest and explore some ideas that may pave the way for solving this difficult problem.

A measure of UI would not necessarily measure quantity but *quality*. For instance, several volumes of repetitive, mundane words may have a lower UI value than a thin brochure containing fundamental scientific equations, measurements, and natural laws about the universe. A qualitative evaluation of UI necessarily involves some parameters that depend very strongly on a subjective appraisal, and this has a significantly aggravating effect on the problem.

---

7. Universal Information (UI) will be identified here as such; any other use of the word "information" is referring to Shannon's or some other definition of information.

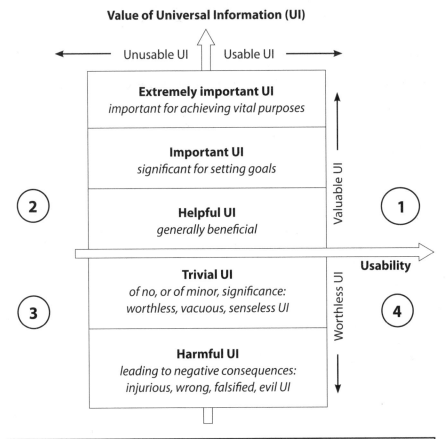

Figure 36: Coordinate system representing the value of UI (Y axis) and usability (X axis). There is no indication of scale on the axes because we are dealing with a qualitative evaluation of UI. Valuable UI is accorded a positive sign and worthless or harmful UI a negative sign. Usable and unusable UI are also distinguished by their positive and negative signs.

In an attempt to remedy this, Figure 36 depicts a graph showing the **value** of UI (Y axis) and its **usability** (X axis). The Y axis shows the following five levels:

**1. Extremely important UI:** This is the highest level of UI because of its high apobetic content (e.g., a search for essential UI regarding ultimate truth).

**2. Important UI:** This involves UI that is required for achieving significant lifetime goals (e.g., subject matter related to a person's selected career/profession, how to select and develop a good relationship with a marriage partner).

**3. Helpful UI:** This includes UI that is of general value in the sense of being informative, constructive, edifying, or amusing (e.g., daily news, weather reports, and general knowledge).

**4. Trivial UI:** Insignificant, hollow, or worthless UI (e.g., redundant UI, clichés, banalities, and small talk).

**5. Harmful UI:** The destructive nature of this level of UI leads to false results, misconceptions, and other negative effects. Harmful UI includes lies (e.g., deliberate or unintentional misinformation, slander, and propaganda), agitation, malicious gossip, expletives, occult doctrines, unbiblical theology, pornographic material, and astrological publications.

Valuable UI (1 to 3) is accorded a positive sign, and worthless or harmful UI (4 & 5) a negative sign, so that now we can regard UI as an entity that can carry a sign. In the X axis (Figure 36) we distinguish between usable UI (positive sign) and unusable UI (negative sign). Thus, the four quadrants for evaluating UI are characterized as follows.

**First quadrant:** This is the most important domain, since it comprises all UI that is both usable and valuable. "Usable" means that the UI is available, accessible, and may be utilized. Usability is an objective property, but the concept of value is always subjectively related to a person, a process, a plan, or a goal.

**Second quadrant:** As in the first quadrant, the UI in this quadrant is also valuable but it is unusable. There are various reasons for this:

- It is not yet available (e.g., a definitive cure for cancer, a book on an important theme that has not yet been written).

- It cannot be located or retrieved from the numerous and gigantic stores of UI that may also be physically inaccessible (e.g., retrieving the May 1885 edition of *Scientific American*).

- It is known to an author, but it has not yet been transmitted (published).

- It is no longer of current interest.

**Third and fourth quadrants:** This is the domain of worthless or harmful UI. At the trivial level, this comprises meaningless or insignificant UI, i.e., valueless, inane, or nonsensical information. At the amplified harmful level, UI can be inadvertently false, deliberately false, or outright evil, often resulting in negative effects. The fourth quadrant indicates that such UI exists, while the third quadrant depicts UI that is not yet available or accessible (e.g., unpublished trash literature). According to certain statistics, upon completing high school the average American youth had watched TV for 22,000 hours, during which time he heard 350,000 promotional slogans and saw 20,000 murders. Unquestionably, a huge amount of harmful UI must have been transmitted to this youth during that time. It is imperative to avoid/not indulge in the fourth quadrant in human affairs, since the results will likely be negative, possibly even tragic. When it comes to technology, security measures must be implemented against fourth quadrant UI. Such measures include error-detecting codes in data processing systems and anti-virus/anti-spyware software to combat spyware, viruses, malware, worms, Trojan horses, etc. It should be noted that harmful UI such as that contained in a computer virus, worm or spyware, is *itself* conveying highly sophisticated UI, purposefully and ingeniously designed to accomplish the goal of the person(s) that created it.

## The value and usability of UI in the Bible

We graphed the value of Universal Information and its usability in Figure 36 by means of four quadrants. According to biblical assertions, we may conclude that God puts a value on every kind of information.

**Worthless UI:** We subdivided "worthless UI" into the categories of trivial and harmful UI. God provides a permanent standard in His commandments: "You shall not give false testimony against your neighbor" (Exod. 20:16) because "The Lord detests lying lips" (Prov. 12:22). Such people are described in Jer. 8:6:

> I have listened attentively, but they do not say what is right. None of them repent of their wickedness, saying, "What have I done?" Each pursues his own course like a horse charging into battle.

James 3:5–6 states,

> The tongue is a small part of the body, but it makes great boasts. Consider what a great forest is set on fire by a small spark. The tongue also is a fire....

These quotations are restricted to cases where we, as senders, send harmful information. Nevertheless, God also wants to protect us from being receivers of such information and He warns us emphatically against association with such senders:

> Proverbs 1:10: "My son, if sinful men entice you, do not give in to them."

> Proverbs 14:7: "Stay away from a fool, for you will not find knowledge on their lips."

> Psalm 1:1: "Blessed is the one who does not walk in step with the wicked or stand in the way that sinners take or sit in the company of mockers."

In this regard, I should point out that Adam and Eve's sin was introduced by the wicked information: "Did God really say…?" (Gen. 3:1). Adam and Eve's response to this harmful UI (that questioned the reliability of God's Word) had unimaginable consequences: it resulted in sickness and pain, death and suffering, war and uproar, and we are all still suffering from the disastrous effects of sin because of it. Man is able to send harmful UI (lies, provocation, slander, mockery, and cursing) and receive, listen, and respond to harmful UI. Both are contrary to God's will. His archives have recorded them all — these books will one day be opened (Rev. 20:12) — and we will be called to account for them. As Jesus said:

> But I tell you that everyone will have to give account on the day of judgment for every empty word they have spoken. For by your words you will be acquitted, and by your words you will be condemned (Matt. 12:36–37).

**Valuable information:** The most valuable information that has ever been sent is the Word of God. Never has a better or more joyful message been given to mankind. There is no unhelpful or false information in the Bible because God's Word is absolutely true:

> God is not human, that he should lie, nor a human being, that he should change his mind. Does he speak and then not act? Does he promise and not fulfill? (Num. 23:19).

Here we find certainty and truth, timelessness, and divine majesty. The Bible contains certainty and truth, as well as eternal and divine words.

No other source of knowledge comes even close to this. The Psalmist testifies from his personal experience: "I rejoice in your promise like one who finds great spoil" (Ps. 119:162). Paul also knows the value of what he has found: "But we have this treasure in jars of clay" (2 Cor. 4:7). God wants us continually to be receivers and transmitters of this Universal Information because He has invested it with the greatest of promises.

1. *As receiver:* Many people make great efforts to improve their qualifications in order to be successful in their private and professional lives. But in the Old Testament God has already given easy-to-follow, simple advice that can have a great effect: "Keep this Book of the Law always on your lips; meditate on it day and night, so that you may be careful to do everything written in it. Then you will be prosperous and successful" (Josh. 1:8). Everything depends on the way we treat the Word of the living God: "Obey me, and I will be your God and you will be my people. Walk in obedience to all I command you, that it may go well with you" (Jer. 7:23). The Word brings understanding and wisdom, and it keeps us from going the wrong way (Ps. 119:104). It renews (Ps. 19:7), enlightens (Ps. 119:130), shows us the way of salvation (James 1:21), and makes us wise unto salvation and thoroughly equips us for every good work (2 Tim. 3: 15–17). Since, according to Figures 32 and 36, we are dealing with Universal Information of the highest value, we are unambiguously instructed to "Let the message of Christ dwell among you richly" (Col. 3:16). During a talk, Helmut Matthies, Director of Information Services of the Evangelical Alliance of Germany, stated that the average German works 38.5 hours per week and watches television for 17.5 hours per week [M1]. Statistics indicate that the latter figure is constantly increasing, indicating more exposure to enormously harmful influences and less attention to God's Word. God wants something else for us: that we should be conformed by His Holy Spirit, in line with His Word (Rom. 12: 2).

2. *As sender:* In our role as senders, we will only pass on the UI that has influenced us. Jesus expresses this with the words: "For the mouth speaks what the heart is full of" (Matt.

12:34). The Psalmist always concerned himself with the Word so that he was always able to draw from this source: "May my tongue sing of your word" (Ps. 119:172). This not only means that no worthless UI should come from the mouths of Christians, but that they should be bearers of good news. God expresses His appreciation of them through Isaiah (Isa. 52:7): "How beautiful ... are the feet of those who bring good news, who proclaim peace, who bring good tidings, who proclaim salvation." This good news is the gospel of Jesus Christ, which saves all who put their trust in it. Jesus often gave the instruction that we should be carriers of this message (Matt. 28:19–20, Mark 16:15, Luke 10:3, and Luke 12:8–9). When the Samaritan woman met Jesus at Jacob's well and recognized Him as the Christ, she put her jar down and immediately went back to the town to proclaim the message of salvation (John 4:25–30). Paul also tried any possible way of winning over different people of all backgrounds (1 Cor. 9:19–22), and he even tells himself: "Woe to me if I do not preach the gospel!" (1 Cor. 9:16). He combines the assignment and contents in the following words: "We implore you on Christ's behalf: Be reconciled to God" (2 Cor. 5:20). This message is not only the most important and the most urgent one there is, it is also the most certain. C. H. Spurgeon implores us [S9]:

> If you don't have an eternal gospel to proclaim, then your message is only worth 20 pennies. You can get uncertainties elsewhere and everywhere but matters of eternal life are only found in the Bible.

### Answer 23, Part 2 — Six suggested measurement parameters for Universal Information (UI)

After considering the value of UI in Part 1, Answer 23, we can now begin to explore other measurement aspects for UI. We will define and use the following six measurement parameters: quality, $q$; relevance, $r$; timeliness, $t$; usability, $u$; existence, $e$; and comprehensibility, $c$. Each of these parameters considers the UI predominantly from the receiver's *subjective* viewpoint and appraisal. All parameters are normalized on a scale from 0 to 1 (except for $q$ (defined below); $q$ ranges from -1 to 1). We will briefly discuss these six parameters below:

**1. Quality, q** (subjective term, receiver-oriented): This is used as a measure of the importance of the meaning of certain UI. Different criteria can be considered according to the goal and the type of UI. Some criteria of production UI are depicted in Figure 23, chapter 5.9.1. For example, in a computer program the following criteria are relevant and crucial at the semantic level and partly at the pragmatic level:

- Efficacy of the applied algorithm (e.g., simplicity of method of solution, speed of convergence, and absence of instability)

- Minimal computing time (this can be a decisive cost factor when time has to be paid for)

- Portability, meaning that the program can be run on different computer systems

- Reliability, meaning that the program has been tested comprehensively and is fully debugged so that the desired results will be obtained with a high degree of certainty

- The programming language used

The weight of each criterion depends on both objective and subjective criteria. For trivial or nonsensical UI, **q** is taken as zero, while for the best possible UI, **q** = 1 and the worst possible UI, **q** = -1.

**2. Relevance, r** (subjective term, receiver-oriented): This parameter reflects individual interests in particular and includes its relevance for achieving some set purpose (e.g., an economical, technical or strategic goal, collector's value, or a goal in life). Whatever may be extremely important UI (**r** = 1) for one person may be completely irrelevant UI (**r** = 0) for another person. The weather forecasts for Australia are normally of no importance for someone in Europe (**r** = 0), but their relevance can increase dramatically when that person is planning to travel there. For a farmer, the agricultural news would have relevance completely different from the latest research results in physics. It is clear that relevance is entirely receiver-oriented. A hurricane and storm tide warning over the radio is substantially more relevant for inhabitants of a coastal island than for inland residents. The main issue of relevance is to judge it correctly; a false appraisal might have catastrophic effects. Sadly, there are many cases in human history where wrong decisions were made based on a faulty appraisal of the relevance of UI. These decisions have sometimes resulted in painful costs in terms of lives and property. An example of this was the Space Shuttle Challenger disaster that occurred in 1986. In this case, the UI regarding the weather and the O-ring seals in the solid rocket boosters (UI that was fully available at the time) was improperly evaluated or dismissed altogether. Some of the engineers communicated the critical relevance of low ambient temperatures to the seal's function, but this UI was not heeded. On the day of the launch, very low temperatures caused a failure of the O-ring seals, resulting in the total destruction of the shuttle and the loss of the seven-person crew.

**3. Timeliness, t** (subjective, receiver-oriented): It is often necessary for relevant UI to be available at the right time. Newsworthiness is time-dependent, so that yesterday's news is often $t = 0$ and highly relevant UI received at the right moment is $t = 1$. When a person is standing in the rain and somebody tells him that it is raining, the newsworthiness of this UI is zero ($t = 0$), even though it is accurate and relevant.

**4. Usability, u** (subjective, receiver-oriented — this concept was introduced in Part 1, Answer 23): The most important UI is worthless if it cannot be used; $u = 0$ means the receiver is not able to use the UI, and $u = 1$ when the receiver is fully able to use the UI transmitted by the sender. We are being overwhelmed by an ever-increasing flood of UI. One newspaper wrote: "We are thirsty for knowledge but we are drowning in the flood of information." One Member of Parliament complained during an address: "I have collected all the information that was sent to me last week from the European Parliament. I did not read it, I weighed it. There were 5.5 kg [12 lbs.] of paper."

We are being overrun by so much information that we do not know where to begin with it. How much worse must it be for members of government?

Due to the existing and ever-increasing mountains of information, it is equally important that there be systems for rapid, efficient information retrieval. In the age of the computer and internet, this role is increasingly taken over by databases and search engines. Associative storage would be a great help, but as yet only the brain can provide this ideal access principle. In the early days of the internet, there were around 10,000 pages that could be used; now we have available for use a global library of 600 *billion* pages and counting.

Although the UI exists, its usability, **u**, may nevertheless be zero when:

- the UI cannot be seen by the receiver (e.g., he is dying of thirst in the desert close to a spring but he does not see the sign pointing to it)

- the UI is coded in a language that the receiver does not understand (e.g., an English tourist in China who cannot read Chinese)

- the UI is written in technical terms that can only be understood by experts in that technical field (e.g., legal texts that non-lawyers cannot follow or a mathematical book that is "Greek" to the uninitiated)

- the amount of UI is so overwhelming that time constraints do not allow it to be used

- the sender deliberately excludes some potential receivers (e.g., information encrypted for secrecy, data protection in Information Technology Systems or a sealed letter)

**5. Existence, e** (subjective, sender-dependent)**:** Usability involves the possibility that an individual can obtain UI that, in principle, is available. Existence, on the other hand, concerns the basic question as to whether the UI even exists. Usability involves the receiver only, but existence depends solely on the sender. The value of **e** lies between 0 and 1 and it indicates how much of the potential or desired UI about the present case has been obtained (e.g., the fraction that has already been researched). The existence, **e**, is zero for questions that are completely unanswered (whether there is life on any of Jupiter's moons (**e** = 0)), and, **e** = 1 if something is fully known. At the time of writing, for example, the UI needed to cure primary cancer of the liver is essentially **e** = 0. In the case of stomach cancer, **e** lies somewhere between 0 and 1 depending on the stage of its development. It is quite difficult to make an estimate of the value of **e** since the totality of relevant UI is generally not known at a given moment. The great physicist Isaac Newton estimated his contribution to scientific research as having a very low **e** value in spite of his many valuable findings. Newton said [M3]:

> I do not know what the world thinks of me; but to myself I appear as a little boy playing on the beach and who finds joy in

discovering a smoother pebble or a prettier seashell than the ordinary, while the great ocean of truth lay undiscovered before me.

**6. Comprehensibility, c** (subjective concept, both sender- and receiver-oriented): This factor describes the intelligibility of UI. When the UI cannot be understood at all, $c = 0$; when it is completely understood, $c = 1$. Both sides may be at fault if the UI intended for transmission does not completely reach the receiver. The sender might not have expressed himself clearly enough and, as a result, the receiver grasps the intended semantics only partially in spite of being highly intelligent; or it could be that the receiver may not be intelligent enough to understand everything correctly. The mental capacity of the receiver is also important for another reason: verbally formulated UI (the explicit part) often contains implicit UI that has to be read "between the lines." The receiver only receives this latter part by contemplation and having suitable background knowledge.

**NOTE:** Many of the above-mentioned parameters cannot be distinguished sharply and may overlap. The many questions concerning the interrelationships and correlations between these six parameters will not be discussed any further here but may be a rewarding field of research in the future. For now, we can say that any UI may be analyzed in terms of each of these six parameters. Combining these analyses with "value" and "usability," considerations from Answer 23, Part 1 should provide at least a starting point for "quantitatively" comparing UI content and worth.

## Applying the six measurement parameters of Universal Information to the Bible

In the preceding section, we described six parameters that seemed appropriate for the quantitative evaluation of Universal Information, namely quality, relevance, timeliness, usability, existence, and comprehensibility. Let us now investigate the role of these parameters in the Bible.

**1. Quality, q:** The special semantic quality of the Bible is characterized as follows:

- *It is divine:* "This is the word that came to Jeremiah from the LORD" (Jer. 7:1). "I want you to know, brothers and sisters, that the gospel I preached is not of human origin. I did not receive it from any man, nor was I taught it; rather, I received it by revelation from Jesus Christ" (Gal. 1:11–12).

- *It is true:* "Sovereign LORD, you are God! Your covenant is trust worthy" (2 Sam. 7:28). "Your word is truth" (John 17:17).

- *It comprises the message of man's salvation:* "And you also were included in Christ when you heard the message of truth, the gospel of your salvation" (Eph. 1:13a).

**2. Relevance, r:** The message of the Bible is relevant for each and every person because God's judgment is the same for everyone: *"For no one living is righteous"* (Ps. 143:2); "all have sinned and fall short of the glory of God" (Rom. 3:23). Even so, God has provided one way of salvation for everyone through His Son Jesus: "Salvation is found in no one else, for there is no other name under heaven given to mankind by which we must be saved" (Acts 4:12). Numerous other passages point in the same direction; e.g., John 3:16, 18; 14:6, 1 John 5:12. We will obtain the greatest benefit from them if we comprehend their relevance correctly. The attitude of the Thessalonians (1 Thess. 1:4–9) and the Philadelphians (Rev. 3:7–11) is highly commended in this respect.

The Bible warns very explicitly against an erroneous evaluation of its relevance, because this will lead to the greatest possible loss. Paul and Barnabas told the people of Jerusalem: "We had to speak the word of God to you first. Since you reject it and do not consider yourselves worthy of eternal life, we now turn to the Gentiles" (Acts 13:46). The rich wheat farmer made plans for his life without considering God, and was told: "You fool! This very night your life will be demanded from you" (Luke 12:20). The rich man in hell (Luke 16:19–31) was not lost because of his wealth — Abraham and Job were richer in their lifetimes — but because in his sinfulness he misjudged the relevance of the information at his disposal.

**3. Timeliness, t:** Certain passages of the Bible are the most ancient extant writings known to man. All of the New Testament (excluding Luke) and most of the Old Testament authors belonged to an insignificant, small nation of the Middle East. In the light of these facts, one might conclude that such a book could now only be of historical interest, and its contents would have been outdated long ago. One might expect that, at most, the authors' fellow countrymen could regard it as being of some cultural interest. Contrary to all such considerations, millions of people all over the world concern themselves with this book. It is read and loved by people irrespective of age, language, and level of education. No other book in history is so timely, timeless, and relevant. What is the reason? Martin Luther commented: "The Bible is not an antique, neither is it modern; it is eternal."

The message of the Bible is relevant for all times. It is always up-to-date and topical; it has the timelessness of eternity about it. In Matthew 24:35 Jesus expresses it thus: "Heaven and earth will pass away, but my words will never pass away." In this world everything is perishable except the Word: "The grass withers and the flowers fall, but the word of our God endures forever" (Isa. 40:8). Because of this exceptional character, God's Word remains always up-to-date. The oft-cited word "today" in the Bible has never lost its significance over thousands of years. Joshua's entreaty to the Israelites: "Choose for yourselves this day whom you will serve" (Josh. 24:15a) is God's entreaty to us today. What a blessing if we were to give the same reply as Joshua: "But as for me and my household, we will serve the LORD" (Josh. 24:15b). When Zacchaeus experienced a complete change in his life after meeting Jesus, Christ told him: "**Today** salvation has come to this house" (Luke 19:9). This salvation is ours also, today, when we turn our lives over to Jesus. Whoever makes this discovery will be nourished continuously by the timeless Word of God: "Man shall not live on bread alone, but on every word that comes from the mouth of God" (Matt. 4:4).

**4. Usability, u:** At present, the total volume of knowledge is doubled every seven years, in electronic technology every five years, and even more frequently in the case of information technology. If a scientist wanted to really keep abreast of everything in his field, he would have to do the impossible — namely, spend many more hours each day than the 24 it contains just reading! It becomes very difficult, even nigh impossible, to access the relevant information given the present-day explosion of knowledge. In light of this, usability of UI has become a major problem to overcome in most disciplines.

In the case of the Bible, the situation is quite different: The *wisdom* it contains is complete and permanent, and is thus essentially different from human knowledge. God's Universal Information is contained in one book so that we can always use any part of the Bible at any time. This "continuous use" has been commanded by God:

Joshua 1:8: "Keep this Book of the Law always on your lips; meditate on it day and night."

Jeremiah 22:29: "O land, land, land, hear the Word of the LORD!"

Colossians 3:16: "Let the message of Christ dwell among you richly."

1 Peter 2:2: "Like newborn babies, crave pure spiritual milk, so that by it you may grow up in your salvation."

Furthermore, following the commendable example of the Bereans, we are encouraged to read the Bible daily and to verify what a preacher says. "Now the Berean Jews … received the message with great eagerness and examined the Scriptures every day to see if what Paul said was true" (Acts 17:11). The Psalmist longs for the Word (Ps. 119:81) because he finds renewal (Ps. 119:25), strength (Ps. 119:28), hope, and salvation (Ps. 119:81).

**5. Existence, e:** There is one further important question: Does the Bible really contain *all* the information required to know God and ourselves, to live according to God's standards, and to achieve His eternal purpose for us? Yes! All-important questions are answered clearly and unambiguously as they are revealed to us by the Holy Spirit (2 Tim. 3:15–17). Only critics and doubters introduce uncertainties and vagueness. Spurgeon rightly concluded, "Nothing is easier than doubting. A poorly educated person with mediocre abilities can raise more doubts than can be resolved by the cleverest men of science from all over the world."

Because of the completeness of the biblical message, we may not delete anything from this message, nor add anything (Rev. 22:18–19); and for every interpretation the fundamental rule holds: "Do not go beyond what is written" (1 Cor. 4:6).

**6. Comprehensibility, c:** This has already been discussed in chapter 9.5 under "Examining UI Attributes in the Bible."

Summarizing the evaluation of biblical information, we reach some remarkable conclusions:

- The Bible contains the *most valuable Universal Information* (UI) conceivable. It is divine in essence and shows us the way to our Father's house.

- The UI of the Bible is of the highest relevance ($r = 1$) for every person. It comprises the best advice for this life, and is the only compass pointing to heaven.

- The UI of the Bible is *always timely* ($t = 1$). Whereas most scientific publications become outdated after ten years, the Bible is never out of date.

- We can *readily* access and use the UI of the Bible ($u = 1$). A copy in their own language is readily available to the great majority of the world's people. China is an authoritarian state that seeks to suppress allegiance to anything other than the Communist party. Even there, millions of Bibles are printed *legally* each year, in addition to underground or imported copies — 100 million would likely be a conservative estimate of the Bibles in existence there.

- The UI of the Bible is *comprehensive and complete.*

- The Bible contains no false UI; it is the *only* Book of Truth (John 17:17).

We find the highest semantic density of UI in the Bible ($q = 1$) as well as the best pragmatic UI ($q = 1$); e.g., commandments, rules for living and for our relationship with God and other people. It comprises the highest possible goal — apobetics ($q = 1$) — namely, an invitation to heaven!

### 10.2.2 Software complexity and specified complexity

**Q24:** The concept of "complexity" has always played an important role regarding information. What role does complexity play in Universal Information (UI)?

**A24:** The short answer is that UI exhibits complexity, always implicitly and almost always explicitly. The lengthy answer will be in two parts, below.

**Answer 24, Part 1: Software complexity**

Since UI is a non-material entity, it cannot be directly quantified using any of the standard units of measurement as can be done with material entities. However, when a symbol set is used to encode a sequence onto a material medium, the statistical attribute of UI can be quantified in units of "bits" (see A1). Although it is not possible to fully treat UI mathematically, there have been numerous attempts to quantify at least one characteristic of Universal Information, namely, its complexity. Dr.

Horst Zuse summarized all of these attempts in his comprehensive work *Software Complexity* [Z1]. It is possible to distinguish five types of software complexity:

- *Structural* — topological relationships between system components

- *Algorithmic* — related to the computational methods used

- *Logical* — the relative difficulty of logical decisions or processes or branching within a system

- *Conceptional* — has to do with psychological perception or integration of a system

- *Textual* — statistical analysis of a program source code

Quantifying complexity is a very difficult task because there are many ways to measure complexity. For example, software may be regarded as more or less complex depending on the amount of time that it takes to execute, or the number of operations involved in the execution, or the space (memory) requirements. Thus, we find that more than 200 different metrics for complexity have been suggested in the literature; e.g., process metrics, product metrics, statistical and descriptive metrics, black box metrics, quality metrics, and design metrics. The confusion is so great that a programmer would have a very difficult task trying to compare the complexity even between simple programs. In summary, there exists no *single* definition of complexity with which the statement *"program A is more complex than program B"* may be universally valid.

We must consider the following fact: programming languages have always been conceived within a limited, goal-oriented scope of application; e.g., to perform calculations, solve administrative problems, draw graphics, and many others. This gives them a considerably narrower vocabulary, structure, syntax, and expressive range than natural languages. If it is not even possible to universally measure the complexity of these artificial computer programs, then how far are we from being able to quantify the distinguishing attributes of UI? We can easily imagine the difficulty of bringing the syntax, semantics, pragmatics, and apobetics of Universal Information into the realm of the measurable (see Answer 23, Part 2 pg. 312).

## Answer 24, Part 2: Specified complexity

The American scholars William A. Dembski and Stephen C. Meyer have, in a sense, amalgamated the terms "specified complexity" and "information" (Leslie Orgel originally coined the former term in his book, "Origin of Life," in 1973). According to Dembski and Meyer, "information" is created in the most general sense, while imposing the fewest restrictions possible, whenever at least one possibility is excluded from the set of all possibilities. So, for example, a die tossed once will yield one element from the set **S** = {1, 2, 3, 4, 5, or 6}. **S** represents the set of all possibilities. If you are told that a "3" came up when the die was tossed, then you have acquired "information" — all other possibilities in **S** have been excluded. It is in this sense — and only in this sense — that Shannon, Dembski-Meyer, et al. define, quantify, measure, and use the term "information."

Dembski and Meyer wanted to express the idea that a system exhibiting "contingency," "complexity," and "specification" (as these concepts are defined) could *only* have originated from the activity of an intelligent agent [D3]. The word "design" is used to express this. Stated differently, an object, structure, or event that exhibits contingency, complexity, and specification is said to be "designed" or (what amounts to the same thing) is said to contain "Complex Specified Information" (CSI). Thus, CSI is a specific type of information — specific in that it is information (due to its contingency) that is both complex and specified. This definition applies to human languages, computer codes, machines, works of art, and even to the natural world as, e.g., DNA, proteins, scales on butterfly wings, and animal migrations. Following this definition, the 18.3-meter-high faces of the four American presidents on Mount Rushmore in South Dakota are determined to contain complex specified information because these faces satisfy the three attributes (contingency, complexity, and specification) of CSI. Dembski generalizes this example by showing that the only known source of *de novo* CSI is intelligence. Dembski demonstrates that DNA qualifies as CSI and since all the proposed materialistic models of the last forty years for the origin of genetic information have failed, intelligence remains the only viable cause.

## Concluding remarks

Dembski's Complex Specified Information (CSI) differs from Universal Information (UI) primarily because CSI is a less-restrictive definition of information than the definition of UI. Concisely, all UI is CSI but not all CSI is UI. The four *distinguishing* attributes of UI — syntax, semantics, pragmatics, and apobetics — must always be explicitly present in UI. In CSI, all of these four attributes may be present but only purpose (apobetics) **must** be explicitly present (in the form of a specification). For example, a fighter jet (hardware only) exhibits CSI but not UI since syntax and semantics are not explicitly present. In the Mt. Rushmore example, only apobetics is explicitly present. Nonetheless, it is perfectly clear that UI was used in the design, manufacture, and maintenance of the fighter jet, and in the design and sculpturing of Mt. Rushmore. In that sense, it is possible to say that entities exhibiting CSI were preceded by and implicitly "contain" UI.

Taking this one step further, we observe that there is a good amount of common ground between Complex Specified Information and Universal Information. One way to accentuate this commonality is by making a distinction between what may be called *Primary* CSI and *Secondary* CSI.

Primary Complex Specified Information is CSI explicitly exhibiting all of the distinguishing attributes of UI; in other words, there is no distinction between *Primary* CSI and UI. Secondary Complex Specified Information is CSI in which one or more of UI's distinguishing attributes are not *explicitly* manifested. In the earlier examples, the fighter jet and Mt. Rushmore exhibit *Secondary* CSI. It goes without saying that Primary CSI was created by an intelligent agent since Primary CSI is equivalent to UI. It should also be noted that Primary CSI (i.e., UI) is required for the design, construction, and maintenance of all entities exhibiting Secondary CSI.

In any event, whenever we detect Secondary CSI in an entity, we know three things:

1. The Secondary CSI was created by an intelligent agent.

2. The intelligent agent used UI (or some other form of information that exhibits semantics, pragmatics, and apobetics) to design and create the Secondary CSI.

3. An intelligent agent can closely examine and measure the Secondary CSI in an entity and, from that examination, reverse-engineer/reconstruct the original Primary CSI (UI) used to design and create the entity.

#  EPILOGUE

You have reached the end of this long book. Much of it was scientific, but hopefully I have made the science understandable. I trust that your efforts were rewarded. It has also been my goal to let science speak through the facts and conclusions that have come to light since Darwin's time. Darwin had no knowledge of these scientific insights that not only refute his theory of evolution but also refute all materialistic/atheistic views of the world (see Appendix 4). Perhaps you have gained a new perspective towards life that is both scientifically and biblically sustainable in this twenty-first century.

We have established that the Bible is an extraordinary and trustworthy book in which God, who has revealed Himself in Jesus Christ, personally speaks to us. God Himself invites you to turn to Christ and enjoy eternity with Him in heaven. According to 1 Corinthians 2:9, heaven is indescribably beautiful: "What no eye has seen, what no ear has heard, and what no mind has conceived — the things God has prepared for those who love Him." The invitation stands! When you accept it, you receive many spiritual gifts from God. The following encounter is an example of just how easily you can respond to this invitation.

## The necessary initial spark

I was speaking on the subject "Looking forward to heaven" at a church in North Germany. At the end of the talk, I encouraged people in the audience to accept God's invitation to join the eternal celebration in heaven.

A young couple remained behind to talk about it. I asked them both directly whether they wanted to spend eternity in heaven. The husband, having already spoken to a friend about this, was well informed and said, *"Yes!"* His wife, on the other hand, was rather skeptical, explaining her indecision with the fact that she had not heard much about faith until then. She thought that faith had to grow first so that she could think about it and decide later. I sat at the head of the table, André on my right and Sandra on my left. She was obviously at a late stage of her pregnancy. In response to her argument about faith having to grow first, I told her: you will soon be having a baby. Now it is still growing in your womb. This growth had to start with an initial spark, as it were, and that is the same with faith in Christ. Without the initial spark there is no growth. In the case of faith, turning to Jesus Christ is this spark. She immediately understood this allegorical explanation. During that conversation, both of them experienced that initial spark that leads to eternal life. About one year later, I met them both again at a birthday party. He enthusiastically told me that they had grown in faith and enjoyed working in their church. It had all begun with that initial spark.

## How can I get to heaven?

We come now to the most important question of all: How can I be sure that I will get to heaven? Jesus said very clearly: "I am the gate [to heaven]" (John 10:9) and "I give them eternal life" (John 10:28). You can do this now just as if you were reading an instruction manual.

***Recognize yourself in the light of the Bible:*** Let us together read Romans 3:22–23: "There is no difference between Jew and Gentile, for all have sinned and fall short of the glory of God." This scripture shows that from God's perspective we are all lost and cannot come to Him, because sin separates us from Him. In brief: we lack all merit before God and we possess nothing that can reconcile us to Him. Since the Fall, a chasm has existed between the living God and sinful mankind. Do you agree with God's appraisal that mankind is fallen and sinful?

*The only way out:* There is only one way out of this plight, and it is entirely dependent upon God. His Son willingly received our punishment on the Cross for our sins. Jesus came to save what was lost (Matt. 18:11). Salvation is found in no one else nor in any other way (Acts 4:12). Can you accept this fact as well?

*Confess your sins:* We read in 1 John 1:8–9: "If we claim to be without sin, we deceive ourselves and the truth is not in us. If we confess our sins, he is faithful and just and will forgive us our sins and purify us from all unrighteousness." Jesus has the authority to forgive sin. If we trust in His promise and confess our sin to Him and ask His forgiveness, we can be assured of His faithfulness. We can rely on the fact that He will truly set us free from the burden of our sin and its eternal consequences. But thinking about this is not enough. You need to act! Are you willing to do that? Let us now tell the Lord Jesus all this in prayer (below is a suggested basis for a freely formulated prayer):

> *Lord Jesus Christ, I have lived my life as if You did not exist. I now recognize You for who You are and I turn to You in prayer for the first time. I now know that there is a heaven and there is also a hell. Please save me from hell, the place I deserve to go as a result of all my sins, especially that of my unbelief. It is my desire to be with You in heaven for all eternity. I understand that I cannot enter heaven by my own merits, but by faith in You alone. Because You love me, You died for me on the Cross and took upon Yourself my wrongdoings and paid for them in my stead. I thank You for that. You see all my transgressions, even those of my childhood days. You know all the sins I have committed, not only those which I can remember, but also those that I have long forgotten. You know everything about me. Every notion of my heart is known to You, be it joy or sadness, happiness or despair. I am like an open book before You. Because of the way I am and the way I have lived so far I cannot come before You and the Father God and, so, I cannot enter heaven. Therefore I beg You to forgive me all my sins, which I deeply regret. Amen.*

You have told the Lord everything that is necessary for now (1 John 1:8–9). God Himself vouches for His promise. How much of your guilt do you think He has forgiven? 80%? 50%? 10%? It is written: He will "purify us from **all** unrighteousness" (1 John 1:9). You have been forgiven **completely**! Yes, all of it, 100%! This is fact (if you sincerely meant that prayer), not just an assumption, a possibility, or a hope! The Bible is adamant about this, we must be certain of this fact. In this context, let us read 1 Peter 1:18–19:

> For you know that it was not with perishable things such as silver or gold that you were redeemed from the empty way of life … but with the precious blood of Christ, a lamb without blemish or defect.

Also 1 John 5:13:

> I write these things to you who believe in the name of the Son of God so that you may know that you have eternal life.

***Surrendering your life:*** The Lord Jesus has forgiven all your sin. Now you can entrust your whole life to Him. In John 1:12 we read: "Yet to all who did receive him, to those who believed in his name, he gave the right to become children of God." All those who invite the Lord Jesus to take over the control of their lives receive the authorization to become children of God. Becoming God's children is not a reward we receive for any of our good deeds or because we are pious or because we go to a particular church. We become children of God if we have entrusted our lives to the Son of God and are willing to obediently follow Him through the power of the Holy Spirit. Let us affirm this in a prayer:

> *I now accept You as my Lord and Savior. Reign over my life. I want to live a life that pleases You. Please help me to give up all that is not right in Your eyes and bless me with new habits. Help me to understand Your Word, the Bible. Help me to understand what You are saying to me and to find new strength and joy in Your Word. Please show me the way I should now go, and give me an obedient heart to follow You. I thank You for hearing me. I believe Your promise that by turning to You I am now a child of God who, one day, will be with You in heaven for all eternity. I recognize this undeserved favor as great gain, and I rejoice in the certain knowledge that You are by my side in every situation, even now. Please help me to find people who also believe in You, and help me to find a church that teaches Your Word faithfully and without compromise. Amen.*

*Accepted:* The Lord has accepted you! He has bought you at great cost to Himself. He has saved you. You are now a child of God. A child is also an heir: heir of God, heir to the heavenly world. Can you imagine what is taking place in heaven right now? In Luke 15:10, we read: "There is rejoicing in the presence of the angels of God over one sinner who repents." All of heaven is involved when one person takes the message of the gospel seriously and accepts it into their life. The Bible calls this process of turning to Jesus *conversion* — we give Him our guilt and He removes it. At this point in time we become born again: He gives us new life (a new spirit and soul). Now we are His children. Conversion and rebirth belong together — they are the two sides of one and the same coin.

*Thanksgiving:* Salvation is God's gift to us. Only through His love has this path of salvation been made possible. We cannot contribute anything to this act of redemption. Everyone who receives a gift says, "Thank you!" Tell the Lord Jesus now — just pray in your own words.

**What comes next?** The Bible compares your situation now as a new believer, spiritually born again, to that of a newborn child. As a newborn child clearly belongs to its family, you also belong to God's family. Newborn children find themselves in a critical phase of life. The same applies to our life of faith. Through conversion, a new spiritual child is born. There is new life. Now nourishment, care, and attention are absolutely necessary for this child. God has, naturally, made provision for this, too, and has done everything so that you can develop in the right direction. Harm to our infant faith can be avoided if we follow God's commands. The following aspects are not only important for life as a disciple of Jesus, they are indispensable prerequisites for everyday life with Him. If we adhere to these five points, we have God's guarantees that we will reach our designated goal:

### God's Word

You have made your decision based on God's Word, the Bible. The Bible is the only book that is authored and authorized by God. All of the world's books together do not even come close to the Bible in terms of truth, and the amount of vital information. Reading and comprehending God's Word is absolutely necessary to nourish your new life. In 1 Peter 2:2, this aspect is emphasized and clearly expressed: "Like newborn babies, crave pure spiritual milk." Make it a habit each day to read the Bible in order to get to know about God's will. Preferably, start by reading one of the Gospels (for example, the Gospel of John). There are certain habits in your life that you never forget. Be just as faithful in reading the Bible so that it is an essential part of your day.

## 1. Prayer

Speak with God every day. He speaks *to us* through His Word, and He wants us to speak *to Him*. It is a great privilege to tell Him everything. According to the Bible, prayer can only be directed to God, who is now your Father, and to Jesus, your Savior, your Good Shepherd, your friend — your everything. The Bible specifically tells us not to direct our prayers to anyone or anything else. Prayer will give you strength. It will change you in a positive manner. Everything in your daily life can become a subject for prayer: your sorrows, pleasures, and plans. Thank the Lord for all the circumstances in your life. Pray for other people and their difficulties. Pray to the Lord that the people surrounding you will also find faith. Prayer and reading God's Word are the pumps for the "spiritual circulation" that is necessary for a healthy spiritual life.

## 2. Obedience

When reading the Bible, you will find many useful instructions and commands for all areas of your life, including how to live with God. Put into action all that you have understood and you will be blessed by the Lord. God takes pleasure in our being obedient children who live according to His Word and heed His commands. The best way to show our love for the Lord is by obeying Him: "This is love for God: to keep his commands" (1 John 5:3). This world offers many paths that reflect the spirit of our times, but do not prove their worth in practice. The Bible sets a standard that is blessed by the Lord: "We must obey God rather than human beings!" (Acts 5:29). We must be careful, however, not to give way to the desires of what the following Bible verse calls the "flesh" (Gal. 5:16–17):

> So I say, walk by the Spirit, and you will not gratify the desires of the flesh. For the flesh desires what is contrary to the Spirit, and the Spirit what is contrary to the flesh. They are in conflict with each other, so that you are not to do whatever you want.

## 3. Fellowship

God created mankind with a need for fellowship. Therefore, you should look for other Christians who have surrendered their lives to God and keep in touch with them. These are the people with whom you can pray and talk about your faith. If a glowing coal is taken out of a fire, it will soon grow cold. As a rule, our love for Jesus will also grow cold if it is not kept alive through fellowship with other believers. Join a Bible-believing church and take an active part in this community. A good evangelical church where people believe in the whole Bible is so important for our Christian walk. Don't neglect fellowship with believers committed to a straightforward understanding of God's Word!

## 4. Faith

After our conversion and rebirth it is vitally important that we continue to grow spiritually. Paul wrote to Timothy: "But as for you, continue in what you have learned" (2 Tim. 3:14). Carefully read Ephesians 4:17–32, which lists practical truths about your lifetime sanctifying walk in the Spirit. At the end of his life Paul could say: "I have fought the good fight, I have finished the race, I have kept the faith" (2 Tim. 4:7). Let us follow his example and also remain faithful.

Conversion is not an end but rather the *beginning* of a new life. You are now able to be God's co-worker (1 Cor. 3:9). Be active in ensuring that others might also experience salvation in Jesus. Conversion has two amazing consequences: 1) our earthly life takes on a whole new meaning and, 2) we become God's children, heirs to eternal life, with Him in heaven.

# APPENDICES

*Appendix I*

# THE STATISTICAL VIEW
# OF INFORMATION

## A1.1 Shannon's Theory of Information

Claude E. Shannon (1916–2001) formulated a mathematical definition that includes a measure of information in his well-known paper, *The Mathematical Theory of Communication* [S7]. His measure of information, the "bit" (binary digit), had the advantage of allowing the properties of strings of symbols to be quantified. The disadvantage is just as plain: Shannon's definition of statistical information does not take into account any meaning or content in the information, but only the limited aspects that are necessary for evaluating its transmission and storage. Questions about meaning, comprehensibility, correctness, worth, or worthlessness, the origin (sender), and for whom it is intended (receiver) are not necessary for this kind of analysis. For Shannon's purpose, it is completely irrelevant whether a sequence of symbols represents meaningful text or whether it was produced by a random process. Because a random process may well be harder to compress for the purposes of transmission than a meaningful text, that random text will often have a higher "information" content than a meaningful text having the same number of symbols.

## Shannon's concept

His basic concept addresses an engineering problem in the communication of a message, namely, the determination of the maximum transmission speed, fidelity of the transmission (i.e., accurate reproducibility), and storage requirements. For these engineering purposes, the meaning and importance of a message are of no concern and, therefore, Shannon did not consider these aspects. According to Shannon's definition, information is present only if a sequence of symbols cannot be completely predicted. Thus, information is linked to the improbability of a set of symbols (letters, numbers, etc.). In English, "klamciny 9ucezdj" would be unlikely, so it contains a lot of Shannon "information." However, "The cat ate 9 mice" is much more likely and so contains *less* information. Clearly, Shannon's concept does not indicate the semantic content of a set of symbols.

In order to understand what Shannon was concerned with, we need to distinguish between the source of the symbols and the source of meaningful information. Meaningful information always comes from an intelligent source (a machine can, of course, reproduce or transmit such information, but not generate it in the first place). Strings of symbols, however, can be generated by machines, whether or not an intelligent source is operating them. Since Shannon was concerned with the symbols, the predictability of one symbol following another was important to him. Before a discrete source of symbols (N.B.: not a Universal Information source) delivers one symbol (Figure 37), there is uncertainty as to which symbol from the available symbol set (alphabet: $a_1$, $a_2$, $a_3$, ..., $a_n$) it will be (e.g., it could be symbol $x_1$). When that one symbol arrives, the uncertainty is resolved. For example, consider the letter "A" in English. There is a set of probabilities regarding what letter will follow it. If the source is not generating random sequences, then the next letter, which could be almost anything, will dramatically reduce the number of possibilities for accurately predicting the third letter. If, for instance, the second letter is a "P," then, again assuming that the sequence is not random, only the words in the dictionary which start with "AP" will be part of the probability set. If the third letter is also a "P," then the number of possibilities is even further reduced. Thus, words such as "apply," "applicable," "apple," etc. are the only ones now in the running. If, however, the sequence is random, then there is no reduction of probability at any point, so the series of letters is said to have high "information" content for the purposes of storage and transmission.

For the mathematically inclined reader, below are the derivations of a few of Shannon's basic formulae that may contribute to a better understanding of his reasoning.

## The information content of a sequence of symbols

Because Shannon was seeking to resolve a specific engineering problem, he needed to only be concerned with the statistical dimension of information. If one assumes that the probabilities of the appearances of the symbols are mutually independent of each other (e.g., "q" is not necessarily followed by "u") and that all N symbols have an equal probability of appearing, then the probability $p_i$ of any chosen symbol $x_i$ arriving is given by $p_i = 1/N$. Shannon defines information content in such a way that three conditions must be met:

1. The information content of k independent messages[1] (symbols or sequences of symbols) shall be summed, that is, the total information content is given by $I_{tot} = I_1 + I_2 + \dots + I_k$. This summation condition regards information as quantifiable.

2. The greater the element of surprise, the more information content is ascribed to a message. The surprise effect of the seldom-used letter "z" (low probability) is greater than for "e," which appears more frequently (high probability). It follows that the information value of a symbol $x_i$ increases when its probability $p_i$ decreases. This is expressed mathematically as an inverse proportion: $I \sim 1/p^i$.

3. In the simplest symmetrical case where there are only two different symbols (e.g., "0" and "1") that occur equally frequently ($p_1 = 0.5$ and $p_2 = 0.5$), the information content of such a symbol will be exactly one bit.

---

1. **Message:** In Shannon's theory, a message is not necessarily meaningful; it simply refers to a symbol (e.g., a letter) or a sequence of symbols (e.g., a word). In this sense the concept of a "message" is even included in the DIN standards system (recognized and applied in most countries) as DIN 44 300: *"Symbols and continuous functions employed for the purpose of transmission of information on the basis of known or supposed conventions."*

## A1.2 Mathematical treatment of statistical information

### A1.2.1 The bit: A unit of statistical information

One of the chief concerns in science and technology is that results, as much as possible, be expressed in a numerical form or as formulae, whereby the choice of units is important. This is comprised of two parts: the quantity and the unit. The unit is predetermined for purposes of comparison (e.g., meter, second, watt) and can be used to express other similarly measurable entities.

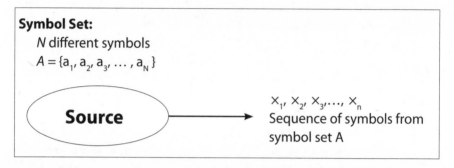

**Symbol Set:**
$N$ different symbols
$A = \{a_1, a_2, a_3, \dots, a_N\}$

**Source**

$x_1, x_2, x_3, \dots, x_n$
Sequence of symbols from symbol set A

Figure 37: Model of a discrete source for generating sequences of symbols. The source has a supply of N different symbols (e.g., an alphabet with 26 letters), of which a long sequence of n symbols is transmitted one after the other. The source could be a symbol generator that releases random sequences of symbols according to a given probability distribution, or it could be an unknown text stored on magnetic tape that is transmitted sequentially (i.e., one symbol at a time).

The unit used for measuring information content is called a "bit" (abbreviated from **b**inary dig**it**). In data processing systems, information is represented and processed in the form of electrical, optical, or mechanical signals. For this purpose, it is technically most advantageous, and therefore customary, to employ only two defined (binary) states or signals, similar to a switch being either "off" or "on." This means that only one of two values needs to be considered at any one time. One state is designated as binary one (1) and the other as binary zero (0). These two states may represent a variety of binary conditions such as YES and NO, TRUE and FALSE, 12V and 2V, and others. The bit is thus the smallest unit of information that can be represented in a digital computer. When text is entered in a computer, it is transformed into one of several predetermined binary codes, such as ASCII, and stored in this form. Thus, one letter of the English alphabet in ASCII requires 8 binary storage positions, known as a byte (8 bits = 1 byte). The information storage requirement of a text is then described in terms of the number of bits or bytes required. Different texts of the same length are thus accorded the same information content regardless of sense and meaning. The number of bits only measures the statistical quantity of the material medium used for information storage and transmission, not its meaningfulness.

The following two examples will illustrate the advantages (e.g., of calculating the amount of storage space) and the disadvantages (e.g., of ignoring the semantic aspects) of Shannon's definition of information.

## Example 1: Storage of biological information

The total length of all of the human DNA molecules in the nucleus of one cell (two molecules for each pair of chromosomes) is about two meters when fully stretched. They contain approximately $6 \times 10^9$ nucleotides with their chemical letters: adenine (A), cytosine (C), guanine (G), and thymine (T). How much statistical information is this according to Shannon's definition? The $N = 4$ chemical letters (A, C, G, and T) are nearly equal in their frequency distribution. Hence, their mean information content, I, is $I = -\log2\ p = -\log2\ (¼) = 2$ bits. The entire nuclear DNA thus has an information content of $Itot = 6 \times 109$ nucleotides $\times 2$ bits/nucleotide $= 1.2 \times 1010$ bits. This is equal to the information contained in 750,000 typed pages (US, 8 ½ × 11 inches). Taking 1,024 bits as 1Kbit, the total statistical information content of human DNA is $1.2 \times 1010/1024 = 1.172 \times 107$ Kbit = 11,720 megabits. This exceeds the capacity of a 512-megabit storage chip by a factor of almost 23.

## Example 2: The statistical information content of the Bible

The King James Version of the English Bible consists of 3,566,480 letters that make up 783,137 words [D1]. When the spaces between words are also counted, then n = 3,566,480 + 783,137 - 1 = 4,349,616 symbols. Taking into account the frequency of occurrence of letters (including spaces) in the English language, the average information content of a single letter thus amounts to i = 4.046 bits. The total information content of the Bible is then given by $I_{tot} = 4,349,616 \times 4.046 = 17.6$ million bits. Since the German language contains more letters than English, each

340 • Information: The Key to Life

| | |
|---|---|
| 1 | 1 Hụrẹ ụmọrụmọ, d'a va yẹ ka aa mẹ ẹhẹ, Ịrẹyị Ohomorihi hụrẹ yà ịzọọ nị. Ịrẹyị ọnọọ vi ana yà ịda Ohomorihi, Ịrẹyị ọnọọ gẹdẹ-gẹdẹ vị Ohomorihi. 2 Hụrẹ ụmọrụmọ ọnọọ, Ịrẹyị ọnọọ hụrẹ yà ịda Ohomorihi nị. 3 Inị oze Ịrẹyị ọnọọ Ohomorihi zị mẹ avaba ịsa nị. Inị avaba ịsa on 'Ohomorihi tú saka-saka, ayị nyị ikonya ẹnẹ ẹyị vị ini oze Ịrẹyị ọnọọ ọ yà túọọ. 4 Ịrẹyị ọnọọ ọ mẹ ka ịsavị-savị è yàra nị. Ọyịyàra ọnọọ aa sị etohueyii zù aza nị.<br><br>(EBIRA, Nigeria; 86 words, 325 letters) |
| 2 | 1 Bunso zaa piiligu, so ba n boona Yelibii n daa n na, o ba Naawun saani, ka o ni Naawunni niŋi lunko, 2 ka o ni Naawunni daa n ba niŋi piiligu maa. 3 0 zu n na, bunso zaa daa n maali, ka pa o zu, bunso zaa daa n ki maali. 4 A kpali o zu, bunso zaa n daa n maali la marini nyevuri, ka nyevuri maa mi ti nisaaldima paaligu, ba nyaara.<br><br>(HANGA, Ghana; 73 words, 240 letters) |
| 3 | 1 A daarra jày pî yèy tâaye nà, tâanjirre nà ni Fay. Yèy gi tâage Fay. 2 A daarra tâanji ni Fay. 3 Jày pî mbangsi ni erra. Cen jày mbangsi, to naa ni erra gi ba. 4 E hîige gŭyrra. Gŭyrra maan tâage kayang da nit ây.<br><br>(FALI, Cameroon; 44 words, 155 letters) |
| 4 | 1 Aullaġniisaqqaaġataqman ittuq uqałiq, uqałiq, iqatauplunĭ Agaayutmĭ, suli uqałiq Agaayutaupluni. 2 Ilaa piqatauniqsuq Agaayutmĭ aullaġniisaqqaaġatałiġmĭ. 3 Ilaa piqatigiplugu Agaayun iñiqtaqaqtuq supayaamĭk. Atausriq-unniiñ ilugaaniñ iñiqtaġikkaŋanin iñiqtauṅĝitchuq piilaaġlugu. 4 Uqałiq iñugutiqaqhuni iŋmiñi, taavruma iñuułhum iñuich qaġgutigai, kaŋiqsiłiksraŋatnun Agaayutmĭk.<br><br>(KOBUK RIVER Eskimo, Alaska; 33 words, 332 letters) |
| 5 | 1 Ja Joi Ibo yoiquinra, en mato yoiai. Jabichoressiqui, jahuequescarin Dios iśhon, jan jato quiquinshamanhaquin onanmai; noa yoyo icatoninbi huetsabaon non icábo onancanai quescáaquin. Ja Joi Ibora, Diosen nato nete joniaamatianbi jaa iqui. Jara jatíbitian Dios betanbishaman jaconhirai jaque. Jainoaś jaribi iqui, Dios betan senenribi. 2 Jascara iquenra, en mato banebainquin yoiai. Ja Joi Ibora, Diosen nete joniaamatianbi jaa iqui. Jascara icaśhśha, jaribi iqui Dios, jainoaś ja betanbishamanribi jatíbitian jaque. 3 Ja Joi Ibo betan rabéanan jatíbi jahuéquibo jonianośhonra, Diosen shinana iqui. Jascara icaśhśhiqui, jatíbi non oinai jahuéquiboyabi nato neten jaa jahuéquibo, ja Joi Ibon joniaabires; jascáanon iśhon Diosenbi imaa icaś. Jatíbi jan joniayamaquetianra, jahuebi yamaqueanque. 4 Jascati jatíbitian jaa iśhonra, joniboribi jan joniaa iqui. Jascara iśhonra, jatíbitianbiressibi noa jatíbi jonibo jan jamai. Jascáaquin noa jatíbitian jan jamai iśhonra, jatíbi noabo jan acai noa aconquin onanmaquin; jahuequescarin Dios iśhon. Nato netemea jahuéquibo joecan tenaquetian non oinai quescáaquinra, jan noa Dios onanmai.<br><br>(SHIPIBO-CONIBO, Indian, Peru; 147 words, 944 letters) |
| 6 | 1 Topẽ tỹ nén ũ kar han ja tũg ki tóg nĩ ja nĩ, ẽg tỹ ũ to: "Topẽ vĩ," he mũ ẽn ti, hã to ẽg: Jesus, he mũ. Topẽ mré tóg nĩ nĩ. Topẽ vỹ tỹ ti nĩ gé. 2 Topẽ tỹ nén (ũ) kar han tũg ki tóg Topẽ mré nĩ nĩ. 3 Ti hã tugrĩn tóg nén ũ kar han, Topẽ ti, ẽg tỹ ũ to: "Topẽ vĩ," he mũ ẽn tugnĩn. A pir mỹ Topẽ tóg nén ũ han tũ nĩ, ti hã mre tóg nén kar han kãn. 4 Ẽg tỹ ũ to: "Topẽ vĩ," he mũ ẽn vỹ rĩr nĩ, hã kỹ tóg ẽg rĩnrĩr han mũ gé. Jẽngrẽ ri ke ti nĩ, ũ tỹ ẽg rĩnrĩr han mũ ẽn ti. Ti tỹ ẽg kanhrãn to ken hã vẽ.<br><br>(KAINGANG, Indian, Brazil; 132 words, 335 letters) |
| 7 | 1 C?ia⁴ nca³ to²ts?in³ -le⁴ cjoa⁴ to⁴c?oa⁴ ti¹jna³je² en¹. Je² en¹ ti¹ -jna³t?a³ Ni³na¹. Je² en¹ ña³qui³ Ni³na¹ ni¹. 2 Je² -vi⁴ ×i³ ti¹ jna³t?a³ Ni³na¹ c?ia⁴ nca³ to²ts?in³ -le⁴ cjoa⁴. 3 Je² tsa³c?e¹nta³ nca³yi³je³ tso³ jmi². Tsa² tsin² je², ni⁴to⁴ jme³ -jin² ×i³ tjin¹ ×i³ qui³s?e³nta³. 4 Je² ×i³ tjin¹ -le⁴ cjoa⁴vi³jna³ chon³. Je² cjoa⁴vi³jna³chon³ je² I?i¹ ×i³ si¹?i³ sen³ -le⁴ cho⁴ta⁴.<br><br>(MAZATECO, Indian, Mexico; 54 words, 212 letters) |

The author is sincerely grateful for the Bible texts made available by Mr. Andreas Holzhausen, Wycliffe Bible translator, Burbach/Germany.

Table 4: John 1:1–4 in different languages

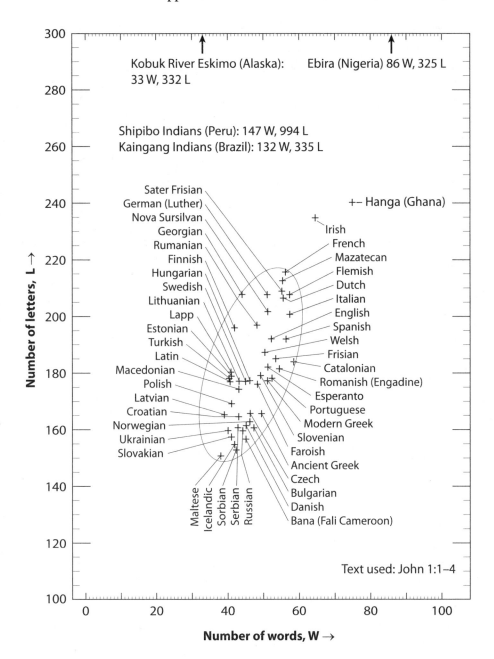

Figure 38: The number of letters, L, and words, W, illustrating statistical properties of the indicated languages in their translations of John 1:1–4.

German letter will have higher average information content, although
the actual information content in either language is the same in terms of
meaning. This difference becomes extreme when we consider the *Shipibo*
language of Peru (see Figure 38 and Table 4 on pages 340–341). The
*Shipibo* Bible contains (by simple extrapolation) about 5.2 (= 994/191)
times as much "information" (measured in the purely statistical sense) as
the English Bible. Thus, even when the meaning of the contents is exactly
the same (as in the case of John 1:1–4 in different languages), Shannon's
theory yields appreciably different estimates of the information content.

In Table 4, the first four verses of the Gospel of John are rendered
in three African and four American languages. In my book, *So Steht's
Geschrieben, (It is Written)*, [G18], p. 105–108, the same verses are given
in 47 different European languages for purposes of comparison. The seventh language in Table 4 (Mazatecan) is a tonal language.

Figure 38 plots the various values of W and L for John 1:1–4 for
the following languages: 47 European and 7 African and American. It
is remarkable that the coordinates of nearly all European languages fall
inside the given ellipse. Of the 54 languages, the Maltese language uses
the least number of words and letters while the *Shipibo* Indians use the
largest number of words and letters for expressing the same semantic
information.

### A1.2.2 The information spiral

Table 5 lists an abundance of examples from the fields of language, everyday events, electronic data processing, and biological life in which the
statistical information content is given in bits. A graphical representation
of the full range of values requires more than 24 orders of magnitude
(powers of ten) so a logarithmic spiral has been chosen for Figure 39. A
selection of values from Table 5 is shown in Figure 39, where each scale
division indicates a tenfold increase from the previous one.

Next, we will focus on two distinct regions of Figure 40, where two
different storage media are shown:

- the storage technology used in a computer — exemplified by
  the microchip

- biological storage in the DNA molecule — represented by
  the ant (A1.2.3).

Table 5: An extensive list of examples from fields of language, everyday events, electronic data processing and biological life in which the statistical information content is given in bits.

| Bits or bits/s | Comparison of various information quantities | |
|---|---|---|
| | $I$ = total statistical information content (unit: bits)<br>$i$ = statistical information content per symbol (unit: bits)<br>$S$ = memory (unit: bits)<br>$v$ = transmission speed (unit: bits/s or bits/minute) | |
| | **Standard information units:** | |
| 1 | 1 bit | |
| 1024 | 1 Kbit* | = $2^{10}$ bits = 1024 bits |
| $1.049 \times 10^6$ | 1 Mbit* | = $2^{20}$ = 1024·1024 bits = 1,048,576 bits |
| $1.074 \times 10^9$ | 1 Gbit* | = $2^{30}$ = $1024^3$ bits = 1,073,741,824 bits |
| $1.100 \times 10^{12}$ | 1 Tbit* | = $2^{40}$ = $1024^4$ bits= 1,099,511,627,776 bits |
| 8 | 1 byte | = 8 bits (= 1 octet = 2 nibbles) |
| $8.192 \times 10^3$ | 1 Kbyte | = 1,024 bytes = 8,192 bits |
| $8.389 \times 10^6$ | 1 Mbyte | = 1,048,576 bytes = 8,388,608 bits |
| $8.590 \times 10^9$ | 1 Gbyte | = 1.073742 $\times 10^9$ bytes = 8.5899 $\times 10^9$ bits |
| $8.796 \times 10^{12}$ | 1 Tbyte | = 1.099512 $\times 10^{12}$ bytes = 8.796 $\times 10^{12}$ bits |
| | * Technically, $2^{10}$ = 1024 bits is actually 1 Kibit, not 1 Kbit. Similarly, $2^{20}$ = 1,048,576 bits is 1 Mibit, not 1 Mbit. The same for $2^{30}$ and $2^{40}$ bits (1 Gibit and 1 Tibit, respectively). However, common practice is to allow the nearest power of ten to be used. For example, a processor designated as '64Kb' actually contains 65,536 bits instead of 64,000. | |
| | **Information content of a single letter or groups of letters:** with an alphabet of 27 characters (26 letters and 1 space): | |
| 4.76 | a) | uniform frequency of all letters:<br>$i = \log_2 27$ = 4.755 bits/letter |
| 4.113 | b) | taking into account the frequency distribution of letters in the German language (see [G14, p. 178]):<br>$i = \Sigma p_i \log_2 (1/p_i)$ = 4.113 bits/letter |
| 4.05 | c) | taking into account the frequency distribution of letters in the English language (see [G14, p. 178]):<br>$i = \Sigma p_i \log_2 (1/p_i)$ = 4.05 bits/letter |
| 3.32 | d) | taking into account groups of two English letters (see [G14, p. 201]):<br>$i$ = 3.32 bits/letter |
| 3.1 | e) | taking into account groups of three English letters (see [G14, p. 201]):<br>$i$ = 3.1 bits/letter |
| 1 to 2 | f) | considering the redundancy of the language:<br>$i$ = 1 to 2 bits/letter |

| Bits or bits/s | Comparison of various information quantities | |
|---|---|---|
| | **Information content of a number in various number bases:** | |
| 1 | a) | Binary system: 2 different symbols (0 and 1) $i = \log_2 2 = 1$ bit/symbol |
| 3.32 | b) | Decimal system: 10 different symbols (digits) (0, 1, 2 ... 9) $i = \log_2 10 = 3.32$ bits/digit |
| 4 | c) | Hexadecimal system: 16 different digits (0, 1, 2, 3, 4, 5, 6, 7, 8, 9, A, B, C, E, F) $i = \log_2 16 = 4$ bits/digit |
| | **Genetic code:** Nucleotides of the DNA molecules contain four chemical letters: A, C, G, T, where a triplet (3 nucleotide letters) codes for a single amino acid. | |
| 2 | a) | Information content of one letter (uniform frequency): $i = \log_2 4 = 2$ bits/nucleotide letter |
| 6 | b) | Information content of a triplet within the DNA molecule: $i = 3$ letters/triplet $\times 2$ bits/letter $= 6$ bits/triplet |
| 4.32 | c) | Statistical information content of one amino acid (of a possible 20) (for simplification here, we assume uniform distribution): $i = \log_2 20 = 4.32$ bits/amino acid |
| 1.44 | d) | Statistical information content of one nucleotide letter assuming the above amino acid: $i = \log_2 4.32$ bits/amino acid $= 4.32$ bits/triplet $= 1.44$ bits/nucleotide letter |
| | **Some everyday examples:** | |
| 198 | Counting numbers for one minute: approximately $v = 3.3$ bits/s $= 198$ bits/minute | |
| 960 | Typing for one minute: $v \approx 16$ bits/s $= 960$ bits/minute | |
| 1,320 | Playing the piano for one minute: $v \approx 22$ bits/s $= 1,320$ bits/minute | |
| $3.5 \times 10^4$ | Information collected by the human ear in 1 second: $v \approx 3.5 \times 10^4$ bits/s | |
| $1.6 \times 10^4$ | One typed 8.5 × 11 (American) page with 2,000 characters: $S = (2,000 \text{ symbols}) \times (8 \text{ bits/symbol}) = 1.6 \times 10^4$ bits. | |
| $1.28 \times 10^4$ | Computer screen: $S = (20 \text{ lines}) \times (80 \text{ characters}) = 1,600 \text{ bytes} = 1.28 \times 10^4$ bits | |
| $9.22 \times 10^6$ | TV screen: 300 Kbit in 1/30 second $v = 300 \times 1,024 \times 30 = 9.216 \times 10^6$ bits/s | |
| $3.33 \times 10^4$ | Hi-fi long-playing record: 2 Mbit in 1 minute $= 3.33 \times 10^4$ bits/s | |
| $5.87 \times 10^9$ | Compact Disc (CD): $S = 700$ Mbyte $= 5.87 \times 10^9$ bits | |
| $4.04 \times 10^{10}$ | Digital Versatile Disc (DVD): $S = 4.7$ Gbyte $= 4.04 \times 10^{10}$ bits | |
| 5,120 | Telephone conversation: 300 Kbit/minute $v = 300 \times 1,024 = 307,200$ bits/minute $= 5,120$ bits/s | |

| Bits or bits/s | Comparison of various information quantities | |
|---|---|---|
| | Telephone communication via satellite: | |
| $3.1 \times 10^5$ | a) | First communications satellite, Telstar (1962): 60 telephone calls $v = 60 \times 307{,}200$ bits/minute/60 $= 3.072 \times 10^5$ bits/s |
| $1.23 \times 10^6$ | b) | First fully commercially utilized satellite (Early Bird = Intelsat I; 1965): 240 telephone calls simultaneously $v = 240 \times 307{,}200$ bits/minute/60 $= 1.228 \times 10^6$ bits/s |
| $1.69 \times 10^8$ | c) | Intelsat VI (1986): 33,000 telephone calls simultaneously: $v = 33{,}000 \times 307{,}200$ bits/minute/60 $= 1.69 \times 10^8$ bits/s |
| $5.1 \times 10^6$ | d) | Intelsat 17 (2011), 66 degrees east, 1.5 GHz bandwidth: 100,000 telephone calls simultaneously $v = 100{,}000 \times 307{,}200$ bits/minute/60 $= 5.1 \times 10^6$ bits/s |
| | In the field of computers: | |
| $1.6 \times 10^4$ | Main memory of the first generation ESDAC computer: 2,000 bytes = 16,000 bits | |
| $1.007 \times 10^7$ | 5 ¼" diskette for PC: 1.2 Mbyte = $1.2 \times 8.389 \times 10^6$ bits $= 1.007 \times 10^7$ | |
| $1.174 \times 10^7$ | 3 ½" diskette for PC: 1.4 Mbyte = $1.4 \times 8.389 \times 10^6$ bits $= 1.174 \times 10^7$ bits | |
| $1.258 \times 10^7$ | Main memory of the early main frame computers (e.g. TR440; 1970): 256 KWords each of 48 bits length $= 1.258 \times 10^7$ bits | |
| $4.54 \times 10^7$ | Storage capacity of a magnetic tape: length 720 m, storage density 1,600 bits per inch $S = 1{,}600$ bpi $\times 720 \times 10^3$ mm/(25.4 mm/inch) $= 4.54 \times 10^7$ bits | |
| $9.6 \times 10^7$ | Peformance per hour of early line printers: 1,250 characters/minute; maximum 160 characters/line $v = 1{,}250 \times 160 \times 60 \times 8 = 9.6 \times 10^7$ bits/hour | |
| $6.87 \times 10^{10}$ | Main memory of a modern laptop computer (PC; 2010): 8 Gbyte $S = 8$ Gbyte $= 8 \times 8.5899 \times 10^9$ bits $= 6.87 \times 10^{10}$ bits | |
| $4.29 \times 10^{12}$ | Hard disk of a modern laptop computer (PC; 2010): 500 Gbyte: $S = 500 \times 8.5899 \times 10^9$ bits $= 4.29 \times 10^{12}$ bits | |
| $2.75 \times 10^{11}$ | USB stick (2010): 32 Gbyte $S = 32 \times 8.5899 \times 10^9$ bits $= 2.75 \times 10^{11}$ bits | |
| $10^{12}$ | Theoretical capacity of holographic memory: $10^{12}$ bits/cm$^3$ | |

| Bits or bits/s | Comparison of various information quantities |
|---|---|
| | **In the fields of science and literature:** |
| $4.8 \times 10^6$ | Electronics terms: 60,000 terms (*Duden*, Vol. 1), ca. 10 letters/word $S = 60{,}000 \times 10 \times 8 = 4.8 \times 10^6$ bits |
| $1.28 \times 10^7$ | *Meyers Großes Universallexikon* in 15 volumes: $S = 200{,}000$ key words = $200{,}000 \times 8 \times 8 = 1.28 \times 10^7$ bits |
| $2 \times 10^7$ | Medical terms: 250,000 terms (according to Duden, Vol. 1) $S = 250{,}000 \times 10 \times 8 = 2 \times 10^7$ bits |
| $4.2 \times 10^8$ | Names of compounds in organic chemistry: 3.5 million (according to *Duden*, Vol.1), 15 letters/name: $S = 3.5 \times 10^6 \times 15 \times 8 = 4.2 \times 10^8$ bits |
| $3.47 \times 10^7$ | Bible, English King James version 783,137 words, 3,566,480 letters $I = (3{,}566{,}480 + 783{,}137 - 1)$ characters $\times 4.05$ bit/character = $17.6 \times 10^6$ bits $S = (3{,}566{,}480 + 783{,}137 - 1) \times 8 = 3.47 \times 10^7$ bits |
| $8 \times 10^8$ | 100 ring binders = 50,000 typewritten pages $S = 50{,}000 \times 2{,}000 = 10^8$ characters = $8 \times 10^8$ bits |
| $5.76 \times 10^{12}$ | Current number of scientific journals: 100,000 Assumptions: 100 pages/journal; 6000 characters/page; publication monthly. Annual growth of volume of information: $S = 100{,}000 \times 100 \times 6{,}000 \times 12 \times 8 = 5.76 \times 10^{12}$ bits |
| $4.02 \times 10^{11}$ | Number of book titles at the Frankfurt book fair of 2009 Total number of book titles 402,000, of which 120,000 were new appearances $S = 402{,}000$ books $\times 10^6$ bits/book = $4.02 \times 10^{11}$ bits |
| $6.2 \times 10^{11}$ | 620,000 book titles are currently available in German $S = 620{,}000$ books $\times 10^6$ bits/book = $6.2 \times 10^{11}$ bits Each year more than 60,000 new titles appear on the market |
| $10^{13}$ | Library of Congress, Washington, USA $10^7$ volumes [S4] $S = 10^7$ volumes $\times 10^6$ bits/book = $10^{13}$ bits |
| $10^{18}$ | Total knowledge of mankind in books: $10^{18}$ bits. By comparison: 1 book containing 100 pages of text = 200,000 characters = $1.6 \times 10^6$ bits. Thus $10^{18}$ bits correspond to 625 billion such books. Assuming each book to be 1.5 cm thick, then the length, L, of the bookshelf is L = $625 \times 10^9$ books $\times 1.5$ cm/book = $937.5 \times 10^9$ cm = 9.4 million km = 235 times around the equator |
| $9.06 \times 10^{12}$ | Daily data volume from satellite pictures: Transfer rate: 100 Mbits/s $v = 100 \times 1.048 \times 10^6 \times 86{,}400 = 9.055 \times 10^{12}$ bits/day |
| | **Examples from the Life Sciences:** |
| $3.9 \times 10^6$ | According to Küpfmüller [S4], the number of mother tongue words stored in a person's memory is 100,000: (by comparison, the German Lexicon "Volksbrockhaus" contains 250,000 words). Taking one letter: 1.5 bits required for the memory of its sound and 5 bits (= $\log_2 32$) for the memory of its shape, at 6 letters/word: $S = 100{,}000 \times 6 \times (5 + 1.5) = 3.9 \times 10^6$ bits |

| Bits or bits/s | Comparison of various information quantities |
|---|---|
| $2.65 \times 10^{20}$ | The memory capacity of the human brain from a purely physical viewpoint, is according to [S4]:<br><br>a) McCullach: $10^{13}$ to $10^{15}$ bits<br>b) Küpfmüller: $3.9 \times 10^6$ bits (word memory only)<br>c) Müller: 1,500 bits per complex $\times$ 1,000 cognitive complexes = $1.5 \times 10^6$ bits<br>d) v. Neumann: $10^{10}$ nerve cells in the brain, 14 bits/s for a standard receptor.<br><br>*In 60 years:*<br>$S_{max} = 10^{10} \times 14$ bits/s $\times$ 60 years $\times$ 365 days/year $\times$ 24 h/day $\times$ 3,600 seconds/hour<br>$S_{max} = 2.65 \times 10^{20}$ bits<br><br>As expounded in depth in [G16], the information capacity of the human brain cannot be explained solely in terms of neural switching. |
| $3.76 \times 10^{18}$ | The storage capacity of 1 mm$^3$ of DNA: $3.76 \times 10^{18}$ bits<br>(DNA = DeoxyriboNucleic Acid; calculated for the nucleotides in both strands) |
| $3.5 \times 10^{19}$ | The daily unconscious flow of information in the human body [S4, p. 81] such as the immense production of macro-molecules:<br>$v = 3 \times 10^{24}$ bits/day = $3.5 \times 10^{19}$ bits/s |
| $7.14 \times 10^8$ | Images received by the human eye, assuming 14 images/second [S4]:<br>$v = 10^{10}$ bits/s<br>$I = (10^{10}$ bits/s)/(14 images/s) = $7.14 \times 10^8$ bits/image |
| $1.2 \times 10^{10}$ | Human cell: $6 \times 10^9$ nucleotides in the nuclear DNA<br>$I = 6 \times 10^9$ nucleotides $\times$ 2 bits/nucleotide = $1.2 \times 10^{10}$ bits |
| $9.4 \times 10^6$ | The DNA of *Escherichia coli*. This bacterium weighs $10^{-23}$ g and has a length of only 2 µm. Its DNA molecule is 1 mm long when stretched out and contains<br>4.7 million letters (nucleotides)<br>$I = 4.7 \times 10^6$ nucleotides $\times$ 2 bits/nucleotide = $9.4 \times 10^6$ bits<br>Cell division takes around 20 minutes and the basic rate of recognition of the letters is around 1,000 times faster. This leads to a reading speed of $9.4 \times 10^6$ bits $\times 1,000/(20 \times 60) = 7.75 \times 10^6$ bits/s. |

**Table 5: Comparison of diverse information statistics**

This table shows a selection of information statistics from a number of domains: the letters of natural languages and of the genetic code, computer technology and science, literature and biological life. The numbers in the left column are the numbers of bits, representing the statistical unit of measurement or the transfer rates of bits/s. A short calculation shows the origin of some of the numbers for better understanding.

## Computer technology

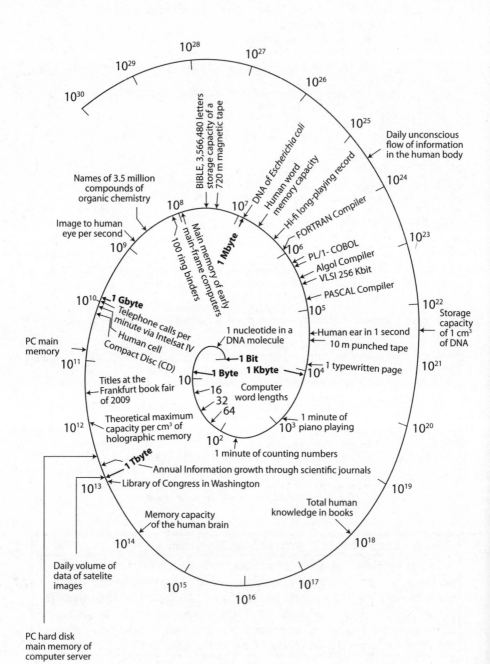

Figure 39: The information spiral

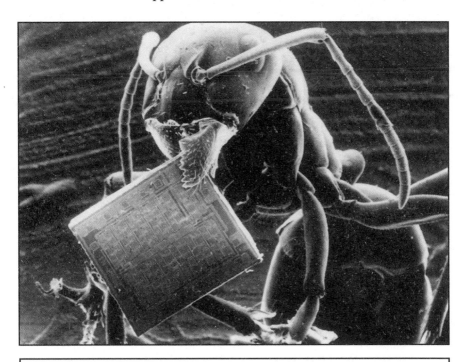

Figure 40: The ant and the microchip. Microchips are the storage elements of present-day computers. What a 30-ton computer at the University of Pennsylvania (USA) could do in 1946 could by 2010 be accomplished by a chip less than six mm² in size. Such a chip could also store all the telephone numbers of a large city and process the words in the entire Bible 200 times in one second. Since then, their performance has grown exponentially.

(Source: "Werkbild Philips"; with the kind permission of "Valvo Unternehmensbereichs Bauelemente" of Philips GmbH, Hamburg.)

The German inventor Konrad Zuse (1910–1996) is recognized as the pioneer of the programmable computer in that he built the first operational programmable electronic computing machine, the Z3, in 1941. It used 600 telephone relays for calculations and 2,000 relays for storage. This was the first functioning, programmable calculating machine based on the binary system. It could store 64 numbers of 22-bit length, and could perform between 15 and 20 arithmetic operations per second.

The next advance was the introduction of vacuum tubes (first generation electronic computers), with the ENIAC computer becoming operational in 1946. It had more than 18,000 vacuum tubes and other components wired together by means of more than half a million soldered connections. One

350 • Information: The Key to Life

addition operation required 0.2 thousandths of a second and a multiplication could be performed in 2.8 thousandths of a second. This installa-
tion utilized a word length[2] of 10 decimal places, weighed 30 tons, and
consumed 150 kW of electrical power. After several years of research,
transistors were invented in 1947. They were much smaller and faster
than vacuum tubes and their introduction as switching elements initiated the second computer generation in 1955.

The next milestone on the way to the powerful computers of today
was the remarkable new idea of integrating different interconnected components on the same substrate. This novel idea, proposed by Kilby and
Hoerni in 1958, led to the first integrated circuit (IC). Further development of this concept, and the steady increase in the number of circuit
elements per silicon chip, led to the advent of the third computer generation. ICs have undergone a rapid development since the first simple ones
introduced in 1958. By 1994, 64-megabit chips were commonplace.
Depending on the number of components per structural unit, we can
distinguish five levels of integration:

SSI    (Small Scale Integration)       1 to 10

MSI    (Medium Scale Integration)     10 to $10^3$

LSI    (Large Scale Integration)       $10^3$ to $10^5$

VLSI   (Very Large Scale Integration)  $10^5$ to $10^{10}$

GSI    (Grand Scale Integration)       $10^{10}$ and upward

Large scale integration (LSI) — with between 500 and 150,000 transistors accommodated on one silicon chip with an area between 5 and
30 mm$^2$ — led to the development of microprocessors. With this technology it was possible to have complete computer processing units and
memory on a single chip. The number of circuits integrated on one
chip has doubled approximately every second year. The first experimental silicon chip capable of storing more than one million bits (1 Megabit
= $2^{20}$ bits = 1,048,576 bits) was developed in 1984 by IBM. The silicon wafer that was used measured 10.5 mm × 7.7 mm = 80.85 mm$_2$,

---

2. **Word length:** A set of bits that is processed as a unit is called a word. The range of
numbers that can be handled, as well as the number of data storage locations that can be
addressed, depends on the length and the structure of the word.

so that the storage density was 13,025 bits per square mm. The time required to access data on this chip was 150 nanoseconds (1 ns = $10^{-9}$ s, a billionth of a second). The integration density has increased steadily in subsequent years and the time required to access data has decreased proportionately.

## A1.2.3 The highest packing density of information

The greatest-known packing density of information is found in the DNA of living cells. The diameter of this chemical storage medium, illustrated in Figure 41, is 2 nanometers (nm) = $2 \times 10^{-9}$ m = $2 \times 10^{-6}$ mm and the spiral increment of the helix is $3.4 \times 10^{-6}$ mm (Greek *hélix* = winding, spiral). The volume of a cylinder (in this case, one turn of the DNA coil) is $V = hd^2 \pi/4$.

$$V = 3.4 \times 10^{-6} \text{ mm} \times (2 \times 10^{-6} \text{ mm})^2 \times \pi/4 = 1.068 \times 10^{-17} \text{ mm3}$$

Thus, the volume of all the coils in the human DNA is about $3 \times 10^{-9}$ mm³.

$$(1.068 \times 10^{-17} \times 3 \times 10^{9} / 10 = 3.2 \times 10^{-9})$$

There are 20 chemical letters (nucleotide "letters") in each turn of the double spiral (10 letters for each strand), giving a statistical information density of $\rho$ = 20 nucleotide letters/($1.068 \times 10^{-17}$ mm³ ) $\approx 1.88 \times 10^{18}$ nucleotide letters per mm³.

If we associate the average statistical information content of six bits with three nucleotide letters (codon) of the genetic code, we arrive at 6/3 = 2 bits per nucleotide letter. We can now use this to express the statistical information density of DNA.

A few further comparisons will help us comprehend the vast storage density of the DNA molecule $\rho_{DNA}$.

$$\rho_{DNA} = 1.88 \times 10^{18} \text{ nucleotide letters/mm}^3 \times (2 \text{ bits/nucleotide letter}) = 3.76 \times 10^{18} \text{ bits/mm}^3.$$

This packing density is so inconceivably large that we need an illustrative comparison to help us grasp it. Figure 41 shows the dimensions of a photographic slide "A" (a mostly outdated technology today) that displays the *entire* Bible (from Genesis through Revelation) on its 33 mm × 32 mm surface, having been reproduced by means of a special microfilm process with a thickness of 0.44 mm [M5]. By computation it follows that the DNA molecule entails an information storage density

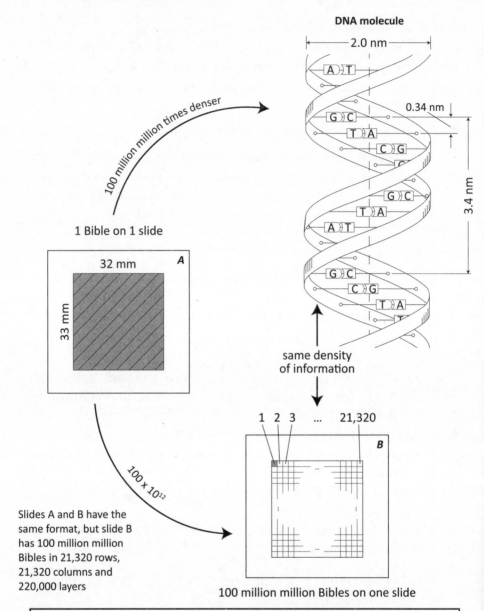

**DNA molecule**

2.0 nm

0.34 nm

3.4 nm

100 million million times denser

1 Bible on 1 slide

32 mm

*A*

33 mm

same density
of information

100 × 10¹²

1  2  3  ...  21,320

*B*

Slides A and B have the
same format, but slide B
has 100 million million
Bibles in 21,320 rows,
21,320 columns and
220,000 layers

100 million million Bibles on one slide

Figure 41: Comparison of statistical information densities. DNA molecules contain the highest known packing density of information. This particularly ingenious storage method reaches the limit of the physically possible, namely down to the level of single molecules, with an information density of more than $10^{21}$ bits per cm². This is 100 million million times the density obtained when the entire Bible is reproduced on photographic slide A. To equal the information packing density present in all cells would require that 100 million million Bibles could be represented on slide B (this is only theoretically possible) having approximately 21,320 rows, 21,320 columns, and 220,000 layers (for the 0.44 mm thickness!), with the entire Bible reproduced in each resultant minuscule rectangle.

of approximately 100 trillion times[3] greater than that of slide "A," which contains the entire Bible.

This comparison is all the more astonishing if we want to achieve the DNA packing density on a similar photographic slide "B" (Figure 41). We would have to divide its surface into approximately 21,320 rows, 21,320 columns, and 220,000 layers with each layer the thickness of the DNA molecule, i.e., 2 nm (throughout the entire 0.44 mm thickness). We would then need to be able to copy *an entire Bible in a readable form* into each of the resulting tiny rectangles on each layer. If this were possible, we would have reached the density of the information carried in every living cell. In any case, we should remember that it is technologically impossible at present to produce slide "B." Even if it were possible to achieve such a photographic reduction, we would still only have a static storage system that differs fundamentally from that of DNA. The DNA molecule is a dynamic memory since its own information is duplicated during cell division by means of complex machinery.

### Further astounding comparisons

a. *A pinhead of DNA:* Let us imagine we had enough DNA to fill the volume of a pinhead with a diameter of 2 mm. How many paperbacks (each with 189 pages as in [G19]) could be represented by the information held in that amount of DNA? Answer: about 25 trillion. That is about 3,000 copies for each of the approximately 8 billion people on earth in 2022. This would make a pile of these books approximately 920 times the distance from the earth to the moon (240,000 miles = 384,000 km).

b. *Drawing a wire:* Now let us stretch the material of the 2 mm diameter pinhead into a wire of the same thickness as the DNA molecule ($2 \times 10^{-6}$ mm). How long would this wire be? Unbelievably, it would stretch 33 times around the equator, which has a circumference of 24,860 miles (40,000 km).

---

3. **Calculation:** $V_{Bible}$ = 32 mm × 33 mm × 0.44 mm = 464.6 mm³. The English Bible has a statistical information content of $17.6 \times 10^6$ bits (see Table 5). Therefore, the information density of the Bible on the slide is given by $17.6 \times 10^6$ / 464.6 mm³ = $3.78 \times 10^4$ bits/ mm3. If we divide $\rho_{DNA}$ by $\rho_{Bible}$ we arrive at $3.76 \times 10^{18}$ bits/mm³ / $3.78 \times 10^4$ bits/mm³ ≈ $100 \times 10^{12}$.

c. *One thousandth of a gram of DNA:* If we were to take a milligram (1 mg = $10^{-3}$ g) of a (double helix) strand of DNA material, it would almost stretch from the earth to the moon!

## Human nuclear DNA

a. *Typed on a typewriter:* The human nuclear DNA contains approximately six billion nucleotide letters. If these letters were 7 letters to an inch and we were to type these individual letters on a single line, this string of letters would stretch nearly 13,530 miles (21,770 km) — which is about 1,100 miles (1,770 km) more than the distance from the North Pole to the South Pole. Four good typists typing at 300 characters (letters) per minute, 8 hours per day, and 220 days a year, would need 48 years to finish typing all of the letters.

b. *Volume:* The storage medium in each human cell in the form of the DNA double helix takes up a volume of only three billionths of a cubic millimeter ($3 \times 10-9$ mm$^3$). To illustrate, suppose that the period at the end of this sentence (having a diameter of approximately 0.3 mm) was actually a sphere of the same diameter. The volume of this spherical "period" would be approximately $1.414 \times 10^{-2}$ mm$^3$. Therefore, one could fit approximately 4.7 *million* human DNA volumes into this "period" sphere, each encoding the complete genetic information for an individual person.

c. *Number of letters:* To try to comprehend the number of letters in the human nuclear DNA encoding one person, consider: it is *six times* the number of minutes that have passed since the birth of Jesus, around 2,000 years ago!

d. *Human nuclear DNA and paperback books:* The number of letters (six billion) contained in the genome of a single human corresponds to those in almost 19,300 copies of a 189-page paperback book [G19].

All of these comparisons have shown us the breathtakingly ingenious information storage concept found in DNA, both in terms of economy of material and miniaturization. This is the densest-known storage of (statistical) information. The highly integrated storage memory of our modern computer systems doesn't come close to matching this.

## Typing speed and error rate

Perhaps the most well-known bacterium is *Escherichia coli (E. coli)*. Under favorable conditions, the doubling time, i.e., the time in which the number of bacteria in a given volume of culture medium doubles, is only 20 to 25 minutes. Since the DNA of an *E. coli* bacterium consists of around 4,720,000 base pairs, the copy rate/bacterium is about 472,000 nucleotide letters per minute. An English Bible has 3,566,480 letters. In other words, an *E. coli* bacterium could "copy" an entire Bible in about 7.6 minutes.

Even more astonishing is the accuracy of the copying (with its built-in error correction) of the whole DNA molecule (replication). The probability that one letter is copied incorrectly is less than one in one billion. Imagine 280 individuals each typing out one Bible (or one typist typing out the Bible 280 times). The precision of the DNA replication is such that there would be only a *single* letter wrong in these 280 copies of the Bible.

## A new coefficient for information density

The density of storage media or degree of integration of computer chips has steadily increased in past years. Until now there has been no suitable coefficient available to allow comparison of this degree of integration between the various technologies. The author therefore made the proposal [G12] to consider the respective storage densities in relation to the highest density known in nature. This was calculated above as $\rho_{DNA}$ = $3.76 \times 10^{18}$ bits/mm$^3$.

The 256-megabit memory (developed jointly by IBM, Siemens, and Toshiba) and introduced in 1995, had a surface area of 286 mm2. If we take the depth as 1 mm, we obtain an information density of this DRAM (Dynamic Random Access Memory) of $\rho_{DRAM}$= $9.39 \times 10^5$ bits/mm$^3$. Analogous to the Mach number ($M = u/v_0$) in fluid physics or the relative velocity in relativity, $\beta$ = v/c, the number q = $\rho_{Sp}/\rho_{DNA}$ was proposed [in G12] as the **coefficient of information density**. The above-mentioned DRAM has a value q = $\rho_{DRAM}/\rho_{DNA}$ = $2.5 \times 10^{-13}$. This extremely small value for q shows how far modern computer technology has yet to go in order to match the storage density of DNA.

Since the dimensions of the DNA molecule can be measured in a precisely definable crystalline state, they are reproducible everywhere. Thus, the particular storage density $\rho_{DNA}$ may actually represent a physical constant.

At the current state of the art, q will always take on a very small value. But since this coefficient is a ratio of the maximum value, there is enough leeway for all future technologies so that $0 < q < 1$ is always guaranteed. This proposal also allows comparisons of the degree of integration of any desired forms of storage media (e.g., DVD, hard disk, magnetic tapes), within as well as between each category.

*Appendix 2*

# ENERGY AND INFORMATION IN BIOLOGICAL SYSTEMS

## A2.1 Energy, a fundamental entity

Energy (from the Greek *energeia* = activity) is a fundamental entity that plays a central role in all natural sciences and belongs to the material domain (the lowest hierarchical level, in Figure 24, chapter 5.4). Energy appears in numerous forms, most of which can be converted into another form. In fact, most physical processes involve the conversion of one form of energy into another. Several important forms of energy are:

- Potential energy
- Kinetic energy
- Radiant energy
- Thermal energy
- Electrical energy
- Chemical energy
- Nuclear energy.

It is important to note that the energy conversion processes in living systems are entirely controlled by "biological information" conveying Universal Information. This is required in order to maintain biological homeostasis, thus opposing the degradation that would otherwise come about according to the Second Law of Thermodynamics. Moreover, from a physical viewpoint, these processes often occur with an optimized consumption of energy. These processes are so ingeniously conceived that all attempts to simulate them technologically have failed to date. For this reason, we will devote Appendix 2 to a few selected biological systems.

All processes in both inanimate and animate systems obey two basic physical laws known as the First and Second Laws of Thermodynamics.

**First Law:** This extremely important law of nature, also called the "Law of Conservation of Energy" (LCE), was first formulated/published in 1841/1842 by the German surgeon Julius Robert von Mayer (1814–1878). The LCE states that in the natural universe, energy can neither be created nor destroyed. This statement is not an axiom but rather a statement of experience (as are all scientific laws — see N1 in chapter 4.3). In every chemical or physical process, the total energy of the system and its environment remains constant as does the total energy of the universe. Energy can be neither destroyed nor newly created but it can be converted from one form to another. Important results can be deduced from the LCE:

- The only processes possible in nature are those in which the net amount of total energy remains unchanged.

> **Mass-energy equivalence ($E = mc^2$):** This connects the concepts of conservation of mass and conservation of energy. Physics allows particles which have rest mass to be converted to other forms of mass which require motion, such as kinetic energy. In a nuclear explosion, some of the mass is converted to energy, but the total amount of mass-energy remains the same. Energy can also be converted into particles which have rest mass. The total mass-energy inside a closed system remains constant over time, as seen by any single observer in a given inertial frame. In other words, mass-energy cannot be created or destroyed, and energy, in all of its forms, has an equivalent mass.

- It is impossible to build a machine in a closed system which, once set in motion, endlessly continues to do work without the supply of more energy from *outside* that system.

- There is a quantitative equivalence between the different forms of energy. These equivalences are backed up by experiment.

**The Second Law:** Whereas the First Law only considers the conversion between, for example, heat energy and mechanical energy or vice versa, the Second Law effectively determines the *direction* of the process. Generally speaking, all natural, unguided processes run in only one direction, and this direction is irreversible. For instance, we know from experience that if a hot block of copper is put in contact with a cold block (Figure 42) in a perfectly insulated container, the hot block will deliver its energy to the cold block *(not the other way around!)* until they both reach the same temperature. Note that it would not contradict the First Law of Thermodynamics if, hypothetically, one block became warmer and the other cooler as long as there was no overall loss or gain of energy. But it would contradict the Second Law.

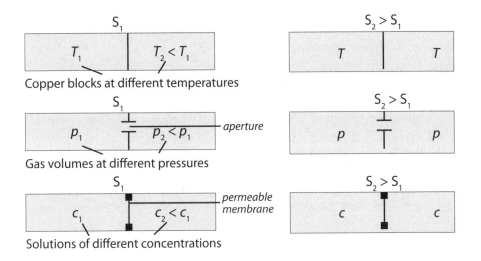

Copper blocks at different temperatures

Gas volumes at different pressures

Solutions of different concentrations

Figure 42: Three processes in closed systems:

- Two blocks of copper with different initial temperatures eventually attain the same temperature.
- The gas pressure of two compartments containing gases, initially at different pressures, will eventually equalize through the opening.
- Two salt solutions with different initial concentrations will attain equal concentrations through a semi-permeable membrane.

In all three cases, the common aspect is that the entropy of later states is greater than for the initial conditions ($S_2 > S_1$).

The Second Law provides us with a criterion for predicting the direction of a given energy process. An abstract and highly useful concept is that of entropy, S. Entropy is, in fact, used to mathematically formulate the Second Law (see Figure 42). In its briefest formulation, the Second Law can be expressed as $dS \geq 0$ (for a closed system), where $dS$ represents a change in entropy. Thus, $dS \geq 0$ means that net entropy (i.e., considering all relevant systems) either stays the same or increases — it never decreases. From this, the following deductions may be made:

- Thermal energy (heat) cannot by itself flow from a cooler body to a warmer one (Rudolf Clausius, 1850).

- A natural, unguided process in which entropy only decreases is impossible.

The following formulation was first proposed by Josef Meixner (1908–1994), a German theoretical physicist [M2]:

In the gigantic factory of natural processes, the function of manager is taken over by the production of entropy because it prescribes the direction and the nature of the entire business. The Energy Conservation Law only plays the role of accountant, being responsible for the balance between assets and liabilities.

**Useful work:** An important consideration is the ability of a system to do *useful* work. It is the flow of heat into a "heat sink," i.e., a cooler area, that produces useful work. This asymmetry of energy conversion is one of the core results of the Second Law of Thermodynamics. This law also means that a closed system will tend toward thermal equilibrium, a state that is characterized by a minimum of energy available for useful work and maximum entropy. The essence of this is that the Second Law places a strict limit on the amount of useful work that may be done. Specifically, "100 units of available work-energy" cannot be used to produce "100 units of work" — the Second Law imposes an unavoidable loss of available energy in all conversion processes. Thus, no machine can be 100% efficient — the Second Law demands that we *always* get less than what we put in. As a common example, consider that we supply gasoline to our cars. Let's suppose that this gasoline contains 100 units of available energy (in the form of chemical energy). This energy is converted into kinetic energy (when the car is in motion) via the car's engine, driveshaft, etc. The conversion efficiency of a car's machinery is probably somewhere between 10% and 20%. The balance of the original (chemical) energy is wasted as heat (mainly caused by friction within the mechanical components). The Second Law takes its toll!

As we will see, however, living organisms have a greater efficiency (useful mechanical work obtained from a given energy input) than the maximum thermal efficiency allowed by the Second Law. This is not a contradiction of this natural law but shows that the Creator has, in a sense, "bypassed" the law by supplying the body muscles with an intricate system that converts chemical energy directly into mechanical work.

*Conclusion:* The Law of Entropy (Second Law of Thermodynamics) prohibits any processes that would result in a net reduction in total entropy (system + surroundings).

## A2.2 Energy: Its generation and utilization in various systems

As per the First Law of Thermodynamics, the generation and consumption of energy is a matter of converting one form of energy into another. Any energy *generation* system must exploit the available energy source as economically as possible, i.e., must maximize the efficiency of energy conversion. The following sections are devoted to a discussion of technological and biological systems where this principle is used. The inverse strategy, a *strategy for energy minimization* is pursued for energy *consumption*, i.e., the available fuel must be used as economically as possible. The required work has to be done with the least possible input of energy. The ingenious methods employed by biological systems, and the superlative results achieved, are also discussed.

Every cell requires energy continuously for its vital functions, such as the synthesis of new molecules, or the production of replacement cells. In multicellular organisms there are other purposeful reactions in addition (e.g., locomotion and the control of body temperature). The conversion of energy in every cell — whether in animals, plants, or microbes — is based on the same principles and mechanisms. Cellular processes are isothermal [B7], i.e., they run at a constant temperature. In this way living organisms avoid over-heating and maximize energy efficiency. Cellular processes take place at optimal temperatures, which are fairly consistent in warm-blooded animals. However, in cold-blooded animals the cells can operate efficiently over a wide range of temperatures.

**Energy concept:** It should be emphasized that energy-carrying nutrient molecules in biological systems release energy by way of extremely efficient, purposeful processes.

Sugar molecules, such as glucose, enter the cell and are broken down in numerous precisely-tuned individual enzymatic reactions that follow one another in exactly the required sequence and employ just as many intermediate compounds. The primary end product formed from the energy released is adenosine triphosphate (ATP), belonging to the group of nucleotides containing adenine, D-ribose, and phosphate groups. The energy stored in ATP can then be utilized subsequently by conversion into chemical work, such as biosynthesis, mechanical actions like muscular effort or osmotic transport. This conversion of energy occurs when the ATP loses one phosphate group and reverts to ADP. The numerous, very complex, intermediate chemical steps in this ATP–ADP energy cycle are catalyzed by a specific set of enzymes. In addition to this general flow of biological energy, there are some very clever special mechanisms for energy conversion.

Electrical fish such as the electric eel, electric ray, or electric catfish can generate pulses of several hundred volts directly from chemical energy. Similarly, light flashes emitted by luminescent organisms are generated by chemical energy converted to light. The bombardier beetle converts the chemical energy contained in the mixture of hydroquinone and hydrogen peroxide into explosive pressure, heat and volume changes.

In order to generate useful work, many man-made machines employ round about methods such as using heat energy to do mechanical work that is used to create electrical energy, which is then used to produce mechanical work (e.g., this is how modern diesel locomotives function). The heat energy, $Q$ (in units of joules, calories, or BTU [British Thermal Units]) may be supplied in the form of fuel (e.g., wood and coal) and can only perform useful work, W, when there is a temperature difference ($T_2 - T_1$) in the system. The theoretical maximum amount of work that can be performed by a heat engine is given by the Carnot formula:

$$W = Q \times (T_2 - T_1)/T_2.$$

$T_2$ could be the initial temperature of the steam entering a turbine, for example, and $T_1$ would be the exhaust temperature. It follows that large temperature differences are required to produce work with a reasonable efficiency. The energy-generating processes in living cells need to be fundamentally different, since all reactions have to take place isothermally, i.e., at the temperature of the cell. In other words, the use of a heat engine in biological processes is forbidden. Instead, chemical reactions are used.

**Cells:** A living cell can be compared to a factory comprising several departments (organelles), each of which has a certain number of machines. The work of the machines in each of the cell's departments (organelles) manufacture end products through a sequence of numerous individual processes that have been optimally planned and coordinated, down to the last detail. We can justifiably claim that we are dealing here with the smallest fully automated production line in the world, which even has its own computer center and its own power generating plants (primarily the ATP-generating mitochondria).

The prokaryotes (single-celled organisms such as bacteria, which do not have an organized nucleus), with diameters of $0.1$ μm, are the smallest cells, while birds' eggs are the largest. Ostrich eggs measure about $0.1$ m = $10^5$ μm, and the average diameter of the cells of multicellular organisms lies between 4 μm and 40 μm. Large living beings consist of exceedingly large numbers of cells (about $10^{14}$ for humans), while the smallest organisms, like bacteria and protozoa, are unicellular. Two large classes of cells are distinguished according to whether they have an organized nucleus (eukaryotic) or not (prokaryotic). Many unicellular organisms, like yeast cells, protozoa, and some algae, are eukaryotic, as are nearly all multicellular forms. Their cells contain a nucleus and mitochondria. The prokaryotes comprise the bacteria (which includes the photosynthesizing cyanobacteria, sometimes still called blue-green algae) and the archea. Compared with the eukaryotes, they are considerably smaller (only 1/5,000 in volume). For a long time they were considered less specialized, but recent research has shown that they are organized differently from the eukaryotes, but are still very complex and organized in their own right.

**Summary:** From the above, let us now summarize the essential characteristics of energy utilization in cells of living organisms that distinguish them from technological processes:

1. *Isothermal energy conversion:* Energy processes in living cells often take place within a narrow range of temperatures in warm-blooded animals. These have circumvented the commonly

roundabout and inefficient technological processes that depend upon the generation of heat.

2. *The greatest possible miniaturization:* One of the aims of technology, the miniaturization of equipment, is realized in cells in a way that cannot be imitated. The energy generating and consuming processes in an organism are coupled at the molecular level. We can rightly speak of "molecular machines," representing the ultimate in miniaturization.

3. *Optimal operation:* Each one of the approximately ten trillion ($10^{13}$) muscle cells in the human body possesses its own decentralized "power generating plants." These mitochondria can vary in their amount of ATP output as required and are thus extremely economical in the process of energy transfer.

4. *The indirect conversion of energy:* Energy is not applied directly because ATP acts as mediator between the energy generating process and the energy consuming reaction. The energy-rich ATP is used for transporting and releasing energy when and where it is needed. The amount of usable energy in the ATP existing in muscle cells at the moment of activation can be used up in 15 seconds. The processes requiring the energy carried by the ATP can be very diverse: mechanical work is performed when muscles contract; many animals have organs that can discharge electrical energy; when substances are absorbed or transported through a membrane, osmotic work is done; and in many cases the result is chemical work, e.g., synthesizing molecules. All of these processes are part of an extensive metabolic chain achieved through extremely complex and incompletely understood enzymatic systems.

5. *High efficiency:* The efficiency of the transport of electrons in the last stage of ATP synthesis is 91%, an efficiency of which engineers can only dream. This fascinating result is achieved by a superbly constructed system that continuously employs the "principle of a common intermediate product for the transfer of energy." ATP is the link between energy-releasing and energy-consuming reactions; in other words, cells have an energy exchange unit that is readily convertible. ATP

channels the transfer of energy, providing the cell with excellent control over the energy flow.

The biological energy conversion system is so brilliantly designed that energy engineers can only watch in fascination. No one has yet been able to copy this highly miniaturized and extremely efficient mechanism.

## A2.3 Conservation of energy in biological systems

With regard to the relationship between physics and biology, Alfred Gierer (1929– ), a physicist from Tübingen (Germany), concluded [G2]:

> Physics is the most general science since it can be applied to all events in space and time, while biology is the most complex science and, at the same time, directed, to a large extent, toward ourselves.

In this context, some important questions now arise: Are there any processes occurring in living organisms where physical and chemical laws do not apply? Is not a living organism fundamentally different from a machine? Is biology solely based on physics? Two points should be considered carefully before we can answer such questions, namely:

1. *Process:* All biological processes obey physical and chemical laws (see N2, N3, and N4 in chapter 4.3). These laws, however, only delineate the external framework within which the relevant events generally occur. Further limitations are imposed by the boundary conditions: environment and the stage of development. Additionally, DNA information guides and controls all functions of living organisms.

2. *Origin:* No man-made machine — from a simple corkscrew to a computer — can be explained in terms of natural laws and environmental conditions *only* — they all required an intelligent inventor. Likewise, all biological systems required an intelligent inventor. Every creator of a technological invention must know at least something of the laws of physics so that the necessary mechanisms can be constructed to achieve the desired goal. He displays his ingenuity best by skillfully integrating the natural laws into his constructional and architectural ideas, thus producing a mechanism that functions

near-optimally. We can certainly say the same for the Creator of biological systems, which display His wealth of ideas and His unfathomable wisdom.

Physical laws provide the boundary conditions for the limits of life processes, but they fail to explain the origin of their complexity and the wealth and diversity of biological structures and functions. Anyone who discusses questions of origin and spirituality on a purely material plane distances himself completely from these realities.

The following examples of energy use and conservation illustrate the inventiveness of the Creator, often seeming to take the laws of nature to the limits of the physically possible.

## A2.3.1 Animals with "lamps"

From the energy viewpoint, there is a most remarkable phenomenon exhibited by many sea animals and some land animals (e.g., glow-worms and fireflies), namely, bioluminescence (Latin *lumen* = light). These animals can emit light of various colors (red, yellow, green, blue, or violet) and in different signal sequences. When it comes to energy efficiency, our technological attempts at generating light look extremely amateurish when compared with bioluminescence. A standard electric light bulb converts only 3 to 4 percent of the energy consumed into light, the rest is heat. And the efficiency of a fluorescent tube is only about 10%. Even LED bulbs are only about double that. The Creator's "cold light" bioluminescent systems, even by conservative estimates, operate with about 85% efficiency (see sciencedirect.com/topics/materials-science/bioluminescence). Our lamps by comparison are perhaps more similar to ovens than light sources.

No man-made light source has even approached the efficiency of bioluminescence. This involves the oxidation of certain fluorescent substances (luciferins) by an enzyme called luciferase. There are three fundamentally different types of luciferin, namely that of bacteria, that of fireflies, and that of *Cypridina* (clam-like creatures). American biochemist Professor W.D. McElroy was able to quantify the efficiency of this type of light production. It was found that each quantum of energy transported to the light organ in the form of ATP[1] was converted to light. The number of oxidized luciferin molecules is exactly equal to the number of

---

1. **ATP** (adenosine triphosphate) is a macromolecule used for the transport and immediate source of energy in living cells (see Section A2.2).

emitted light quanta. It thus seems that the light emitted by a firefly is indeed "cold" light, which means that there is no loss of energy as heat. Here we are confronted with lamps operating at nearly 100% efficiency where the incoming energy is almost completely converted into light.

The Creator has equipped many types of bacteria, microorganisms, insects, and especially deep-sea fish with this method of illumination. The best-known examples are the fireflies and the glow-worms *(Lampyris and Phausis)*. Most of the subtropical and tropical lampyrids differ from the mid-European species in that they can emit deliberate sequences of flashes. In experiments with the pyralis firefly *(Photinus pyralis)* [B8], it was found that the flying male emitted 0.06-second flashes at intervals of 5.7 seconds, and the female on the ground replied after exactly 2.1 seconds with the same rhythm. These flashing signals serve as communication between prospective mates. There also are insects with "lamps" that emit different colors, like the Brazilian railroad worm *(Phrixothrix)*. This larva from the beetle family of snail predators *(Drilidae)* normally carries two orange-red lights in front. At the approach of danger, two rows of 11 greenish lanterns are switched on, one row on each side. This resemblance to a train approaching in the dark gives this larva its apt name, "railroad worm."

During a visit to Israel in 1985 we went to the underwater observatory in Eilath and could watch a flashlight fish *(Photoblepharon palpebratus steinitzi)* that lives in the Red Sea. This fish does not produce its own light but obtains it from symbiotic luminescent bacteria. These bacteria are so small that the light of a single one is invisible, but the light of an entire colony can easily be seen. These bacteria congregate exclusively on an oval light organ situated below the eyes of the fish to receive nutrients and oxygen through a densely branching network of capillary blood vessels. They continuously emit light just like other bacteria, but amazingly, the fish can deliberately switch the light on and off. It does this by pulling a black skin flap over the luminescent organ like an eyelid and is thus able to transmit different flashing signals. It uses these signals to attract its prey.

Bacterial light emission is fundamentally different from that of other luminescent organisms. Whereas bacteria continuously emit light of a constant intensity by day and night without any particular stimulation, other marine organisms only emit light when they are disturbed or stimulated in some way (e.g., by the passage of a ship, a school of mackerel or the breaking of waves on the shore).

The bioluminescence of deep-sea creatures is particularly interesting. A number of them glow, including fish, crabs, arrow worms, and jellyfish. Some species of fish have a single "lamp" on their side while others are equipped with rows of them. The light-emitting organs (photophores) can be arranged in irregular circles, in curves, or irregular patterns. The five-lined constellation fish *(Bathysidus pentagrammus)* has five beautiful rows of lights on each side of its body where each row consists of large, pale yellow lights that are surrounded by serrated, bright purple "jewels."

The luminescent shrimp *(Sergestes prehensilis)* has more than 150 light points, all of which can be instantly switched on and off. Like neon signs in cities, the yellow-green lights flash sequentially and quickly from head to tail for one or two seconds. While some species of fish employ luminescent bacteria to generate light flashes, others have highly specialized organs that produce their own luminous substances. Some fish have intricately constructed light projectors to amplify the light effects, e.g., collecting lenses or other optical equipment for producing a directional light beam. The projectors are constructed in such a way that a mosaic of thousands of minute crystals provides a mirror-like surface behind the luminous tissues to reflect the light. Some creatures even have color filters (pigment membranes) for producing any shade of color.

Although materialists/evolutionists are quite sure all these things evolved over time via the selection of thousands of random mutations, the data do not support this. We can only stand by in amazement at the Creator's limitless inventiveness.

### A2.3.2 The lung, an optimal structure

The construction of an efficient technological plant or a biological system requires that its own consumption of energy should be minimized in relation to the work it does. Special attention has to be paid to irreversible processes, since they cost energy. For instance, in fluid dynamics, friction is the decisive irreversible factor. Frictional losses can be reduced by having large diameter conduits, thereby decreasing the contact areas. But there are constraints: generous dimensions in a processing plant mean higher investment costs, and in living organisms more energy would be needed for maintaining a resting metabolism. The total quantity of energy required by an organ or a muscle consists of two parts, namely, a basic minimum for keeping the tissues themselves functioning plus any extra needed to support added activity.

Continuing the work of Swiss physiologist and Nobel Laureate Walter R. Hess, and using the human lung as an example, E.R. Weibel [W1] showed how remarkably this optimization problem has been solved. The lung is constructed in such a fashion that, with minimal use of living tissue, a minimum of energy is needed to compensate for pressure losses. The air passage (trachea) branches into two bronchi, each of which again branches into two smaller passages with equal diameters. This bifurcation into smaller conduits continues until the 23rd level, which represents the smallest bronchioles. These empty into a duct composed of very thinly lined pouches where respiratory exchange with blood capillaries takes place. The mean ratio in diameters, $d_2/d_1$ of two consecutive sections ($d_2$ following $d_1$) is very close to 0.8. Given that the pressure drop has to be a minimum for a given volume of tubes and that laminar flow must be maintained, the result obtained by optimization calculations in fluid dynamics is found to be $d_2/d_1 = (1/2)^{1/3} = 0.79370$. This is consistent with the measured value of 0.8 and this $(1/2)^{1/3}$ law applies even more precisely for the bifurcations of the blood vessels supplying the lung. The more we study the details of biological systems, the stronger the impression becomes that their Creator is a brilliant designer.

## A2.3.3 The flight of migrating birds

The flight of birds is fascinating. There are numerous mechanisms involved that cannot be imitated technologically [D5], [R5], [S2]. Aerodynamically, birds' wings are highly specialized and optimized structures. The type of wing curvature is especially important, because without it they could not fly. Whereas an airplane is dependent on rather high minimum airspeed to stay airborne, birds can utilize the updraft caused by their wing strokes to fly slowly. Their wings are simultaneously an airfoil and a propeller; the lift is achieved with an efficiency not yet replicated by technological means. Let us take a closer look at two of the many problems solved in the design of bird flight, namely, *precise energy calculations* (A2.3.3.1) and *exact navigation* (A2.3.3.2).

### A2.3.3.1 Migratory bird flight: An accurate energy calculation

Every performance of work requires energy. Frequently, migrating birds have to carry enough energy reserves in the form of fat to complete a long journey. However, the entire structure of the bird has to be as light as possible for flying; superfluous mass must be strictly avoided. Moreover, fuel consumption must be optimal. How did the Creator provide for enough fuel without sacrificing efficient flight? There are two critical factors — flight speed and center of mass.

**The most economical flight speed:** First, flight speed must be optimal. If a bird flies too slowly, it consumes too much fuel to obtain lift. If it flies too fast, then more energy is required to overcome air friction. There is thus a distinct optimum speed for minimum fuel consumption. Depending on the aerodynamics of its body and its wings, every bird has a specific optimal speed for fuel efficiency. For example, it is 28 mph (45 km/h) in the case of the laughing gull and 25.8 mph (41.6 km/h) for a budgerigar (parakeet). It is known that birds keep exactly to their own energy-saving speeds. We have not yet been able to determine how they "know" this.

**Maintaining the height of the center of mass:** The 2002 film *Winged Migration*, by Frenchman Jacques Perrin, is a unique nature film. Using the most modern microlight aircraft, mini-helicopters, and delta kites, he accompanied 44 species of bird at their own flight altitudes and speeds in order to study in detail their elegant flight behavior. Whoever has seen this film has experienced an amazing display of beauty, precision, and technique from the Creator's workshop. It is remarkable, when thinking about the energy equation, how all the large birds (e.g., wild geese, storks, and cranes) are able to maintain their centers of mass at a nearly constant height in spite of the considerable size of the wing strokes. There would be a considerable loss of energy if this condition were not met. Imagine a wild goose weighing 8 kilograms. An additional 2.4 joules of energy, for example, would be consumed at each wing stroke if its center of mass were to drop and rise again by only 1.2 inches (3 cm). This means that 100,000 wing strokes would use 240 kJ, requiring the goose to carry an extra 6 grams of fat.

**The fuel needed:** We now consider a specific energy problem in more detail — the amount of fuel that the Pacific golden plover *(Pluvialis fulva)* takes with it. These birds migrate from Alaska to spend the northern winter in Hawaii. They have to fly non-stop over the ocean without resting because there are no islands en route, nor can they swim. During the journey of up to 2,800 miles (4,500 km), they beat their wings an incredible 250,000 times without interruption in a flight lasting 88 hours. Their average weight at the start, $G_0$, is 200 g, 70 g of which is fat that serves as fuel. It has been found that these birds "burn" 0.6% of their weight per hour (fuel consumption $\rho$ = 0.006/h) to produce flight propulsion and heat. Assuming no wind, the fuel required in the first hour, $\times_1$ amounts to

$$\times_1 = G_0 \times \rho = 200 \times 0.006 = 1.2 \text{ g fat.}$$

Since its weight diminishes as it burns fat, it consumes somewhat less energy during the second hour than during the first hour (i.e., the bird weighs less and so it needs less energy to propel it). The same is true during every subsequent hour — less energy is required than in the previous hour of flight. Given these facts, the mathematical analysis reveals that these birds *should not* have enough fuel for the flight since they burn 82 g of fat, while having only 70 g in their "fuel tank" (details are provided below). The number of hours that these birds can fly with the given amount of fuel that they have at the start should only be 72 hours, not the 88 hours of flying time that they need to reach their destination. Yet we know that they make it — how do they do it?

---

**The mathematics governing the bird's fuel use:** Omitting its derivation, the equation is $G_f = G_0 (1-\rho)^t$ where $G_f$ is the bird's final weight, $G_0$ is the bird's initial weight, $\rho$ is the percentage weight consumed per hour and t is the number of hours. For example, after the first hour (t = 1) the bird's weight will be: $G_f = 200(1 - .006)^1 = 198.8$ g. The missing 1.2 g (from the initial weight of 200 g) is the fat that was "burned" as fuel. Next, after the second hour (t = 2), the bird's weight will be: $G_f = 200(1 - .006)^2 = 197.6$ g. Continuing this process, at the 88th hour, the bird's weight *ought* to be $G_0 (1 - \rho)^{88} = 200(1 - .006)^{88} \approx 117.8$ g. This means that the bird's weight *should have* dropped by approximately 82 g (found by subtracting the final weight (at the 88th hour) from the initial weight: 200 g – 117.8 g $\approx$ 82 g).

**Alternative calculation method:** For ease of understanding, we made the above calculation in discrete one-hour steps. However, we may take the differential equation $dG/dt = - G(t) \times \rho$ with $G(t = 0) = G_0$ to obtain the continuous $G(t) = G_0 \times e^{(-\rho t)}$, where $\rho$ = 0.006/h.

---

Emphasizing this point, these birds should plunge into the ocean 500 miles (800 km) *short* of their destination. Did we make some mistake or did the Creator fail to equip the bird adequately? Neither is the case — no mistake was made; the Creator's work is infallible. God optimizes the use of energy through very important Universal Information that He provided to the birds, namely, "Do not fly *alone* (curve $G_A$ in Figure

43), but fly in a V-formation (curve $G_V$)!" In the V-formation each bird except the leader will save 23% of its energy and will then safely reach winter quarters.[2] Because these birds, like migrating geese, change leadership positions frequently, no bird is forced to burn more fat than the others during the flight. The V-formation results in less air resistance for the birds following the lead bird.

Curve $G_V$ in Figure 43 also shows the weight decrease in V-formation. After 88 hours the normal residual amount of fat is 6.8 g. This is not carried unnecessarily but is a reserve calculated by the Creator in case more is needed to cope with head winds. The extremely low specific rate of fuel consumption ($\rho$ = 0.6% of its weight per hour) is all the more astonishing when we consider that the corresponding values for man-made aircraft are orders of magnitude greater (for a helicopter, $\rho$ = 4% to 5% of its weight per hour; and $\rho$ = 12% for a jet plane).

For someone who does not regard these precise phenomena as the work of the Creator, the following questions remain unanswered:

- How does the bird know the exact energy requirement?

- How is it possible that the bird accumulates the exact amount of fat before the journey?

- How does the bird know the distance and the specific fuel consumption?

- How does the bird know the migration route?

- How does the bird navigate to reach its destination promptly?

- How does the bird know to fly in a V-formation with other birds to reduce fuel consumption?

An adherent to the doctrine of evolution might answer all these questions as follows: "Yes, only a bird with enough fat reserves can reach the destination. The bird does not know the route and it has no navigation system, but some have chosen the correct route purely by chance … ."

With such a series of assumptions and restrictions, it is clear that the flight will succeed only if *all* the above questions are answered positively.

---

2. **Other birds in V-formation flight:** By flying in V-formation, the common Shelduck saves 18% energy and cranes save up to 70% if the group consists of at least two dozen birds flying at three-quarters of maximum speed. Now and again a crane may fly along with a group of wild geese or a duck will "hitchhike" a ride with a formation of cranes.

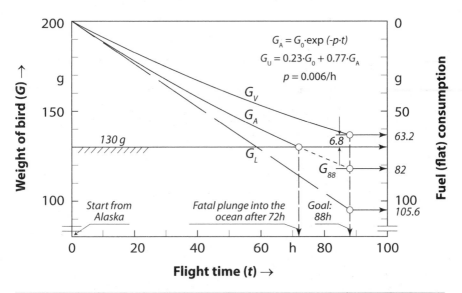

Figure 43: The flight of the Pacific golden plover. For the non-stop flight of up to 2,800 mi. (4,500 km) from Alaska to Hawaii, the amount of available fuel is 70 g. If the bird used the same amount of fuel every hour as in the first hour, we would have the straight dashed line $G_L$ which would require a total of 105.6 grams of fat. If this flight were undertaken by a single bird (curve $G_A$), it would have consumed all its fat reserves after 72 hours and would plunge into the ocean 500 mi (800 km) short of its destination. On the other hand, flying in a V-formation (curve $G_V$) reduces the energy consumption by 23% so that the birds reach their destination safely.

Otherwise, not just a slim majority, but more likely, *most* of the birds would drown. However, we observe that most of the birds arrive safely.

(Based on the above facts about the golden plover, in my book, *If Animals Could Talk* [G21], in which the bird is the narrator, involving the reader in an imaginary dialogue in order to draw his attention to numerous wonders of creation).

Besides the Pacific golden plover mentioned above, there is also the American golden plover *(Pluvialis dominica)*. These birds also undertake a non-stop long distance migration flight from the coast of Labrador across the Atlantic Ocean to north Brazil. Whereas the Pacific plovers follow the same route for both the outward and the return journey, the American plovers use different routes in autumn and spring. On the northward leg they fly back to Canada over Central America and the USA. Some further astonishing migration feats are:

- The Japanese snipe *(Capella hardtwickii)* flies 3,100 mi (5,000 km) to Tasmania (Australia).

- The East Siberian spine-tailed swift *(Chaetura caudacuta)* migrates from Siberia to Tasmania.

- The migration route of the American sandpipers (e.g., *Calidris melanotos* = gray breasted sandpiper) covers 9,950 mi (16,000 km) from Alaska to Tierra del Fuego, at the southern tip of South America.

### A2.3.3.2 Migratory bird flight: a navigational masterpiece

Finn Salomonsen (1909–1983), the well-known Danish ornithologist, writes the following about the in-flight orientation of birds [S2]:

> The ability of birds to find their way while flying is a most puzzling mystery. Few other questions have given rise over the years to so many theories and speculations as this one.

This navigational ability is indeed a supreme wonder since birds do not have complex navigational dashboards, compasses, or maps, and environmental conditions like the position of the sun, wind direction, cloud cover, and day-night rhythms are continually changing. When terrestrial birds have to cross an ocean, as we have seen in the case of the golden plover, a small error in direction would result in their floundering helplessly over the open ocean and finally plunging to their deaths. Keeping an exact course cannot be achieved by trial and error. A large majority of the migratory birds would never reach their destination without navigational measures, and no species could survive such great losses. It has been suggested that juvenile birds are first shown the way by their knowledgeable parents. This idea is refuted by the observation that juvenile golden plovers leave Alaska a few weeks after their parents have already left. We thus have to assume that migratory birds possess an inbuilt sense of direction that enables them to orientate themselves with respect to geographical direction and to stay on course.

Salomonsen bases this sense of direction on his research of two small bird species living in western Greenland, both of which migrate south in autumn. The wheatear *(Oenanthe oenanthe)* and the snow bunting *(Plectrophenax nivalis)* summer in the same region, both often beginning their migration at the same time. However, their ways part after arriving in southern Greenland. The snow buntings continue directly south to spend the winter in America while the wheatears turn southeast, flying right across the Atlantic Ocean to Western Europe and North Africa. Both kinds of birds have a specific sense of direction that determines their different courses.

Detailed insights into navigational precision have been found by transporting different species of bird to distant locations. A noteworthy experiment was undertaken with two kinds of seabirds in the family Laridae, the sooty tern *(Onychoprion fuscatus)* and the brown noddy *(Anous stolidus)*, which breed on the Tortugas Islands in the Gulf of Mexico. The birds were taken by ship in different directions from their nesting place and then released at distances of between 517 and 850 mi (832 and 1,368 km). Although they found themselves in unknown parts of the ocean, most of them unerringly found their way back after a few days to lay their eggs and raise their young on the Tortugas Islands.

Many experiments have been carried out with homing pigeons. Their navigational abilities have been extensively investigated and described. Salomonsen writes as follows about these breathtaking marvels of navigation [S2]:

> Even when pigeons have been transported while anaesthetized or when their cage was rotated so that its orientation changed continuously, when released they were able to fly back home just as readily as undisturbed control pigeons. It can be asserted, therefore, without a doubt that these birds possess a special ability for determining their geographic position; they have a real navigational sense. We know nothing about the actual nature of this sense, and neither do we know where the relevant organ is located.

These birds have exceptional faculties: they can return home over great distances even when they are deprived of any possibility of orientation during transport. Wherever they are released, they have the amazing ability to extract the required data from the environment to determine their position relative to their home. Even after they have oriented themselves in this unknown way, the real problem (namely, en route navigation) has just begun. A simple sense of direction is inadequate for this purpose.

When migrating over vast oceans, where continual winds prevail, the birds have to consider drift. To avoid wasting energy on detours, such factors have to be sensed and corrected continuously as with a techno-logical control system. The Creator provided birds with a very precise "autopilot" which is obviously able to determine the current geograph-ical location, compare the data with the internally programmed home location, and guarantee the quickest and most economical route to the target. As yet, no one but the Creator who conceived it knows the loca-tion of this vital system, nor do we know how its operational informa-tion is encoded. We use a special term to cover our ignorance; we call it "instinct."

### A2.3.3.3 Bird flight — an information-controlled process

According to the theory of evolution, birds are supposed to have evolved from reptiles. In chapter 8 we have already rejected this macro-evolution-ary process with the help of the scientific laws of Universal Information (Deduction 8). However, there is another quite valid objection to evolu-tion in connection with the migration of birds. Let us, for the moment, concede a great deal and accept that an evolutionary process could have produced a bird complete with a flying apparatus. Such a bird, how-ever, would not be able to fly since it would also need a highly complex navigational program (i.e., "biological information" conveying Univer-sal Information) in its brain to enable it to perform all its maneuvers. Even if evolution were able to fulfill all the physiological conditions of the material body, as a purely material process it would never be able to create Universal Information — a *non-material* entity — in accordance with SLI-2 and SLI-3 (chapter 5). We may confidently believe what is written in Gen. 1:21:

> So God created ... every winged bird according to its kind. And God saw that it was good.

*Appendix 3*

# SCIENTIFIC LAWS

## A3.1 The classification of scientific laws

Scientific laws can be grouped into distinct categories by the topics they cover, as follows.

**Conservation laws**: The following description applies to this group of laws: A certain entity is measured in some suitable unit of measurement. If this same entity is measured at any later time and its value remains unchanged from the original, then this may signal a conservation law. The best-known law in this category is the Law of the Conservation of Energy. This is an abstract and difficult conservation law, but at the same time it is one of the most useful ones. It is more difficult to understand than the laws about the conservation of mass (see example 2 in the box "Amendments to formulated scientific laws", p. 121), of momentum, of angular momentum, or of electrical charge. One reason is that energy can exist in many different forms, such as kinetic energy, potential energy, radiant energy, electrical energy, chemical energy, or nuclear energy. In any given process the energy can be distributed among these forms in many different ways, and a number can then be computed for the amount of each kind of energy. The conservation law now states that the sum of all of these numbers remains constant at all times, irrespective of all the conversions that take place. This sum is always the same at any given moment. It is very surprising that such a simple formulation holds for every physical or biological system, no matter how complex it may be.

**Equivalence laws:** Mass and energy can be seen to be equivalent in terms of Einstein's famous formula $E = mc^2$. In the case of atomic processes of energy conversion (nuclear energy) there is a small loss of mass (called the mass deficit) that is equivalent to the amount of energy released according to Einstein's formula.

**Directional laws:** From experience we know that numerous events in this world proceed in one direction only. A dropped cup breaks in pieces. The converse, namely that the cup puts itself together and jumps back into our hand, will never happen, however long we might wait. When a stone is thrown into a pond, concentric waves move outwards on the surface of the water. This process can be described mathematically, and the resulting equations are equally as valid for outward-moving waves as for the reverse case (where small waves would start from the edge and move concentrically inwards, becoming larger as they do so). Although the first event can be repeated as often as we like, the converse process has never been observed. This signals a caveat about mathematical formulations and proofs. They can be very useful when verified by repeated observation and experimentation but, by themselves, mathematical proofs do not necessarily correspond to reality (truth).

For some scientific laws the direction does not play a role (e.g., conservation of energy) but for others the process is unidirectional, like a one-way street. In the latter case one can clearly distinguish between past and future. In all cases where friction is involved, the processes are irreversible — they proceed in one direction only. Examples of such laws are the Law of Entropy (see Appendix 2.1), the chemical principle of Le Chatelier *(the Law of Least Restraint)* (see Appendix 3.3d), and the *Law of Mass Action*.[1]

**Impossibility laws:** Most scientific laws can be expressed as impossibility statements. For example, the Conservation of Energy Law may be stated as follows: *"It is impossible that energy can come into existence by itself."* R. Clausius formulated the Second Law of Thermodynamics as an "impossibility law": *"Heat cannot of itself pass from a colder body to a hotter*

---

1. For a reaction mixture in equilibrium, the rate of a chemical reaction is proportional to the product of the concentrations or activities of the substances reacting, i.e., the ratio between the concentration of reactants and products is constant.

*body."* The impossibility laws are very useful because they effectively distinguish between possible and impossible processes. This type of scientific formulation is encountered frequently when using the Information Laws as premises in chapter 8.

Geometrical impossibilities can also be devised. Three different geometric drawings appear in Figure 44. It is just as impossible to construct such structures in three-dimensional reality as it is to expect results that are precluded by scientific laws.

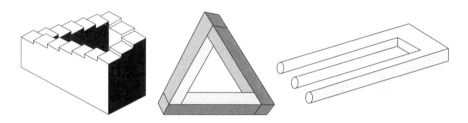

Figure 44: Drawings of geometrically impossible bodies

**Laws that describe processes:** A process law is a formulation that allows the description of future or past states of a system when the values of the relevant variables are known for at least one point in time.

**Co-existence laws:** As opposed to process laws, these laws describe the simultaneous existence of the properties of a system. The Ideal Gas Law, pV = nRT, is a typical physical co-existence law. It is the equation of state of a hypothetical ideal gas. It is a good approximation to the behavior of many gases under many conditions, although it has several limitations. It was first stated by Émile Clapeyron in 1834 as a combination of Boyle's Law and Charles's Law. It can also be derived from kinetic theory, as was achieved (apparently independently) by August Krönig in 1856 and Rudolf Clausius in 1857. In the Ideal Gas Law, the values of four quantities comprise a complete description of the "state" of an ideal gas: pressure, p, specific volume, V, the amount of substance of the gas, n, and the absolute temperature, T. Their values do not depend on the previous history of the gas, nor on the way the present pressure or the present volume has been obtained. Quantities of this type are known as state variables; R is the gas constant.

**Boundary laws:** Finally, there are laws that describe the limitations of our world. In 1927, the German physicist Werner Heisenberg (1901–

1976) published such a law — the Heisenberg Uncertainty Principle. According to this principle it is impossible to precisely determine both the position and the momentum of a particle at the same time. It follows that certain measurements can never be exact. This finding resulted in the collapse of the deterministic philosophy prevalent in the 19th century. The assertions of scientific laws are so powerful that they may cause viewpoints widespread at one time to be subsequently discarded.

**Information laws:** This book comprehensively discusses a series of scientific laws about Universal Information that cannot be ascribed to

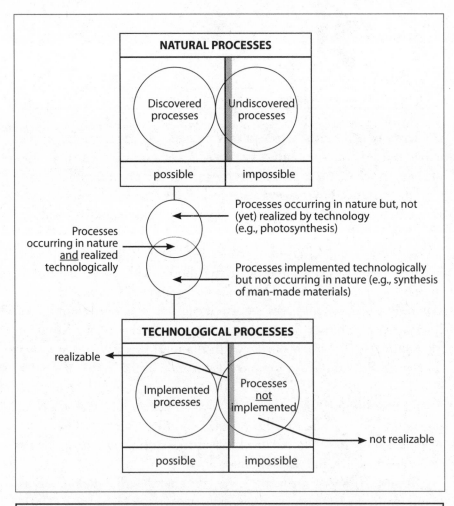

Figure 45: Possible and impossible processes in nature and technology

physics or chemistry. All the previously featured statements **N1 to N10** (chapter 4) about the nature of scientific laws, as well as the statements **R1 to R6** about the relevance of scientific laws (natural laws or laws of nature), are also fully applicable to these Laws of Universal Information.

## A3.2 Possible and impossible processes

The totality of all imaginable events and processes can be divided into two groups as in Figure 45, namely

a. Possible processes
b. Impossible processes

Possible processes occur under the "supervision" of scientific laws, but it is generally not possible to describe all of them completely. On the other hand, impossible processes can be identified by means of the so-called impossibility laws.

Impossible events can be divided into two groups: those that are fundamentally impossible and those that are statistically impossible. For example, events that contradict the energy conservation law are fundamentally impossible because this law even holds for individual atoms. On the other hand, radioactive decay is a statistical process that is subject to the probability laws and cannot be applied to individual atoms. In other words, we cannot know when one particular atom will release some type of radiation in its decay process. But in all practical cases, the number of atoms is so immense that an "exact" formulation can be used, namely, $n(t) = n_0 e^{-kt}$. The half-life as we know it today, T, is given by the formula $T = \ln 2/k$; this indicates the time required for any number of atoms at the start, $n_0$, to diminish to half as many, $n_0/2$. Since we are dealing with statistical events, one might expect that less than half the number of atoms, or appreciably more than half, could have decayed at time T. However, the probability of deviation from this law is so close to zero that we could regard it as statistically impossible. It should be clear that impossible events are not observable, recognizable, or measurable. Possible events have, in general, either been observed or they are observable. However, there are other possible events about which it can be said that they:

- cannot ever be observed (e.g., processes taking place in the sun's interior)

- are in principle observable but have not yet been observed (e.g., processes taking place on the surface of an extrasolar planet)

Thus far we have only discussed natural events but now we can apply these concepts to technological processes (in the widest sense of the word, comprising everything man-made). The following categories are now apparent:

- Possible processes
  – already implemented
  – not yet implemented but realizable in principle

- Impossible processes: Proposed processes of this kind are fundamentally unrealizable because they are precluded by scientific laws.

  The distinctions illustrated in Figure 45 follow from a comparison of possible events in nature and in technology, namely:

- processes that occur only in nature but have not (yet) been realized technologically (e.g., photosynthesis and life functions)

- processes occurring in nature that are also technologically realizable (e.g., industrial synthesis of organic substances)

- processes that have been technologically implemented but do not occur in nature (e.g., synthesis of artificial materials).

## A3.3 Must scientific laws always be expressed mathematically?

I am frequently asked, "Can empirical statements be regarded as scientific laws only when they are expressed mathematically? Are scientific laws always quantifiable?"

Several different language systems are available for making scientific statements but the most common are the natural languages. In addition, diverse artificial languages have been devised for specific purposes, such as notes for coding music or the formula languages of chemistry or mathematics. The latter are designed for describing physical or mathematical relationships. In order to capture any scientific insight, we need some kind of language system, and the corresponding context determines which system is the most suitable, descriptive, or effective. The more or less arbitrarily chosen language system does not determine whether or not an observed phenomenon has the character of a Scientific Law.

In 1604, Galileo Galilei (1564–1642) discovered certain phenomena due to the effects of gravity. He first expressed his discoveries in Italian verbal sentences *(La nuova scienza)* that could then be translated into every other language. Later the sentences were captured in an artificial language, namely, mathematics. The language of mathematics has the advantage over natural language in that it allows a very concise and unambiguous representation. Equations are expressions with quantitative units, but they represent only a portion of the mathematical toolset. Although the formula system used for mathematical logic does not employ standard units of physical measurements, it represents another no less indispensable means of expression. Regarding the questions posed above, two remarks are necessary:

**1.** Not all observations in nature that can be expressed mathematically are necessarily scientific laws. Two conditions have to be fulfilled: the assertions of scientific laws must be universally and absolutely applicable. They must stand on their own and, in particular, not depend on the place and time of their discovery. It should not matter who makes the observation or when or what the current state of the world is. The state of the world is determined by the laws and not the other way around.

**2.** In order to fulfill the conditions for a Scientific Law (see **N1 to N10** in chapter 4.3), it is not necessary that the observed facts be amenable to mathematical formulation. This does not exclude the possibility of later finding a formal representation (see examples a, b, and c, below). Moreover, it may become possible to combine several acknowledged laws into a single, more general principle. A scientific law need not necessarily be represented by quantitatively expressed units and variables. It is sufficient to describe an observation qualitatively and verbally as long as it is valid and can be reproduced arbitrarily often. Above all, there must be no exceptions to the assertions of the law. The following examples provide further explanation.

a. *Direction of rotation of a vortex:* In the northern hemisphere, the water draining out of a very large vessel rotates counter-clockwise, while in the southern hemisphere, it rotates clockwise. If this experiment were conducted on another planet, we would also discover a clear relationship between the planetary rotation and the relative distance of the experiment above or below the planet's equator. This effect is primarily seen on a large scale, such as with whirlpools in the ocean. In the case of small drainage (e.g., from a bathtub), the direction depends primarily on the angle of the drain and any movement in the water prior to draining. The only time this Coriolis Effect *might* be seen on such a smaller scale is under very carefully controlled experimental conditions.

b. *The right hand rule:* In 1831, the English physicist Michael Faraday (1791–1867) discovered that a current is induced in a metallic conductor being moved in a magnetic field. The direction of the current is described in a law known as the "right hand rule," given by the English physicist John Ambrose Fleming (1849–1945) in 1884:

> Position the first three digits of the right hand at right angles to each other. If the thumb gives the direction that the conductor is moved and the index finger the direction of the magnetic field, then the middle finger gives the direction of current flowing in the metallic conductor.

c. *Pauli's Exclusion Principle:* The Exclusion Principle was formulated in 1925 and named after its discoverer, the Austrian physicist and Nobel laureate Wolfgang Pauli (1900–1958). It states that only those electrons can participate in the structure of atoms and molecules that differ in at least one of their four quantum numbers, i.e., no two fully identical electrons can exist together in a single atom. In other words, in no atomic system may there be electrons with identical quantum numbers, $n$, $l$, $m$, and $s$). Or, more graphically, there is "no room" for two electrons with identical properties (quantum numbers).

*Comment:* The verbal formulations of examples a, b, and c were enough for them to be acknowledged as scientific laws before their later restatement with the help of mathematical equations, as discussed in each of the following bulleted items.

- The direction of rotation of the vortex can be derived with the help of equations of mechanics *(Coriolis force)*.

- The English physicist James Clerk Maxwell (1831–1879) succeeded in 1873 in finding a mathematical description of electromagnetic phenomena (published in *A Treatise on Electricity and Magnetism*). Later, the German physicist Heinrich Hertz (1857–1894) converted some of this work into Maxwell's well-known first and second equations.

- *The Pauli Exclusion Principle*, originally discovered by experiment, was later derived mathematically from the wave function of the electron. This mathematical explanation is based on the validity of the wave function, but the law itself is retained in its verbal form.

d. *Le Chatelier-Braun Principle (Le Chatelier's Principle of Least Restraint)*:

This principle, elaborated in 1887 by the French chemist Henry-Louis Le Chatelier (1850–1936) and the German Nobel laureate in physics (1909) Karl Ferdinand Braun (1850–1918), describes *qualitatively* the dependence of chemical equilibrium on external conditions. This equilibrium shifts to counter the effect of imposed changes (e.g., temperature, pressure, and concentration). It is also called the *Law of Least Restraint*.

Example: In the case of a reaction with a related change in volume (e.g., in the spontaneous decomposition of ammonia ($2\,NH_3 \rightleftarrows N_2 + 3\,H_2$) an increase in pressure must lead to a reduction of decomposition rate. Correspondingly, a reduction in volume and increase in pressure leads to an increase in production. Ammonia synthesis $N_2 + 3\,H_2 \rightleftarrows 2\,NH_3$ is achieved by pushing the equilibrium under high pressure toward $NH_3$. This result is used to produce ammonia under high pressure and is called the Haber-Bosch process. According to the principle, by injecting additional heat into exothermic reactions, the equilibrium of reactions can be pushed in the direction of the original components. The *Le Chatelier Principle* applies not only to reversible chemical processes but to reversible physical ones as well, for example, salt water plus heat → water vapor plus salt.

e. *Principle of Minimum Structural Change:* Hine published a law that helps predict the course of chemical reactions. It states that the preferred reaction is the one requiring the least rearrangements of atoms and electrons.

f. The *Third Law of Thermodynamics*: "Absolute zero cannot be attained by any means."

**Scientific laws and mathematics**: The Nobel laureate for physics Richard P. Feynman described mathematics as follows [F1, p. 40]: *"Mathematics is a language plus reasoning; it is like a language plus logic. Mathematics is a tool for reasoning."*

That mathematics is not always necessary to describe natural laws is attested to by Feynman with the following example [F1, p. 36]:

> There is a law in physics called Faraday's Law which says that in electrolysis the amount of material that is deposited is proportional to the current and to the time that the current is acting. This means that the amount of material deposited is proportional to the electrical charge that goes through the system. It sounds very mathematical but what is actually happening is that the electrons going through the wire each carry one charge. To take a particular example, maybe to deposit one atom of the material requires one electron. Therefore, the number of atoms of material that are deposited is necessarily equal to the number of electrons that flow and thus proportional to the charge that goes through the wire. Here we see that a mathematically appearing law has as its basis nothing very deep, requiring no real knowledge of mathematics.

The above examples demonstrate that scientific laws need not necessarily be expressed mathematically or be quantifiable. Mathematical formulae are not always appropriate to describe the course of chemical reactions or preferred directions of rotation or general principles. In some cases, the experimentally observed laws can also be derived from more general laws. In this way, for example, Maxwell's Equations led to the Induction Law.

It is important that we neither underestimate nor overestimate the possibilities of mathematics. Two divergent views may help us come to a balanced assessment. Kant provided one extreme standpoint when he expressed that "Any scientific discipline is only as much real science as the amount of mathematics contained in it" [*Metaphysische Anfangsgründe der Naturwissenschaft* (Metaphysical Foundations of Natural Science — 1786)]. In contrast, the French mathematician and physicist Blaise Pascal (1623–1662) wrote in a letter to Pierre de Fermat (1660):

> To be honest about mathematics, I regard it as the highest school of the human mind; but at the same time it is so useless that I would hardly differentiate between a man who is only a mathematician and a skilled craftsman. I call it the most beautiful pastime in the world, but it is only a pastime, and I have often said that it is good for testing our strength but not to be used, so that I would not lift a finger in favor of mathematics.

The points concerning the nature and relevance of the scientific laws of physics and chemistry that we have discussed in chapter 4 (4.3 and 4.4) apply also to the scientific laws of Universal Information. The statements/laws about Universal Information are observable and most have yet to be quantified. Although these statements are verbal, the language used is no criterion to judge whether a statement is a Scientific Law or not. We are not yet able to determine if non-material entities will be quantifiable in the future. In the case of information, its engineering in material media during storage and transmission is statistically quantifiable (see Appendix 1.2).

*Appendix 4*

# WHAT DARWIN COULDN'T HAVE KNOWN[1]

## A4.1 Who are we to thank?

On December 31, 2008, in perfectly timed anticipation of 2009's "year of Darwin," the German newspaper *Die Zeit* ran a four-page item devoted to the theme of evolution, with the double-spread header, "Thank you, Darwin!" The gratitude was directed at a man born 200 years ago, whose revolutionary book *On the Origin of Species* was published 150 years ago.

German philosopher Immanuel Kant (1724–1804) proudly declared, "Give me matter, and I will build a world out of it!" French mathematician and astronomer Pierre-Simon Laplace (1749–1827) wrote extensively on the universe and its origins. Asked by Napoleon why he made no mention of its Creator, he famously responded, "I have no need of that hypothesis." These and other pioneers of scientific atheism searched for an explanation of life origins in which God was no longer required. Seemingly coming to their rescue was Darwin, who provided a way to imagine how living things arose by "natural processes" alone.

---

1. This text of Appendix 4 is also available in a variety of languages as a colorful tract that can be ordered from the "Missionswerk DIE BRUDERHAND" (email: bruderhand@ bruderhand.de, homepage: www. bruderhand.de, address: Am Hofe 2, 29342 Wienhausen, Germany).

While Darwin himself may have regarded the implications of his message with some trepidation, today's ever-more-godless world adulates its patron saint in an endless parade of journalistic jubilation.

Until Darwin's voyage to the Galápagos islands (1835), the teaching of the Greek philosopher Aristotle — that species were fixed and could not change — had held sway. From the varying beak forms of the finches living there, Darwin correctly concluded that species could change and adapt. However, his further conclusion, that all species could be traced back to a single common ancestor, is not scientifically sustainable. Even Darwin was aware of a great weakness in his theory — that there were next to no fossils that could be claimed as transitional forms, when there should have been vast numbers. Nonetheless, after Darwin, mankind lost its special status of being created in God's image, becoming instead a mere upstart of the animal kingdom.

## A4.2 Making evolution happen

Today, mutation, selection, isolation, long time periods, chance and necessity, and of course death are claimed to be the only factors necessary to drive evolution. Though all are real enough, none have ever been observed to generate new creative information.

- **Mutation** can only change hereditary information that is already present. Without the DNA information system already in existence, biological evolution could not even get started. Mutation is, by definition, a *random* process, without any conceivable goal orientation. So, in principle it could never produce new functional systems (e.g., the invention of new organs).

- **Selection** favors those organisms more capable of surviving, ensuring that their hereditary material has a better chance of propagating itself. However, this process only sorts or culls information that is already there, neither improving the information nor adding anything new.

- Like mutation and selection, none of the other factors listed earlier have any creative function.

Let's look at a few examples in living things to see if such purposeless factors could have brought the following systems into being.

## A4.3 Sexual reproduction

According to evolutionary teaching, the "invention" of sex was a crucial necessity for the development of higher organisms. Through repeatedly new combinations of genes, many varieties emerge, from which the selection process ensures that those best adapted to their environment are more likely to survive and propagate. But this process is ruled out as an explanation for the desired upward trend in evolutionary complexity, for two reasons.

1.  Sexual reproduction itself could never have arisen via an evolutionary process. It would only be possible if both sexes already possessed functionally complete and complementary reproductive organs. But evolution, by definition, permits no goal-oriented strategy or plan. How can such organs develop by such a gradual process over thousands of generations, when the organisms cannot reproduce sexually without them? If the gradual action of selection is ruled out in favor of some rapid chance process, then how could such complex complementary structures arise, since they are so different, yet suited to each other down to the last detail? Additionally, they must arise at more or less the same time and place in separate organisms.

2.  Even if we assumed that sexual reproduction somehow just miraculously arose, such mixing and recombining of hereditary information would still not be capable of producing any fundamentally new information. Plant and animal breeders have shown, through innumerable efforts, that highly bred cows still remain cows, and wheat never gives rise to sunflowers.

    So-called microevolution, better called programmed variation within a kind, is easily observed, but we never see one kind of creature give rise to a different kind, as macroevolution would have it.

## A4.4 Technological ingenuity in red blood cells

Each mm³ (= 1 µl = 1 microliter) of our blood contains five million red blood cells — so there are 150 million of them in each drop of blood. These highly specialized cells perform functions vital to life.

- Throughout their 120-day lifetime, while circulating through the lungs, they are refueled with oxygen 175,000 times, while simultaneously offloading carbon dioxide, the waste product of oxidation.

- Red blood cells are so tiny, they can squeeze through narrow capillaries to reach every part of the body.

- Our body produces two million new red cells every second and each cell is rich in hemoglobin, a remarkably complex chemical compound.

**Hemoglobin** is used for transporting oxygen, even during development of the embryo. Up to about the third month of pregnancy, the embryo's oxygen needs are distinctly different from those in the ensuing fetal stage, which are different again from the needs of the infant and adult. All three stages — embryo, fetus, and adult — require the production of chemically different forms of hemoglobin. Shortly before birth, for example, the body's "factories" start switching to top production mode of the third (adult) type of hemoglobin. These three types of hemoglobin could not have arisen by trial-and-error evolutionary processes because none of the other mutant forms of the hemoglobin molecule could carry enough oxygen, and would thus be deadly. Even if the right forms of hemoglobin were to somehow arise to supply the first two stages, but without the genetic coding to produce the third form, the outcome would still be certain death. Each of these three stages of our development requires fundamentally different DNA coding to produce each of the three different hemoglobin molecules. Further, each set of different DNA coding, and its biomachinery that synthesizes the hemoglobin molecules, must be switched on and off at the right point in time.

Where did such a complex system of information-controlled machinery come from? All conceivable evolutionary explanations fail miserably because any partially completed transitional stage required by evolution would not permit the organism to survive. The whole complex of information and machinery must be present and functional from the start.

This concept of "irreducible complexity" also applies to the immune system, and to the flagellum that many bacteria use to propel themselves. In each case, the organisms "on the way" to their completed state would not have been able to survive. A more obvious explanation is that this information-controlled machinery was initially complete — something only possible if a wise Creator conceived and made everything fully functional in the beginning.

## A4.5 Is evolution a workable paradigm?

In addition to the above brief glance at the realm of living things, one can point to many other examples of high-level goal-oriented systems.

- The **sperm whale**, though a mammal, is so equipped as to be able to surface rapidly from a depth of 3,000 meters (1.86 miles). Yet it shows no signs of that dreaded nemesis of divers, "the bends," which would kill most other mammals attempting this feat.

- Many of the **bacteria** in our bowels are propelled by miniature built-in electric (proton-powered) motors, which can run forwards or backwards.

- In all cases, life itself depends on the functionality of the body's major organs (heart, liver, kidneys, etc.). Unfinished organs, yet to be developed, would be useless. Those wanting to think along Darwinian lines need to be reminded that evolution by definition excludes any specific direction towards an ultimate goal or target in the form of a finished product. German evolutionary biologist Günther Osche (1926–2009) rightly stated: "Of course, unlike a business enterprise, organisms undergoing certain phases of evolution cannot be temporarily shut down while being rebuilt." Each intermediate "stage" must be capable of fully surviving in its own right.

The intelligence and wisdom expressed in the works of creation is nothing short of overwhelming. The conclusion that there was an original Creator is more than just obvious. It also fits with what the Bible states in its very first verse: "In the beginning, God created"!

Because of Darwinism, the theology of higher literary criticism has flourished. This liberal theology dismisses the idea that the creation account is an accurate revelation from God. But we would do well to "believe everything ... that is written" (Acts 24:14), for "God is not human, that he should lie" (Num. 23:19).

## A4.6 Where does information come from?

The strongest arguments in science are always those in which scientific laws can be invoked to preclude the possibility of a proposed process or event. Scientific laws know of no exceptions. This is why a perpetual motion machine, one that runs continually with no external input of energy, is impossible.

Today, we know what Darwin could not know — that the cells of all living things contain an unimaginable amount of information stored in DNA in the most compact form known to us so far. The development of all organs is information-directed, and all processes and functions in living things are information-controlled, including the manufacture of all the substances that make up our bodies (for example, thousands of different proteins). The whole concept of evolution would only be feasible if there were some property in matter that permitted information to arise through chance processes. This is absolutely essential, because all the body plans of individuals, and all the complex processes in cells, are information-based.

**Information is a non-material entity, thus not a property of matter.** The scientific laws about Universal Information state that purely material processes can never generate a non-material entity and that information is a non-material entity, which can only arise from an originator with intelligence and will. We can see, then, that someone who thinks evolution is possible must believe in a "perpetual motion machine of information," i.e., in something strictly forbidden by the universally applicable scientific laws. This is the Achilles' heel of Darwinism; at this point, evolution requires science itself to be abandoned. This is explained in detail in this book.

## A4.7 Where did life come from?

All the evolutionary bluster of our day has never really answered this question. Evolutionists have not the faintest notion of how dead matter could have given rise to life.

Stanley Miller's (1930–2007) "primordial soup" experiment (1953) began to be featured in all biology textbooks and yet, 40 years later, he admitted that none of the contemporary hypotheses about the origin of life were convincing. He described them collectively as "nonsense" and "paper chemistry." The microbiologist Louis Pasteur (1822–1895) scientifically established at the microbial level what we now call the biogenetic law: "Life can only come from life."

There was only One who could say, "I am ... the life" (John 14:6), and that was Jesus. Of Him it says in Colossians 1:16: "For in him all things were created: things in heaven and on earth, visible and invisible," and further in John 1:3: "Through him [the Word = Jesus] all things were made; without him nothing was made that has been made." Every theory of origins that does not have Jesus as the source and foundation of life and the universe is thus a stillborn notion, one that must inevitably founder on the Rock that is Jesus.

Darwin could not have known these and many other things because technology had not made them available (e.g., high-powered microscopes). However, Darwin could have, and should have, known other things simply by reading the Scriptures and remaining faithful to what God's Word clearly says. So, in the end, even Darwin is *without excuse*.

Evolution is therefore shown to be one of the greatest errors in the history of the world, and it has drawn millions of people into the abyss of unbelief. Unfortunately, many today do not take into account that this abyss of unbelief is followed, after death, by the abyss of being eternally lost (hell). A real tragedy in today's world is that journalists pay widespread homage to Darwin instead of proclaiming the real Originator of everything, saying, **"Thank You, Jesus!"**

*Appendix 5*

# POST-PUBLICATION REVIEW

Since its original publication in German, this book has appeared in several languages. At the time of writing this appendix, it was already in its seventh German edition. It has aided and guided many in their search for God. Even believers challenged by the strong influence of evolutionary theory and materialism have found many scientific arguments that align with the biblical account.

With such a radically fundamental book presenting many scientifically new ideas, it is inevitable that skeptics will arise and critically question these. Such questioning has always led to a theory either being consolidated and put on a firm footing, or to the model being formulated more precisely, or having to be discarded because of recognized errors. Every new scientific idea has to face this process, and this is no exception, but rather, it is what should happen.

**Questioning relativity:** Einstein's Theory of Relativity, published in 1905, was also massively questioned. The well-known physicist and Nobel laureate Ernest Rutherford (1871–1923) apparently said: "Oh, that stuff! We never bother with that in our work." Fellow Nobelist Wilhelm Roentgen (1845–1923), the discoverer of X-rays, criticized Einstein, saying, "I can't get it into my head that one has to use such quite abstract considerations and concepts to understand natural phenomena." It was not until 1919 that an astronomical verification of the Theory of Relativity was provided by measurements during an eclipse showing that the sun's gravity bent light as Einstein had predicted on the basis of his theory.

I have accrued the main objections, which seem justified in each case, and will now answer them in detail. I trust the following explanations will aid better understanding of the overall concept of this book.

## A5.1 Proofs and refutations

**Objection O1:** *You keep referring to "proofs," and claim to have thereby refuted the theory of evolution, atheism, and materialism. Isn't that rather over the top? In my opinion, real proofs only exist in mathematics.*

**Answer to O1:** The following answer will no doubt become understandable if, concerning "proofs," we:

- Rigorously distinguish between **hard** and **soft** proofs, and **hard** and **soft** refutations, respectively. This necessary distinction is introduced here for the first time.

- Clarify what a proof is based on.

- Clearly define the term "proof."

**Definition D11:** A **proof** is the error-free derivation of a statement from established facts.

**Definition D12:** A **refutation** is the error-free proof that an asserted statement can be shown on the basis of established facts to lead to a contradiction.

In order to draw a clear dividing line between that which is irrefutable, and that which can potentially be corrected thanks to better knowledge, we introduce two new terms here: Hard and soft proofs (or refutations).

### A5.1.1 Hard proofs and hard refutations

**Hard proofs** and **hard refutations** only exist if they are based on absolutely established facts. There are only three areas in our world that meet this requirement:

1. The structural sciences (axioms) — e.g., mathematics
2. The laws of nature (reality)
3. The Bible (God)

What is the established basis for each of these three areas? Point 1 is based on *axioms*; the basis of point 2 is *observed reality*; and in point 3, all statements are anchored in *God*.

Since the concepts of **hard** and **soft proofs** are newly introduced here, a more precise definition is in order.

**Definition D13: Hard proofs** (and also **hard refutations**) are new statements that are based on such a firm foundation that they can no longer be refuted.

We have only been able to identify three areas in which this strict condition is fulfilled. We will now name one such proof, that cannot be refuted, from each of the three areas.

**1. Mathematics.** If in a right-angled triangle the two sides that form a right angle with each other are designated a and b (= the catheti) and the side opposite the right angle is designated c (= the hypotenuse), then the theorem proved by Pythagoras applies: In all plane right-angled triangles, if a square is drawn based on each side, the sum of the areas of the two smaller squares (drawn on each cathetus) is equal to the area of the largest square (that drawn on the hypotenuse). This is succinctly expressed as $a^2 + b^2 = c^2$.

**This proof cannot be refuted.**

**2. Laws of nature:** According to the Second Law of Thermodynamics, no process is possible in this world in which heat exchange occurs with decreasing entropy (see Appendix 2, A2.1). This proves that heat energy can never flow by itself from a cooler body to a warmer one.

**This proof cannot be refuted (by any experiment!).**

**3. Bible:** In John 10:35, Jesus speaks of the prophecies of the Old Testament and says about them: "… Scripture cannot be set aside." This means that all prophetic predictions will come true, which of course includes also the prophecies about Jesus.

**This statement has so far never been refuted.**

**Definition D14:** We speak of **soft proofs** (and also **soft refutations**) in all other cases that do not belong to the three areas above.

A soft proof can be applicable in most cases, but something proven in this way is not necessarily true. For example, we classify all legal and historical proofs as soft, since they are based neither on mathematical logic nor on natural laws.

Let us now turn to the three fields whose characteristics include hard proofs and hard refutations.

## 1. The structural sciences

The structural sciences such as mathematics and computer science work detached from the reality of all that happens in this world. Albert Einstein (1879–1955) rightly said, "As far as the laws of mathematics refer to reality, they are not certain, and as far as they are certain, they do not refer to reality." The derivation of a theorem, whether it is a true or false one, follows from a certain number of axioms which are assumed to be true, and further from theorems which have already been proved.

**True theorems** can be **proved** by various methods (e.g., complete induction[1]) — for example, "The number $\pi$ is an irrational number"; Fermat's famous Last Theorem: "No three positive integers a, b, and c satisfy the equation $a^n + b^n = c^n$ for any integer value of n greater than 2."

The mathematician Kurt Gödel (1906–1978) was able to prove with the help of his incompleteness theorems that *not all* true theorems in mathematics are provable or disprovable.

A **false theorem can be disproved** by showing mathematically that the statement asserted leads to a contradiction.

## 2. Natural laws

According to the knowledge of the natural sciences that has been established to this point, the laws of nature and the natural constants are not subject to change in space and time. **Natural laws** have such a pervasive effect in the material world that they are valid even in the most distant corners of the universe. Not a single atom can escape their influence. All processes — and there are thousands at work in just a single living cell — are under the absolute supremacy of the laws of nature. No process on this earth and in the vastness of the universe is disregarded or overlooked by them for even a fraction of a millionth of a second. One can only marvel in the highest degree that there is something so fundamental, so all-encompassing and all-pervasive across all boundaries of space and time.

---

1. Mathematical induction is not to be confused with inductive reasoning.

The significance that axioms have in mathematical reasoning is the same significance that the laws of nature have in regard to the reality that surrounds us. **If our argumentation is based on natural laws, we have arrived at the strongest scientific form of proof.**

In chapter 4.3, we stated and expounded a series of principles (N1 to N14) concerning the attributes or nature of physical laws. The following principle N15 adds to that list, and it applies to all natural (scientific) laws.

**N15:** Natural laws have both a **permissive** and **prohibitive** quality (nature), or stated otherwise, a **proving** and also a **disproving** quality.

(*Note:* Only the author of the laws of nature can change or override them for His purposes. This is the case with the miracles of the Bible — see 4.4 in chapter 4).

The principle expressed in **N15** will now be expressed via different formulations in order to cover different applications.

**N16:** One can **prove via natural laws** that an imagined process is in principle possible in reality, if no natural law is contradicted in the process. All engineering is based on the fact that processes (e.g., ammonia synthesis) and machines (e.g., aeroplanes, turbines, cars, rockets) can be calculated and planned in advance according to the laws of nature. If everything takes place within the framework of natural law, then the plans can also be implemented in reality, unless other restrictions prevent this (e.g., cost too high, distances too great).

**N17:** One can **prove by natural laws** that an imagined process or an imagined machine cannot be implemented or occur in reality if even one natural law is contradicted in the process.

**N18:** If someone imagines a process or a machine in which a law of nature is demonstrably violated, this idea can be **disproved with the aid of natural laws**.

**N19:** Whether an imagined process or machine is **impossible** in reality can be **proven** by showing that a law of nature would be violated in the process.

**Two new natural law proofs from this book:**

**P1: Impossibility of macroevolution:** According to T3, the process of biological evolution (macroevolution) has never taken place because it would violate a natural law of Universal Information (violation of SLI-4: *"Universal Information can only be created by an intelligent sender"* and cannot arise by itself).

**P2: Proof of God through information:** Since living cells contain a huge amount of Universal Information, but all the encoded concepts have no human origin, a (divine) intelligent sender (originator, God) is required as the source. (Necessity of the existence of an originator per SLI-4: *Universal Information can only be created by an intelligent sender.*)

P1 and P2 make use of the above statement **N15:** Natural laws have a **proving** and also a **disproving** character.

## 3. Bible

Every atheist can agree with the two previously mentioned possibilities of proof with the help of the structural sciences and the laws of nature. However, to recognize the Bible as an absolute source of truth can only be understood by those who believe everything in the Word of God, as Paul states that he does in Acts 24:14. Jesus is equally clear in His prayer to the Father: "Your word is truth" (John 17:17). With this clarity, we have found another firm foundation for engaging in proof and disproof with the help of the Bible.

We see this proving or refuting approach in Jesus' use of the Word of God, especially when He argues his case to His interlocutors with the words "Haven't you read?" (Matt. 12:3) or "Scripture cannot be set aside" (John 10:35).

**Example 1: Proof of resurrection**
Jesus was approached by the Sadducees with a trick question to argue against the resurrection of the dead. They asked him (Matt. 22:23–33), if seven brothers marry one and the same woman in succession and she finally dies herself, whose wife will she be in the resurrection? Jesus rebutted their objection by saying that in the hereafter, the marriage union no longer exists, and added a thought exercise by quoting from Exod. 3:6, where God says, "I am ... the God of Abraham, the God of Isaac and the God of Jacob." But since Abraham, Isaac, and Jacob had died, they must logically be resurrected from death because God "is not the God of the dead, but of the living" (Matt. 22:32b). Thus, Jesus proved the fact of resurrection to His critics with the help of the Bible.

**Example 2: Refutation of a false hope**
After Jesus' crucifixion, the Emmaus disciples were deeply disappointed: "But we had hoped that he was the one who was going to redeem Israel" (Luke 24:21). They had firmly expected that Jesus would free Israel from the occupying Romans. When the risen Jesus joins the disciples unrecog-

nized on the road to Emmaus, Jesus refutes their wrong way of thinking with Scripture:

"Did not the Messiah have to suffer these things and then enter his glory?" And beginning with Moses and all the Prophets, he explained to them what was said in all the Scriptures concerning himself (Luke 24:26–27).

## A5.1.2 Soft proofs and soft refutations

Under the terms **soft proofs** or **soft refutations** we include all other forms of evidence that are based on less strong statements than the three sources of truth mentioned above. This category includes, for example, **historical evidence** and **circumstantial evidence**. In a court case, one speaks of circumstantial evidence when (ideally, multiple) facts can be cited to establish the action to be proven. However, because the risk of misinterpretation remains (miscarriage of justice[2]), we speak here of a "soft" form of proof.

## A5.2 Is God provable?

**Objection O2:** *God cannot be proven. He is infinite, and therefore one cannot prove Him by finite means.*

**Reply to O2:** Indeed, emotions are readily inflamed when it comes to the provability of God. Since ancient times, people have tried to "prove" God. We list here only some of the attempts in times past:

- The cosmological proof of God
- The causality proof
- The ontological proof of God (Anselm of Canterbury; 1033–1109)
- The teleological proof of God (Thomas Aquinas; 1225–1274)

*First, an important note:* The short phrase "proof of God" can be misunderstood if taken in the sense that it is possible to make God provable in His entire nature. This is impossible to begin with, because God has revealed of Himself:

"For my thoughts are not your thoughts, neither are your ways my ways," declares the LORD. "As the heavens are higher than the

---

2. There are countless examples of miscarriages of justice worldwide. A far from exhaustive list is found at: en.wikipedia.org/wiki/List_of_miscarriage_of_justice_cases.

earth, so are my ways higher than your ways and my thoughts than your thoughts" (Isa. 55:8–9).

With the help of the laws of nature we can prove only a few of the characteristics of God, such as:

- His existence (chapter 8.3, SF1)
- His omniscience (chapter 8.4, SF2)
- His eternal nature (chapter 8.4.3, SF2c)
- His omnipotence (chapter 8.5, SF3a)

Thus, with each form of proof, it is absolutely necessary to state in addition which of God's attributes is being referred to. The attributes of God revealed in the Bible, such as love, mercy, goodness, truth, and saving grace, are not accessible to any scientific form of proof.

When we think about proofs of God, we cannot avoid talking about the well-known philosopher Immanuel Kant (1724–1804). He is considered the great demolisher of all proofs of God. Kant has become viewed as one of the leading figures of the Enlightenment's humanistic assault on belief in the God of the Bible.

Kant maintained that our cognitive faculties are extremely limited. Our brain nonetheless constantly throws up questions which — according to him — overtax its capacity: questions about the purpose of life, about the universe, about eternity, the soul, immortality, and God.

The Bible on the other hand says that we are well able to know things about God: "Be still, and know that I am God" (Ps. 46:10); "What may be known about God is plain to them" (Rom. 1:19).

In his "Critique of Pure Reason," Kant maintained that we can in any case not recognize the world as it is, but only how it appears to us. "When contemplating God and the soul, reasoning falls short. We cannot know whether there is a God, whether He is loving or harsh, or whether He punishes sin or not. Equally we cannot know whether there is a soul, and whether it lives on after death." Though he never embraced atheism, with these fundamental statements, Kant places himself in clear opposition to the Bible.

Many today increasingly declare themselves to be agnostics, claiming not to know whether God exists. But since in Paul's Letter to the Romans it is so strongly emphasized that God's "invisible qualities ... have been clearly seen, being understood from what has been made," and that therefore "they knew [about] God" (Rom. 1:20–21), then this is more than a mere reference to God, but a very strong form of statement about the existence of the Author of all things.

## Proofs of God in scientific terminology

Whether we can speak of a **proof of God** in scientific terms or not depends on the form of that proof.

We have shown in A5.1.1 above that we can only speak of "hard" proofs in three areas, namely in the structural sciences of mathematics and computer science, or when the proofs are based on natural laws, or when biblical references are applied.

In chapter 8.3 (Deduction 1), based on applying a natural law of information to the DNA information found in all living things (SLI-4: *"Universal Information [UI] can only be created by an intelligent sender"*), we concluded that there must be an Intelligent Sender who created this UI.

This is a proof of God in the sense that a God who is an Intelligent Sender must exist. This result, based on natural laws, leads to two direct conclusions:

**DC1:** Atheism is refuted.
**DC2:** The existence of God is confirmed.

The conclusion derived from SLI-4 is initially only the proof of the existence of a God. That it is the God of the Bible cannot be concluded from this. In the further course of the conclusions, it was possible to show that this God must be omniscient (chapter 8.4, DC2) and eternal (chapter 8.4.3, SF2c).

We can thus describe the proof of God presented in chapter 8.3 as **the proof of God's existence through a natural law of information.**

A special form of proof of God is presented in detail in chapter 9.3. It is the **prophetic-mathematical proof of God**. Since this proof starts from the fulfilled prophecies of the Bible, this is a proof of God that clearly goes beyond natural law conclusions in its statements. Thus, this proof is able to prove the God of the Bible as the **only** existing one, and it confirms the Bible as a book of truth.

*Purpose of a proof of God:* Is it even necessary to construct a proof of God? What is gained thereby? In the so-called Christian West, only a small percentage of the population still reads the Bible. Many have no religious affiliation; the vast majority are atheistic or agnostic, and experience shows they are barely reachable any longer through just proclaiming the Bible. A proof of God can persuade some that they are on the wrong track as an atheist or agnostic, so they then have a serious reason to concern themselves with the Bible and the Gospel.

*Falsifiability of proofs of God:* We have here already (in A5.1) distinguished between hard and soft proofs. This also draws a sharp dividing line between the two types of proofs of God. Hard proofs of God are based on natural laws. Since, scientifically speaking, there is no higher authority than the laws of nature, there is also no criterion by which such proofs of God could fail. There is another reason why a hard proof of God cannot be disproved: If the existence of God has been established though natural law, one will never find another natural law which could refute this outcome, since by definition there is no such thing as a natural law which contradicts another (see chapter 4.3, statement N9, and question Q1 in chapter 10.1).

Soft proofs include all those proofs of God not based on natural laws. Even when these are ever-so-plausibly formulated, they always carry the risk of refutation, as they are not based on an absolutely immutable foundation. If Kant is referred to as the refuter ("demolisher") of proofs of God, that can only refer to soft proofs, which are not based upon natural law. Note that Kant may have criticized one or the other soft proof of God, but if he only argued philosophically and not from the standpoint of natural law, one cannot speak of refutation or "demolition." No one can refute God's existence, since it has already been proven on the basis of natural law. Since natural laws are immutable, and cannot contradict one another, refutation is in principle no longer possible.

*Proof of God and salvation:* Through the acceptance of a proof of God one has not yet come to saving faith. It still requires the revelation through the Holy Spirit that Jesus must be accepted as personal Savior through a free decision. Although proofs of God do not directly lead to faith, they are nonetheless able to clear a number of obstacles to faith out of someone's way. Saving faith is dependent on Jesus. This is established by two passages from the New Testament: "Whoever has the Son has life; whoever does not have the Son of God does not have life" (1 John 5:12). "Whoever believes in him is not condemned, but whoever does not believe stands condemned already because they have not believed in the name of God's one and only Son" (John 3:18).

### A5.3 From a mathematical point of view, can prophecies be regarded as independent events?

**Objection O3:** *In the ant model used to illustrate the "prophetic-mathematical proof of God," probability calculation is used (chap. 9.3.3). Strictly speaking, however, this method may only be used if the individual events are independent of each other. In my estimation, biblical events are not independent of one other.*

**Answer to O3:** Since mathematics is a purely theoretical science that is conducted detached from all reality, at best it only approximates reality. Nevertheless, mathematics has proven itself countless millions of times over in the real sciences as an extremely effective tool for the quantitative evaluation of processes. In particular, it plays a central and indispensable role in the description of real-world processes in the natural and engineering sciences, and also in economics. Because of their complexity, real processes often cannot be idealized in such a way that mathematical formulae can be applied exactly. In such cases, one avails oneself of the help provided by mathematical models. Although these do not describe the process exactly, they do so with sufficient precision.

If individual parameters are unknown in the modeling, it often helps to use an upper limit value, for example, such that all real values will always lie below it. Then one is on the safe side when drawing conclusions. This is exactly what was strictly observed in the calculations for the "Prophetic-Mathematical Proof of God." Since the probability to be applied for *each individual* prophecy is unknown, we applied an extremely high value for its fulfilment (by chance) with $p = 0.5$ (upper limit!).

In no case will the actual individual probability be higher than $p$ (see chapter 9.3.2). Thus, we can be assured that the actual total probability that all the prophecies involved would have been fulfilled — in the biblically indicated way, but by chance — is still significantly smaller than the value of $P = 10^{-984}$ found by our model calculation. Since the conclusions (see chapter 9.3.4) are based on this "too high" value, we have erred on the safe side in what is in fact an extreme way.

Actually, given the multitude of fulfilled prophecies, a mathematical treatment should not be necessary. Their sheer number speaks so strongly for itself that everyone who is confronted with it would have to be overwhelmed, and at the same time convinced that here the living God of the Bible knows all events in advance due to His omniscience — and is furthermore able to put the predicted statements into action due to His omnipotence.

Nevertheless, we want to go down the mathematical route as well, because such a quantitative approach doubtless calls for renewed amazement from us. I realize that the **prophetic-mathematical proof of God** cannot be an exact mathematical representation of biblical reality. This will be explained here by two points.

**Point 1:** The number of fulfilled prophecies used is based on a meticulous count by the American Bible teacher Finis Jennings Dake (1902–1987). In the meantime, further prophecies have been fulfilled which could not be taken into account here. It is also possible that Dake considered some prophecies fulfilled that another Bible scholar would consider not yet fulfilled. We have taken this variation into account too, by carrying out the calculation with half the number of fulfilled prophecies (see Calculation 1, chapter 9.3.3). This does not change the conclusions at all.

**Point 2:** There is still a semantic fuzziness in dealing with biblical texts. Unlike a secular book, the full content of the Bible is only revealed to the believer in Christ (1 Cor. 2:13). Jesus made an important statement about understanding the Old Testament in John 5:39: "You study the Scriptures diligently because you think that in them you have eternal life. These are the very Scriptures that testify about me."

To the one who does not believe in Jesus as the Son of God, the promises of the Old Testament that refer to Jesus remain closed. The Pharisees and scribes of Jesus' time are an eloquent example of this. In modern times, there are many other groups that reject Jesus as the Messiah who has already come. Years ago, when I wanted to publish the Prophetic-Mathematical Proof of God in a physics journal, I received a negative response from the editors on the grounds: "We have many Jewish readers, and they would feel their faith violated."

**Event independence:** An important condition for the application of probability theory is that the individual events should be independent of each other. We can consider the prophecies as historical events because they occur in our world in space and time. Historical events take place either in parallel[3] or in a temporal sequence, one after the

---

3. For example, in the year 1492 the following parallel events took place: • Christopher Columbus (1451–1506) discovered America. • Leonardo da Vinci (1452–1514) drew his designs for a flying machine. • Queen Isabella of Castile (1451–1504) drove the Moors out of Granada, their last foothold in Spain.

other[4] — and this is also true for the prophecies. We can regard the parallel events as independent of each other. For those with a temporal sequence, we have the intuitive impression that there could be an event-dependency. Thus, it is necessary to verify this.

The throwing of dice is the prime example of the fact that the individual throws are to be regarded as mathematically independent of each other. In all practical applications, it must be checked whether this event independence is also guaranteed. In the case of the ant model, too, it is necessary to check whether event independence applies. For this purpose, we pick out the most striking prophetic chain of events in the Old Testament for which we would be intuitively the most likely to assume an event dependence. It is the numerous predictions about the coming of the Messiah that we now want to take a closer look at. At first glance, there seems to be a fixed coupling of the generational sequence of the family tree of Jesus according to Matt. 1:1–17, for this forms a fixed linear sequence that begins with Abraham and then continues steadily through Isaac, Jacob, Judah, ... Jesse, David, Solomon....

For proof of event-independence, we will take only ten links out of the long chain of progenitors from Adam to Jesus in order to make the essentials clear. Immediately after the Fall, God announces His intention to save, which He then increasingly unfolds over many centuries in the course of the Old Testament. This happens in gradual, successive revelations, whereby each individual step — mathematically speaking — corresponds to a new throw of the dice. When calculating probabilities in dice throws that take place one after the other, it no longer matters what numbers came up in previous throws. The new dice throw is and remains independent of the previous one (event independence!). It is the same when looking at the individual chain links with regard to the progenitors in the line of salvation. Mathematically, games of dice that take place one after the other in time are independent of each other. If by prophetic decision "the die is cast" for the progenitor $S_k$, then this "chain link" can be regarded as settled. Now nothing stands in the way of the probability calculation for the following progenitor $S_{k+1}$, because $S_k$ belongs to the past dice-throwing process and does not influence the new one.

---

4. For example, three successive U.S. presidents were involved in consequential events surrounding WW2 (the dates in brackets refer to their time in office): Franklin D. Roosevelt (1933–1945), Harry S. Truman (1945–1953), and Dwight D. Eisenhower (1953–1961).

Since the progenitors had different numbers of descendants, it was initially impossible to know which of the n sons would continue the family tree of Jesus. Thus, each son has the probability p = 1/n of entering the family tree of the line of salvation. Only prophecy narrows down the number of independent possibilities to the **one single one** in each generation.

**1.** We begin with Genesis 3:15, the very first, still cryptic, announcement of the Savior:

> And I will put enmity between you and the woman, and between your offspring [or "seed"] and hers; he will crush your head, and you will strike his heel.

With the help of the New Testament, we know that the Messiah comes both as the **Son of Man** (e.g., Matt. 18:11, 24:30; Luke 6:22; John 3:14), but at the same time as the **Son of God** (e.g., Matt. 14:33, 16:16; John 3:18). However, in order to be both human and God at the same time, He had to have both a human and a divine origin. This seems to rule out a married couple as a gene source. If a human father and mother each contributed half of His genes, as is normally the case, Jesus would then be purely human in nature. As we know from Luke 1:35, the Holy Spirit takes on the role of divine lineage-bearer. The human genealogical role can therefore be assumed by **only one person** — either a man or a woman. In other words, before it is known that it is to be a woman, the probability of being the seed of the woman was w->p = 0.5. In Genesis 3:15, God decides in favor of the woman: the Messiah is to come explicitly **from the offspring (seed) of the woman.**

**2. Noah** had three sons: Shem, Ham, and Japheth. Since only one of the three can continue the line of blessing, up to this point the probability for each son is w->p = 1/3. By the following still somewhat concealed prophecy, the Semites are named the bearers of the line of blessing; at the same time two-thirds of the nations (Hamites, Japhethites) are excluded:

> "Praise be to the LORD, the God of **Shem**! May Canaan [= son of Ham] be the slave of Shem. May God extend Japheth's territory; may Japheth live in the tents of Shem" (Gen. 9:26–27).

**3.** In the course of time, the **Semites** branched off into hundreds of individual people groups. No one knew which of these peoples would continue the family tree of Jesus; thus, the probability for each people up to that point is w->p < 1/100. Only through the prophecy of Gen. 22:18: "...and through your [= **Abraham's**] offspring all nations on earth will be blessed, because you have obeyed me" does the choice fall on Abraham, thus excluding all other Semitic peoples from the family tree of Jesus.

**4. Abraham** had eight sons (Gen. 16:11, 21:3, 25:1–2), so for each son the probability of belonging to the line of blessing was exactly w->p = 1/8. In Genesis 17:19, God says to Abraham:

...your wife Sarah will bear you a son, and you will call him **Isaac**. I will establish my covenant with him as an everlasting covenant for his descendants after him.

So, through this prophecy, the choice now clearly falls on Isaac.

**5.** Of **Isaac's** two sons, Esau and Jacob, the latter is chosen by prophecy: "A star will come out of **Jacob**; a scepter will rise out of Israel" (Num. 24:17).

**6. Jacob** had twelve sons, each of whom could have continued the line of salvation with probability w->p = 1/12. Through the prophecy of Genesis 49:10 it is now established that it will be the tribe of *Judah* from which Shiloh (an epithet of the Messiah) will later come forth:

The scepter will not depart from **Judah**, nor the ruler's staff from between his feet, until he to whom it belongs shall come and the obedience of the nations shall be his.

**7.** From the by-now **thousands of families of Judah**, the coming of the Savior from the lineage of *Jesse* is promised by the following prophetic determination:

A shoot will come up from the stump of **Jesse**; from his roots a Branch will bear fruit. The Spirit of the LORD will rest on him — the Spirit of wisdom and of understanding, the Spirit of counsel and of might, the Spirit of the knowledge and fear of the LORD (Isa. 11:1–2).

**8.** According to 1 Samuel 16:10–11, **Jesse** had eight sons. The names of seven of these are given in 1 Chronicles 2:13–15: Eliab, Abinadab, Nethanel, Raddai, Ozem, and David. Since only one of them can continue the family tree of Jesus, initially (one likely died prior to the writing of 1 Chronicles) for each of them the probability is w->p = 1/8. By way of the prophecy of 1 Samuel 16:11–12, **David**, as the youngest of them, is chosen: "Rise and anoint him; this is the one."

**9. David** had 19 sons: Amnon, Chileab, Absalom, Adonijah, Shephatiah, Ithream (2 Sam. 3:2–5), Shammua, Shobab, Nathan, Solomon, Ibhar, Elishua, Nepheg, Japhia, Elishama, Eliada, Eliphelet (2 Sam. 5:14–16), and Elishama and Nogah (1 Chron. 3:5–8). Since all are sons of David, for each of them the mathematical probability of belonging to the line of salvation at this time is w->p = 1/19. Only the prophecy of 1 Chronicles 28:5, 7 makes it unambiguous — it will be **Solomon**:

> Of all my sons — and the LORD has given me many — he has chosen my son Solomon to sit on the throne of the kingdom of the LORD over Israel.... I will establish his kingdom forever.

In Isaiah 7:14, God's prophetic words focus on a single person: a virgin: "The **virgin** will conceive and give birth to a son, and will call him Immanuel." The recipients of this message at that time must not have been able to grasp what was being said, because God was asking them to accept something humanly impossible, a pregnant virgin! Even Mary cannot grasp the message of the angel when she says: "How will this be, since I am a virgin?" (Luke 1:34). She is given the answer: "For no word from God will ever fail" (Luke 1:37).

As we have seen, after a time lag, each new prophecy establishes a new link in the line of salvation. After the line of salvation has been revealed through prophecy, link by link, up to the progenitor $P_L$, there is nothing by which it is possible to infer which of the sons of the progenitor $P_L$ will now be the next link $P_{L+1}$ in the line of salvation. From a mathematical point of view, depending on the number of sons n of the lineage-bearer $P_L$, the probability for each of his sons to be the one to continue the lineage is w->p = 1/n. It is only through the new prophecy that the next chain link $P_{L+1}$ is determined. Thus, we have positively verified the event-independence of all the chain links.

Another aspect of event-independence that needs to be considered is the fact that most of the prophets lived in different centuries and therefore never met in person.

## A5.4 Is theistic evolution refutable by natural laws?

**Question:** *You have shown that biological evolution in its atheistic form can be refuted by the natural laws of Universal Information. Now, there is a theistic variant, which unfortunately quite a few Christians follow, which says that God used evolution to create life. Can evolution be refuted by hard evidence in this theistic form, as was possible in its atheistic form?*

**Answer 1 — Natural law refutation:** In chapter 8 we were able to show by hard evidence that for life to have originated there must be an originator (SF1), and that this originator must necessarily be omniscient (SF2) and omnipotent (SF3a). With increasing intelligence $\times$ and simultaneously available power, the time needed to solve a task decreases according to the relationship $1/\times$. At infinite $\times$, the time required $T$ becomes zero, according to this hyperbolic function $T \sim 1/\times$. Since theistic evolution adopts the creation times of millions of years from the atheistic theory of evolution, it contradicts the above derivation and is thus refuted.

**Answer 2 — biblical refutations:** Two refutations may be pointed out here.

**R1:** The long periods of time adopted in theistic evolution from the atheistic version contradict the biblically attested total creation time of six days: "For in six days the LORD made the heavens and the earth, the sea, and all that is in them" (Exod. 20:11). According to the considerations in A5.1.1, this is a hard refutation.

**R2:** According to the view which theistic evolution of necessity adopts from the atheistic doctrine of evolution, life paved its way to upward development with a tremendous amount of pain, suffering, and death. This is in clear contradiction to the biblical teaching according to which death is a consequence of the sin of an already-created human being, and therefore cannot be a principle of creation.

## A5.5 What is fundamentally new about this book?

**Objection O4:** *I cannot accept the natural laws of information, set up by you, as being natural laws, because information is a non-material quantity. Laws of nature always refer to matter.*

**Answer to O4:** The objection raised here is quite understandable. In today's sciences, materialism and methodological atheism have been unilaterally elevated to the status of an all-superior paradigm. To deviate from this paradigm would require overcoming a not-inconsiderable mental hurdle. The questioner in **O4** may have felt some of this.

Although will, consciousness, and information are clearly non-material quantities, they are interpreted in the corresponding sciences solely within materialistically oriented models. Thus, information is almost exclusively reduced to Shannon's level (see Appendix 1, A1.1).

To avoid confusion, the term **"Universal Information"** (UI) was introduced to distinguish it from all other situations in which one speaks of information. With regard to this UI, four fundamentally new research results are conveyed in this book, which have been unknown in the established sciences up to now:

1. After information has already been defined in many ways, a comprehensive definition for UI is provided here for the first time, with the specific property that with it, one is able to formulate natural laws of information.

2. Scientific proof is provided (chapter 5.4) that this information (UI) is a non-material quantity and can in no way be assigned to matter.

3. Furthermore, the reader learns something completely new: laws of nature can also be formulated for non-material quantities, which have all the qualities and characteristics that are also valid for the material laws of nature (in physics and chemistry) — see chapter 4.3: *The nature of physical laws.* It is important to emphasize this again and again and to make people aware of it, because new scientific territory has been embarked on here.

4. The conclusions that can be drawn with the help of *the natural laws of Universal Information* are particularly far-reaching (see chapter 8). As we showed in this appendix at A5.1.1 (under point 2, "Natural laws"), statements based on natural laws provide us with the strongest form of scientific reasoning.

The information concept put forward in this book has been presented worldwide — in numerous countries on five continents — at specialized institutes of various universities (see "Scientific lectures" following this appendix). Nowhere has anyone been able to refute by way of a counter-example the natural laws of Universal Information presented. This is significant in that a single counter-example is sufficient to bring down a merely supposed law of nature.

Two proofs of God are further presented in this book. The first is based on a natural law of Universal Information (see chapter 8.3) and the other looks at fulfilled prophecies from the point of view of mathematical probability theory (see chapter 9.3).

Finally, it is shown that Life (upper case "L") is also a non-material quantity (see chapter 6.3). An attempt was made to formulate the first scientific laws of Life.

# SCIENTIFIC
# LECTURES

# Scientific Presentations by Werner Gitt on the Theory of Universal Information

I am often asked how long since I developed and published the Theory of Universal Information as described in this book, and whether I have discussed the results with other scientists. I will try to answer this question exhaustively here. The first time I presented the basic ideas to a scientific audience was under the title "Ordnung und Information in Technik und Natur" ("Order and Information in Technology and Nature") during a two-day symposium organized by me on October 7–8, 1981. It was the 37th PTB Symposium entitled "Struktur und Information in Technik und Natur" ("Structure and Information in Technology and Nature") held at the Physikalisch–Technische Bundesanstalt in Braunschweig (Federal Institute of Physics and Technology, Brunswick, Germany). All nine contributions appeared in the report, *PTB–Bericht* ATWD 37, 1981 [G6]. Later, the lectures were published in a book [G7]: *Am Anfang war die Information — Forschungsergebnisse aus Naturwissenschaft und Technik* (In the Beginning was Information — Research Results from Science and Technology), Technischer Verlag Resch KG, Gräfelfing/München, 1982, 211 p., (out of print).

Over the years, I have presented this Theory of Universal Information to scientists in various countries on five continents, in particular to the scientific faculties of universities and other tertiary institutions. I have used titles such as (translated here from the particular language where relevant):

• Information — the Third Fundamental Quantity besides Mass and Energy

• Scientific Laws about Information

• Information — a Fundamental Entity in Science and Technology

• The Origin of Life from the Viewpoint of Information

• A New Answer to the Question of the Origin of Life

420 • Information: The Key to Life

- What Scientific Laws say about Information

- Information — a Fundamental Entity in Natural and Technological Systems

- Scientific Laws about Information

- In the Beginning was Information — the Origin of Life

- Scientific Laws about Information

- Information: a Fundamental Entity in Science and Engineering

- In the Beginning was Information

- Information — a Central Quantity in Nature and Technology, Linguistics and Biology

The many lively discussions that followed, with scientists of various disciplines, and the ideas provided by their provocative questions, have increasingly convinced me that the scientific laws of information are equivalent in their nature to the natural laws as we know them from physics and chemistry (see Part I of this book).

Here, in chronological order, are the lectures held before scientific institutes. The numerous other talks before a wider public are not mentioned here:

1. Physikalisch-Technische Bundesanstalt (Federal Institute for Physics and Technology), Braunschweig (Brunswick), Germany, October 8, 1981. (First presentation of these new ideas about Information to a scientific audience. Lecture title: "Order and Information in Technology and Nature", published in [G6] and [G7]).

2. Rhein-Ruhr district chapter of the Association of German Electrical Engineers, Münster, Germany, November 1987.

3. Institute for Broadcasting Technology, München (Munich), Germany, June 20, 1988.

4. Southern Bavarian district chapter of the German Association of Electrical Engineers, Munich, Germany, March 15, 1988.

5. Television and Cinema Technical Society, Mainz, Germany, October 12, 1989.

6. Electrotechnical colloquium of the Faculty of Electrical Engineering, University of Stuttgart, Germany, April 30, 1991.

7. Skotschinski Institute, Academy of Sciences, Moscow, Russia, May 14, 1991.

8. Institute for Theoretical Electrical and Optical Communications, University of Kaiserslautern, Germany, December 10, 1992.

9. Institute of Electrical Engineers, University of the Witwatersrand, Johannesburg, South Africa, February 20, 1992.

10. Institute of Electrical Engineers, University of Cape Town, South Africa, March 5, 1992.

11. Department of Computer Science, University of the Western Cape, Cape Town, South Africa, March 10, 1992.

12. Institute of Physics, University of Karaganda, Kazakhstan, April 14, 1993.

13. Medical Institute of the University of Karaganda, Kazakhstan, April 14, 1993.

14. Polytechnical Institute of Karaganda, Kazakhstan, April 15, 1993.

15. Institute for Information Technology, Karaganda, Kazakhstan, April 17, 1993.

16. Technical University of Bishkek, Kirghizia, April 20, 1993.

17. University of Architecture and Civil Engineering, Bishkek, Kirghizia, April 20, 1993.

18. Institute of Agricultural Science, University of Bishkek, Kirghizia, April 21, 1993.

19. Institute of Medicine, University of Bishkek, Kirghizia, April 22, 1993.

20. Lomonosov Moscow State University, Moscow, Russia, April 23, 1993.

21. University of Salzburg, Austria, October 18, 1994.

22. Faculty of Mathematics and Physics of the University of Kaliningrad, Russia, May 9, 1994.

23. Department of Electrical and Electronic Engineering, University

of Pretoria, South Africa, February 23, 1995.

24. Rand Afrikaans University of Johannesburg, South Africa, February 28, 1995.

25. University of Namibia, Windhoek, Namibia, March 16, 1995.

26. Second Conference on the Foundations of Information — The Quest for a Unified Theory of Information, Vienna University of Technology, Austria, June 11–15, 1996.

27. University of Kaliningrad, Russia, June 21, 1996.

28. Faculty of Mathematics, Vilnius University, Lithuania, June 24, 1996.

29. Faculty of Information Technology, Queensland University of Technology, Brisbane, Australia, April 11, 1997.

30. Department of Computer Science, Curtin University of Technology, Perth, Australia, April 21, 1997.

31. School of Physical Sciences, Engineering and Technology, Murdoch University, Perth, Australia, April 22, 1997.

32. Department of Physics and Mathematical Physics, The University of Adelaide, Australia, April 24, 1997.

33. School of Electronic Engineering, Faculty of Science and Technology, La Trobe University, Melbourne, Australia, April 29, 1997.

34. School of Physics and Department of Electrical and Electronic Engineering, University of Melbourne, Australia, April 30, 1997.

35. School of Information Technology and Mathematical Sciences, University of Ballarat, Australia, May 1, 1997.

36. Department of Software Development and Computer Technology, Faculty of Computing and Information Technology, Monash University, Melbourne, Australia, May 2, 1997.

37. Department of Electrical and Electronic Engineering, University of Tasmania, Hobart, Australia, May 5, 1997.

38. School of Computing Sciences, University of Technology, Sydney, Australia, May 7, 1997.

39. Department of Computer Science, University of Sydney, Australia, May 9, 1997.

40. Faculty of Information Sciences and Engineering, University of Canberra, Australia, May 13, 1997.

41. IDE-colloquium, IBM Deutschland Entwicklung GmbH, Böblingen, Germany, February 6, 1997.

42. PTB-colloquium, Physikalisch–Technische Bundesanstalt (Federal Institute of Physics and Technology), Braunschweig (Brunswick), Germany, June 18, 1997.

43. Pacific Symposium on Biocomputing, Kapalua, Maui, Hawaii, USA, January 4–9, 1998.

44. University of Lisbon, Portugal, September 18, 1998.

45. Lusíada University, Porto, Portugal, September 19, 1998.

46. Association of German Engineers, München (Munich), Germany, December 12, 1998.

47. Department of Electrical and Electronic Engineering, University of Witwatersrand, Johannesburg (South Africa), March 2, 1999.

48. Library of Pietersburg, South Africa, March 3, 1999.

49. Faculty of Mathematics and Natural Sciences, University of the North, Pietersburg, South Africa, March 4, 1999.

50. Department of Electrical and Electronic Engineering, University of Pretoria, South Africa, March 5, 1999.

51. Glenwood High School, Durban, South Africa, March 11, 1999.

52. George Campbell Technical High School, Durban, South Africa, March 12, 1999.

53. University of Natal, Durban, South Africa, March 12, 1999.

54. Department of Mechanical Engineering, University of Stellenbosch, South Africa, March 18, 1999.

55. University of Namibia, Windhoek, Namibia, March 25, 1999.

56. University of Silesia, Katowice, Poland, May 9, 2000.

57. Main School of Economics, University of Warsaw, Poland, May 10, 2000.

58. Portland University, Oregon, USA, September 14, 2000.

59. Los Alamos National Laboratory, New Mexico, USA, September

16, 2000.

60. University of Missouri, USA, September 19, 2000.

61. Ohio State University, Columbus, Ohio, USA, September 20, 2000.

62. Pennsylvania State University, University Park, Pennsylvania, USA, September 25, 2000.

63. Mathematics and Computer Science Department, University of Canterbury, Christchurch, New Zealand,March 7, 2001.

64. Department of Electrical and Electronic Engineering, University of Canterbury, Christchurch, New Zealand, March 9, 2001.

65. University of Otago, Dunedin, New Zealand, March 13, 2001.

66. Department of Information Sciences and Technology, Massey University, Palmerston North, New Zealand, March 16, 2001.

67. Departments of Physics and Electronic Engineering, University of Waikato, Hamilton, New Zealand, March 21, 2001.

68. Department of Computer Science, University of Auckland, New Zealand, March 26, 2001.

69. Department of Chemical and Materials Engineering, University of Auckland, New Zealand, March 27, 2001.

70. Teacher's Conference in the Chaco, Fernheim, Paraguay, August 17, 2001.

71. Pedagogic Institute of the University of Brest, Belarus, September 2, 2002.

72. Institute of Mathematics, University of Brest, Belarus, September 3, 2002.

73. Belarusian Engineering Academy, Minsk, Belarus, September 6, 2002.

74. Polytechnic and University for Banking Education, Pinsk, Belarus, September 10, 2002.

75. National University of Asunción, Paraguay, August 18, 2004

76. Department of Genetics, Faculty of Biological Sciences, Federal University of Paraná, Curitiba, Brazil, March 8, 2005.

77. University of Posznan, Poland, May 18, 2005.

78. Polytechnical Institute, University of Elblag, Poland, May 20, 2005.

79. Technical College of Gdansk, Poland, May 24, 2005.

80. Technical University, Karaganda, Kazakhstan, May 5, 2006.

81. Medical College, Temirtau, Kazakhstan, May 10, 2006.

82. Pharmaceutical Institute, University of Karaganda, Kazakhstan, May 12, 2006.

83. Medical Institute, University of Karaganda, Kazakhstan, May 12, 2006.

84. Chair of Computer Science, Kazakh-Russian University, Karaganda, Kazakhstan, May 15, 2006

85. University of Oviedo, Coronel Oviedo, Paraguay, August 21, 2006.

86. Polytechnic, University of Asunción, Paraguay, August 22, 2006.

87. UCSA University, Asunción, Paraguay, August 23, 2006.

88. Interfaculties (UNI), University of Encarnación, Paraguay, August 24, 2006.

89. UTCD (Technical University of Marketing and Development), Caaguazú, Paraguay, August 26, 2006.

90. Commonwealth International University, Simferopol, Crimea, Ukraine, May 14, 2007.

91. Faculty of Informatics, Crimean Industrial-Pedagogical University, Simferopol, Crimea, Ukraine, May 15, 2007.

92. S. Seifullin Kazakh Agrotechnical University, Astana, Kazakhstan, May 5, 2008.

93. North Kazakhstan State University (University of Petropavlolvsk), Petropavlovsk, Kazakhstan, May 7, 2008.

94. University of Kokshetav, Kazakhstan, May 8, 2008.

95. Karagandan Medical College, Karaganda, Kazakhstan, May 12, 2008.

96. Medical Academy of Karaganda, Kazakhstan, May 14, 2008.

97. Karaganda University of Business, Management and Law, Kazakhstan, May 14, 2008.

98. Institute of Technology, Precision and Intelligence, Tokyo University, Japan, June 6, 2008.

99. Wasedo University, Tokyo, Japan, June 7, 2008.

100. Kyoto International University, Ichinotsubo Kusauchi Kyotanabe, Kyoto, Japan, June 12, 2008.

101. Nagoya University, Japan, June 14, 2008.

102. Chitose Institute of Science and Technology, Chitose, Japan, June 16, 2008.

103. Hokkaido University, Sapporo, Japan, June 17, 2008.

104. University of Agriculture, Sapporo, Japan, June 18, 2008.

105. Aoyama Gakeun University, Tokyo, Japan, June 25, 2008.

106. Toyo Eiwa Jogakin University, Yokohama, Japan, June 25, 2008.

107. Sophia University, Tokyo, Japan, June 25, 2008.

108. Vienna Technical University, Austria, 1March 16, 2009.

109. Technical University of Gdansk, Poland, June 12, 2009.

110. Various cities in Bulgaria, August 16–24, 2010.

111. University of Jena, Germany, October 14, 2010.

112. University of Bielefeld, Germany, January 30, 2011.

113. Cornell University, New York, USA, May 31 to June 3, 2011.

114. University of Szeged, Hungary, September 20, 2014.

115. University of Debrecen, Hungary, September 23, 2014.

116. University of Miskolc, Hungary, September 24, 2014.

117. Budapest Technical University, Hungary, September 25, 2014.

118. Corvinus University, Budapest, Hungary, September 26, 2014.

119. University of Regensburg, Germany, November 20, 2014.

120. Leuphana University, Lüneburg, Germany, May 18, 2015.

121. Technical University of Chemnitz, Germany, June 10, 2015.

# Bibliography

[B1]   BAM: (Federal Institute for Materials Research and Testing, Germany) "Informationsversorgung — neue Möglichkeiten in der Bundesanstalt für Materialforschung" (Information supply — new possibilities in the Federal Institute for Materials Research), *BAM-Information* 6/81.

[B2]   Batten, D., Ham, K., Sarfati, J., Wieland, C.: *Fragen an den Anfang — Die Logik der Schöpfung* (German adaptation of *The Answers Book*), Christliche Literatur–Verbreitung, Bielefeld, 2nd revised edition 2004, 281 p.; W. Gitt: "Was ist ein wissenschaftliches Modell?" (What is a scientific model?) p. 275–279.

[B3]   Blechschmidt, E.: *Die pränatalen Organsysteme des Menschen* (The Prenatal Organ Systems of Humans), Hippokrates Verlag Stuttgart, 1973, 184 p.

[B4]   Bleeken, S.: "Welches sind die existentiellen Grundlagen lebender Systeme?" (What are the existential foundations of living systems?), *Naturwissenschaften* 77, 277–282 (1990).

[B5]   Born, M.: "Symbol und Wirklichkeit" (Symbol and reality), *Physikalische Blätter* 21 (1965), p. 53–63.

[B6]   Borstnik, B. *et al.*: "Point mutations as an optimal search process in biological evolution," *J. Theor. Biol.* (1987) 125, p. 249–268.

[B7]   Broda, E.: "Erfindungen der lebenden Zelle — Zwölf epochale bisher nicht nachgeahmte Prinzipien" (Inventions of the living cell — twelve epochal, previously unimitated principles), *Naturwiss. Rundschau* 31 (1978), p. 356–363.

[B8]   Buck, J.B.: "Synchronous flashing of fireflies experimentally produced," *Science* 81 (1935), p. 339–340.

[C1]   Chaitin, G.J.: "Randomness and mathematical proof," *Scientific American* 232 (1975), p. 47–52.

[D1]   Dake, F.J.: *Dake's Annotated Reference Bible*, Dake Bible Sales, Inc., PO Box 173, Lawrenceville, Georgia 30245, 1961.

[D2]   Dawkins, R.: *Der blinde Uhrmacher — Ein Plädoyer für den Darwinismus* (The Blind Watchmaker), Kindler-Verlag, München, 1987, 384 p.

[D3]   Dembski, W.A.: *No Free Lunch — Why Specified Complexity Cannot Be Purchased Without Intelligence,* Rowman & Littlefield Publishers, Inc., Lanham, Boulder, New York, Oxford, 2002, 404 p.

[D4]   Dose, K.: "Die Ursprünge des Lebens — Tagungsbericht über den ISSOL-Kongress in Mainz vom 10. bis 15. Juli 1983" (The origins of life — proceedings of the ISSOL Congress in Mainz 10–15 July 1983), *Nachr. Chem. Techn. Lab.* 31(1983), No. 12, p. 968–969.

[D5]   Dröscher, V.B.: *Überlebensformel,* dtv — Taschenbuch, 2. Auflage (Survival Formula), dtv — paperpack1982, 329 p.

[D6]   de Duve, C.: *Vital Dust,* Basic Books, 1995, 362 p.

[E1]   Eichelbeck, R.: *Das Darwin-Komplott — Aufstieg und Fall eines pseudowissenschaftliches Weltbildes* (The Darwin Conspiracy — the Rise and Fall of a Pseudoscientific Worldview), Riemann Verlag (Bertelsmann), 1st edition 1999, 380 p.

[E2]   Eigen, M.: "Self-organization of matter and the evolution of biological macromolecules," *Naturwissenschaften* 58 (1971), p. 465–523.

[E3]   Eigen, M.: *Stufen zum Leben — Die frühe Evolution im Visier der Molekularbiologie* (Steps to Life — Early Evolution in the Crosshairs of Molecular Biology), Piper-Verlag, München, Zürich, 1987, 311 p.

[F1]   Feynman, R.P.: *The Character of Physical Law,* The M.I.T. Press, 2001.

[F2]   Fischer, *Der Fischer Weltalmanach 2001 — Zahlen, Daten, Fakten,* (The Fischer World Almanac 2001 — Figures, Dates, Facts), Fischer Taschenbuch Verlag, Frankfurt/M., Oct. 2000, 1407 p.

[F3]   Flechtner, H.-J.: *Grundbegriffe der Kybernetik* (Basic Concepts in Cybernetics), Wissenschaftliche Verlagsgesellschaft mbH, 4th edition 1969, 423 p.

[F4]   Forrest, S.: "Genetic algorithms: principles of natural selection applied to computation," *Science,* Vol. 261, August 13, 1993, p. 872–878.

[F5]   Fricke, J.: "Biomasse" (Biomass), *Physik in unserer Zeit* (Physics in our Time), 15 (1984), H. 4, p. 121–122.

[G1]  Gallager, R.G.: "Claude E. Shannon: A retrospective on his life, work, and impact," *IEEE Transactions on Information Theory*, Vol. 47, No. 7, November 7, 2001.

[G2]  Gierer, A.: *Die Physik und das Verständnis des Lebendigen* (Physics and the Comprehension of the Living), Universitas 36 (1981), p. 1283–1293.

[G3]  Gilbert, W.: "DNA-Sequenzierung und Gen-Struktur (Nobel-Vortrag)" (DNA sequencing and gene structure (Nobel lecture), *Angewandte Chemie* 93 (1981), p. 1037–1046.

[G4]  Gipper, H.: "Sprache als Information (Geistige Prägung)" (Language as information (mental imprinting)) in: O.G. Folberth, C. Hackl (editors): *Der Informationsbegriff in Technik und Wissenschaft* (The Concept of Information in Technology and Science), R. Oldenbourg Verlag, München, Wien, 1986, p. 257–298.

[G5]  Gitt, W.: "Information und Entropie als Bindeglieder diverser Wissenschafts Zweige" (Information and entropy as links between various branches of science), *PTB-Mitt.* 91 (1981), p. 1–17.

[G6]  Gitt, W.: "Ordnung und Information in Technik und Natur" (Order and information in technology and nature), p.165–204, in: W. Gitt (Ed.): *Struktur und Information in Technik und Natur*, (Structure and Information in Nature) (lectures from the 37th PTB seminar, October 7–8, 1981, at the Federal Institute of Physics and Technology, Brunswick, Germany), *PTB-Bericht* PTB-ATWD-18, 1981, 204 p., ISSN 0341-6682.

[G7]  Gitt, W.: *Am Anfang war die Information — Forschungsergebnisse aus Naturwissenschaft und Technik* (In the Beginning was Information — Research Results from Science and Technology), Resch-Verlag, Gräfelfing/München, 1982, 211 p.

[G8]  Gitt, W.: "Ein neuer Ansatz zur Bewertung von Information — Beitrag zur semantischen Informationstheorie" (A new approach to the evaluation of information — a contribution to semantic information theory) in: H. Kreikebaum *et al.* (Eds.), *Festschrift Ellinger* (Ellinger Commemorative Publication), Verlag Duncker & Humblot, Berlin, 1985, p. 210–250.

[G9]  Gitt, W.: "'Künstliche Intelligenz' — Möglichkeiten und Grenzen" ("Artificial intelligence" — possibilities and limitations), *PTB-Bericht* TWD-34, 1989, 43 p.

[G10] Gitt, W.: "Information — die dritte Grundgröße neben Materie und Energie," *Siemens-Zeitschr* (1989), H. 4, p. 2–8. English translation of [G10]: "Information: The Third Fundamental Quantity," *Siemens Review*, Vol. 56, No. 6, November/December 1989, p. 2–7.

[G11] Gitt, W.: "Naturgesetze über Information" (Natural laws of information), *Jahresbericht 1996 der Physikalisch– Technischen-Bundesanstalt in Braunschweig (*1996 annual report of the Federal Institute of Physics and Technology, Brunswick, Germany), p. 280, ISSN 0340-4366, March 1997.

[G12] Gitt, W.: "Neues Maß zum Vergleich hoher Speicherdichten" (A new metric for comparing high storage densities), *Jahresbericht 1997 der Physikalisch–Technischen Bundesanstalt in Braunschweig (*1997 annual report of the Federal Institute of Physics and Technology, Brunswick, Germany), p. 307, ISSN 0340-4366, March 1998.

[G13] Gitt, W.: "Ist Information eine Eigenschaft der Materie?" (Is information a property of matter?), Westdeutscher Verlag, *EuS 9* (1998), Vol. 2, p. 205–207.

[G14] Gitt, W.: *In the Beginning was Information* (a) Christliche Literatur-Verbreitung, Bielefeld, 3rd English edition, 2003, 256 p. (b) First Master Books printing, 2006, 264 p.

[G15] Gitt, W.: "Zur Präzisierung des Informationsbegriffs" (Towards greater precision of the term information), Westdeutscher Verlag, *EuS12* (2001), Vol. 1, p. 22–24.

[G16] Gitt, W.: *In 6 Tagen vom Chaos zum Menschen — Logos oder Chaos — Aussagen und Einwände zur Evolutionslehre* (From Chaos to Man in 6 Days — Logos or Chaos — Assertions and Objections to the Theory of Evolution), 5th revised edition 1998, Hänssler-Verlag, Holzgerlingen, 238 p.

[G17] Gitt, W.: *Wunder und Wunderbares* (Miracles and wonders) Christliche Literatur-Verbreitung, Bielefeld, 2nd edition 2007, 319 p.

[G18]  Gitt, W.: *So steht's geschrieben — Zur Wahrhaftigkeit der Bibel* (It is Written: The Veracity of the Bible), 7th expanded and revised edition 2008, 255 p.

[G19]  Gitt, W.: *Questions I Have Always Wanted to Ask,* Christliche Literatur-Verbreitung, Bielefeld, 2nd expanded English edition 1998, 189 p. (22nd edition in German, 2009).

[G20]  Gitt, W.: *Did God Use Evolution?* Christliche Literatur-Verbreitung, Bielefeld, 2nd English edition 2002, 152 p. (8th edition in German, 2009).

[G21]  Gitt, W.: *If Animals Could Talk — Creation Speaks for Itself* (a) Christliche Literatur-Verbreitung, Bielefeld, 4th English edition, 2001, 124 p. (b) First Master Books printing, 2006, 115 p. (16th edition in German, 2009).

[G22]  Gitt, W.: *Stars and their Purpose — Signposts in Space,* Christliche Literatur-Verbreitung, Bielefeld, 2nd English edition, 2000, 217 p. (5th edition in German).

[G23]  Gitt, W.: *The Wonder of Man,* Christliche Literatur-Verbreitung, Bielefeld, 2nd expanded and updated English edition 2003, 156 p. (2nd edition in German, 2003).

[G24]  Gitt, W.: *Time and Eternity,* Christliche Literatur-Verbreitung, Bielefeld, 1st English edition 2001, 150 p. (4th edition in German, 2011).

[G25]  Gitt, W.: *Am Anfang war die Information* (In the Beginning was Information), Hänssler-Verlag, Holzgerlingen, 3rd revised and expanded edition 2002, 360 p.

[G26]  Gitt, W.: Scientific laws of information and their implications — part 1, *J. Creation* **23**(2):96–102, 2009; Scientific laws of information and their implications — part 2, *J. Creation* **23**(2):103–109, 2009.

[G27]  Goel, N.S. and Thompson, R.L.: *Computer Simulations of Self-Organization in Biological Systems,* Croom Helm Ltd, Beckenham, Kent BR3 1AT, 1988.

[G28]  Guinness: *Das neue Guinness Buch der Rekorde 1994* (Guiness Book of Records). Ullstein Verlag Berlin, 1993, 368 p.

[H1]  Halstead, B.: "Popper: good philosophy, bad science?" *New Scientist*, 17 July 1980, p. 215–217.

[H2]  Herschl, A.: *Das intelligente Genom* (The Intelligent Genome), Springer Verlag, Berlin, Heidelberg, 1998, 391 p.

[H3]  Horgan, J.: *An den Grenzen des Wissens — Siegeszug und Dilemma der Naturwissenschaftern* (German version of Horgan's *The End of Science: Facing the Limits of Knowledge in the Twilight of the Scientific Age*), Fischer-Taschenbuch, Frankfurt/M, 2000, 463 p.

[H4]  Hoyle, F.: "The Big Bang in astronomy," *New Scientist* **92**(1280):527, November 19, 1981.

[J1]  Janich, P.: "Informationsbegriff und methodisch-kulturalistische Philosophie" (The concept of information and methodological-culturalist philosophy), Westdeutscher Verlag, *EuS 9* (1998), Issue 2, p. 169–182.

[J2]  Jones, E.S.: *Das frohmachende Ja — Das Vermächtnis des bekannten Missionars und Evangelisten* (The Joyful Yes — the Legacy of the Famous Missionary and Evangelist), Christliches Verlagshaus GmbH, Stuttgart, 1975, 95 p, 6th edition, 2006, 336 p.

[J3]  Junker, R., Scherer, S.: *Evolution — ein kritisches Lehrbuch* (Evolution — a Critical Textbook), Weyel Biologie, 6th edition 2006, 328 p.

[K1]  Kaplan, R.W.: *Der Ursprung des Lebens* (The Origin of Life), dtv Georg Thieme Verlag, Stuttgart, 1st edition 1972, 318 p.

[K2]  Kessler, V.: *Ist die Existenz Gottes beweisbar?Neuere Gottesbeweise im Licht der Mathematik, Informatik, Philosophie und Theologie* (Is God's Existence Provable? New Evidences for God in the Light of Mathematics, Informatics, Philosophy and Theology), Brunnen-Verlag, Gießen, 1999, 125 p.

[K3]  Knippers, R.: *Molekulare Genetik* (Molecular Genetics), Thieme Verlag, Stuttgart, New York, 7th edition 1997, 508 p.

[K4]  Küppers, B.-O.: *Der Ursprung biologischer Information — Zur Naturphilosophie der Lebensentstehung* (The Origin of Biological Information — Towards a Natural Philosophy of the Origin of Life), Piper-Verlag, München, Zürich, 1986, 319 p.

[K5]   Küppers, B.-O.: *Leben = Physik + Chemie?* (Life = Physics + Chemistry?), Piper-Verlag, München, Zürich, 2nd edition 1990, 256 p.

[K6]   Kuhn, H.: "Selbstorganisation molekularer Systeme und die Evolution des genetischen Apparats" (Self-organisation of molecular systems and the evolution of the genetic apparatus), *Angewandte Chemie* 84 (1972), p. 838–861.

[K7]   Kreeft. P.: *Three Philosophies of Life*, Ignatius Press, 1989, 140 p.

[L1]   Lehninger, A.L.: *Bioenergetik* (Bioenergetics), Georg Thieme Verlag, Stuttgart, 1974, 261 p.

[L2]   Lexikon der Biologie: *Lexikon der Biologie in 9 Bänden* (Encyclopedia of Biology in 9 Volumes), Spektrum Akademischer Verlag, Heidelberg, Berlin, Oxford, 1994.

[L3]   Lwoff, A.: "Virus, Zelle, Organismus" (Virus, cell, organism), *Angewandte Chemie* 78 (1966), p. 689–724.

[M1]   Matthies, H.: "Satellitenfernsehen ist Fingerzeig Gottes" (Satellite TV is God's pointer), *Christen in der Wirtschaft* (Christians in Business), (1986). Issue 1, p. 7–9.

[M2]   Meixner, J.: "Die Thermodynamik irreversibler Prozesse" (The thermodynamics of irreversible processes), *Physikalische Blätter* 16 (1960), p. 506–511.

[M3]   Meschkowski, H.: *Mathematiker-Lexikon* (Mathematician's Encyclopedia), Bibliographisches Institut, Mannheim, Wien, Zürich, B. I.-Wissenschaftsverlag, 3rd revised and expanded edition, 1980, 342 p.

[M4]   Meyer, S.C.: "DNA and the origin of life: information, specification, and explanation," discovery.org/articlefiles/PDFs/DNAPerspectives.pdf, 2002, 44 p.

[M5]   Minibibel: Die kleinste Bibel der Welt auf einem Dia (Mini-Bible: The smallest Bible in the world on a single slide). Obtainable from: Ernst Paulus Verlag, Haltweg 23, 67434 Neustadt/Weinstraße, Germany.

[M6]   Mohr, H.: "Der Begriff der Erklärung in Physik und Biologie" (The concept of explanation in physics and biology), *Naturwissenschaften* 65 (1978), p. 1–6.

[M7] Monod, J.: *Zufall und Notwendigkeit — Philosophische Fragen der modernen Biologie.* (Chance and Necessity — Philosophical Questions of Modern Biology), dtv-Verlag, 3. Auflage 1977, 173 p.

[O1] Ohta, T.: "A model of evolution for accumulating genetic information," *J. Theor. Biol.* (1987) 124, p. 199–211.

[O2] Osawa, S. *et al.*: "Recent evidence for evolution of the genetic code," *Microbiological Reviews*, March 1992, p. 229–264.

[O3] Osche, G.: "Die Vergleichende Biologie und die Beherrschung der Mannigfaltigkeit" (Comparative biology and the mastery of diversity), *Biologie in unserer Zeit* 5 (1975), p. 139–146.

[P1] Peierls, R.E.: "Wo stehen wir in der Kenntnis der Naturgesetze?" (Where do we stand in our knowledge of the laws of nature?) *Physikalische Blätter*, (19) 1963, p. 533–539.

[P2] Peil, J.: "Einige Bemerkungen zu Problemen der Anwendung des Informationsbegriffs in der Biologie. Teil I: Der Informationsbegriff und seine Rolle im Verhältnis zwischen Biologie, Physik und Kybernetik, p. 117–128. Teil II: Notwendigkeit und Ansätze zur Erweiterung des Informationsbegriffs" (Some remarks on the problems of applying the concept of information in biology. Part I: The concept of information and its role in the relationship between biology, physics and cybernetics, p. 117-128. Part II: Necessity and approaches to the enlargement of the concept of information), *Biometrische Zeitschrift* Vol. 15, p. 199–213, (1973).

[P3] Penzlin, H.: *Ordnung — Organisation — Organismus — Zum Verhältnis zwischen Physik und Biologie* (Order — Organisation— Organism — on the Relationship Between Physics and Biology), Akademie-Verlag Berlin, 1988, 32 p.

[P4] Planck, M.: *Vorträge und Erinnerungen* (Lectures and Memories), S. Hirzel-Verlag, Stuttgart, 1949.

[P5] *P.M. Perspektive* (P.M. Perspectives): "Das Wunder der Evolution" (The miracle of evolution). C 7382 F, 96/044, 1996.

[R1] Rentschler, W.: "Die Erhaltungsgesetze der Physik" (The conservation laws of physics), *Physikalische Blätter* 22 (1966), p. 193–200.

[R2]  Ripota, P.: "Was Charles Darwin uns alles verheimlichte" (What Charles Darwin kept from us), *P. M. Peter Moosleitners Magazin– die moderne Welt des Wissens*, Issue 4/2002, p. 22–29.

[R3]  Rokhsar, D.S., *et al.*: "Self-organisation in prebiological systems: Simulations of a model for the origin of genetic information," *J. of Molecular Evolution* (1986) 23, p. 119–126.

[R4]  Ropohl, G.: *Der Informationsbegriff im Kulturstreit* (The Concept of Information in the Culture Wars), Westdeutscher Verlag, EuS 12 (2001), H. 1, p. 3–14.

[R5]  Rüppell, G.: *Vogelflug* (Bird Flight), Rowohlt Taschenbuch Verlag GmbH, 1980, 209 p.

[S1]  Sachsse, H.: "Die Stellung des Menschen im Kosmos in der Sicht der Naturwissenschaft" (The place of man in the cosmos in the light of science), Herrenalber Texte, HT33, *Mensch und Kosmos* (Man and Cosmos), 1981, p. 93–103.

[S2]  Salomonsen, F.: *Vogelzug* (Bird Migration) from the series: *Moderne Biologie* (Modern Biology), BLV Munich, Basel, Vienna, 1969, 210 p.

[S3]  Sanford, J.: *Genetic Entropy & The Mystery of the Genome*, Ivan Press, a division of Elim Publishing, Lima, New York, 2005, 233 p.

[S4]  Schäfer, E.: "Das menschliche Gedächtnis als Informationsspeicher" (The human memory as information repository), *Elektronische Rundschau* 14 (1960), p. 79–84.

[S5]  Scherer, S.: "Photosynthese — Bedeutung und Entstehung — ein kritischer Überblick" (Photosynthesis — significance and origin — a critical overview), *Wort und Wissen — Fachberichte* (Bible and Science — Technical Reports), Vol.1, Hänssler-Verlag,Neuhausen-Stuttgart, 1983, 74 p.

[S6]  Schneider, H.: "Der Urknall" (The Big Bang), *Factum* magazine (1981), No. 3, p. 26–33.

[S7]  Schrödinger, E.: *What is Life? — The Physical Aspect of the Living Cell,* Cambridge: At the University Press; New York: The Macmillan Company, 1945, 91 p.

[S8]  Shannon, C.E. and Weaver, W.: *The Mathematical Theory of Communication*, Urbana (USA), University Press 1949.

[S9] Sösemann, F.: "Information, physikalische Entropie und Objektivität" ((Information, physical entropy and objectivity), *Wiss. Zeitschrift der Techn. Hochschule Karl-Marx-Stadt* 17 (1975), p. 117–122.

[S10] Spurgeon, C.H.: *Das Buch der Bilder und Gleichnisse — 2000 der besten Illustrationen* (English original: *The Book of Pictures and Parables — 2,000 of the Best Illustrations*), J.G. Oncken-Verlag, Kassel, 1900, 731 p.

[S11] Spurgeon, C.H.: *Es steht geschrieben — Die Bibel im Kampf des Glaubens* (It is Written — the Bible in the Battle of Faith), Oncken-Verlag, Wuppertal und Kassel, 1980, 94 p.

[S12] Steinbuch, K.: *Falsch programmiert* (Wrongly programmed), Deutscher Bücherbund, Stuttgart, Hamburg, 1968, 251 p.

[S13] Strombach, W.: "Philosophie und Informatik" (Philosophy and informatics), Research report no. 122 of the Department of Informatics, Dortmund University, 31 p.

[T1] Theimer, W.: *Was ist Wissenschaft?* (What is Science?) Uni-Pocketbooks 1352, Francke Verlag Tübingen, 1985, 163 p. Arizona, 1953, 285 p.

[V1] Vollmert, B.: *Das Molekül und das Leben — Vom makromolekularen Ursprung des Lebens und der Arten: Was Darwin nicht wissen konnte und Darwinisten nicht wissen wollen* (The molecule and life — the macromolecular origin of life: What Darwin couldn't know and Darwinists don't want to know), Rowohlt-Verlag, 1985, 256 p.

[V2] Völz, H.: *Information II.* Akademie-Verlag, Berlin, 1983, 367 p.

[V3] Völz, H.: *Information verstehen* (Understanding Information), Vieweg Verlag, 1994, 184 p.

[W1] Weibel, E.R.: *Morphometry of the Human Lung*, Springer Verlag, Berlin, 1973.

[W2] v. Weizsäcker, E.: *Offene Systeme I — Beiträge zur Zeitstruktur von Information, Entropie und Evolution* (Open Systems I - Contributions to the Time Structure of Information, Entropy and Evolution), Ernst Klett Verlag, Stuttgart, 1974, 370 p.

[W3] Wieland, C.: "Superbugs — Not super after all. Why drug-resistant germs in hospitals don't show that Darwin was right," *Creation* Vol. 20, No. 1, p. 10–13, 1998.

[W4] Wieland, W.: "Möglichkeiten und Grenzen der Wissenschaftstheorie" (Possibilities and limits of the philosophy of science), *Angewandte Chemie* 93 (1981), p. 627–634.

[W5] Wiener, N.: *Cybernetics or Control and Communication in the Animal and the Machine*, Hermann & Cie Editeurs, Paris; The Technology Press, Cambridge, Mass.; John Wiley & Sons Inc., New York, 1948.

[W6] Wills, P.R.: "Scrapie, ribosomal proteins and biological information," *J. Theor. Biol.* (1986) 122, p. 157–178.

[W7] Wuketits, F.M.: *Biologie und Kausalität* (Biology and Causality), Verlag Paul Parey, Berlin und Hamburg, 1981, 165 p.

[X1] "Energie aus Sonne und Wind: Raum nicht in der kleinsten Hütte" (Energy from sun and wind: space not in the smallest hut), magazine "tag+nacht" (day+night) of the Braunschweig (Brunswick) municipal utility, IV 1983, p. 3.

[Y1] Yockey, H.P.: "Self organization, origin of life scenarios and information theory," *J. Theor. Biol.* 91 (1981), p. 13–31.

[Z1] Zuse, H.: *Software Complexity — Measures and Methods*, Walter de Gruyter, Berlin, New York, 1991, 605 p.

# General Index

SLI–5b: A functioning machine means that UI is affecting the material domain, 164
SLI–5c: Machines operate exclusively within the physical-chemical laws of matter, 164
SLI–5d: Machines cause matter to function in specific ways, 164
SLI–6: Existing UI is never increased over time by purely physical, chemical processes, 166
Examples of converse formulations:
SLI–3C: It is impossible to generate UI by purely random processes, 167
SLI–4C: It is impossible to create UI without an intelligent sender, 167
SLI–4aC: It is impossible to establish a code system without an intelligent sender, 167
SLI–4bC: It is impossible that a UI chain exists without an intelligent source, 167
Shannon's Theory, 6, 41, 137, 335
sexual reproduction, 7, 76, 391
Software Complexity, 6, 320–321, 437
SOS signal, 301
sound arguments, 5, 16, 80, 222, 253
source of information, 5, 33, 178, 184, 212, 228, 239, 256
specified complexity, 6, 320, 322, 428
sperm whale, 393
statistics, 3, 37, 40, 68, 137, 258, 275, 277, 309, 311
substitutive function, 83–84, 86–88, 91, 94, 102, 200, 297
synthetic life, 4, 178
Terminology used in science:
fiction, 114, 116–117,
hypothesis, 115, 118, 129–130
model, 114–115, 125, 127, 130,
paradigm, 3, 115–118, 171, 175, 177, 393, 413–414
scientific law, 4, 7, 16–17, 24, 36, 68, 113–115, 119–134
speculation, 114–116, 127, 130–131, 221, 247–248
theory, 223, 225–226, 242–243, 245–249

Theory of Universal Information (TUI), 76, 142
transcription, 180, 189, 193, 196, 234
translation, 13, 38, 51, 55, 176, 180, 189–190, 193, 196, 200, 234, 277, 430
transmitter, 104, 155, 159–160, 230
UI:
measurement parameters of, 316
existence of, 17, 23–24, 47, 63, 99, 126, 164, 174–175, 181, 202, 204, 227, 233, 236, 266–268, 295–296, 379, 402, 405–406
extremely important, 212, 313, 358,
harmful, 173, 307–311,
helpful, 43, 138, 160, 266, 275,
important, 40–41, 48, 50, 54–55, 60, 65–66, 68–69,
quality of, 5, 161, 225, 316,
relevance of, 4, 109, 128, 314, 317, 381, 387,
trivial, 66, 231, 300, 308–309, 313,
usability of, 306, 309, 318,
valuable, 117, 124, 139, 167, 258, 277, 308, 310, 315, 319,
worthless, 124, 291, 307–309, 312, 314, 335,
Uroctea, 3, 28
vase on Mars, 99
V-formation, 372

# Index of Names

# About the Author

Werner Gitt was born February 22, 1937, in what was then Raineck, East Prussia, Germany. In 1963 he enrolled at the Technical University of Hanover and in 1968 he completed his studies as an engineering graduate (Diplom Ingenieur).

Thereafter he worked as an assistant at the Institute of Control Engineering at the Technical University of Aachen, Germany. Following two years of research work, in 1970 he received his doctorate *summa cum laude*, together with the prestigious Borchers Medal, from the Technical University of Aachen.

Werner was appointed Director and Professor[1] at the German Federal Institute of Physics and Technology in Brunswick (Physikalisch-Technische Bundesanstalt Braunschweig) in 1978. He has written numerous scientific papers in the field of information science, numerical mathematics, and control engineering.

In 1990 he initiated the Conference for Information Science which is attended annually by around 150 participants. Its goal is to link biblical principles with scientific questions (in particular, in the information sciences). Since 1984 he has been a regular guest lecturer at the State Independent Theological University of Basle, Switzerland, on the subject of "The Bible and Science."

He has given many lectures in Germany and in many other countries on all five continents. He has been married to his wife, Marion, since 1966. His son, Carsten, was born in September 1967 and his daughter, Rona, in April 1969.

Werner Gitt's homepage: wernergitt.de. Downloads of many of his articles and books in English, German, Russian, Spanish, and other languages are available. Tracts such as "How can I get to heaven?" "Who is the Creator?" "Crib, Cross and Crown," and "What Darwin couldn't know" can be downloaded in more than 60 languages.

---

1. Three prerequisites must be fulfilled in order for the German Ministerium to award the title "Director and Professor" at a German research institute, on the recommendation of the Praesidium. The person concerned must be:
   • A scientist, i.e. it is definitely an academic title.
   • One who has published a significant number of original research papers in the technical literature.
   • Must head a department of that institute in his area of expertise, in which several working scientists are employed.

# TRACED

*Human DNA's Big Surprise*

## Nathaniel T. Jeanson

## This amazing discovery is the Rosetta Stone of human history

Dr. Nathaniel Jeanson has discovered the Rosetta Stone of human history — a DNA-based, generation-by-generation family tree of global humanity. Jeanson reveals how this tree uncovers the geneaological links between ancient civilizations and the peoples of today, in ways that dramatically rewrite our understanding of race and ethnicity.

Master Books®
A Division of New Leaf Publishing Group
www.masterbooks.com

ISBN-13: 978-1-68344-291-2

Also available from Dr. Werner Gitt

¹In the beginning
was information

*A Scientist Explains
the Incredible Design
in Nature*

Dr. Werner Gitt

Master
Books®
A Division of New Leaf Publishing Group
www.masterbooks.com

ISBN-13: 978-0-89051-461-0